A
History of
ITALIAN
LAW

A
History *of*
ITALIAN
LAW

VOLUME II

By *Carlo Calisse*

PROFESSOR OF LAW IN THE UNIVERSITY OF ROME
AND SENATOR OF THE KINGDOM OF ITALY

Translated By Layton B. Register
LECTURER ON LAW IN THE UNIVERSITY OF PENNSYLVANIA

WITH INTRODUCTIONS BY
Frederick Parker Walton
FORMERLY DIRECTOR OF THE KHEDIVIAL SCHOOL OF LAW, CAIRO
AND
Hessel E. Yntema
PROFESSOR OF LAW IN COLUMBIA UNIVERSITY

BeardBooks
Washington, D.C.

Copyright 1928, Boston: Little, Brown and Company
Reprinted 2001 by Beard Books, Washington, D.C.
ISBN 1-58798-111-4

Printed in the United States of America

PART III
THE PHILOSOPHIC PERIOD

PART III

THE PHILOSOPHIC PERIOD

INTRODUCTION [1]

§ 266. The Close of the Neo-Roman Period. | § 267. New Principles.

§ 266. **The Close of the Neo-Roman Period.** — From the foregoing exposition, necessarily brief, of the general rules and applications of the criminal law in the Neo-Roman period, it may be seen that the result obtained was largely contrary to the purpose in view. Though penalties were multiplied and sharpened, crimes diminished neither in number nor gravity; society was not reformed, however much men thought to do so; laws were constantly re-enacted, a fact which in itself demonstrated their insufficiency; the learned men of the times produced enormous volumes, in which they deplored the increasing frequency of every crime within the field of their study and continued to invoke new preventives.

They did not, and perhaps could not, bring their investigation to bear upon the serious defects of the system.

On examining their penalties, it is observed that they were not fixed by any reference to the needs which they were to satisfy, but were ordinarily based upon rules or maxims of the Roman or canon law, if indeed they were not left to the harsh vengeance of the injured party. Montesquieu declared that, to punish one criminal action, another yet more criminal was committed. There was no clear and real understanding of crime; morals and law were confused, thus bringing within the sphere of civil repression what can not without harm be taken from the field of conscience. Between crime and penalty there was not the correspondence and balance necessary for punishment to be effective; the death penalty was abused, often being applied to minor transgressions; for graver crimes, or those believed to be such, death was made more terrible by barbarous means. The familiarity thus bred left criminals indifferent before the threat and fact of punishment; the public,

---

[1] [English §§ 266, 267 = *Calisse*, Part III, §§ 155–175.]

through a feeling of reaction, sympathized with the condemned, so
that the purpose of example through the publicity given to inhu-
man executions was rendered vain.   In the application itself of
penalties there was on the one hand the unlimited discretion of the
judge, endangering the secure and impartial administration of
justice, and on the other, because of the legally recognized inequality of social classes, the penalty for the same crime did not fall
alike upon all, but weighed heaviest upon those who, through
poverty and ignorance, might have some excuse.   Nor must it be
forgotten that above law, magistrate and citizen stood the prince,
who in the penalties of the criminal law possessed a weapon for
defense of his political interests, which were but too often confused
with his personal ambitions.   No procedure bound him, he feared
no appeal, he was not limited by any other jurisdiction; all punishments were within his arbitrary hands, and unless he recognized
some restraint within himself, criminal law represented for him only
a powerful instrument of absolute power.

The causes of these defects may be reduced in the main to three.
First was the condition of legislation, derived from divers and
discordant sources, based upon artificial reasons, bewildered by the
opinions of the writers, who, when they came upon the Roman law,
made no effort to interpret it according to its spirit but looked to its
literal expression.   The second cause was the then composition of
society, made up not of citizens all equal before the law, but of
classes which the law itself held as distinct.   The third cause is
to be sought in the domination of the political over every other
concern.   The State did not exist for the citizen, but the citizen
for the State; the preservation and prosperity of the State, considered above and beyond its citizens and personified in the prince,
were the supreme ends for which the legislator and magistrate must
strive, without regard for any other interest which might seem
contrary.

§ 267.   **New Principles.**[1] — There now gradually appeared, independent of legislator and judge, a new class of persons who occupied
themselves with public affairs but with quite new principles and
aims.   They sought to renovate society through philosophy; for
this purpose they studied the life of society as a whole, and espe-

---

[1] Besides *Pertile* and *Salvioli, op. cit.*, and the other authors and treatises
on criminal law already cited, may be consulted to advantage for this
period: F. *Sclopis*, "Storia della legislazione italiana", vol III (Turin,
1864); C. *Cantù*, "Beccaria e il diritto penale" (Florence, 1862); E.
Pessina, "Dei progressi del diritto penale in Italia nel secolo XIX"
(Florence, 1868).

cially the aim, scope and reason of the criminal law, as its guardian
sentinel. The new theories, laid as a foundation for an edifice
which they earnestly strove to raise upon the fragments of the old,
rapidly affected the criminal law; and their consequences were
fuller and more immediate in measure as they directly contradicted
the principles which we have just enumerated as the causes of the
earlier defects.

To the early legislative theory was now opposed the doctrine that
law must be based upon human nature, considered in its essentials,
and must therefore be constant and the same for all. The existing
criminal system then fell, in so far as it was derived historically
from ancient laws, was linked with the supernatural, inspired by
political interests, was the fruit of personal zeal, or adapted only
to the special conditions of a determined society. In denial of the
unequal composition of society, the equality of all persons was
proclaimed, and thus ceased the reasons for weighing penalties
upon uneven scales; and finally against omnipotent " reasons of
state ", utilized by the prince, was set up the " Rights of Man ",
whereby the State was made for him and not vice versa, and whereby it became the task of the State to guarantee and develop the
faculties of the individual, and not to make them the stool for its
own artificial ambitions. The natural faculties of the individual
were not to be limited save when they damaged those of another.
This harmful exercise of one's own powers was the reason that
transformed an act into a crime, which thus was something
conceivable only in a state of society. Outside society, in a natural state, crime was impossible, for there were no other rights, by
their own proper development, to limit the powers of the individual.
While the older society, therefore, acted upon the notion of original
sin and so assumed the duty of improving mankind, the new
philosophical schools, on the other hand, set out from the concept
of a state of primitive innocence, because of absolute natural
liberty. Man emerged from this state into that of society, and so
created the possibility of crime; and crime must be punished, as a
violation of the compact upon which society was formed, or because through crime society would return to a state of dissolution.
The penalty thus acquired a social quality, in the sense that it
existed for, and in defense of, society. As crimes could be only
such facts as directly injured the civil community, many acts now
escaped that category which formerly were forced within it.
Only such penalty might be given as was suited to effect its purpose, and to exceed this limit was tyranny and injustice.

It may easily be understood how such ideas, derived from the philosophical theories which had become general in the second half of the 1700 s, quickly accomplished a complete overturn of the criminal law.   At first, as usual in violent reactions, men fell into excess and exaggeration in their mania for the new and in the application of principles which in themselves had great power for good.   But with time they moved toward greater moderation; from these same principles sprang yet more useful results, which at no very remote day were to form the foundation and doctrines of the present criminal law.

Chapter XVII [1]

THE NEW PENALISTS

§ 268. **The Encyclopedists.** — The doctrines which the diffusion and application of the principles just outlined carried with them, belonged to the philosophical period, commonly called the period of the Encyclopedists. Around them were grouped all who, towards the middle of the 1700 s, adhered to the new philosophy. But the work of preparation had been going on for a considerable time: to be exact, from the time of the rise of the school of "natural law", so called because it studied the nature of man, whom it was intended to serve. From the 1600 s criminal law had felt the influence of this school. Hugo Grotius, who may be considered its founder, pointed out the new course to be followed. In the penalty he saw only "malum passionis, quod infligitur ob malum actionis"; for it he found justification in the principle of natural law: "qui male fecit malum ferat"; he conceived of crime solely as the violation of an obligation, undertaken by everyone in civil society, not to injure another; he did not believe that inward acts were punishable, for "Naturae humanae congruum non est ut ex actibus internis jus vel obligatio inter homines nascatur." He even declared that sins were not punishable in so far as "nec directe nec indirecte spectant ad societatem humanam." The penalty, consequently, should have no other aim than the common good; otherwise it was not permissible; the idea of clemency should always dominate, so that in repairing one evil another graver should not be committed.[2] In substance, two points especially were studied by Grotius and his followers, Hobbes, Puffendorf and Thomasius: to find a scientific and wholly satisfactory basis for the right and purpose of punitive law,

---

[1] [English Chap. XVII, §§ 268–275 = *Calisse*, Part III, Chap. I, §§ 158–165.]
[2] "De iure belli ac pacis", bk II, c. 20, "De poenis."

and, contrary to the habits of their times, to render punishments, so far as possible, less severe.

In Italy also writers were not lacking who, directly or indirectly, put forward the same ideas. To mention only the more important, Vico had already declared that " Jure naturali necessario poena manet "; and that its varying particulars should depend upon accessory circumstances, among which the most important was the character with which, at any given time, public power was invested.[1] Muratori, in his treatise on " Public Welfare " (" Della Felicità publica "), also exposed the evils of the existing system, and in his other book, " Shortcomings of Our System of Justice " (" Dei difetti della giurisprudenza "), he combatted their causes, among which he named first the confusion of opinions among writers and the uncontrolled discretionary power of the judge.

So the great reform was prepared. But on examining the writers, properly belonging to the revolutionary period of the 1700 s, it is found that the movement, until then slow and cautious, attained precipitous speed. The new writers, less erudite and less legalistic than their predecessors, because trusting more to their own rational powers than to positive knowledge, were eloquent, impassioned, pleasing and popular and so obtained a maximum result in a short time by interesting public opinion in their discussions and turning it openly in their favor. The centre of this movement was France. Voltaire, Rousseau, Helvetius, Montesquieu, included the penal law within their universal analyses and gave it a new direction. But from France this early intellectual revolution spread into Italy as into other countries. There, in so far as it touched the penal law, it is fair to note that its writers did not remain the modest disciples of foreign doctrines, but during this important period gained a leadership to which all Europe turned attentive ear.

§ 269. **Beccaria.** — No book, indeed, upon penal law created a greater stir in Europe, was more read, or brought greater fame to its author than " Crimes and Penalties " (" Dei delitti e delle pene "), published in 1764 by Beccaria. He was born at Milan in 1738. Scorning the conventional type of education planned for him, he gave himself over to the French writers, then coming into fashion.[2]

---

[1] "De uno universi·iuris principio et fine uno", chaps. LXIX, CCIV.
[2] He so declared, writing to his French translator Morellet: "I owe everything to French authors; they have revealed to me human feelings that eight years of a fanatical education had suffocated . . . D'Alembert, Diderot, Helvetius, Buffon, Hume, glorious names that none can hear

Beccaria was ranked among those who, in the name of philosophy, demanded the complete renovation of society. It was natural that he should soon ally himself with those having ideas common with his own. But they must have been few, if his statement may be believed that " In a capital (Milan) numbering 120,000 inhabitants, hardly a score may be found who thirst for knowledge or would make a sacrifice for virtue and truth." [1] Thus Beccaria found himself one of a small group of friends, who discussed among themselves the dominant questions of the day, planned to form a colony, based upon French philosophy, " in distant America ", and who, " persuaded that periodical literature was the best means of tempting minds, incapable of serious application, to undertake some reading ",[2] printed serials under the title " The Cafè " (" El Caffè "), through which, in the flamboyant style of the day and in imitation of French examples, they succeeded in disseminating the principles of which they were such fervent apostles. In this company was Alessandro Verri, who held the position of prison inspector. As such, under the old prison system (§ 247), he visited the prisons, discovered and reported abuses, hastened trials, recommended pardons and gave what aid he could to the unfortunate inmates. The spectacle which his duties thus presented every day was made the subject of his conversation with his friends; conditions were discussed, existing evils were deplored, and radical changes were urged. Their imaginations were stirred and Beccaria, preaching a philosophy of the heart rather than the mind, felt that first passionate spark that led him to write " Crimes and Penalties."

§ 270. **Beccaria's " Crimes and Penalties."** — The book is wholly given to the application of contemporaneous philosophical doctrines to the criminal law, with the view mainly of effecting a complete reform. But, as was common with all the Italian writers who followed the new philosophy, Beccaria had the wisdom to avoid the extreme consequences of his French masters. In place of the fanatical and relentless destruction of the whole existing order, he desired improvement. Certainly his aversion to the past was great, whenever it involved the cause of the evils which

without emotion! Your immortal works are my constant reading, the object of my labors by day and of my thoughts in the silence of the night! It was but five years ago that I became the convert of philosophy, and this I owe to the 'Lettres Persanes.' The second work, which completed the revolution in my mind, was that of Helvetius. It urged me with irresistible force into the road of truth and for the first time awakened my attention to the blindness and the wrongs of humanity." *Cantù, op. cit.*, pp. 66–69.   [1] *Cantù, cit.*, pp. 66–69.   [2] *Ibid.*

he would remove.   Toward the Roman law as then studied, and its learned followers, he was therefore implacable.   "A few remnants," as he described it in his preface, "of the laws of an ancient conquering people, compiled at the command of a prince who reigned twelve centuries ago in Constantinople, later mingled with Lombard rites and collected into jumbled volumes by private and obscure interpreters, form the tradition which, in a large part of Europe, still enjoys the name of law.   It is sad, though a common thing today, that an opinion of Carpzov, an antiquated practice referred to by Clarus, a torture suggested with cruel complacency by Farinacius, should constitute the law, followed with confidence by those who would use fear to rule the lives and fortunes of men."   He, therefore, followed a different goal.   In disregard of common opinion, courageously attacking where others had feared, following his own inspiration, speaking with frankness and passion, he obtained in the field of criminal law what others were proclaiming in the civil and political field.

His point of departure was the social contract.   From the necessity of defending the social order so established he drew his fundamental concepts of crime and punishment and from them he derived all other consequences.   There is no crime save in so far as there is injury to some right which society is bound to defend for its own preservation and to insure the exercise of the individual faculties of others.   Crimes, therefore, are acts which tend to destroy society or its representative; or endanger the citizen with respect to his life, property, or honor; or finally, are contrary to each man's duty to do or to refrain from doing, in the light of the public good.[1]   All other acts, even when not in themselves good, are nevertheless not punishable; particularly are exempt those qualified simply as sins.   "I speak," said Beccaria, "only of offenses that arise from the nature of man and the social contract, not of sins, whose temporal penalties should be regulated by principles other than those of a limited philosophy."[2]   The main object of those who rule society is to prevent violations of the social contract, to hinder, that is, the commission of crime, seeing to it that the laws are clear and simple, that all take an interest in their execution, that no inequality of treatment exists among men, that education and culture are made as general as possible.[3]   If this means does not succeed, recourse is had to punishment.   But, before applying it, there must be certainty as to the crime, and this

---

[1] *Beccaria*, "Dei delitti e delle pene", § 25.
[2] *Id.*, § 37.   [3] *Id.*, § 41.

must be sought by quite other methods than those then in practice. He proscribes secret accusations, which encourage men to false and covert actions;[1] leading questions and judicial discretion;[2] oaths intended for the accused's own harm.[3] Above all he condemns torture, the destroyer of truth, the sure means of absolving the courageous criminal and condemning the weak and innocent.[4] Credible witnesses and secure facts are the road to the determination of crime, for, to merit punishment, offenses must be certain.[5] And when they are such, the penalty must strike them " in order to dissuade the obstinate mind of every man from resubmerging the laws of society into primal chaos "; that is, to prevent anyone from taking to himself, to another's injury, that portion of his liberty which in the measure of strict necessity he yields in order to render social life possible. " The aggregate of these minimum portions constitutes the field of punishment; all beyond is abuse and injustice; fact but not law. Penalties that go beyond the preservation of the requirements of public safety are of their nature unjust." [6] " The aim (of punishment), therefore, is solely to prevent the criminal from further harming his fellow citizens and to deter others from doing the like. Those penalties and methods of infliction should be chosen which, aside from the question of proportion, will create the most effective and lasting impression upon men's minds and be least painful to the body of the criminal." [7] From these principles the consequence easily followed that punishment should not be needlessly inhumane; that confiscation was improper because it struck at the innocent besides the guilty;[8] that the death penalty was unjust and injurious in that it could not be supposed that man, in constituting society, had by any reasoning whatsoever renounced the natural right of self-preservation; and in that this punishment failed of its object, since, both for the individual who suffered it and for others for whom it was to serve as an example, it was but a momentary impression less effective than other penalties, such as life imprisonment, which was continuing and visible. Only in two cases might death be necessary: when the criminal, though imprisoned, continued to possess such relations and power as to be able to produce a revolution, dangerous to the established government; and when his death was the sure and only means of diverting others from crime.[9] These two reservations, it is evident, greatly circumscribed the ideal of

---

[1] *Beccaria*, " Dei delitti e delle pene ", § 9.
[2] *Id.*, § 10.   [4] *Id.*, § 12.   [6] *Id.*, § 2.   [8] *Id.*, § 17.
[3] *Id.*, § 11.   [5] *Id.*, § 7.   [7] *Id.*, § 15.   [9] *Id.*, § 16.

the abolition of the death penalty, and as a consequence, Beccaria concluded : " In order that no penalty should be an act of violence by one or many against a private citizen, it is essential that it be public, prompt, necessary, the minimum possible under the circumstances, proportioned to the crime and commanded by law." [1]

§ 271. **Beccaria's Merits.** — That the stir over Beccaria's book was tremendous was not to be wondered at. On the one hand he had the sympathy of great numbers, who felt inwardly what he first had the courage to say publicly ; each of these discovered his own thoughts in Beccaria's pages and at once enlisted under his standard. On the other hand he rendered a service to those who would direct the philosophic movement and who were shaping public opinion throughout Europe. For, accepting their rules, he applied them to the criminal law and showed the great power for good which they contained because of their successful adaptability to every argument of social interest. To such an extent were the Encyclopedists recognized in " Crimes and Penalties ", that it was even said they had written it, though the risk incurred in publication was credited to Beccaria. D'Alembert, who with Diderot founded the Encyclopedia, was unstinted in his praise of its truth, logic, philosophy and humanity. Voltaire made it the object of a special study in which he declared that in morals it was what few prescriptions were in medicine, and prophesied that alone it would eliminate every trace of barbarism from the law. No sooner had Beccaria arrived at Paris than Baron d'Holbach invited him to his suppers, where Helvetius, Rousseau and all who called themselves followers of the philosophy of humanity met and by their discussions prepared the social revolution. Malesherbes inspired Morellet to translate Beccaria into French ; Diderot added notes which appeared in the edition by Röderer. The latter, when sending a copy to Julia Beccaria, declared that so great was the effect of her father's book in France that ten years before the Revolution the criminal courts had lost all semblance of what they had been, since the younger judiciary drew guidance more from the principles of his treatise on crime and punishments than from the laws. As many as six translations have been made into French ; translations into other languages also appeared, including one into Spanish by Charles III's Minister, Campomanes, to whom had been entrusted the compilation of a criminal code. With the acceptance of philosophic opinion, Beccaria's book spread throughout the whole of Europe. The Society of Economics of Berne

[1] *Beccaria,* " Dei delitti e delle pene ", § 42.

voted him a gold medal for the courage of his protest in aid of humanity against deep rooted prejudices. Even the Empress of Russia, who enjoyed corresponding with the French philosophers, learned through them of Beccaria and desired him at her Court. Though D'Alembert advised against it, he decided to accept the invitation and had already set out upon his journey when Lombardy, recognizing in him the trained mind capable of rendering a great service to his country, and fearing criticism should he be lost through the invitation of a foreign country, succeeded in holding him in Italy by creating for him in 1768 a professorship in the political sciences, later known as political economy. It was proof that Beccaria was honored for his book even by his government, although perhaps also prompted by the desire to avoid his traveling over Europe with the possibility of his accomplishing a still greater revolution. Beccaria in fact remained in undisturbed and easy relations with his government. In the replies to the criticism of his book he declared himself a Catholic and a faithful subject. This he repeated in later prefaces so that editions and commentaries were also published with governmental authorization in the various States of Italy, while in his own State he held honorable though always modest positions, and such as kept him out of the public eye. He died suddenly on the 28th of November, 1794, unnoticed and obscure, while over the world swept the reverberations of the Revolution, among whose makers he had but a short while since been enthusiastically proclaimed.

§ 272. **Beccaria's Opponents and Critics.** — The applause given Beccaria's " Crimes and Penalties " did not drown other voices, raised not in praise but in condemnation, sometimes violent. From 1765 to the end of the century much was written in refutation, entire or partial. This was truer of Italy than elsewhere. Naples, Sicily, Rome, Tuscany, and even Lombardy produced defenders of what were regarded as Italian institutions and which Beccaria, censured by all who did not support the foreign novelties, had condemned. Two institutions, or rather two forces, had been the particular objects of his attacks, because in his opinion they had done the greatest harm in criminal matters; the authority of the Roman law and reasons of State. Two writers, strongly contrasted in sentiment and doctrine, now came forward in their defense from different parts of Italy. The theory of reasons of State was championed at Venice, where the very method of procedure and sentence most forcibly condemned by Beccaria was so closely followed in the Tribunal of the Ten that he was believed to have been attacking it directly.   A defender was needed and found in Angelo Fachinei, who in his "Notes and Observations" ("Note ed osservazioni"), which appeared in 1765, violently and abusively attacked Beccaria's work and eulogized torture, secret accusation, executive interference in the administration of justice, — in short, the procedure followed by the Venetian court.   Beccaria's temperate and clear replies won him praise and victory. From Rome came a defense of Roman law.   In 1784 was published "An Apology of Roman Jurisprudence or Critical Notes on the Work Entitled 'Crimes and Penalties'" ("Apologia della giurisprudenze romana o note critiche al libro intitolato Dei delitti e delle pene"), an anonymous work, but known to have been written by Antonio Giudici, who described it as a study of the basis of the Roman law, sovereignty, innocence, and public welfare.   His work was the opposite of that of Fachinei.   Giudici admitted and condemned the abuses of torture, the death penalty, judicial discretion, privileges, and others.   But because of the abuses he did not believe that logically the institutions themselves could be condemned.   It was not Roman jurisprudence that was pernicious, but the accumulation of commentaries that suffocated it; courts should not be reduced to a simple instrument for the mechanical application of laws: " Scire leges non est verba earum tenere sed vim et potestatem "; torture might be useful when the clearly guilty criminal persisted in silence; equal penalty for all was not always just, because some punishments, such as outlawry and infamy, were more serious for persons of one rank than of another; the death penalty was necessary for crimes which attacked the basis of society or with premeditated malice disturbed public or private security.   These and similar principles were defended by Giudici with a restraint and moderation which, however, did not hide his strong aversion to the fundamental ideas which the new philosophy was proclaiming concerning the origin and aims of society, the essential nature of crime and the justification of punishment.

§ 273. **Renazzi.** — Contemporaneously with Giudici's there appeared at Rome another deservedly celebrated work on criminal law: the "Elements of Criminal Law" ("Elementa juris criminalis"), of F. Maria Renazzi.[1]   He went beyond Giudici, because his greater sympathy led him to profit more by the new direction taken by penology.   His attack upon the past, however, led him into a middle path of compromise.   If compromise had been pos-

[1] Published at Senis, 1794.

sible, it would have been effected by Renazzi, for he presented a
system of penal law, well ordered in every part, inspired by a humane sentiment and a philosophic spirit, moderate in its refutation
of opposing opinions, and frank in recognizing and condemning
existing abuses.   Renazzi, too, placed the blame for these upon
the jumble of commentators.   Of Clarus, while superior to the
others, he said no more than that he deservedly lost the fame
enjoyed during his life; but to Farinacius, he declared, must be
laid the blame for the shocking corruption of penal science, of
which he had not only written unsoundly and obscurely, but which
he had rendered variable and uncertain, so that from his works
nothing of use could be derived.   His learning was commonplace,
he added; he contributed nothing at all in the needed fields of
principles; he stole from the works of others what little merit
can be found in his own; finally so small was his critical judgment that he dared apply to himself the Horatian motto " Exegi
monumentum aere perennius." [1]   So severe a criticism of one who
had occupied a position of first rank among criminalists, throws
light upon Renazzi, especially when these words are compared with
his estimate of writers of the school of natural law.   Three he
admired: he praised Grotius, Puffendorf and Montesquieu, declaring them the great masters, in all cases save where, contrary to
his own policy, they departed from religious principles.   He
commended Beccaria but dared not let it be known to what extent,
merely saying of him that without a doubt it was he who first
courageously gave a new course to criminal science.[2]

This course, in substance, he aimed to follow.   He proposed,
he said, to cleanse the criminal law of the filth with which, like the
Augean stable, he found it cumbered.[3]   He wished to purge it,
that is, to preserve existing institutions in substance, but through
philosophy to disengage them from the Roman and canon law,
theology, politics, medicine and every other art or science that had
come to attach itself injuriously.[4]   Renazzi's book is divided into
four parts.   The first deals with crimes in general.   His classification includes the religious crime, which Beccaria had excluded.
Here his purpose of punishment is not, however, to revenge an
offended divinity, but to repress acts harmful to society.[5]   In the
second part, which treats of penalties, he admits that the object of
the punitive power is to obtain peace; he accepts the idea of the

---

[1] "Praef.", Part I, pp. xvi–xvii.   [3] Ibid., p. xxvii.
[2] Ibid., pp. xxiv–xxv.   [4] "Prolegomena", c. ix–xxiii.
                 [5] Part I, pp. 47, 232; IV, pp. 61, 62.

passage from a state of nature to one of society and the necessity of penalties to prevent, " comminatione et repraesentatione sensibilium malorum ", the resumption of surrendered liberties.   In a word, he admits the social contract, and joins Beccaria in advocating that more attention be paid to the prevention of evil, especially by proper education, than to the sharpening of punishment; that laws should be few and clear; that penalties should be proportioned to crimes; that they should not be crueler than necessary, and that they should never be inflicted unless the crime was proved with certainty.[1]   Thus, in the third part he comes to the reform of procedure.   Prisons should be light and healthy; the keep of the prisoners should be in the charge of the State; the old methods of trial are condemned, torture especially because of its cruelty and the untrustworthiness of the evidence claimed to be obtained by it; and on this last point he cites Becarria.[2]   Upon the question of the death penalty Renazzi would not speak, though his disapproval may be implied.   He pleads that he has not the spirit to write upon so cruel a subject, and in a note he prays the reader not to take his statement as pretense.   But it is difficult to believe this protest when the preceding chapters show that his spirit was undismayed by a minute description of all the terrible methods by which death was customarily inflicted.[3]   In the fourth part he comes to the application of his principles to the several kinds of crimes and penalties and throughout shows the same desire to breathe a new life into the old body of the criminal law.   An example is furnished by his words upon the crime of magic.   He admits its existence, as did the earlier criminalists, and grants them even the satisfaction of describing with particularity the manner and effects of the crime.   Then he declares that " probi et doctissimi viri gravissimique jurisprudentes " laugh at these follies and protest against their cruel penalties.   He concludes that if magic were made manifest in acts of themselves indubitably criminal, such as poisoning, rape, heresy, deceit or otherwise, it should undoubtedly be severely punished; but if such a criminal consequence was lacking, an accusation of magic should be dealt with very cautiously, in order not to incur the just rebuke of those who denied the existence of the crime and held that the accused should be sent to the doctor rather than to the executioner, in order by diet and drugs to be restored to normal life.[4]

[1] Part II, pp. 22, 154, 198, 222, 223.   [3] Part II, p. 155.
[2] Part III, pp. 96, 100, 150, 221–228.   [4] Part IV, pp. 61, 62.

In all this is clearly seen one who understood his age but who, on the other hand, because of attachment to the institutions about him, or because he foresaw the exaggerations into which the innovators would be led, maintained a prudent reserve, marked, however, by good judgment and dignity. This estimate is confirmed by the honor in which he was everywhere held. Catherine of Russia invited him to reorganize the criminal procedure of her Empire; Austria desired him to teach at Pavia; Napoleon in 1803 named him a professor at Bologna. He remained, however, faithful to the University of Rome, where he continued until his death in 1808.

§ 274. **Filangieri.** — A somewhat similar movement appeared in the Neapolitan school, where the doctrines of Beccaria had found both champions and foes, and where, among such names as Genovesi, a commentator of Beccaria,[1] Melchior Delfico, Dragonetti, Cirillo, Mario Pagano, all of whom in different ways wrote upon the criminal law, there rose to special prominence Filangieri, who in himself epitomized all the characteristics of this school. Part Three of his " Science of Legislation " ("Scienza della legislazione ") he dedicated entirely to the criminal law. To it he applied the same principle which should govern legislation in general, namely, that, to be useful, it should make for the safety and tranquillity of the citizen,[2] by combining at once two virtues, one absolute, consisting in harmony with the universal moral law, the other, relative, residing in concordance with the conditions of the place and people whom the law governs.[3]

Under the veil of such expressions are easily recognized the predominant theories of natural law and of the defense of society as the object of punishment. Through them is also recognizable at once the character of Filangieri, who, while in substance following and using the new philosophy, sought to moderate it and harmonize it with existing social institutions, especially with ecclesiastical and political authority. To this end he sought to give to legislation a basis of philosophy, not derived solely from reasoning, but sustained by revelation [4] and confirmed by history. In this he opposed the pure rationalists and the method of reasoning then in vogue;[5] but he also departed from the Roman school, in that whereas, especially under Renazzi, it turned to history to show that the institutions still in use were in themselves good but had

---

[1] *Cantù, op. cit.*, pr.
[2] Book I, chap. 1.
[3] Book I, chaps. 4, 5.
[4] Book I, chap. 4.
[5] Book III, chap. 2, last note.

become bad only by the incrusting growth of innumerable abuses, now Filangieri, without limiting himself to any definite historical period, examined the whole of the past in search, among the fragments left by the memory of time, of something which would satisfy the essential requirements of good legislation and could be usefully adapted to the conditions of his day.

It should be observed that the innovations which Filangieri effected, or thought to effect, were more apparent than real. An example will illustrate this. He denied a state of nature preceding that of society; he declared himself the first " to believe that society was born with man." But what was that society? It was a " purely natural " one in which " magistrates, laws, penalties, and civil duties were unknown "; in which " no other inequality was recognized but that born of physical force, no law save that of nature "; in which " each was sovereign, magistrate, judge, and the revenger of his own injuries "; it was a society that exposed the weak " to the caprice of the strong "; where honor and life were " insecure possessions " and " distrust, uncertainty and fear disturbed " at every moment the individual's peace; in short a society from which it was well to emerge and for which, to avoid its defects, " civil society " was substituted, whereby natural liberty was sacrificed to insure safety and tranquillity.[1] What difference, save in words, between original society as described by Filangieri and savagery? Between his theory and that of the social contract? In substance, therefore, the consequences in the criminal field are no less alike. The right to punish results from the formation of a moral entity, representing the will of all and possessed of the aggregate of all private forces.[2] The object of punishment is to insure peace and it should not, therefore, be regarded as revenge for a crime committed, but as a means to prevent the delinquent from further harming society and to deter others from imitating his example, by keeping before them a picture of the pain that swiftly and surely will follow crime.[3] Crime can not exist unless it involves in itself an injury, a violation of the law: that is, of the contract by which society is governed.[4] Only by such a test may crimes against religion also be punished.[5] As a corollary to these principles, it was shown that penalties should not be severer than needed for the object in view, or than the damage demanded; that there should be no punishment until

[1] Book I, chap. 1.   [3] Book III, chap. 27.
[2] Book III, chap. 26.   [4] Book III, chap. 25.
                [5] Book III, chap. 44.

the wrong had been ascertained by means satisfactory to the general principles of natural law; that all discretionary power should be withdrawn from the application of the law, which should be cleared from the rubbish of so many different systems and the " stupid " veneration of ancient use, so that all men should hold it in faith, without fear that the innocent might be convicted or the guilty acquitted. He showed, in short, that legislation should be reformed upon the guiding principle that the absolute must be coupled with the relative good.[1] From this rule Filangieri derived many inconsistent consequences. It led him, for example, to the abolition of torture, against which he inveighed bitterly on the ground that, being contrary to natural law that one should accuse oneself, no right existed to force an act which was a violation of the inviolable.[2] On the other hand, by the same rule he justified the death penalty for homicide, since, being a law of nature to kill in self-defense, if society, the depositary of individual rights, did not kill the slayer, the latter would enjoy the advantage of being relieved from the reaction of the injured: that is, he would have wholly consummated his fatal design.[3] Turning thus to every branch of the criminal law, but especially to procedure, which he thought too much neglected in favor of other branches,[4] Filangieri concludes that society should aim for the reform of legislation, in accord with his principles, employing the powers already existing, rather than surrendering to the extreme theories that demanded the remorseless destruction of all that had been so laboriously constructed.

§ 275. **Romagnosi.** — Of these theories the best were brought together by G. D. Romagnosi. He rejected all that did not conform to a rigorous metaphysic; to the rest he gave a full scientific demonstration and, so, a durable stability. In his " Genesis of the Criminal Law " ("Genesi del diritto penale"), he went beyond the observable; he studied the phenomena of criminal law by abstract speculation, and therein departed from all existing schools, including that of the " social contract ", which he called fictitious. He declared men's renunciation of a part of their rights in order to form society a fiction; men associated together by the necessity of their nature; outside of society man had no rights (though he had moral claims), and therefore had none to yield. Law evolved in society merely as a " useful regulative

---

[1] Book III, chaps, 1, 12, 15, 25, 27, 39. [4] Book III, chap. 1.
[2] Book I, chap. 4; III, chaps. 10, 11.
[3] Book III, chap. 29.

force ",[1] and especially from society's necessity of defending itself and its members.   In the right of defense, which is inherent in and not derived from society, and which is legitimate because necessary and because the ideal to be defended, namely, social life, is just, he found the basis and justification of the criminal law.[2] Therefore defense was not limited solely to the actual repression of a crime, by preventing its accomplishment, but extended also to its punishment when committed.   In this way society repelled the evils which would arise from impunity, for to remove the fear of suffering following surely upon crime, would be to release from restraint the tendency to procure by crime gratifications otherwise unobtainable.[3]   And this right of defense resulted from yet another social right, namely that of men to safeguard their happiness.   It emerged as a direct emanation, an acquisition of society from the relationship of men in association, without the need of any transfer or surrender; it was enlarged proportionately to the need of punishment to preserve the legitimate well being of man; it resided in the " totality " of the social group, to the exclusion of any private individual; its aim was not to torment the sensitive being, or to satisfy a sentiment of vengeance, or to recall from the order of accomplished things a crime already committed, but to inculcate fear in the delinquent, in order that in the " future " he might not again offend society.[4]   It is apparent that the ideas of expiation, amends, compensation for damage and absolute justice were entirely abandoned.   As to penalties, it was shown that they should satisfy certain general requirements.   They must be necessary, the mildest possible, and at the same time they must be made the most effective, by properly proportioning the quantity of fear possible to inspire to the quantity of " criminal impulse " actuating the crime.[5]   It was necessary, therefore, to understand well how to weigh that impulse, as also to understand well the elements of the crime, and these Romagnosi acutely examined under the different situations of commission, attempt, failure, wrongful intent and damage, in order to make possible an effective and warranted proportionment of punishment to crime.   The just penalty was one which, based on the authority of society for a violation of a clear social duty, proved in practice the most appropriate to preserve the general safety.[6]   If it fulfilled these conditions any punishment was justified including

[1] § 151.
[2] Part II, chap. 8.
[3] §§ 332, 390.
[4] §§ 391–395.
[5] §§ 400, 404, 430, 460.
[6] § 1577.

death;[1] and the greater became its justification as all members of society became persuaded of its justice.[2]   On the other hand, prevention was more necessary than punishment.   Here the essential condition was a politically strong government.   But physical force was not alone sufficient; to complete the force of the State, manifesting itself in punishment, there should concur other subsidiary sanctions: religion, social convention, and honor.[3]   These sentiments, derived from a right conscience, healthy public opinion and social respect, were the obstacles which the criminal impulse had to overcome along the path towards crime.   They also, therefore, together with fear of punishment, were to act as a " counter-impulse " upon the mind of one disposed towards crime, cause him to discover his error and to refrain.[4]   It was thus the idea of the co-operation of the psychological factor that Romagnosi developed as a supreme corollary from his philosophy of criminal law.   It followed that the individual, who gave nothing juridical to society while he received from it the fullest legal protection, lost in importance in competition with society, and through society with the State: a consequence contrary to the then prevailing theory that the individual was everthing and that the State could possess or do nothing save within the limits of what was first yielded to it by the individual.

[1] § 346.
[2] §§ 666, 679, 743, 746 *et seq.*

[3] §§ 907, 920, 921.
[4] § 1579.

CHAPTER XVIII [1]

REFORM OF THE CRIMINAL LAW

§ 276. Eighteenth Century.
§ 277. Peter Leopold, Tuscany.
§ 278. Joseph II, Lombardy.
§ 279. The French Revolution.

§ 280. Kingdoms of Italy and of Naples; the French Penal Code.

§ 276. **Eighteenth Century.** — So great an intellectual movement, wherein the most robust minds of the period participated, could not remain confined within the circle of speculation and theory, especially when supported by a favorable public opinion. In Italy, as already stated, the destruction of the existing order was not preached; on the contrary it was claimed that the then State had within itself power to reform political and social conditions and therefore it was everywhere urged to exert its power. The enlightened princes who were then governing, supported by able counselors, did not decline the invitation. Whether by conviction or to control a movement the extent of whose force they realized, they lent their labor to many reforms, among which those concerning the penal law had particular importance. Naturally this recreative spirit was not equally intense and effective in all the Italian States. The temperament of the ruling princes, the intellectual development of the people, the particular political conditions, all made for varied applications in different territories.

The States of the Church remained faithful to the principles of the canon law, slowly coördinating with them the betterments that were taking place. And it must be granted that those principles had, on the whole, during the preceding period, checked those excesses and abuses complained of elsewhere. Nor did Piedmont advance far along the path of reform, although one entire section, the fourth, of the Royal Law of 1770, was devoted to the penal law. The spirit of the new age had penetrated but little; and the same may be said of the Modenese laws of 1771, which were but imitations. While on the one hand it was accepted that "infamy" should not attach to the family of the criminal, and

[1] [English Chap. XVIII, §§ 276–280 = *Calisse*, Part III, Chap. II, §§ 166–170.]

470

that no composition might be made with the culprit himself as to his punishment, aside from exceptional cases which it was desirable to retain; on the other hand judicial discretion remained undisturbed, as also inequality of treatment depending upon social rank, the death penalty for numerous and even minor crimes and deliberately made more painful, torture, mutilation and many other sad inheritances of the preceding period. At Naples, however, Charles III and Ferdinand IV, under the ministry of Tanucci, accomplished important liberal reforms. Torture, after 1738, was retained chiefly merely to exhibit the machines that might be used; unity was given to the many jurisdictions within the Kingdom; judges were obliged to declare the reasons of their decisions and to base them solely upon the authority of the statutes of the State or the common law; the sanitation and morality of prisons were improved. Terrible, indeed, however, was Ferdinand's reaction, involving the field of the criminal law, when he felt himself in the coils of the great revolution. In two other States of Italy, Lombardy and Tuscany, on the other hand, reforms had a wider and more fertile field of application and greater sincerity and stability.

§ 277. **Peter Leopold, Tuscany.** — From the time when he took over the government of Tuscany, the Grand Duke Peter Leopold contemplated the reform of criminal legislation. He recognized that the existing law was too severe, that it was cumbered with the contradictory rules of remote and contrasting periods, ill adapted to a population whom he characterized as gentle and kindly. Encouraged by the very excellent results of some partial reforms, he prepared for a general restatement of the whole body of criminal law. On November 30, 1786, was published his " Reform of the Criminal Law of Tuscany " (" Riforma della legislazione criminale toscana ").[1]

The philosophy and philanthropy then dominant contributed largely to this work, but not to the point of excluding all independence of action by this ruler, who, while frequently adopting the new ideas, moderated them, combined them with others or rejected them altogether, according to their fitness. Reference has already been made to Leopold's consideration for the temper of the population to be served by his code. He therefore departed from the system of pure natural law and approached Filangieri's doctrine of the relative good, thus anticipating the reaction which

[1] "Introduction" to the "Riforma della legislazione criminale toscana", published in Siena; it contains 119 sections..

was to reach its height in the "historical school." In punishment he did not see, as did most, merely a means of social defense, but aimed to use it at once as a satisfaction for private and public injury, a corrective of the criminal and a public example.[1] In crime he saw always a hurt to social interests: if public or private security was disturbed, there was a delict; if a regulation for the greater well-being of society was infringed, there was a transgression. The two classes had different penalties and jurisdictions.[2] If there was no direct violation of a social interest, there was no crime. Following Beccaria[3] and Filangieri,[4] Leopold did not enumerate suicide and duelling; crimes of "lèse majesté" were abolished;[5] but he recognized those against religion and punished them severely, provided they were evidenced by external acts and were such as to cause injury to society's interest in general order and tranquillity.[6] On the other hand, he departed from the accepted opinion in punishing offenses against public and private morality by very severe penalties, even that of forced and hard labor for life.[7] This was the maximum penalty in the Leopoldine system, which, having abolished the death penalty, justified this severe provision upon reasons similar, even in phraseology, to those of Beccaria.[8] Together with death, he proscribed mutilation, branding, infamy, torture and confiscation, as involving the innocent with the guilty.[9] Pecuniary penalties were retained; compositions with the judge were prohibited, although latitude of judgment was preserved.[10] The proceeds of fines were devoted to the compensation of those proved innocent in the course of process.[11] The major penalties were paid in prison. The maximum, as already noted, was forced labor for life, in double chains, bare feet, a special uniform and a placard worn on the breast bearing the words "Extreme Penalty" ("ultimo supplizio").[12] In the condition of the prisons great improvement was made. It was provided that they should be dry, airy, and lacking in nothing which made for salubrity.

Great benefits were said to have followed the Leopoldine reforms; the prisons were indeed almost emptied; and it is certain that his people were appreciative. But since the reforms were obtained through the generous concession of the sovereign, no right could

[1] § 51.
[2] §§ 3, 109.
[3] "Dei delitti e delle pene", §§ 29, 35.
[4] "Scienza della legislazione", Bk. III, chaps. 51, 55.
[5] § 62.   [7] §§ 96–101.   [9] §§ 45, 54, 57.   [11] § 46.
[6] § 60.   [8] § 51.   [10] § 96.   [12] § 55.

be set up in opposition whenever the prince thought it proper to change or revoke them. The fact is that Leopold began to tear down his own edifice by re-establishing the death penalty in 1790 for incitement to rebellion, and later for murder and attempt to destroy the religion of the State.

This reaction became still more marked under the government of Ferdinand III, who, by an edict of August 30, 1793, extended the application of the death penalty and adopted other severe provisions, following especially the recommendations contained in the report made at his request by Professor Ranucci of Pisa, under the title " Study on the Form of the New Criminal Code " (" Saggio per la forma del nuovo codice criminale ").

§ 278. **Joseph II, Lombardy.** — Though more guarded and less inclined to the new systems, Lombardy found a great reformer in Joseph II, who in 1787 published his Code of Crimes and Penalties (" Codice dei delitti e delle pene "). The need for his reform rested upon the same reasons as that of Leopold, and on many points the two lawmakers agreed. In withdrawing discretionary power from the judge, in following Beccaria's method of classifying crimes, in considering crimes against religion as disturbances of social tranquillity, in his prison reforms, abolition of torture, proportioning of penalties to crimes, divesting general opinion of authority, in his investigation of the constituent elements of crimes in order to determine their quality and gravity, — in all these matters Joseph II's legislation conformed with his time, though different from that of Leopold and not infrequently superior from the point of view of scientific exactness and practical judgment.[1] Where Leopold had courageously made an end, Joseph II stopped at mitigation. Branding and infamy remained;[2] confiscation, even where the accused had children, was retained for crimes of sedition and high treason;[3] crimes of " lèse majesté " found a place, although subjected to the ordinary procedure and cleared of many features that had accompanied them;[4] suicide and the duel were punished;[5] fines were abolished except for prohibited games;[6] but on the other hand we find chains, beating and the gallows;[7] the death penalty was preserved for those guilty of sedition,[8] and Joseph took care to declare that, if abolished for most crimes, he had not done so out of regard for the principles of the philosophers, but had followed his own belief that his substituted

[1] I, §§ 13, 22; II, §§ 64 etc.   [5] I, §§ 105, 125.
[2] §§ 24, 39.   [6] II, § 10.
[3] I, §§ 42, 46, 53.   [7] I, § 21.
[4] I, §§ 41, 42, 44.   [8] I, § 20.

punishment would be felt even more powerfully, because of its duration, and because better suited to instill terror in evil doers. Upon these points Joseph's Code did not escape criticism; and it seemed so just that he was disposed to make his penal reform correspond more nearly to the conditions of his country and the character of his people. The collected criticisms were referred to a commission which, besides being versed in theory, and possessed of qualities both philosophic and exact, was without prejudice as to any determined system. It, therefore, was to choose from the old laws and the new codes all that was best and most suitable to the new era. Beccaria was a member of this commission, which began its labors in 1791; he was in fact its reporter upon several questions, though not always successful in imposing his views. But no practical results came of the long drawn out discussions, for they were interrupted by the French Revolution, which swept across the Alps.

§ 279. **The French Revolution.** — Beyond the Alps the Revolution had already transformed criminal law, from the day when, in the " Declaration of the Rights of Man ", the principle was proclaimed that law might prohibit only actions harmful to society and should establish only penalties strictly and evidently necessary. It was the application of already professed doctrines, in conformity with which a general penal reform was to be effected as part of the program of all parties of the Estates General. Many professed theories, nevertheless, never came into practice. The death penalty is an example. The Convention, which had promised to abolish it before adjourning, defeated the proposition six times during 1793 and, on adjourning, postponed action until a general declaration of peace. Meanwhile France was decimated by executions, because the defence of society was confused with the political interests as they arose from time to time, and because in the general chaos no higher necessity was recognized than the destruction of personal enemies, who were seen as enemies of the people.

Into Italy also the Revolution carried the impulse to destroy all that belonged to the past. The criminal law was not spared. And yet in this regard Italy found herself amid peculiar conditions. Here a rich treasure of science, accumulated through centuries, although rendered obscure by an overgrowth of literature and by despotic courts, saved the tradition of Italian superiority in the field of penology. To Italy belonged the names and experience of the two greatest writers upon the criminal law produced by the revolutionary philosophy, Beccaria and Romagnosi, about whom a very large number of other illustrious penalists had grouped themselves; here a broad and fertile spirit of rivalry developed in the universities, courts and legislative bodies, from which, without foreign aid, the criminal law felt the refreshing influence of the most recent scientific discoveries; here, finally, there was a just appreciation of the reality of things so that none sought to destroy existing institutions merely to realize innovations, whose worth could only be theoretically appraised.   There was consequently in Italy a strong desire for a native criminal law, and it sought, so long as possible, to resist the will of the French conqueror.

§ 280. **Kingdoms of Italy and of Naples; The French Penal Code.** — In the Kingdom of Italy [1] two drafts were begun, one of a code of criminal law and the other of a code of criminal procedure. For this work Romagnosi was in 1806 called to Milan from Parma, where he was teaching public law.   The illustrious philosopher, though not without powerful opposition, succeeded in introducing many of his own ideas concerning punishment, criminality, rehabilitation and numerous other questions of great interest. But the compilers had before them the French laws, whose severity they were not allowed to ignore.   In consequence the Italian draft retained the death penalty, aggravated by the mode of execution; deportation, internment, branding, gallows, confiscation, civil degradation, barring from the professions and arts, were retained; crimes of " lèse majesté ", enumerated at length and severely punished, also found a place.   Even thus dressed in foreign style, these drafts did not meet with favor from the conquerors.   From Paris, where they were sent for approval, came the order that in their place should be substituted a simple translation of the French Penal Code, and by an Imperial Decree of December 6, 1810, this command was put into effect.   Of the labor of the Italians there remained only their preparatory studies, printed in Brescia in 1807, to serve as a guide and basis for subsequent legislators.

Somewhat greater results were obtained in the Kingdom of Naples.   King Joseph, who had already put forth great efforts to expedite procedure, to improve the prisons, and to remove ancient defects from the administration of criminal justice, promulgated in 1808 the Code of Procedure in Criminal Trials (" Regolamento

---

[1] [The Kingdom of Italy was erected as an imperial dependency by Napoleon I.   It comprised principally the northeastern countries of Italy: Venetia, Lombardy, Modena, Romagna and the Marches.]

di procedura nei guidizi criminali ") and the Law of Crimes and Penalties (" Legge sui delitti e sulle pene "). The Italian school openly avowed their leaning towards the Neapolitan writers. Notwithstanding, or rather perhaps because of, its Italian quality, this Code also was abolished in 1812 under the reign of Joachim Murat and the French Code of 1810 was substituted. Thus throughout the firmest years of Napoleon's domination, this Code held sway over all parts of Italy subject to him and again revived, in large part, those systems and theories which shortly before seemed forever condemned and rejected. Force had indeed returned as the dominating principle. Of clear ideas concerning the nature of crime and the purpose of punishment there was none; the elements constituting the crime and the various phases by which its consummation was reached were not well analyzed and co-ordinated; imputability was not always related to the causes which determined it with certainty; punishments were many and severe, e.g. branding, confiscation, loss of all rights, mutilations, death extended to many more crimes than had for long been the case; reasons of State dominated and were confused with the will of the conqueror, who at times knew no restraint in his transports of anger. The famous example may be cited of the Commune of Crespino which, during the war, had shown favor to Napoleon's enemies. A Decree of February 11, 1806 provided that its inhabitants, no longer considered as citizens of the Kingdom and excluded in consequence from the enjoyment of constitutional rights, should, as a colony of persons without a country, be governed by a commandant of police, invested with the offices appropriate to municipal authorities; that they should be subjected to double the ordinary land tax and to the penalty of flogging in cases where imprisonment was ordinarily imposed; and finally that, in commemoration, a stone should be placed over the entrance to the city's seat of government.

CHAPTER XIX [1]

THE RESTORATION GOVERNMENTS AND UNITED ITALY

§ 281. General Observations.
§ 282. Lombardy, Venetia, the Two Sicilies, Parma and Dependencies, Tuscany, States of the Church, Kingdom of Sardinia.
§ 283. Period Following 1848.
§ 284. The Scientific Movement, Pellegrino Rossi.

§ 285. Carmignani and his School; other Philosophic Criminalists.
§ 285 a. Codes of the 1800 s and 1900 s.
§ 285 b. The Positive or Anthropological School.
§ 285 c. The Ferri Draft of a Criminal Code.

§ 281. **General Observations.** — With the end of French domination in Italy, the restored governments were in general moved by two contrary tendencies, which, because they determined the character of the period up to 1848, were of great importance in the development of the criminal law. On the one hand, they were inflamed by reaction, that is, hatred of the principles, political and social, which had brought about their fall; and love of the ancient traditions by which they had been previously ruled. Self-interest and the desire that the population should forget the recent changes, made the governments turn eagerly towards the past in the hope of recalling it once more to life. On the other hand the governments saw a new field opened before them by the progress already accomplished, in which that in penal science was of such a nature that, while possible to retard, it could not be halted. In Italy this science had prospered even before the changes of the Revolution. These gave it fresh nourishment and, after the restoration of the old order, handed down to it various and important subjects of research and discussion. The reaction provoked by past extremes even aided science, especially through the historical method, which sought out of the past as also from pure reason, for precedents and principles through which to accomplish the reforms demanded by the times. So great was the authority and force of this scientific movement, supported as it was by the better part of public opinion, that the governments could not wholly ignore it and were

[1] [English Chap. XIX, §§ 281-285 = *Calisse*, Part III, Chap. III, §§ 171-final 175. English Sections 285 a-285 c have been contributed by the Translator, in order to bring the history down to the advent of the Fascist government.]

forced, some more some less, some sooner and some later, to follow it and to co-ordinate their own interests with it.   In the matter of political and religious crimes, that is, crimes directly touching the interests of the State religion, no concessions were made; but in other fields of the criminal law the governments were, generally speaking, inclined to ameliorations.   Thus may be explained that confusion, sometimes even inconsistency and instability, revealed in the criminal legislation following the Restoration.

§ 282.   **Lombardy, Venetia, the Two Sicilies, Parma and Dependencies, Tuscany, States of the Church, Kingdom of Sardinia.** — In the Lombard and Venetian provinces, the Austrian Penal Code of 1803 was promulgated, April 24 and May 31, 1815.[1]   This contributed to the diffusion in Italy of the results of the German penal school, just as in the preceding period those of the French school had received circulation.   After an introduction, this Code divides into two parts, corresponding to the separation of punishable acts into " delicts " and " transgressions."   Great care was bestowed upon the establishment of the requisites of criminality and upon the determination of the elements which constitute and modify crime.   But punishments were severe: among them were death and the harshest form of imprisonment.   Subject to these penalties were acts which of themselves would not seem to deserve them, but which the legislator placed there on the ground of defending society against a future danger, as Romagnosi had done.   For example, the drunkenness of a laborer at work was punished because the danger of fire might result.   Procedure was also harsh, for not only was publicity of arguments denied, but the accused was even denied the protection of counsel, in order, as was said, that he should not have advice or aid in hindering the course of justice.   Nevertheless the practical result of the Code was good and its severe terms had seldom to be executed, though it remained in force until the publication of a new code in 1852.

The Two Sicilies were governed by the Code of 1819,[2] of which the Second Part dealt with criminal law and the Fourth Part criminal procedure.   It was one of the best codes of the period and from it may still be gained fruitful counsel and example.   An unfailingly humane spirit inspired it, if we except the crimes freshly enumerated under the title of " lèse majesté ", offenses against God and those relating to political interests.   It was a perfectionment of the French Code, to which important principles were

[1] "Codice dei delitti e delle gravi transgressioni di polizia" (Venice, 1815).
[2] "Codice per il regno delle Due Sicilie" (Naples, 1819).

added, such as one regarding accomplices and another attempt, which from the Neapolitan Code passed into all others published later.   It was declared a rule of public law that the trial of the proof of all crimes should be open to the public, and oral procedure was retained without limitation in the criminal courts.   The death penalty remained, but confiscation and branding were abolished, and the equality of all before the courts was declared.   It should be added that the work of the courts was sound and beneficial.   Having by their decisions laid the basis of the legislation of 1819, with the same good intentions they dedicated themselves to its proper interpretation and application, and they thus succeeded in mitigating some of the harshness of the law, in meeting some of its deficiencies and in establishing rules of great importance.[1]   Unfortunately political interests soon resumed unrestrained ascendancy.   Not only was the promise of the law's progress arrested, but a disastrous reaction set in, when by decrees, rescripts, exceptional laws, special commissions and changes in the fundamental political institutions, the Code of 1819 was repealed substantially in its entirety.   The fleeting and ephemeral liberties of 1848 did not suffice to revive it.

The good provisions of the Neapolitan Codes were employed in the codes of criminal law and procedure given to Parma in 1820, as also in the drafts that were unavailingly prepared for the Kingdom of Italy.[2]   In the neighboring State of the Este family [3] the laws of 1771 were revived, and no native penal code was adopted until 1855.[4]

In Tuscany the old Leopoldian legislation of 1786 was restored. Its relative mildness had been departed from by the French government, for capital sentences, very rare until 1808, became frequent from that year until 1814.   After the restoration the death penalty was at first extended, by the Law of June 22, 1816, to crimes which hitherto had not been subject to it ; but later, though not abolished, it was made less and less frequent.   The important Ducal Decree of August 2, 1838, in the preamble of which Leopold II declared his desire to conform the administration of justice with the principles best adapted to the state of society and to insure due protection to public order and private property, introduced

---

[1] *E. Pessina*, "Dei progressi del diritto penale in Italia nel secolo XIX", pp. 16 *et seq.*
[2] "Codice penale e codice di procedura criminale per gli Stati di Parma, Piacenza e Guastalla" (Parma, 1820).
[3] [Parma and Modena.]
[4] "Codice criminale per gli Stati Estensi" (Modena, 1855).

notable reforms in criminal procedure, which were generally understood as the preparation for many other desirable provisions; for
the legislation of 1786, though good, was not without defects and
had not progressed with the times.[1]   In fact by the Ducal Decree
of May 31, 1847, a commission was named to draw up a penal code.
In July of the same year the commission received the report of
some of the higher judges who had been called upon to submit their
opinions; that of the criminalist Carmignani was also submitted;
and as real conditions were to continue as the chief criterion and
guide, the commission was asked to consider all the improvements
effected or proposed, especially by the judiciary, as also to give
particular attention to the question of the graduation of penalties,
the substitution of cellular prisons for the galleys ("bagni") and
public labor then in use, and also the complete abolition of the
death penalty.[2]   This penalty was, however, abolished by the
Ducal Decree of October 11, of the same year.   By it Leopold
extended to the Duchy of Lucca, of which he had taken possession, the benefit of the abolition, already in fact enjoyed throughout the rest of the State, under the constant decisions of the courts
and in conformity with the purposes of the government.   All
this was altered after the political events of 1848.   The death
penalty was restored by the Decree of November 18, 1852, without even the limitations formerly surrounding it.   Because of the
same political reaction, the draft of a penal code prepared by the
commission of 1847 was never put in force.   Its labors, however,
were not lost, because they were largely used for the Code of 1853,
until then one of the best that Italy had [3] and which, amended in
1859 and 1860, chiefly by removing the death penalty and reform-
ing the law relating to prisons, governed Tuscany even after
national unification and until recent times.   Valuable commentaries upon the Tuscan Criminal Code were prepared by Mori,[4]
one of the commissioners of 1847, by Bonfanti [5] and Puccioni.[6]

The States of the Church long remained loyal to the laws inspired
by the old system, although the Decree of Pius VII, of July 6, 1816,
provided among other things for the organization of criminal

---

[1] *Ademollo*, "Il giudizio criminale in Toscana secondo la riforma leopol-
dina del 1838."   A theoretical and practical outline (Florence, 1840).
[2] Decree of July 30, 1847.
[3] *Pessina, op. cit.*, p. 49–64.
[4] "Teorica del Codice penale toscano" (Florence, 1854).
[5] "Teoria del Codice penale toscano" (Lucca, 1854).
[6] "Il Codice penale toscano illustrato" (Pistoia, 1855); *F. Carrara*,
"Francesco Puccioni e il diritto penale in Toscana" (Florence,   "Nuova
Antologia", 1866).

courts;[1] better government was promised and the study of wider reforms undertaken.[2] A commission was in fact appointed to prepare a code of criminal law and procedure; but none was ever published. Leo XII favored the reaction; Gregory XVI, by the "Regolamento di procedura" of November 5, 1831, and by the "Regolamento dei delitti e delle pene" of September 20, 1832, though in part reproducing the French Criminal Code and drawing also upon the Austrian, was also faithful to the reaction, preserving inquisitorial and secret procedure, ecclesiastical courts with jurisdiction determined by reason of the parties and the matter, loss of family rights for political crimes, judicial discretion, the death penalty, aggravated for its admonitory value, higher courts presided over by prelates, the Court of the Cardinal Vicar for crimes against morals, and of the Holy Office for offenses against religion. Pius IX showed a desire to move more in step with the changed social conditions of his time, but the political events of his reign prevented.

Not unlike in principle was the attitude of the government of the Kingdom of Sardinia. After the restoration of 1814, the laws of 1770 were declared again in force and long remained unchanged. In practice, however, ways were constantly sought to mitigate their severity, by utilizing the discretionary power confided to the court or by recourse to the right of pardon. To that extent the spirit of the period asserted itself effectively. And it was because of this discord between the written law and real social needs that Count Balbo, when made minister by Victor Emanuel I, interested himself very especially in legislative reforms. His designs were carried out and on February 25, 1820, a high legislative commission was appointed. But in 1821, at the end of Victor Emanuel's reign, the Balbo ministry retired, and his whole project was laid aside, not, however, without having planted seed that was to bear fruit. Charles Felix, pursuing his predecessor's plans, published in 1827 a new compilation of laws, civil and criminal, for the Island of Sardinia,[3] which, though leaving untouched no small part of the old institutions, nevertheless accomplished a substantial improvement in criminal law and served as preparation for those more general and significant reforms for which the credit is due to Charles Albert. On coming to the throne Charles Albert turned his thought to the improvement of his country's laws, by bringing

---

[1] Title III, arts. 76–101
[2] "Disposizioni generali", art. 242.
[3] F. Sclopis, "Storia della legislazione italiana"; cit., Bk. II, c. 2.

them into harmony with the times.   June 7, 1831, he named a
commission, the fourth section of which was charged with the
preparation of codes of criminal law and procedure, upon the bases
set forth in the preamble of the decree creating the commission.
According to it, the laws were to be the same for all, founded upon
ascertained principles, co-ordinated one with the other, and yet
such as to permit the judge to adapt his decision to changing states
of fact; penalties were to aim at reform, were to be proportioned
to the crime, graduated according to the age and physical condition of the offender and according to whether it was a case of commission or attempt, complicity or recidivity.   By October 26,
1839, the commission's labor was completed and the Penal Code
for the States of the King of Sardinia (" Codice penale per gli
Stati di S. M. il re di Sardegna ") was published.   It was favorably received and declared superior even to the French Code,
of which it was largely an imitation.   But it was not without
defects and did not escape criticism for perpetuating many vestiges
of earlier institutions and for its large use of the death penalty.
The Code of Criminal Procedure (" Codice della procedura criminale ") was published by the Edict of August 30, 1847, and came
into force March 1, 1848.

§ 283. **Period following 1848.** — This was the year when enthusiasm
burned high throughout all Italy.   Although soon cooled elsewhere, it continued strong in Piedmont and under the new orien-
tation of the times it gave fresh life to legislation as well as politics.
Charles Albert's Penal Code no longer appeared, as in fact it no
longer was, a reflection of the changed ideas and the new needs.
On November 13, 1859, therefore, after various separate laws had
been passed in harmony with the developments of the period and
after the parliamentary debates of 1857, amidst the serious crisis
of the nationalist movement, Victor Emanuel II, then invested
with dictatorial powers, published the new Penal Code.   It introduced notable improvements over the prior Albertine Code, from
which it freely borrowed, and governed throughout the greater
part of the new united Kingdom of Italy until the publication
of the Code now in force.   In the same year the Code of Criminal
Procedure was published.

§ 284. **The Scientific Movement ; Pellegrino Rossi.** — The
general characteristics of the penal legislation of the first half of
the 1800 s were also found in the scientific works which prepared
and accompanied it.   They showed a frank reaction against the
excesses of the schools of the 1700 s, though friendly to the more

important principles then proclaimed; they always strove to reconcile existing arrangements, actual social conditions, and the postulates of abstract reason; they manifested a tendency to seek perfection, without any illusion that a point, when gained, was the best. While in general up to this time, the senses, social instinct, and utility had served as the main guides in the study of penal systems, now, without abandoning these, man's spiritual and moral side were also considered. The illustrious champion of this system was Pellegrino Rossi, whose work closes the philosophic period and ushers in the changes which were to follow.

In 1829 Pellegrino Rossi published his Treatise on Criminal Law (" Trattato di diritto penale ").[1] It was divided into four parts; in the first he examined the foundations of the penal system, in the second crime, in the third punishment, and in the fourth the criminal laws. Rossi's was in substance an eclectic system, since many others, when properly understood, may easily be related to it and were related at the time it appeared, and because it went beyond the others and reached new conclusions.

He sets out from the premise that social justice is necessary, because without it society could not exist and society is, as Romagnosi had said, a will of human nature. But since the exercise of this justice is in the hands of men, always fallible and capable of abuse, it must be limited within reasonable bounds, that it may not become injustice and so destroy the essentials of political liberty. These bounds must be furnished by moral principles since man, before being a member of society, is a moral being, and, therefore, the social order must be a means of realizing that morality, rather than an end in itself. Punitive justice, as guardian of the social order, must therefore maintain itself in harmony with the moral principle, towards which it is directed. Under any other condition and especially in view of the force of example of the government, punitive justice would minister to a decline of the moral sense and turn men from the path of civilization, which " is but the manifestation and rule of the good and the true." [2] But if criminal justice is founded on morals, its purpose must be the protection of the social order : in other words, the moral necessity of punishment may not be separated from its political necessity. This comes close to the idea of defense as the justification of the right to punish. But, instead of making social protection the sole

---

[1] "Traité de droit pénal" (Paris, 1825); was translated into Italian and went through several editions; the references here used are to the Sienese edition of 1853.
[2] "Introduzione," § 2.

purpose of the right, he uses it as a limitation, as the measure of its exercise. For, when it is affirmed that justice should serve the moral order, it is not to be understood that all moral principles are to find their sanction in human laws, but that justice should not remain alien to them, that those who make and execute the laws should not violate them. On the other hand, to hold utility, that is social utility, as the goal, as did other systems, too often destroyed the link between morality and justice. By itself, utility can make nothing lawful, because, had it such power, it could make anything lawful: punishment of the guilty and of the innocent, punishment with and without limit. On the other hand, if the idea of utility is wholly ignored, the law falls into the vague domain of morals without means of knowing where to place restrictive bounds to the field of legislation.[1] In conclusion, therefore, morals must be the region beyond whose boundaries we may not pass; within this field social utility should be the guide along the way which alone is proper to legislation. This link between the moral and the social appears the more evident and necessary when it is considered that the social order itself is a moral obligation from which man may not withdraw. For man, not a brute, but intelligent and free, is governed by the moral law in all that constitutes his nature, and, therefore, in his social life, which is for him one of the greatest of the natural laws. To preserve society is in consequence to support a moral law, which, in turn, cannot be disassociated from the means necessary to preserve society, namely, the right to punish.[2] Man has then, by the same moral law, social duties which may be exacted of him and the violation of these constitutes crime. This does not mean that the violation of the other moral duties is not an evil, but that, not being a legal wrong, it does not fall under the sanction of social justice, since the social order is not thereby damaged.[3]

In accord with this view of crime, the penalty also, which society prescribes, is of a kind with that which in general attaches to every act contrary to morals:[4] the penalty perfects the law and is characterized by certain determinate qualities, of some of which it may not be deprived: viz., it must be moral, personal and of a nature to serve as an example; with respect to its other qualities it should but become more charitable, by being revocable, reformative, capable of removing the power to harm.[5] Thus the effects

[1] Book I, chap. 7.   [3] Book II, chap. 1.
[2] Book I, chap. 12.   [4] Book III, chap. 1.
                [5] Book III, chap. 13.

which punishment aims to produce are many. There is the instruction which the legislator thereby addresses to the public, the fear inspired in one meditating crime, the reform of the guilty, the moral satisfaction of the public conscience, the sense of security derived from the application of the penal sanction.[1]

§ 285. **Carmignani and his School ; Other Philosophic Criminalists.** — Such were the fundamental principles which Pellegrino Rossi put to logical application in his examination of the elements of crime, of the penalties most in use and of the existing body of law. To these same principles substantially all arrived who during the middle of the 1800 s studied the criminal law, especially upon philosophic bases. The moral principle was not discussed ; men sought only to find a surer foundation and to apply it in the best possible way. To this end, alongside the moral and in addition to the social and political principle, a place was sought for still another. Taparelli thought he had found it in theology, on the theory that society and the governing ideals of justice emanate from God.[2] Others, with greater success, sought it in the sphere of law. Chief among these was Giovanni Carmignani, first publicly known for his oration at Pisa in 1836 in favor of the abolition of the death penalty. He also postulated juridical necessity as the basis of the right to punish. As Pellegrino Rossi had found in morals the limitations to the punitive right, which arose, according to Romagnosi, from a social necessity, Carmignani sought these same limits in the idea of law, which is natural to man, not in discord with the moral principle, but in furtherance of its more exact determination, by a specification of what legislative sanction should embrace.[3] Carmignani thus became the founder of an important school of penalists which performed great service for Tuscan criminal legislation and which survives in the illustrious name and work of Francesco Carrara.

Elsewhere there arose other remarkable writers upon criminal law and philosophy. Besides Rosmini, must be mentioned Giuliani,[4] Mancini, Mamiani,[5] Buccellati,[6] and others who, writing at different times and with different purposes, were one in recogniz-

[1] Book III, chap. 3.
[2] "Saggio teoretico di diritto naturale" (Palermo, 1842).
[3] "Teoria delle leggi sulla sicurezza sociale" (Pisa, 1831–1832).
[4] "Istituzioni di diritto criminale" (Macerata, 1856).
[5] "Intorno alla filosofia del diritto e singolarmente intorno alle origini del diritto di punire", letters of *Count Mamiani della Rovere* and of *P. S. Mancini*, lawyer and professor (Naples, 1844).
[6] See the complete list of his works in the "Memorial" by *P. del Giudice* in the "Rendiconti" of the "Reale Istituto Lombardo", for 1891.

ing the moral principle.   Reference must also be made to the subsequent appearance of another school, which, following a course in contrast to the classical, took the name of " Positive ", setting up the experimental principle in place of those that had prevailed in other systems of criminal science.   From this school also history will record real achievements, for its members do not rush into bold deductions before having that full and sure equipment of facts necessary to work of this sort, and they are persuaded that the safe and the beneficial are to be found in what criminal science has in the course of centuries laboriously built up upon a basis of morals and philosophy.

§ 285 a. Codes of the 1800 s and 1900 s.[1] — From the end of the Napoleonic period and the restoration of the petty Italian States (following the Congress of Vienna), to national unity in 1859, there was no greater unification of criminal law than of private law.   In the Kingdom of the Two Sicilies fairly progressive codes of criminal law and procedure were adopted in 1819 ; reactionary codes appeared in the States of the Church in 1832 and 1831 ; in 1853 Tuscany adopted the best Italian criminal code of the period ; Modena adopted a progressive code in 1855 ; Parma enacted codes of both law and procedure in 1821 ; in Lombardy-Venetia the reactionary Austrian code of 1804 was put into effect in 1815 and displaced by a more liberal one in 1852 ; in the Kingdom of Sardinia, which embraced Genoa and Piedmont, Charles Albert produced a criminal code in 1839 and a code of criminal procedure in 1848, modeled somewhat after the French codes.

Thus when national unity was won, there was system without uniformity.   In 1865 a Code of Criminal Procedure was adopted for the whole realm, by extending the Sardinian Code of 1839 over northern Italy, the States of the Church, and to a certain extent over southern Italy, Tuscany preserving her own code.   In 1890 the present Penal Code was put into force generally.   In 1913 a new Code of Criminal Procedure was adopted.[2]

The latter Code simplified procedure and accelerated sentences. An effort was made to strike a better balance between individual

---

[1] [This section is contributed by the Translator. See "Continental Legal History Series", Vol. I, "General Survey", p. 192, abridged from *Calisse*, "Sources" ("Fonti").]

[2] [October 5, 1913.   Commissions had worked on the Code since 1892, *i.e.* two years after the adoption of the Penal Code.   It was introduced in the legislature in 1912.   *See* the speech of *Enrico Ferri*, in full in "La Giustizia Penale", Aug. 29–Sept. 5, 1912.   Notice of the Code will be found in Journal of Criminal Law and Criminology, vol. 3 (1912), p. 920; *E. Storoni*, "La riforma dei codici. Il codice di procedura penale" (1924).]

and social rights, but the tendency towards the accusatorial rather than the inquisitorial type of criminal trial remains apparent, inherited from the philosophy of the 1700 s, — Beccaria, Pagano, and Filangieri. The strict regulation of the judicial police, and of the power to interrogate the accused, and the maintenance of the presumption of innocence, go far in protecting the individual. Bail is related to the kind of crime and kind of punishment rather than the kind of criminal.

§ 285 b. **The Positive or Anthropological School.**[1] — The Positive or Anthropological School was founded a half century ago by Cesare Lombroso (1836–1909), with the publication in 1876 of the first edition of his great work " Criminal Man " (" L'Uomo delinquente "). Working and studying as a physician among criminals in penal institutions, he concluded that actions and modes of thinking are conditioned by physical structure and that the criminal is physically abnormal. This abnormality he regarded as an arrested development, an atavistic reversion to a lower type, constituting a kind of moral insanity.

Inspired by the labors of Lombroso, Enrico Ferri began his many important works on criminal law and criminology by the publication of " New Horizons of Criminal Law and Penal Procedure " (" Nuovi orizzonti del diritto e procedura penali ") in 1884. He carried Lombroso's positivistic philosophy forward by his formulation of the criminal "factors" or causes, in which he numbers not only the physiological and psychic but gives a large place to the individual's social history, including his physical environment. His extended classification of criminals, founded in the main on a differentiation between the habitual and occasional, had a most important bearing on his theory of penology, wherein he stresses the degrees of dangerousness of criminals and limits the functions of law to social protection, while leaving prevention to "penal substitutes."

Where Lombroso is the anthropologist and Ferri the sociologist, Raffaele Garofalo, the last great name associated with the Positive School, is the jurist. His " Criminology " (" Criminalogía ") appeared in 1885. With the works of these three men the creative period of the Positive School closed, the later years being rather an

[1] [This section is contributed by the Translator. See *Lombroso*, "Crime, its Causes and Remedies" (translated as Vol. III, "Modern Criminal Science Series", Little, Brown & Co., Boston, 1911, with extended bibliography); *De Quiros*, "Modern Theories of Criminality" (translated as Vol. I, *id.*, 1911), pp. 10 *et seq.*; *Garofalo*, "Criminology" (translated as Vol. VIII, *id.*); *Ferri*, "Difese penali" (3d ed., Turin, 1925).]

absorption and working out of the positive method in the light of new scientific discoveries.   Garofalo brought forward the theory of the " natural crime ", *i.e.* an act considered punishable at all times and in all places.   With it was contrasted the artificial or positive crime, peculiar to a particular nation.   It was a juristic duality analogous to the " jus gentium " and " jus civilis " of the Roman law and the " malum in se " and the " malum prohibitum " of the Classical School.   Natural crime is " an offence against the fundamental altruistic sentiments of pity and probity in the average measure possessed by a given social group."   The fundamental commandments of pity and probity are an evolutionary result, not a divine command.   Crime becomes an anomaly of the moral sense, an ethical degeneration in the evolutionary process.   Repression thus requires a necessary artificial selective means, amounting to a radical elimination of those unfit for the social group.

§ 285 *c*. **The Ferri Draft of a Criminal Code, 1921.**[1] — The Positive School may be said to have received official recognition when a Royal Decree of September 14, 1919, entrusted the task of suggesting necessary legal reforms for social defense against criminals to a Commission presided over by Enrico Ferri.[2]   The Pre-

---

[1] [This section is contributed by the Translator.   For the Italian and English text of the Report and Draft, see the publication of the Ministry of Justice (printer: "L'Universelle" Imprimerie Polyglotte, Rome, 1921): "Relazione sul progetto preliminare di codice penale Italiano" (English translation by *Edgar Betts*); "Atti della Commissione" (Ministerio della Giustizia e delle Grazie, Rome); notices by *Ferri*, in "Journal of Criminal Law and Criminology", vol. 11 (1920), p. 67, and "Law Quarterly Review", vol. 37 (1921), p. 63; *A. M. Kidd*, "California Law Review", p. 384 (1921). For a criticism in English, see "On the Reform of the Italian Code", by the faculty of the Catholic Univ. of the Sacred Heart in Milan, translated by *Arthur J. Todd*, "Journal of Criminal Law and Criminology", vol. 14, p. 524 (1923–24).   See also *Ferri*, "La riforma della giustizia in Italia", in "Scuola Positiva" (1919); *id.*, "I lavori della commissione per la riforma delle leggi penali", *ibid.* (1919); *id.*, "I lavori della commissione", *ibid.* (1920); *id.*, "La réforme de la justice pénale en Italie", in "Revue de droit pénal et de criminologie" (1920); *id.*, "Saggio di applicazione delle norme generali di libro primo ai responsabili di taluni delitti secondo il progetto di codice penale Italiano", *ibid.* (1923); *Santoro*, "La nomina di una commissione per la riforma del codice penale", *ibid.* (1919); *Fernand Collin*, "Enrico Ferri et l'avant-projet de code pénal italien de 1921" (thesis, Louvain, 1924–25); *A. Rocco*, "Il progetto preliminare del codice penale italiano" (Naples, 1924); *E. Altavilla*, "Il progetto Ferri nelle critiche di Arturo Rocco" (Naples, 1924); *M. Manfredini*, "Sopra alcune critiche ad progetto di codice penale" (1924); *G. Battaglini*, "Il progetto di codice penale positivista" (Foro Umbro, 1924); *G. A. Palazzo*, "I delitti colposi nel diritto romano e nel progetto di codice penale", in "Scuola Positiva", N. S. IV, nos. 4–6 (Milan, 1925).]

[2] [See "Gazetta Ufficiale", Sept. 19, 1919, no. 231.   Other members of the Commission were: Raffaele Garofalo, Agostino Berenini, Enrico de Nicola, Augusto Setti, Raffaele de Notaristefani, Biero Alberici, Eugenio Florian, Giulio C. Ferrari, Alessandro Lustig, Sante de Sanctis, Salvatore Ottolenghi.]

liminary Draft of a new Criminal Code was presented to the legislature January 12, 1921. The following year the Fascist government came to power and the Draft of 1921 did not receive its approval. On January 13, 1925, the Fascist Minister of Justice Rocco presented to the Chamber of Deputies a bill, superseding the decree of 1919, giving the Government authority to amend the two present Codes of Criminal Law and Criminal Procedure.[1] It seems proper, nevertheless, to terminate this history of Italian criminal law with a brief notice of the so-called Ferri Draft of 1921, which, in legislative form, reflects strongly the conclusions of the Positive School and is Italy's latest important contribution to this field of law.

Criminal law had long passed from the theory of defensive vengeance by the victim and his family to one of penitence and chastisement commensurate to the gravity of the offence. The decree of 1919 and the draft of 1921 both illustrate the passage to a third conception, that of adequate social protection against the dangerous individual. Social defence is a fundamental, constant and practical duty of the State. This duty should not be affected by religion, philosophy or doctrine. Protection should not be allowed to wait upon moral responsibility, which never can be accurately assessed; legal follows upon factual imputability; the prevalent hesitancy to choose between the moral and the factual, in so far as the law is concerned, is frankly discarded in favor of society. For crime has both causes and effects, and it is with the latter that the criminal law should properly concern itself; the causes lie without and must be met by those methods of gradual amelioration of man's biological, physical, economic and social conditions which the positive method of observation and experiment point to. The new legislation's first concern is to determine the degree of dangerousness of the individual offender to society and to fix at once a legal responsibility for the commission of the criminal act without reference to moral responsibility; in the determination of sanctions or penalties, its major concern is again with the individual as a social danger. The fundamental processes of criminal procedure are of necessity retained, namely, proof of the act, its determination as a crime, proof that the accused committed the crime. These points once established against the accused, his responsibility follows as a matter of course,

[1] [On this reform of the Penal Code of 1890 and the Code of Criminal Procedure of 1913, see the notice in "Revista internazionale di filosofia del diritto" (October–December, 1925), vol. V, no. LV, p. 627.]

regardless of personal circumstance, sex, mental condition, etc. It is a responsibility founded on social danger and not on the subjective idea of sin. The legal responsibility of the delinquent and his subsequent treatment become clearly separate matters, and only in the latter does consideration for the personality of the individual enter. The term " penalty " and " punishment " are, indeed, discarded and a " sanction " is sought, in the light of scientific observation and study of the individual and his history, which is best adapted to safeguard society, to restore the individual where possible, and to recompense both the State and the victim of the crime. Individual guarantees are sought in the control of a technically trained personnel rather than in rigid legal limitations.

Book I, a general part dealing with the offender and sanctions, that is, with the perilousness of the criminal and social defense against it, is the only completed part of the draft. Book II was to deal with the definition of particular offenses and was to contain little new ; Book III was to contain special provisions for the reform of the judiciary, judicial police, magistrates, administrative officials and attorneys, which would insure a sympathetic atmosphere for the application of the new law.

The idea of social defense has thrown special emphasis on three distinctions made in the draft, that between (1) the common criminal, actuated by a selfish motive, and the socio-political criminal, actuated by an altruistic motive; (2) the occasional and the habitual criminal; (3) the criminal under and over 18 years of age, since the particular limit of civil majority has been shown to have no relevancy to criminal conduct. The classification of offenders keeps steadily in view the objective element of peril to society, while the subjective element of moral responsibility is made relevant, not to the question of guilt, but only to treatment. Corresponding radical changes are therefore introduced in the matter of sentences and penal institutions. The short jail sentence is abolished as a propagator of crime ; for it is substituted obligatory residence away from the locality of the crime, and forced day-labor, generally in the open air, with isolation only at night. Serious offenses, especially if habitual, receive sentences of forced labor or rigorous segregation for life. The death penalty and corporal punishment are not restored. Obligatory labor in the open, where possible, is very largely substituted for the cell. Psychopathic criminals are cared for in special institutions. All criminals are subject to close and constant physical and psychical observation, with a view to limiting sanctions strictly to what social safety requires.   The minor under 18 receives guarded freedom or care in a correctional school or labor colony.   Probation and parole are used guardedly, always with an eye to society's protection. Sentences are classified by the legislator, but their application to the offender is discretionary with the judge and reviewable from time to time in the light of a constant scientific observation of the individual.   Every sentence carries with it an order of reparation to the victim.   To provide for this, penal labor is paid at full current market rates, one half the wage going to the victim and one half to the offender's family or to a fund for his rehabilitation on liberation; profits go to the State and are to be used in part to support a reparation fund for persons improperly accused of crime.   The plan of the Commission includes the inaugurating of special university courses for those entering the profession of criminal law and administration.   This means the judiciary, prosecuting and defense attorneys, judicial police and institutional administrators; defense attorneys are enrolled in a special bar.

It has been said that crime accompanies society like its shadow. At a time when this shadow seems to be lengthening in every land and the fear of the criminal enters increasingly into the hearts of men, this latest contribution from the Positive School of Italy, calm, objective, scientific, even though it may not ever receive legislative sanction, can not be without wide influence.

BOOK III
PRIVATE LAW

PART I
PERSONS

BOOK III

PRIVATE LAW [1]

PART I

PERSONS

INTRODUCTION

§ 286. **Person and Capacity.** — The ancients gave the name *person* to the mask worn by the actor upon the stage, and from this first meaning was derived the other, indicating a certain quality investing the individual. For the jurists such a quality was the aggregate of conditions requisite to legal capacity. Thus the word *person* came to signify one capable of rights, and this remains its true meaning.

Even in Germanic law — though in this respect less strict than the Roman — to be a man was not of itself to be a person; he must have certain special juridical attributes. This conception was maintained unaltered until the abolition of slavery and, in certain of its applications, even afterwards, until acceptance of the principle at the basis of modern systems, that all men are equal before the law.

On the other hand, given the essentials of the person as residing in certain juridical facts, it might be conceived, in whole or in part, independently of human existence. Thus a man might represent more than one person, as where he added to his own juridical capacity that of some office which he held; or it might be that more than one individual gave life to but a single person, as happened in the case of associations having a recognized legal existence.

The fundamental distinction was, therefore, preserved between the physical and the juridical person, a distinction derived from the diversity of their component elements: in the latter, the artificial element alone was necessary, namely legal capacity; in the former the natural element, human existence, must unite with other qualities required by the law.

---

[1] [Book III is a translation of Vol. III, of Professor *Calisse's* "Storia del diritto italiano" (Florence, 1891, ed. Barbèra). Part I, §§ 286–313 = *Calisse* Part I, §§ 1–26, pp. 7–50.]

TITLE I

HUMAN EXISTENCE [1]

§ 287. Its Beginning. | § 288. Its End.

§ 287. **Its Beginning.** — The unborn, though conceived, was not a person; the fœtus was a part of the mother, as unseparated fruit is part of the plant. The principle of the Roman law that the unborn child should be considered as born, when to its advantage, was unknown to Germanic law. The separation of the child from the mother was an absolute condition for the beginning of its existence as a person. In later times, when Roman theories and canon law prevailed, the ancient principle was again accepted, though with some limitations. For conception alone was not enough; there must be a presumption of life, and this was supposed to exist at the end of a certain period, — to be precise, forty days for a male and eighty for a female, according to the long-respected canonical teaching. Limitations of this sort have disappeared from modern law, which has restored the Roman principle.[2]

The child must also be born alive, the still-born not being regarded as a person. It was necessary, therefore, to ascertain the presence of life, and for this the Germanic laws provided different tests. Some required the child to move its eyes in such wise that it would seem to have seen the ceiling and the four walls; some that its voice should have been heard by all present in the room; others that it should remain alive at least an hour. In subsequent legislation the question was left to the testimony and judgment of experts.

Besides life, vitality was required, that is, the physical possibility of continued life. To raise such a presumption, some among the Germanic peoples, the Visigoths, for example, required that the child should live ten days; but others, and they were the majority, were content if the child was not born prematurely and was of proper physical proportions. After the Germanic period, legal

[1] *Pertile*, "Storia del diritto italiano", § 104; *Salvioli*, "Manuale della storia del diritto italiano", part IV, chap. I; *Tamassia*, "L'assenza nella storia del diritto italiano", in "Archivio giuridico", XXXVI (1886).

[2] Civil Code, art. 724, sec. 1.

presumptions as to these questions also gave away to the determination of experts.

Life and vitality — to which should be added human form, for a monstrosity was not considered a person by Germanic law — were then the conditions of human existence qualified to possess legal capacity.

§ 288. **Its End ; Absence.** — When human existence came to an end, the person ceased with it. The natural cause of the end was death, which, however, was not presumed, as was true of life; proof was demanded of one who asserted the fact in his own benefit.

Nevertheless, absence was sufficient grounds for a presumption of death. Under Germanic law if a person was away from home and no word was had of him for three years, his property was given to his children or his brothers, or his nearest relatives, or if there was none such, to the State; the king might give the wife license to remarry.[1] But these provisions did not result from a presumption of the death of the absent, but were in fact a punishment for his disobedience of the law, which did not permit of an absence of more than three years without notice to the magistrates of the province. So true was this that, if he returned, the law did not permit him to repossess himself of his former rights, but threatened him with such punishment as the king might fix.

The statutes of the mediaeval cities returned to the Roman theories. For a judicial declaration of absence in the interest of those living, it was declared that a certain period should run from the date of the last news received of the absent. This was always a longer period than that admitted by the Lombard law, but varied, being seven, ten, fifteen, twenty, twenty-five, and often thirty years, by analogy to the prescriptive period. But this might be shortened if the absent person would first reach an age beyond which death was presumed. Such an age was first fixed at one hundred years, following the Roman law,[2] but later it was more commonly fixed at seventy to accord with the Ninetieth Psalm,[3] which was very widely known in the Middle Ages.[4]

The Glossators also held to the Roman theories, with the result that they were rejuvenated in the legislation of the principalities

---

[1] *Liutprand*, 8.

[2] *Justinian*, Digest, VII, 1, 56; XXXIII, 2, 8.

[3] [v. 10 "The days of our years are three score years and ten; and if by reason of strength they be four score years, yet is their strength labour and sorrow; for it is soon cut off and we fly away."]

[4] *Dante*, "Inferno", I, 1.

more than in the statutes of the mediaeval cities. In fact it became the general rule, that the rights of the absent were not extinguished but must be restored upon return. This meant that the entrance of his presumed heirs into his estate was only in order to administer it in his interest, and it only became an hereditary right upon proof of death or upon the conclusion of the period after which death was presumed. Upon these foundations the jurists gradually developed a complete theory of absence, which was accepted by the French Code and passed from it into the present Italian Code.[1] There the differences in the length of the periods, the presumptions consequent upon each, the aim of safeguarding on the one hand the interests of the absent and on the other of the present, were all combined in the expedient of dividing the absence itself into several periods, having different effects. These periods may be compared to those of past systems of law : the first, a triennial period, similar to that of the Lombard law ; the second, a triennial period, like that of the statutory enactments of the mediaeval cities.

[1] Civil Code, arts. 20–47.

TITLE II

LEGAL CAPACITY

§ 289. **Course of development.** — Juridical capacity was not united by nature to human existence; it was the artificial element of the person and required the concurrence of several conditions. Of these some were necessary for its mere existence; others were necessary for its full and unrestricted presence and for its exercise. Only the last have been preserved in modern law; the others, of great importance in past legal systems, are no longer requisites of juridical capacity. Since the abolition of slavery, the grant of civil rights to foreigners, and the equality of all before the law, they have become, when they exist at all, mere individual qualities.

CHAPTER I

CONDITIONS OF LEGAL CAPACITY [1]

TOPIC 1: FREEDOM

TOPIC 2: CITIZENSHIP

TOPIC 1.   FREEDOM

§ 290. **Freedom the Basis of Capacity.** — In Germanic law, as in Roman law, in fact as in every system of law, so long as slavery existed, freedom was the first requisite for the enjoyment of rights. While Roman law held rigorously that the man who was not free

---

[1] *Pertile, cit.* §§ 87–100; *Salvioli, cit.*, part IV, chaps. 4, 7, 9, containing a very specialized bibliography.

was not a man but a thing, Germanic laws were milder, in that, only in varying measure, did they deny to slaves the rights of human personality. But that was a long way from recognizing in them the rights of freemen.

The application of such principles belongs to distinct subdivisions of private law: the family, property and others. Here, under a general consideration of the division of persons into free and slave, it is important to note merely by what means one became a slave and by what means one acquired freedom.

§ 291. **Sources of Slavery.** — Among its causes should be distinguished those which produced perpetual slavery and those which placed a person in a state of temporary servitude. Of the former captivity in war should be given first place as most ancient and wide spread. While the opinion that the conquered Romans were reduced to slavery by the Germanic invaders cannot be accepted,[1] it was certainly true of prisoners taken on the field of battle, who belonged to the victor by right of occupation. There was the example of the Romans themselves, who were taken in great numbers by the Lombards to be sold in foreign markets. But this practice was not in general prolonged beyond the Germanic period, since on the rise of feudal knighthood, the foundations were laid for the application of milder principles towards prisoners. But for a long time the right to make slaves of infidel prisoners of war endured. In the 1500 s it was still solemnly recognized by both princes and Church and its end did not really come until the beginning of the 1800 s, when new ideas forced a change in the policies of governments, and the power of the European nations on the African and Asiatic littorals brought an end to piratical incursions and with them the principal occasion for continued encounters between Christians and Mohammedans.

Another cause of perpetual slavery might be birth; the issue of slaves were always slaves. On this point, the Germanic peoples were at first even more rigorous than the Romans, since they did not distinguish according to whether the mother was or was not slave from the time of conception until birth. For the child to be slave it was enough that the mother bore that status at confinement. Later, however, this rule was moderated. When marriage was tolerated between the free woman and a slave,[2] their children occupied the intermediate condition of the half-free " aldii ";[3] the children of a freeman and a female slave were legitimatized, when the latter was restored to liberty by her husband; the

[1] *Ante* § 7.   [2] *Post* § 322.   [3] *Ante* § 40.

children of a half-free mother ("aldia") and a slave father were not slaves, unless the master of the father, during the latter's life, exercised a proprietary right over them.[1] Thus, through these and other similar ameliorations, there came about a gradual return of the Roman principle that children, following the status of the mother, were free if she was free, or was so at any time between conception and birth.

Certain crimes also brought perpetual slavery upon the offender. They were in general those profoundly disturbing the political order, religion, or morality. Slavery was in fact the penalty for high treason, falsification of money or public documents, incest, slaying of a relative, repeated robbery, sale of Christians to infidels, and like offences.[2]

Lastly, slavery might also arise from prescription; and this accorded with the power of disposing of one's own freedom. Whoever occupied a servile condition during the whole of the prescriptive period, actually became a slave in fact. The Lombard law fixed this period at thirty years;[3] but a law of Astolf declared that no such pretension against one born free could be tolerated and provided that none should suffer injury, if, born free, he entered slavery without condemnation or other legal cause.[4] Nevertheless traces of such slavery remained. There were examples, in the statutes of the mediaeval cities, of binding to slavery those who had lived as such for ten years; and this happened even more frequently, through the power of the feudal lords, to those who had passed a certain length of time, even as short as a year and a day, as a slave upon feudal lands.

§ 292. **Temporary Slavery.** — The origins of temporary slavery were many. One was voluntary subjection, which was possible under Germanic law. The impossibility of procuring a subsistence in times of distress and the need of finding a protector, in the then turbulent state of society, were the chief motives that urged men to give themselves into slavery. To help back to liberty those who by poverty had been forced to sell themselves, general affranchisements frequently took place,[5] and slaves were then always given the right to repurchase their freedom by offering their owner the same price at which they had been acquired, though a law of Charles the Bald required an increase of a fifth, in order to prevent the hope of profit.[6] Prohibition against this form of slavery

[1] *Rothar*, 216–222.
[2] *Liutprand*, 80, 85; *Arechi*, 13; *Charlemagne*, 104; *Lothar*, 89, 91.
[3] *Grimwald*, 1.   [4] *Astolf*, 22.   [5] *Louis the Pious*, 4.
[6] "Edictum Pistense", of the year 864, chap. 34.

became constantly more rigorous; nevertheless even in the period
of the statutes of the mediaeval cities there were still examples of
persons who, through need, though supported by relatives or the
State, gave themselves into slavery.   And a very persistent trace
endured until times not so distant in the so-called " bonavoglia ",
i.e., those who, to procure money for gambling or for an honest
reason, went as oarsmen into the service of the galleys, mingling
with slave infidels, until, by surrendering their pay, they should
have means of satisfying their debt and returning to liberty.   Governments in need of oarsmen, encouraged this form of slavery in
many ways.   Indeed the galley crews of Venice, Rome, Naples
and elsewhere were constantly reinforced by the " bonavoglia ",
until navies substituted other 'means of propulsion than oars.

Another cause of temporary slavery, debt, differed only in the
element of intent.   In Germanic law slavery had already been
recognized as a natural consequence of non-payment of the composition for a crime.   The insolvent criminal was handed over to
the injured party, that he might by his labor pay for the damage
caused.[1]   But in addition to this, debts civilly contracted could
be paid by slavery; for gambling debts there is evidence of this
method as late as Tacitus.[2]   The creditor had the right to seize the
person of the insolvent debtor and to obtain payment through his
labor.   The wife of such a slave was, by some laws, also made a
slave, in order to hasten by her work the redemption of her husband.[3]   From these conceptions may have arisen the strong disfavor which the laws in later periods manifested towards insolvent
debtors by limitations of their rights and by the mark of "infamy", which was hard to lose.   The last trace of the debtor's
person as guaranty of his obligations may be seen in arrest for
debt, which disappeared from private law in modern times.[4]

§ 293. **Extinguishment of Slavery ; Public Manumission.** —
Slaves could gain their liberty in several ways, but all were
traceable to two main sources, the will of the owner and a provision of law.

A master might be moved by various reasons to free his slave :
as by religious sentiment, especially on the point of death, or as
recompense for services, or because he wished to give him some
office, such as that of guardian, priest or other, or because of the
slave's own right of redemption.   The owner, however, must not
find himself in any of those situations in which the law limited his

---

[1] *Cf.* "addictio in servitutem" of the Roman law.
[2] "Germania", 24.   [3] *Arechi*, 6.   [4] *Post* § 496.

right. He might not, for example, manumit his slaves in such a way or in such numbers as to injure the rights of his heirs, depopulate the fields, diminish the property of the churches, cause the loss of testimony, or in general any complication disapproved by the law. Furthermore, for the slave to be freed, the mere wish of the master was not enough ; his will must be manifested by an act of manumission, the formalities and consequences of which were varied.

Some types of manumission were of Germanic origin and solemn in their nature.[1]

First of these was the presentation of the slave to the assembly, where he was given arms, to indicate that henceforth he was admitted to the class of freemen and might defend his own rights. But this mode of manumission was not commonly used, except when there was reason, for some national need, to make soldiers of a large number of slaves.

The most frequent form of manumission was that called " in quarta mano " or " per sagittam." The master gave his slave to a freeman, by whom he was passed on to a third and then a fourth, who led him to a cross-roads, and there, armed, he was allowed to go where he wished, as proof that he was free to act according to his own judgment.

There was yet another form, called " in votum " or " in manu regis ", consisting in a commendation of the slave to the king who then gave him his liberty. According to Frankish law, the king, by a light blow given in his presence, caused a coin to be knocked from the slave's hand, thus signifying that he disclaimed the services, represented by the money, which the slave would otherwise have had to perform.

To these solemn Germanic forms of manumission was added the Roman form by religious rites, called for that reason " in sacrosanctis ecclesiis." It was in use, though without the full effects of the Germanic forms, prior to its acceptance by the Lombard law. This took place under Liutprand, who first made it a royal privilege, decreeing that full liberty should result only when the king himself presented the slave for manumission before the altar. Later the power was accorded to all, so that this form of manumission was placed on an equal footing in its effects with the other solemn forms.[2] Indeed it became the principal method, when persons on the point of death were permitted to exercise it by merely designating the priest at whose hands the slave was to be

[1] *Rothar*, 224.   [2] *Liutprand*, 9, 23, 55.

enfranchised, and when the law provided that this form necessarily resulted in full liberty, so that agreements were not possible, as they were in the other forms, whereby the enfranchised slave continued subject to duties towards his former owner.[1]

It is apparent that a feature common to all these modes of manumission was the owner's recourse to a third person, a private citizen, the king, or the Church represented by the priest. By giving the slave into the dependence of a third party, the purpose was to free him from subjection to his owner.

§ 294. **Private Manumission.** — Besides the solemn forms, there were private forms of manumission. Their distinguishing trait was that the owner did not have recourse to an intermediary but accomplished the manumission himself. They were mostly of Roman origin. In substance they always consisted of a declaration by the owner of his intention that the slave should be free, made either in the presence of witnesses ("inter amicos"), or by giving the slave a writing ("per epistolam"), called a "charta", from which arose the name of "chartularii", applied to slaves so liberated.

Just as in Roman law, however, this private form did not, under Germanic law, have the full effect of solemn manumission. By the latter full liberty was gained; by the former ordinarily only the half-freedom of the "aldius."[2] The owner, therefore, must choose the form whose effect corresponded to the status in which he wished to place his slave. Thus the law itself gave warning that one who wished to make of his slave an "aldius" should not manumit him by taking him to the cross-roads, because he would thereby be wholly free. And so too the solemn forms might give rise to different consequences. Some, properly Germanic, besides resulting in full liberty, also freed the slave from every duty to his owner as his patron, making him, as was said, "fulfreale" and "amundius."[3] Others made him merely "fulfreale", that is, completely free in himself and yet not released from that power of guardianship and protection which prohibited him from bringing an action involving "infamy" against his patron; which obliged him to procure his patron's consent to marry; and according to which he owed the latter respect and service. The patron, for his part, had the right to claim the "guidrigild" and inherit the manumitted's estate if he died without legitimate descendants.

[1] *Astolf*, 11.
[2] [*Ante* § 40, abridged from §§ 130 *et seq.* of *Calisse*, vol. II, "Diritto publico."]
[3] *Post* § 338.

These and other obligations of the slave, enfranchised without being made " amundius ", were recorded in a document, the " tabula ", which gave the name " tabularii " to the class thus manumitted. For the most part, this effect, especially in the Frankish period, arose from manumissions by religious rites, which conferred upon the manumitted the " defensio " or protection of the Church, subject tò a right to his services, as determined by the " tabulae." In later periods, however, with the fusion of laws, differences of effect disappeared along with those of form, while manumission itself lost importance in proportion as the end of slavery approached. The ancient solemnities were abandoned and the modes most commonly in use in the last manumissions of the 1200 s and 1300 s were those by declaration in writing before a magistrate.

§ 295. **Liberation by the Action of Law.** — Slaves could obtain freedom without, and even against, the consent of their owner, by force of a provision of law. There were several motives for this. Sometimes it was desired to reward a slave for some special merit, as for disclosing a conspiracy, or a serious crime of his owner, or, in the case of the slave of a Jew or infidel, for converting the owner to Christianity ; or for other similar reasons. Sometimes the law aimed to punish the master by freeing the slave. This happened if the master had been guilty of treason, prevented the slave's recourse to the king's justice, sold him to an infidel, committed adultery with his wife, or had attempted to convert him from Christianity, or had in any other way subjected him to serious abuse. For it has already been pointed out that the Roman principle of denying to slaves even the rights inherent in human nature was not accepted by the laws governing Italy, so long as slavery endured there.

It might also happen that liberty came by right to the slave, because of a new status which he might come to occupy and which was incompatible with slavery. One such was the priesthood, whereby, as soon as admitted, he acquired freedom. To avoid injuring the master, his consent to the ordination was required. But the ordination was always the cause of the liberation ; on the owner's part no act of any sort was necessary ; it sufficed that he did not oppose if asked, or that he did not, within a year, reclaim the slave ordained without his knowledge. If he did so, the ordaining priest was punished and the slave, according to Lombard law,[1] was restored to his owner. But since he could not be deprived of

[1] *Liutprand*, 53.

his newly acquired status, rather than restore him, the expedient was later adopted of compensating the owner for his loss, such compensation being made by the bishop or the church to whom the new priest belonged.

Lastly, freedom could be acquired by a prescription of the owner's right. By Lombard law a man who lived as a free man for thirty years remained such, no matter what the contrary proof.[1] Under the Carlovingians an opposite tendency appeared. The Lombard rule governed Lombards and Romans, but for those living under Frankish law Charlemagne decreed that prescription should not benefit a fugitive slave;[2] Louis the Pious,[3] later confirmed by Lothar,[4] extended the principle to all persons. Nor was feudalism favorable to this mode of enfranchisement, especially since the parcelling of feudal territories made it easy for a slave to escape from the master's house and live in fact in freedom. On the other hand the mediaeval communes showed themselves well disposed, since one of their important policies was to enfranchise the feudal lower classes; they therefore welcomed all such fugitives and declared them free by the mere fact of residence in the city, separated from their owners.[5]

When later the slavery of Christians was abolished and servitude remained solely a consequence of the permanent state of war with the Mohammedans, this system of considering fugitive slaves as free became a sort of renewal of the Roman " jus postliminii ", in that a return to Christian territory meant the reacquisition of complete freedom for those who had been taken in slavery by an enemy.

§ 296. **Intermediate Status.** — In Germanic society there was also a status which oscillated between free and slave and partook of the character of both. This was the status of the half free, *e.g.* the " aldii " or the " coloni " or dependents of whatsoever sort. The study of these half free classes as part of the population, and of their relations to social ordinances, belongs to public law.[6] So far as it related to private law, their condition, generally speaking, appeared only as a reason to limit the scope and exercise of legal capacity but never as a cause for its complete absence. In contrast with slaves, those occupying any one of the positions just referred to were truly persons, and the numerous traces of slavery attaching to their status concealed without totally extin-

[1] *Grimwald,* 2; *Astolf,* 13, 22; *cf. Justinian,* Code, VII, 22, 2.
[2] *Charlemagne,* 87.   [5] *Ante* § 92.
[3] *Louis the Pious,* 55.   [6] *Ante* § 40.
[4] *Lothar,* 100.

guishing their free status.   The half free (" aldii "), for example, in their private relations, had capacity to own property, have a family and contract, though not to the same extent as persons wholly free.

TOPIC 2.   CITIZENSHIP

§ 297. **Significance.** — The doctrines of citizenship have lost all importance in Italian private law, since present day acceptance of the principle of unconditional admission of foreigners to the civil rights of the citizen.[1]   But this stage was reached only with modern civilization; it was either entirely unknown or but partially applied throughout the whole historical course of the law; the more remote the period, the greater was the foreigner's legal incapacity, until in the very earliest antiquity he is found to occupy a position wholly outside the law.

In the history of law citizenship was, therefore, another prerequisite of juridical capacity, a necessary condition of legal personality.   Considered in its effect, that is, in its relation to capacity for civil rights, citizenship might be lacking in the individual for any one of several causes: for example, because he did not belong to the State by origin, i.e. was a foreigner; or because, though a citizen by birth, he had lost that status by judicial sentence or a provision of the law.

§ 298. **Foreigners ; " Albinaggium."** — Since a person was not considered a part of the society to which he stood in the relation of foreigner, he could not enjoy the protection of the law which that society had created for its own exclusive benefit.   Thus he found himself in the condition of one outside the law, whom any might kill, enslave, or despoil of his possessions without any ensuing legal repression.   To use a Latin phrase, he was " res nullius " and so belonged to the first who seized possession of him.

To relieve so serious a hardship, the institution of hospitality was held in high honor by all ancient peoples, including the Germanic.[2]   Through hospitality towards the foreigner, a citizen became his protector, and along with protection, he assumed the burden of representing him before the law, defending him from injuries others might do him and standing guarantor of his conduct.   Traces of this institution were long preserved.[3]   But very early the particular protection by a private individual was replaced

[1] Civil Code, art. 3.
[2] *Caesar*, "De bello gallico", VI, 23 ; *Tacitus*, "Germania", chap. 21.
[3] *Rothar*, 358 ; "Divisio Rudelgisi et Siginulfi ducatus beneventani", of the year 851, chap. 3.

by the general protection of the king, or public protection, since the character of defender of those who could not defend themselves belonged properly to the royal power.[1] Among such persons foreigners were certainly numbered. From this protection they undoubtedly gained advantages, such as security, justice, facilities in commerce, and the like; on the other hand, they necessarily suffered a certain subjection. For if the foreigner gained legal recognition through his protector, it was the latter's law by which he was recognized and defended, and not his own, which had no effect. The first consequence was, therefore, that he lost the use of his own law, unless the king especially conceded it to him.[2] Furthermore, as the foreigner's defense fell to his protector, the latter was entitled to claim the " guidrigild ", if he were killed, and the compositions for other injuries suffered. He thereby came to have a power of guardianship, the " mundium ", over the foreigner, even becoming thereby his legal heir, for the law recognized no other bond as possible to the foreigner except that through which he had secured recognition. Thus the protector inherited his estate, even though he left sons. But the Lombard law made an exception of this case,[3] and it is thus apparent that, in general, the foreigner had just so much legal capacity as was conceded to him. Alone he would have had none, but he obtained it in greater or less measure through another's protection, which, however, became a cause of dependence. Thus the various rights which his protector, henceforward the State, had over the foreigner and which were the basis of the right of " albinaggium " (" jus albinatus ") — so called because it related to the " alibi natus " — were derived from an intention to benefit him and were the necessary consequence of the protection accorded him. They were soon turned to his disadvantage and became, contrary to their original purpose, a means of oppression, which it took long for subsequent civilization to remove.

In fact, the laws of the Franks soon began to show themselves severer towards foreigners, for they did not admit the Lombard mitigation whereby sons were preferred to the State in the succession of a foreigner. At the creation of the Empire, the condition of foreigners was not improved by the generalization which the principle of " personal law " had received, because their law was of necessity that of the law of their protector, the king. This prepared the way for the marked debasement of their status, suffered under feudalism, when the seigniors were substituted as guardians

[1] *Ante* § 29.   [2] *Rothar*, 367.   [3] *Ibid.*

in place of the king and an institution intended for the foreigners' advantage was turned to their harm. It was in this period that the right of " albinaggium " came to have as its sole purpose the profit of the person exercising it. This right arose from the legal incapacities which bore upon the foreigner. The greatest of these was certainly the denial of the right to transmit property by will or to inherit, the king or the feudal lord being the heir. But there were others that were also serious, such as disability to participate in civil rights; fewer means of defence and less credibility than citizens before the courts; incapacity sometimes to own land; imposition of higher taxes; in some cases the payment of exceptional burdens, as, for example, that of obtaining consent to marry; and, in general, exposure to the mercy of the seigniors, who sought to make personal slaves of foreigners who put foot upon their soil.

Furthermore it must not be forgotten that it continued a fixed principle that, if the foreigner was without a protector, who was in fact the cause of so much harm to him, he was regarded as outside the law. This is apparent from the " jus naufragii." Like a foreigner, one who had been shipwrecked and had not had time to place himself under the protection of the seignior of the locality upon whose shores misfortune had thrown him, fell, both as to his person and his goods, into the power of the first comer, and it was later looked upon as a mark of progress that he should be given his freedom, subject only to the confiscation of his goods to the State.

Against such customs, which, however, had never had the same extension in Italy as elsewhere, the law soon came to protest. By the 800 s, in the so-called "Lex Romana of Udine", and in the treaty between the Beneventine prince, Sicard, and the Neapolitans, provisions were found prohibiting and punishing the exercise of the " jus naufragii ";[1] in the 900 s and 1000 s, popes and Church councils repeatedly endeavored to obtain for foreigners the right to dispose by will and to have their sons inherit from them;[2] Frederick II enacted laws against the right of " albinaggium " and the " jus naufragii ";[3] the Italian republics followed, then the princes, and finally in the 1500 s the Emperor Charles V. But the evil was not thereby extirpated, as evidenced by the constant need of reënacting these repressive measures. Sentiments

[1] "Lex Romana Udinese", XXIV, 7; "Pactum Sicardi", of the year 836, chap. 13.
[2] Roman Council of 1078, Lateran Council of 1179; Gregory VII, Alexander III, Eugenius III, Pius V, etc.
[3] *Justinian*, Code, VI, 59, 10, Autentica, "Omnes peregrini."

of humanity were overborne by political motives or State greed. For political reasons the mediaeval communes were indisposed to foreigners. Not that at times they did not look upon them with favor for special causes, such as to bring prosperity to their own traders, to attract students to the universities, to obtain, by treaties of reciprocity, favorable treatment for their own citizens abroad. But these were exceptions, limited both as to the persons and to the occasions for which they were established. Outside them, the jealousy between cities caused the foreigner to be regarded almost always as an enemy, against whom they were on their guard, and whose legal capacity they limited not only as to political but also as to such civil rights as property, protection of the courts, giving testimony, marriage portions, marriage itself and so on.

In the governments succeeding the communes, fiscal reasons operated with more damaging effect than others against the foreigner. Governments were reluctant to lose the customary revenue from the right of " albinaggium "; in fact several examples of this use may be found in the following centuries and it was still a subject of legislation in the 1700 s. Victor Amadeus II, for example, decreed that all shipwrecked goods found in the sea and unclaimed within a year and a day, belonged to the State; the Sicilian " sanctiones " of the first half of the 1700 s forbade sales by foreigners within the kingdom without a royal license, so that the treasury should not be defrauded. Piedmontese laws of 1770 still expressly recognized the right of " albinaggium ", while admitting the principle of reciprocity by treaty; and so also did those from 1771, fixing the principle that the foreigner had no capacity to acquire or inherit land within the State. Thus, during all the 1700 s and the first years of the 1800 s, the abolition of the right of " albinaggium " came about only by means of treaties signed by the various States of Italy among themselves and with other European States, all of which were based upon the principle of reciprocity. Reciprocity was not, therefore, a general principle; it was not so even in the Napoleonic Code or those that followed and imitated it. To the present Italian Code belongs the credit of having once for all repudiated the inferiority of status which, in matters of private law, the past had laid upon foreigners in contrast to citizens.[1]

---

[1] [The corresponding right, "droit d'aubaine", was abolished in France by the Law of Aug. 18, 1790.   It was reëstablished in the Napoleonic Code, a distinction being made between foreigners having a fixed authorized residence in France and those who did not. This distinction was done

§ 299. **Civil Death.** — In the same status as foreigners, that is, outside the common law,[1] may also be placed those who lost their rights of citizenship. In Germanic law this was true of one deprived of the " public peace " (" extra sermonem regis "), outlawed from civil society (" forbannitus ", " forjudicatus ", " forfactus "), or declared a public enemy (" faidosus "). He became thereby incapacitated for any juridical act, public or private; he could enjoy no office or authority; he could not appear in court as litigant or witness; he could hold no property or fief; he could not marry or have legitimate offspring; in short he was denied all that the law furnished, including, therefore, even a defense against the damage which anyone might with impunity do him.[2] This penalty was inflicted upon those who, by seriously disturbing it, made themselves undeserving of the "public peace"; and upon the authors of grave crimes, such as an attempt against the king, desertion from the army, or murder of a relative. Condemnation following a serious crime, therefore, gave rise to a condition in which, in the words of the law, he was treated as though dead. Thus arose both the theory of, and the term, *civil death,* which put an end to the person by destroying the basis of legal capacity, as did natural death by destroying physical existence.

Civil death, originating in Germanic concepts and supported also by Roman precedents (cf. " capitis diminutio "), received a development in the period of the mediaeval Italian communes, by which it was classed with all those penalties termed capital, because destructive of the " caput ", that is the capacity for civil rights. These, in addition to death, were perpetual exile, deportation, life imprisonment, and others. The condemned was no longer a person, he could not make a will, his heirs at law at once came into his estate unless already confiscated, and, although living, he lost every right, to the point that his wife was legally a widow and his children born subsequently were not recognized by

away with, in so far as the right to dispose by will and to inherit were concerned, by the law of July 14, 1819, repealing Civ. C., arts. 726 and 912. The Italian Civ. C. came into effect in 1866.]

[1] [The term "common law", used here and elsewhere in this volume, is not of course an exact parallel to the Anglo-American "common" or unwritten law. In Italy it refers to different sources at different periods of history. In general it is describable as the mass of enforceable law, unwritten or written, forming the legal background of the people, and to which reference was had in the absence of special laws. In this sense the Civil Code of Italy is "common law" today. For a description of the "common law" up to and including the period of the Renaissance, in Italy, see *Calisse*, "Fonti", §§ 92 *et seq.*, translated in Continental Legal History Series, vol. 1, "General Survey", §§ 23–34, pp. 108 *et seq.*]

[2] *Cf.* the "sacer" of the Roman law.

the law. Thus strictly the civil death of the Italian laws was different from the Germanic loss of " peace ", according to which, to be outside the law was the necessary consequence of all those privations which formed the very penalty inflicted. Later, on the other hand, civil death became itself a penalty, distinct from the principal punishment, to which it came to be added as an aggravation, though it might also be separate.

Nevertheless, in this respect also, Italian laws never attained the degree of severity of other systems, particularly the French. All, however, recognized so-called civil death, and the term did not disappear from the laws, nor its effect from society, until the period of modern law.

A sort of civil death overtook one who took solemn religious vows, though limited in its effect to property and inheritance. This was not only because such a person had professed a vow of poverty, but because, from the days of the ancient Roman law, the religious order was considered to possess and inherit and so to acquire through him. Admission to a religious order was also an impediment to marriage (§ 320), a disability now no longer existent in Italian law since the suppression of the religious orders.

§ 300. **Religious Difference.** — As some were outside the laws of the State because they did not belong to it (foreigners), or because excluded from it (by civil death), similarly there were those who were outside the community of the Church, having never been a part (Jews, Saracens), or having separated from it (heretics, excommunicants). And just as legal capacity was withheld from the former, so the enjoyment of ecclesiastical benefits was denied those outside the Church. This was not all. State and Church being united, the former did not extend its benefits to those to whom the Church denied its favors. Thus for religious reasons they were also visited with civil incapacity. And just as this might be repaired, in the case of a foreigner, by the protection of public authority, so protection was conceded to the status of those separated off from other citizens by difference of religion or by ecclesiastical sentence.

§ 301. **Jews and Saracens.** — This was best illustrated by the Jews. Against them militated not only diversity of religion but also of race, to which was added popular hate and fanaticism. From Roman times the enjoyment of common rights had been denied them; and if, by special reason of their commercial importance, they obtained protection from rulers, it amounted only to an extension to them of a fraction of the rights which all others enjoyed. Such protection, moreover, was not general but limited to those who had demanded and obtained it, and it was, therefore, always referred to in the laws as a " privilege." [1] It was under the Carlovingians that this protection became a general institution, bringing all Jews within the king's representation, which, because of the benefits obtained thereby, become a regalia ; [2] as such, like all others, it passed to the feudatories, from whom it was inherited by the mediaeval communes, and by them later returned to the succeeding sovereigns.

But, as a general rule, such protection, directed more to the profit of the one granting it than of the recipient, was very far from effecting a full gift of legal capacity. Within the limit pleasing to the grantor, the Jews could, it is true, own property, trade, have a family recognized by law, worship in their own way, and have access to the ordinary courts. But they nevertheless continued in a status markedly inferior to that of other citizens.

In the first place, they found themselves in immediate dependence upon their protector, which obliged them to recompense him in different ways, particularly by the payment of taxes. Of these some were general, payable at one time or at intervals, like the " mano regia " in Rome, the " gisia " in Sicily, or the " contrabando " in Piedmont ; some were special, due, that is, to a particular concession, *e.g.* consent to marry or authority to do something not included among the general privileges, or similar reasons.

Secondly, with the definite aim of keeping the Jews distinct from, and subordinate to, the Christians, certain rights, on the one hand, never came to be extended to the Jews, while on the other hand certain obligations were imposed upon them, restrictive of their personal liberty. As to rights, they were always excluded from those that were political: they might not hold public office, intermarry with Christians, have Christian slaves, conduct public schools, or follow certain professions. The use of their own law, even in the period of the "personality" of laws, was granted them only exceptionally, when they chose from among their number persons who, as arbitrators, should decide their disputes. Ordinarily they were not even admitted to the common courts but to the special jurisdiction of the bishops, who thereby laid claim to rights, among others that of inheritance. Furthermore, even as to the rights conceded, they were not on an equal

---

[1] Edictum Theodorici, chap. 143, ed. *Bluhme*, in M. G. H., "Leges" V, 145 *et seq.*
[2] *Ante* §§ 61–62.

footing with Christians. For the assertion of their rights they did not enjoy all the means given to others; their testimony did not have equal weight; their " guidrigild ", so long as the " guid-rigild " lasted, was made less, in order to show their inferior legal capacity. The obligations, out of which grew restrictions upon their personal liberty, were many and severe. In the public amusements, at times of festivals, they had often to make jests of themselves; they often were forced to take part in Christian ceremonials, such as attending preaching and even receiving for-cible baptism; they had to wear a distinctive mark on their clothes, by which they were at once recognizable; they all lived in a special quarter of the city, the " ghetto ", whose gates were closed at nightfall and opened at sunrise and which none might enter or leave during the interval.

Finally, and most serious of all, this protection, from which sprang so many disadvantages for so few benefits, was never stable or certain. Very frequently it was merely a temporary concession, to be renewed at each expiration by new payments and with new and varying stipulations agreeable to the grantor. This was the custom in Piedmont, Venetia, Sicily and elsewhere. But whether permanent or temporary, nothing prevented the instant revocation of the protection and the placing of all Jews at a stroke beyond the pale of the law. For they were considered slaves of the public, slaves, as was said, of the " imperial household ", of the king's court, or the like, and, therefore, any conduct toward them was deemed lawful, even to the breaking of faith with them for no other purpose than to confiscate their property or to yield to some popular fanatical impulse. Examples of general confiscation and of mass expulsion were frequent in all the Italian States, from the time of Louis in the 800 s until the Jewish emancipation after the French Revolution.

But the reforms of the 1700 s ameliorated the Jews' condition, equalizing it much more nearly to that of other citizens, though still through concessions, by nature revocable, and hence not yet conferring perfect civil equality. The latter first came about through the French legislation in Italy, was again lost under the laws of the restored governments, and finally permanently regained under the constitutional changes of 1848, which became national with Italian unification.

The Saracens, too, were outside the protection of both civil and ecclesiastical laws. In southern Italy, and especially in Sicily, where they were confused with the rest of the population, they were truly placed in an exceptional position, without legal capacity, except as to rights recognized by royal protection.   But elsewhere, and particularly in the States of the Church, where they were found only as prisoners of war, their condition was that of slaves and their lives were spent as oarsmen on the benches of the galleys.

§ 302. **Heretics and the Excommunicated.** — Heretics and excommunicated were also cut off from the communion of the Church.   The Roman emperors, who for political reasons wished to maintain unity of faith within the State,[1] dealt very severely with departures from it and punished dissenters with various penalties, among which was that of almost total loss of civil rights. Those who were ecclesiastically dead were also civilly dead.   This rigor was mitigated under the Germanic rulers, because, though heretics themselves (until the conversion of the Lombards), they were yet obliged to live on good terms with the church of the conquered, which, in turn, avoided constant conflict with the established civil power in Italy.   There thus came about a reciprocal tolerance by which, except for a certain period of friction, the various creeds could be peacefully professed, particularly as such professions were restricted to the remnants of the pagan religions. Against these only, in fact, were the Lombard laws directed under the inspiration of the Church when, after conversion to Catholicism, they became its defenders and missionaries.[2]   During the Germanic period, therefore, it was rather the excommunicated who were reached by the laws.   To lose the " peace " of the Church was to lose that of society, so that one in this condition was outside the law's protection and lost all rights, as well as capacity to acquire fresh ones.   The fact that excommunication pronounced against rulers freed their subjects from the oath of fealty was in fact an application of the rule that excommunication carried with it the loss of all rights.

But there came a change, when true heresies sprang up and religious sects multiplied, especially after the year 1000.   The temporal laws were in every particular an echo of the penalties of popes and councils.   In 1215, the Fourth Lateran Council adopted provisions for the extermination of heresy ; and princes — even those most temporally inclined — imitating their predecessors, gave their support.   Suffice to recall Frederick II, who surpassed even the rigor of the Romans in his enactments against heretics, extending the laws to those who gave comfort or refuge,

[1] [*Ante* § 20, abridged from *Calisse*, "Diritto Publico", § 64.]
[2] *Liutprand*, 84, 85.

515

and in addition to the penalties pronounced by the Fourth Lateran Council, condemned all to the loss of legal capacity.

Thus ecclesiastically and civilly inspired, the statutes of the mediaeval communes followed in the same direction. All alike declared the heretic incapable of any sort of right whatsoever and made him the victim of a persecution, which they intrusted to their highest magistrates, the consul and the podestà. Thus matters continued, so long as the State saw in the tutelage of the faith the promotion also of its own interests. But the time came, with the great religious struggles of the 1500 s, when not only many States withdrew from the ancient faith, but the remainder recognized that, rather than perish in the vain effort to extinguish heresy, it would be in their best interest to seek to remove or lessen the discord, and that this could be accomplished only by substituting tolerance for persecution. This principle has never since been wholly abandoned by the laws, with the exception of a brief interval when, chiefly for reasons of political opportunism, the old road of repression was resumed. Piedmont tolerated the Waldensians; Venice permitted freedom of worship to resident foreigners; full legal capacity was recognized, irrespective of religion, by Grand Duke Ferdinand I of Tuscany; Charles Emanuel II and III, Maria Theresa, and even the popes were tolerant; finally the French Constituent Assembly leveled all differences between dissenters and orthodox and, while this principle was temporarily denied by the laws following the Restoration, it has reasserted itself in the corresponding legislation of present Italy.

CHAPTER II

LIMITATIONS TO LEGAL CAPACITY [1]

§ 303. The "Mundium."

TOPIC 1. PHYSICAL CAUSES

§ 304. Age.   § 306. Infirmities.
§ 305. Sex.

TOPIC 2. MORAL CAUSES

§ 307. Personal and Social.   § 309. Social Inequality.
§ 308. Honor.

§ 303. **The " Mundium."** — To capacity in law there did not always correspond capacity of action. The former might be suspended or limited in scope or exercise by the fact that the individual was under another's authority; that he was not " sui " but " alieni juris ", as the Romans expressed it; or that he was, as the Germanic law put it, subject to the " mundium " of another. The conception of the " mundium " was general and applied to any power, whether marital, paternal or royal, of which the chief attribute was the protection of the person over whom it was exercised. It might arise from various causes, producing differences of duration as well as of kind. But all may be grouped into two categories, according to origin. Some forms were derived from natural facts, that is *physical causes* ; others from the moral qualities of the person, that is, from *moral causes*.

TOPIC 1. PHYSICAL CAUSES

§ 304. **Age.** — To exercise one's rights it was necessary to have attained an appropriate age. The Roman test of ability to act with legal effect was ability to understand all the consequences of one's actions and be responsible for them; in the Germanic nations, the exercise of rights belonged solely to those having capacity to vindicate them, by force if necessary. From this arose all the differences in the two systems as to the age of capacity. While the

---

[1] *Pertile, cit.* §§ 101–103; *Salvioli, cit.* part IV, chaps. 2–3.

Romans recognized several periods, each with a progressive increase of capacity corresponding to the mental and moral development of the individual, the Germanic law made but one distinction: fitness or unfitness to bear arms. So long as a person lacked such capability, he was always under legal age ("infra aetatem"), subject to the authority of father or guardian and to all the consequences of such a status. As soon as he put on arms, a solemn ceremony taking place before the popular assembly, he gained, without having passed through a fixed minority, full legal capacity, without further need of defender or legal representative. There were other consequences of the Germanic system. No age was fixed for the entry into majority, since this depended solely upon the particular qualities of each individual, which might hasten or delay his fitness to receive arms. So also old age, when it deprived of the power to bear arms, resulted in the loss of those rights based exclusively on such capacity.

But upon this point early Germanic law soon changed and, by the date of their first written laws, an age had been fixed for all when the necessary aptitude for the exercise of rights was presumed. These limits, however, varied not only between one Germanic people and another, but also in the laws of a single people, according to the acts to be accomplished. The Lombards at first placed the end of minority at twelve years,[1] but Liutprand, while retaining this term for matrimony and all that related to it, extended it to eighteen for the alienation of property.[2] In Frankish law, majority came at fourteen. And in general all Germanic laws had short terms, because their family organization required even persons of age to act always with the consent of the other members of the family, whenever serious interests were at stake, so that the risks accompanying youthful inexperience were avoided.

Feudalism brought other distinctions. Minority for the nobles was shorter than for the common people. Of this examples were preserved in succeeding centuries, one surviving today in the rule that the age of wardship terminates earlier in reigning families than among private citizens.

Variations in the period were more numerous in the communal legislation of the Middle Ages, since the distinctions of the Roman law were accepted and in different ways combined with those of Germanic tradition. Thus from twelve years, the shortest term of Lombard minority, the period ranged to twenty-five years, at which Roman majority commenced. This last case followed the

[1] *Rothar*, 155.   [2] *Liutprand*, 19, 117.

Roman system of interposing, between the age of puberty and majority, another period, called minority, so that one passed by degrees, rather than at a stroke, from legal incapacity to capacity. Another distinction was added, namely, between civil and political majority, the latter requiring a greater age, in view of the importance of the rights which it gave, among which was that to public office. This could not have been within the Germanic conception, by which a solemn investiture with arms signified introduction into public life.

All these distinctions and differences, inherited also by the legislation following the mediaeval communes, in large part disappeared with the introduction of French law by Napoleon, which, in this respect, has been followed by the Italian legislation of to-day, fixing majority for all at twenty-five. Nevertheless traces of these historic diversities still remain. While the Roman term of twenty-five years has been retained to perfect capacity for all civil acts,[1] an approach to the Germanic basis is evident in the adoption of but two periods, minority and majority, and to the system of the mediaeval communes in the preservation of the distinction between civil and political majority, requiring a special age for certain public offices.

§ 305. **Sex.** — While Roman imperial law succeeded in placing woman in a condition not very unlike that of man, and while Christianity tended to abolish all moral inequality between the two sexes, Germanic law (notwithstanding the honor in which these people held their women[2]), during the turbulent periods of the invasions, hardened the ancient customs, sanctioning woman's inferiority as well in the sphere of public law as in the exercise of civil acts and within the family.

There were mainly two causes for this. The first was the military nature and organization of the people. The exercise of arms, ability to defend one's rights, to carry on blood vengeance for an injury received, were all beyond the capacity of woman. And it was precisely because these constituted the basis of mastership over one's self, that the law always placed the woman in a position of subordination.[3] The second reason was the organization of the family and the necessity, of first importance, of guarding its preservation.[4] Of this woman was quite incapable, because, to have descendants, she had to abandon her paternal family, whose interests, therefore, she could not further. From the first of these rea-

[1] Civil Code, arts. 323, 63.
[2] *Tacitus,* "Germania", 8.
[3] *Rothar,* 204; *Liutprand,* 13.
[4] *Post* § 312.

sons was derived not only lack of political rights, but also incapacity for all those acts which for any reason presupposed the use of arms, such as the collection of the " guidrigild " or compositions, since this right was inseparable from private vengeance; [1] similarly she might not testify in court, because of the application of the principle of mutual defense among members of the family; nor might she institute or defend an action, because this might lead to proof by judicial combat.   The second reason was chiefly responsible for depriving woman of legal capacity with regard to the family estate,[2] the guarantee of the family's continuance.   In consequence, she found herself, within her own family, in a position of personal inferiority, which, aggravated by her need of another's protection, produced her subjection to a permanent guardianship.   This might, depending upon varying situations, be exercised by the father, husband, sons, brother,[3] or other relatives, or finally even by the king.   But, by whomsoever exercised, it always produced on the one hand a limitation of the woman's rights, and was, on the other, always inspired by the idea of protection.   This meant that, for the person wielding it, it was a duty and that from the duty sprang rights.   It was the guardian (" mundoald "), who, on breach of a betrothal, had to force the spouse to payment of the promised dowery (" mefio "),[4] and who had to collect the compositions and " guidrigild " for injuries to a woman.[5]   Thus may be explained the fact, otherwise seemingly in contradiction to what has been previously said, that the " guidrigild " of women was greater than of the men; for whoever injured a woman, besides aggravating his wrong by directing it against a defenceless person, also injured her protector, thereby causing an increase of his penalty.   By Lombard law, the slayer of a woman paid 1200 " solidi ", or four times the " guidrigild " of the highest noble; [6] the Frankish law tripled the ordinary " guidrigild " and the same principle held true of other Germanic laws.

Christianity was not effective in combating this Germanic concept of woman's inferiority, because its consequences were not wholly irreconcilable with Christianity.   In fact her inferiority did not penetrate to the moral sphere; as wife, especially, she had rights against, no less than duties towards her husband,[7] when they did not concern the care of the material interests of the family.   Upon this point even the law of the Church aimed to

[1] *Ante* §§ 46, 47.
[2] *Rothar*, 204.
[3] *Liutprand*, 12.
[4] *Post* § 325.

[5] *Rothar*, 26, 187; *Liutprand*, 31, 60, 93.
[6] *Rothar*, 201; *Liutprand*, 62.
[7] *Post* § 341.

make the husband the head and guide of the household and to subordinate the wife to him.   Besides, to overcome the uncertainty of marriages and to bring them all under a single rule,[1] the canon law favored the property system of the " dos " or marriage portion between spouses, which, borrowed from the Roman law, involved in itself limitations to the wife's powers as to the disposal, management and enjoyment of her property.   It was a maxim of the canon law too, therefore, that woman's condition should be inferior to that of man, both politically and civilly.

This was not altered by feudalism or by the mediaeval communes.   Under feudalism the military ideal, naturally prejudicial to women, prevailed.   It was a principle of this system that the fief, from which women were ordinarily excluded, constituted the completion of legal capacity; she could not, therefore, progress to that point in the acquisition of new rights, but remained in a perpetual wardship.   Yet her inferiority clearly involved no degradation, for it was precisely during the feudal period that a tribute almost amounting to a cult was paid to her through the institutions of chivalry.

The mediaeval communes reached the same result, though upon different reasons.   Not the military spirit but economic interest opposed the acquisition by outsiders of communal wealth through marriage portions or inheritance by women; and it was of political importance that foreigners, through relatives, should acquire no authority in the commune.   These were the causes that kept alive unfavorable traditions towards women, even after the disappearance, under new social conditions, of those other causes which had produced them.   But precisely for this reason the continuance of her inferiority was justified upon new grounds, by which she lost also morally; there was substantial agreement in holding her a source of harm or of dangers to the family, that must be removed at all cost.   This is evident in the writers of the period, whether of literature or of law.   The literature, especially the novels, reverting in this respect towards paganism, lacked the respect for women shown by an earlier Germanic society, while writers on the law, by mistaken interpretations of some Roman jurisconsult, justified her legal incapacity by reasons that dishonored her, such as inconstancy, avarice, caprice, and other supposed evil qualities.   To this tendency was joined the interest of the noble families, who, in the exclusion of the woman, saw a means of assuring the preservation of the family estate.   All this, together with the power which

[1] *Post* § 328.

the aristocracy continued to have in the governments following the mediaeval communes,[1] resulted, until the end of the
1700 s, in excluding women from the exercise of almost every
civil right.

There were, on the other hand, some causes tending, though
slowly, to raise woman's condition. Among them the most important was the Roman law, still in use among the Roman part of the
population, by which the guardianship of the woman was not permanent: by which, indeed, not a few rights were granted her.
Therefore, in the formation of those laws wherein Roman influence was one of the strongest elements, its principles penetrated
and dominated, or at least mitigated the severity of, the Germanic
rules. They prevailed in Venetian territory and Liguria, whose
cities gave woman constantly greater independence in respect to
her civil acts; they moderated the Germanic principles in the
Suabian, Angevin and Aragonese legislation and in the Piedmontese laws, through the creation of exceptions and privileges, permitting the woman, under certain conditions, to dispose of her own
property not included in the marriage portion, to contract, and to
obtain, if damaged, the Roman " restitutio in integrum " or application of the " Senatus-consultum Velleianum "; also to choose
her guardian herself, and to enter, at least provisionally, into certain determined commercial transactions.

But substantial improvement in woman's legal position did not
come until the legislation of the 1800 s. Of this the first was the
French law, the Napoleonic Code, which gave her a plenitude of
legal capacity and also almost full powers to perform civil acts,
excluding her from but a few, such as the giving of public testimony, and in other cases, as a guarantee, restricting her by the
ancient Germanic principle of marital authorization.[2] The subsequent codes followed a different course: the Austrian, in Lombardy,
gave woman a maximum of liberty; others, like the Albertine
and that of the Two Sicilies, for example, retained many of the
rights acquired through the French Code, but also the restriction
by marital or judicial authorization; others finally, and notably the
Papal Regulation, restored the ancient rule of woman's general
incapacity, the necessity of a guardianship, and the distinction
between male and female rights of inheritance. But all these
inequalities have almost wholly disappeared from the present law,
which places woman, with respect to civil rights, almost on a complete parity with man.

[1] *Ante* § 91.   [2] *Post* § 350.

§ 306. **Infirmities.** — Defects arising from infirmities may be physical or mental, and the importance of the one or the other with regard to legal capacity varies with the stage of civilization of a people. Among the Germanic peoples physical strength was held in high esteem, because indispensable to membership in the army, which was the basis of every political and civil right. Consequently physical defects which prevented the bearing of arms were a cause of legal incapacity, total or partial according to their gravity. Considerations of physical weakness gave rise to the large class of " aldii ", intermediate between free and slave.[1] Whoever was not a soldier was not a citizen and, therefore, remained in perpetual dependence within the family. Even temporary infirmity suspended capacity at least for those acts — in the early period the most important — which must be performed before the people in arms, that is, the assembly, *e.g.* a testamentary disposition, which, therefore, could not be made while sick. Some infirmities, such as leprosy and lunacy, caused their victims to be excluded from society. Persons so afflicted were regarded as dead, placed outside the law, driven from home and city, deprived of their rights, and only through pity were they provided with the necessaries of life. And in all this religious superstitions had a hand. Such were the provisions of the Lombard laws,[2] repeated by the Franks and those that followed, though with some alleviations, inspired principally by the Church. During the feudal period the doctrine that a man must be sound to possess rights received re-enforcement from the fact that fiefs might be granted only to those capable of providing the military service inseparable from them. The principle really began to weaken at the time of the mediaeval communes. Not that it was not still applied, for even in the free cities lepers were put away from contact with others. But in so doing the motive was henceforth the care of public health. Special refuges were built for these unfortunates and their plight was not made worse by despoiling them of every right. But in addition the communal legislation was strongly influenced by the Roman law, which sprang from a different conception from that of the Germanic law, in that it held that, for disease to be the cause of legal incapacity, it must result in mental defects. The violently insane and others mentally affected were deprived of the capacity to perform juridical acts. Those having only physical infirmities were shut out merely from those acts for which their physical condition unfitted them : *e.g.* the deaf-mute

[1] *Ante* § 40.   [2] *Rothar*, 176, 180.

and the blind might not testify. And these rules, which alone conform to reason, prevailed henceforth and are those which govern Italian law today.

TOPIC 2. MORAL CAUSES

§ 307. **Personal and Social.** — Besides physical factors, moral qualities might modify a person's legal capacity. Of these some depended upon the individual's habits and were personal; others referred to his relations to the society in which he lived and were social. The former all centered in the person's honor and were the causes of its existence, impairment or destruction; the latter were all comprehended in the distinctions between social classes.

§ 308. **Honor.** — The honor which influenced legal capacity was of a sort given consideration by the law, and was not confused with honor arising out of the appreciation of public opinion, which belonged rather to the sphere of pure morals. It was, as the Romans expressed it, a condition of undamaged personal dignity, which was a juridical fact, because from the law it received rules governing its recognition and its consequences. This did not deprive the basis of such legal provisions of a moral quality, for its moral quality consisted in the fact that the matter dealt with by the provisions was either in harmony or at odds with the moral sentiment of society. Since this sentiment varied, so did the appreciation of the fact in question, and consequently so also the basis and nature of the legal provisions. For the Romans honor was realized by full citizenship; for the Germanic peoples by social recognition of individual valor. The law made this fact its own and from it determined the consequences for the honor of the person. Thus to possess or lose honor there must be either innocence or guilt with reference to the legal command and not merely with reference to moral dictates.

There was a correspondence between honor and legal capacity. One who possessed the former also enjoyed the latter in a full sense; and when honor was impaired or lost, so also was capacity lost in part or in whole. If wholly, there was civil death;[1] if in part, legal capacity was modified.

Under Germanic law, we find in a position of diminished capacity, because of impaired honor, persons who, having been condemned to a penalty destructive of honor, were afterwards pardoned. Under Charlemagne's laws such persons did not re-

---

[1] *Ante* § 299.

acquire the rights which their sentence had removed; they might not again be judges or witnesses, though they might, by pardon, acquire other subsequent rights, such as property and family.[1] A similar consequence befell those who had forfeited public confidence through some legally ascertained act, such as perjury before the court, condemnation for falsification, and the like. Furthermore, if they preserved a part of their private rights, they lost their political rights and also such of their civil rights as involved acts having a public interest, *e.g.* acting as guardian, judge or witness, etc.[2] Traces of this were seen in the statutes of the mediaeval communes: in Venice it was true of one who falsified merchandise. But during the communes, any loss whatever of honor, as conceived by Germanic law, came to be confused with the infamy (" infamia ") of the Roman law,[3] whose principles were spread by the new study. Each communicated its character to the other; differences disappeared and out of them emerged a new institution. The Roman term " infamia " was retained, but the causes and consequences were modified in the process of exchange. As to causes, imitation of the Roman law added to those belonging to the Germanic law, by making infamy arise from a greater number of wrongs than under the latter (*e.g.* breach of contract, by analogy to the ancient " actiones infamantes "[4]), and from other new motives. In the same way the causes already known to the Roman law received additions from those due to Germanic conceptions, which held many more professions derogatory to honor than did the Roman, and which held honor to be compromised by an assignment for the benefit of creditors, by illegitimate birth, by poverty, by insolvency, and by other similar reasons. So also with regard to consequences. To the loss of political rights — " jus suffragii et honorum " — which was the consequence of Roman " infamia ", was added the loss of rights of personal status, as for example, of nobility and of the fief; the limitation upon personal activities, such as exclusion from the legal profession and other pursuits of the nobles; and finally even the suspension of civil rights, such as that of disposing by will, of inheriting, and others.

All this gradually changed in the course of time, because public sentiment altered and fell out of harmony with the provisions of

[1] "Capitulare italicum", 45, 46, ed. *Padelletti*.
[2] *Charlemagne*, "Capitulare Italicum", 138; *Pepin*, 41.
[3] *Ante* § 251.
[4] [Gaius IV, 182. Condemnations in theft, rapine, outrage, partnership, trust, guardianship, agency, deposit, carried infamy.]

the law.   The law then also had to modify its course.   Illegitimate birth was no longer a cause of dishonor, when in the public conscience the feeling prevailed that a penalty should not be visited upon one who had had no part in the fault; no profession was held dishonoring when it was felt that labor, whatever it might be, ennobled and rendered the person useful to society; diversity of religion was no longer a motive for the divergent estimation of the persons, when customs adapted themselves to the principle of tolerance.

So one after another fell away all those motives, inherited from the Middle Ages, whereby the individual was declared undeserving of civil regard.   Honor, properly speaking, has been abandoned by the law and has withdrawn into its appropriate sphere of morals.   The magistrate may give it weight, but only for the better appraisal of those facts with regard to which a certain amplitude of discretion has been granted him.   Like civil death, infamy has disappeared from Italian law.   The " interdiction " of modern law is different.   It arises from a grave penal sentence and produces the loss of only a few rights, considered separately, namely political rights, powers over others, the right of administering the family property, and such others as are neither possible nor compatible in one who has been legally segregated from society.[1]

§ 309. Social Inequality. — The principle of social equality belongs to modern times.   Indeed early societies founded their whole order upon the contrary principle of the inequality before the law of various sorts and conditions of persons, a principle that had penetrated as far as the later Roman law, but which developed chiefly under Germanic institutions and reached its most rigorous application under feudalism.   This inequality showed itself of practical moment not only in public but also in private law, where it produced greater or less capacity for rights, that is, the recognition in each individual of a greater or less extension of legal capacity.   Thus also differences in *social condition*, that is, membership in one rather than in another class of citizens, were reasons for variations of legal capacity.   This principle during the Germanic period found material expression in the " guidrigild ", or valuation of the " caput ", which varied according to social status.[2] Under feudalism the possession of the fief was the criterion for

---

[1] [Civil interdiction results from the condition of a weak-minded person who has attained majority but requires a guardian ("tutor"): Civil Code, arts. 224 *et seq.*; penal interdiction, as a punishment, results from condemnation for certain criminal offenses; Penal Code, arts. 11 and 20.]
[2] *Ante* §§ 38, 39, 40, 50.

evaluating the juridical importance of the person. Many more rights belonged to the holders of fiefs than to those who were not, and, as between feudatories, rights increased as one approached the summit of the feudal hierarchy.[1] Even within the mediaeval communes the citizens were ranged in different classes according to origin and profession, resulting in a variance of legal capacity.[2] And the whole people was divided into estates, for the most part the clergy, the military and the " bourgeoisie " under the governments that followed, up to the time of the French Revolution,[3] during all of which period it was constantly maintained that equality of legal capacity should not exist between the three classes. Those who were at the top of the social scale were alone the " cives optimo jure ", to whom the law not only applied in its entirety, but whom it also invested with privileges. Step by step as the scale was descended, there occurred a corresponding diminution of status in all that affected the exercise of civil rights, until the class dispossessed of both lands and implements was reached, whose condition, except in name, was not that of freemen.

This principle once fixed, its application was apparent in almost every act of civil life : in computing the age of majority, in matrimony, in the " fideicommissa " or entails, in marriage portions, and in many other matters to be dealt with in greater detail later, the extent of the person's rights varied according to the position occupied in society.

[1] *Ante* §§ 38, 39, 40.   [2] *Ante* § 91, 92.   [3] *Ibid.*

TITLE III

JURISTIC PERSONS [1]

§ 310. Early Conception. | § 311. Subsequent History.

§ 310. **Early Conception.** — When the artificial element of juridical capacity was united to an abstract entity, this became a person.   It was not such a person as had as the basis of its being the real existence of the individual; its foundation was the will of the law, by which it was created, and it was, therefore, called a "juristic person."   As such it could have all those rights which did not of necessity presuppose human personality, such for example as rights of family.   Strictly it could have only property rights.

In the early Germanic period entities of this sort were well known.   The family, prior to the formation of the State, was indeed a juristic person,[2] possessing rights of its own independent of those who represented it.[3]   The larger communities which succeeded the decomposition of the family, i.e. the villages, were also subjects of rights,[4] as is amply proved by the fact of collective ownership, which had very enduring and important consequences. When, with the concentration of minor social units into one, the State emerged, it was a juristic person.   When the Germanic races entered upon Roman soil, they found there many other entities created with a personality of their own and these were retained. First in importance was the Church, considered not only as a universal institution, but also in its separate parts; corporations constituting pious foundations, such as bishoprics, abbeys, hospitals, hospices and similar institutions; then there were the associations of private individuals, not wholly unknown to the invaders, who had their own guilds or fraternities [5] and retained those that were Roman, especially the corporations of arts and crafts, which were of advantage to them.[6]

But while there were entities in essence juristic in the Germanic period, the law was as yet very far from that correct notion of them

[1] *Pertile, cit.,* § 106; *Salvioli, cit.,* Part IV, chap. 10.
[2] *Ante* §§ 21, 22.   [4] *Ante* § 22.
[3] *Post* § 312.   [5] *Ante* §§ 38, 39.
                   [6] *Ibid.*

that belongs to Roman and modern law. The idea of the entity was not abstractly conceived; it was confused with the persons who represented its interests and exercised its rights, and of these it was identified particularly with the person who was its head, either in administration, or as representative, or for any other reason that placed him above all other members composing the entity itself. The State was the most obvious example of this. The State was the king, without distinction; hence everything affecting the king was a matter of State, and all that belonged to the State was the king's. And in fact the Germanic king appropriated as his all the income of the public treasury and provided for matters of government out of his own estate; of the public estate he disposed freely; public offices he dispensed as his favors and those who attended his private needs were considered public officials. By this mode of thought there arose the conception of the patrimonial State of the Middle Ages and of the absolute State of later times, until, under the newer theories of modern times, the State came to be regarded as distinct from the person of the prince. In the contrary case, where the legal entity manifested itself in the exercise of certain rights simultaneously by all its members, it became confused with them. The mediaeval commune, for instance, was conceived of only in terms of its citizens, who together enjoyed its pastures, woods and other property and rights.

From this confusion between entity and representatives, there necessarily followed a failure to distinguish their personalities, which resulted in a mode of regulating the relations between the juristic person and its component members and third persons wholly characteristic of the Middle Ages. In fact, the active and passive obligations of the entity extended to all its members individually, and it was for this reason that in the early histories of the communes all the citizens, in mass or through deputies, may be seen binding themselves for their city; summonses were issued against all the citizens for communal debts; all gave their consent to contracts entered into by the commune; penalties were imposed upon all for crimes imputable to the commune; those acts might not be done by the commune which the individual himself might not do as, for example, testifying in court in causes in which the commune was concerned.

§ 311. **Subsequent History.** — So imperfect a conception, with its erroneous consequences, was in time gradually corrected. Ecclesiastical law, which for its own institutions was the conservator of Roman principles, also deserved the credit for this. Even though Germanic law was unable to conceive of juristic personality apart from the physical members, ecclesiastical institutions were not seen through such material eyes. The Church did not come to regard them abstractly as persons, but neither did it confuse them with the visible individuals. It held a middle course, that of considering them personified in the patron saint. The titular saint of a church, the protector of a religious order, in a word, the supernatural entity was the subject of the rights. To him were made the donations, with him contracts were made, and, necessity arising, he had recourse to the courts. Human beings were merely those through whom he manifested himself. The "Patrimony of St. Peter", for example, was all that belonged to the Church of Rome and St. Peter was the incarnation of all its rights; in his name, therefore, gifts were accepted, compromises effected, letters written, treaties stipulated, in short every act of whatsoever nature relating to this patrimony was thus performed.

If this method failed to attain to a complete abstraction of the juristic person, at least it rendered it independent of its physical constituents and this aided in finally reaching the perfected conception. This was gained through the revived study of Roman law. As early as the 1200 s there were instances in which the entity had come to be considered quite independently of the persons composing it. It required only the strengthening of this principle for the consequences of the contrary theory to be discarded, and for minds to turn at once to distinguishing the rights, interests and responsibilities of the entity and its representatives. And as conceptions cleared, since the number of juristic persons was increasing with the constantly growing tendency to associate for common benefits, a tendency which developed from the time of the communes, and especially with the gradual multiplication of interests as civilization progressed, writers and legislators found a vast material to occupy them in this field. They revived all the principles of the Roman law, among them the necessity of recognition by the State to give constitution and life to the juristic person. These principles once regained, were not again lost and have been again confirmed in the contemporary law of Italy.[1]

[1] [Civil Code, art. 2.]

PART II
THE FAMILY

PART II

THE FAMILY[1]

INTRODUCTION

§ 312. General Character of the Germanic Family. — When history throws its first light upon the Germanic family, we see it in a state of transformation, of transition from its primitive natural state to that of a social institution. It still preserved the mark of its first form, when maternity was its basis. But the principle of agnation had also already emerged with the domination of the paternal authority over all natural ties. The legal and social unit was still the family and not the individual, its successor. At the same time, with the multiplication of descendants the family had become part of a vaster society, of a relationship derived from a common ancestor, considered the founder of the stock, of the "gens", as the Romans would have said, of the "sippe", according to the Germanic tongues; for this society had as its principal purpose the maintenance of "peace" by reciprocal defense of all its members.

These included all who were born in the family or attached to it, and who were not beyond that limit where kinship ceased to be recognized. But it was not merely the aggregate of its members which formed the family, but also and rather the sum of its interests, including not only the interests of those actually in the family, but also those who had been and those who some day would become members. For the interests of all, and in a special manner for those of each of its parts, the family provided.

To its *past* members it owed a *cult*, and in this the family appeared as a *religious association*. Death did not break all family

---

[1] [Part II, §§ 312–371 is a translation of *Calisse*, part II, §§ 27–86.]
Pertile, cit., part II, chap. 2; *Salvioli, cit.*, part IV, sec. 2; *Schupfer*, "La famiglia presso i longobardi", in "Archivio giuridico", I (1868); *Salvioli*, "La responsabilità della famiglia e dell' erede nel delitto del defunto", in "Revista italiana delle scienze giuridiche", II (1886); *Brunner*, "Deutsche Rechtsgeschichte", §§ 12, 13, 28; *Schulte*, "Lehrbuch der deutschen Rechtsgeschichte" (Leipsic, 1887–89), bk. III, chap. 4.

ties; between the dead and the surviving there was a continuing communion. As the living must respond for, or might glory in, the good or evil acts of their ancestors, so these shared the merits and demerits of the conduct of the living. Such a participation imposed upon the family a cult of the dead,[1] and that this might not fail, artificial families, especially adoptive, were also formed as a substitute for the natural. In the family thus considered, the father was the priest, also among the Germanic peoples. In matters of major family interest he took the auspices. Having first pronounced an invocation, with eyes raised to heaven, he threw three times into the air small twigs, upon which characters had first been marked, and from the manner in which these symbols fell he formed his judgment.[2]

To its *present* members the family owed *defense*. In this aspect it was a *political association*, a league for peace, an association of mutual help, thus substituting for the State, which was as yet but imperfectly developed. Defense presupposed force and the family was therefore also a union of armed men. In battle the combatants were not aligned by chance but by families.[3] Private vengeance for an offense offered to a single member became a rigorous duty for all; so vengeance sought by one family for an act committed by a member of another must fall upon all of the latter.[4] Composition, as a substitute for the blood feud,[5] was similarly either a family right or obligation, with the exception, however, of the women and others, incapable of vindicating themselves by arms. Defense at law fell equally upon all for the act of a single member. Thus the guardianship of women and minors belonged to the family,[6] as also the right of punishing those members who by their acts had sullied the family honor.[7] For the defense of the individual was the defense of the family, since, by the solidarity of its members, all individual interests became collective and, for good or evil, involved family consequences that might be grave.

Finally, for its *future* members, the family owed the *conservation of the family estate*, and in this purpose it was an *economic association*. Property belonged collectively to the family and not to its constituent individuals,[8] and in its preservation lay the safety of the family itself. Hence the prohibition against alienation, especially by gift, even of a part. Rather than as owners, the living appeared as life-tenants of the domestic estate, under a duty to

[1] *Cf.* the "sacra" of the Romans.
[2] *Tacitus*, "Germania", 10.
[3] *Id.*, 7.
[4] *Id.*, 21.
[5] *Ante* §§ 46 *et seq.*, 155 *et seq.*
[6] *Post* § 364.
[7] *Rothar*, 189, 193, 221.
[8] *Post* § 408.

hand it down intact to those who would come after them to represent the family.

§ 313. **Historical Development of Family Law.** — The arrival of the Germanic invaders in Italy did not alter the characteristics of their family, except in so far as its place gave way to State action in proportion as the latter became more defined and powerful.[1] This process found a perfect reflection in the laws, in that these, while embodying the changes demanded by social and civil progress, accepted and so sanctioned, either in themselves or their consequences, most of the principles already existing in Germanic customs.   Thus the blood feud was repressed, but the composition, which developed from it, remained a family right; the State drew to itself the right of punishment but retained it in the nearest relatives with respect to matters affecting domestic peace and honor; judicial procedure was reformed, but it was left to the relatives to support by their own oath any among them who required it; the position of woman was improved, but she was not freed from the guardianship of her relatives or placed upon a footing with man; the family estate was freed from its chains, but the notion of community of family interests remained firm and continued to produce important effects.

In these traces of its ancient physiognomy, the family was still seen, not greatly altered, in the statutes of the mediaeval communes. Males continued to receive preferential rights of inheritance; the responsibility of relatives continued; the consent of all was still demanded in matters affecting the patrimony; a right of preëmption and redemption was given to members of the family over its property when about to be alienated. Finally, in public life also the effects of the ancient family organization were still felt, in that the factional grouping of citizens was supported and extended by the idea of the solidarity of kinsmen and by the obligation, which each still felt within himself, to avenge an offense to a relative.

Such principles, however, came to be radically changed when the revived study of the Roman law made its effect powerfully felt. For this the way had already been prepared, ever since the Germanic period, by the work of the Church, which imparted milder and more moral qualities to the Germanic customs. Much was accomplished, too, by the rise, through industry and trade, of a form of wealth free from those family chains which bound property acquired by inheritance; and social progress contributed

[1] *Ante* §§ 21, 22.

by investing the State with rights over the family, from whom the individual was thereby unshackled and freed in his social relations.

But stronger than all else was the return to the principles of Roman law, whose application to the new conditions made an end to the complicated organization of the Germanic family. This took place especially by substituting for the interests and authority of the collective entity, the simple individual, who himself became the subject of rights and duties, responsible for his own acts, and filling a legally recognized position in the face of society, which, by means of the State, penetrated the family, assumed many family functions, especially that of guardianship, withdrew from it many others as unsuited to its nature, and, from the political institution that it had been, reduced it to a social and ethical organism.

To reach this stage a long evolution was naturally necessary, during which all traces of the ancient condition were not obliterated; indeed, those relating to property and sex preference endured most tenaciously. Today these differences have disappeared. Now that all those institutions which assured the triumph of agnation have been abolished as having no legal importance, the family has been relieved of its artificial structure, the law has been made to accord with nature, and even within the ranks of the family the rule has been extended that all are equal before the law.

TITLE I

FORMATION OF THE FAMILY

CHAPTER III

MARRIAGE [1]

§ 314. **General Character.** — Marriage aimed at the attainment of the ends for which the family was formed, through the procreation of descendants, who assured both the ceremonial due to ancestors and the continuation of the family name. Like that of the family, the Germanic conception of marriage was dignified and vigorous.[2] At the same time, the control of marriage, in place of being independent of the head of the house, was considered his right, because he had to direct t toward the advantage of the house, of which he was the representative. A marriage, therefore, which was not in the interest of the family, such, for example, as a sterile marriage, could be dissolved by the husband.

The coming of the Germanic tribes to Italy and their conversion to Catholicism caused new ideas to prevail over the old. This change was especially due to the Church, which seriously engaged

---

[1] *Pertile, cit.*, §§ 108–109; *Salvioli, cit.*, chaps. 12, 13; *Schupfer*, "Il diritto privato dei popoli germanici, con speciale riguardo all' Italia"; *Tamassia*, "Osculum interveniens", in "Rivista di storia italiana" (1885); *Scaduto*, "Il consenso nelle nozze, nelle professione, etc." (Naples, 1885); *Calisse*, "Diritto ecclesiastico e diritto longobardo ", chap. 5 (Rome, 1888).

[2] *Tacitus*, "Germania", 18.

in making its views upon matrimony penetrate the Germanic customs and laws. The effects were seen from the time of the Lombards, whose laws accepted many of the church principles concerning matrimony, purified its concept and raised it, as an institution having an independent existence, above all considerations of person. Still more was accomplished during the period of the Carlovingians, who adopted in their capitularies the precepts of the canons without alteration, so that thereafter the Church took over wholly to itself the regulation of marriage, and finally, when in the 1000 s it obtained exclusive jurisdiction over all matrimonial cases, excluded every rival from the field.

§ 315. **Civil and Religious Marriage.** — The ecclesiastical law, which governed marriage, had incorporated, in so far as compatible with Christianity, many principles of the Roman law and had preserved, with respect to the visible acts, those rites and forms of Germanic law whose abolition would have resulted in irritation and suspicion and so harmed rather than furthered the cause which the Church had proposed. From this law, derived from many sources, arose a perfect product; it was free from local controversies and diversities; it was in all respects certain in substance and form; it was made common and universal for all Christendom by the Council of Trent. Thus the way was made fitting for the Reformation to dispose many European countries again to regard marriage as a simple civil act, to withdraw it from control of the Church and entrust it to the State. In Italy, as in other countries that remained Catholic, this tendency developed rather slowly and was always combated by the Church. The State, however, had come to a consciousness of its rights and never again ceased to demand them. The method sought, in order to conciliate the two opposing tendencies, was that of granting due consideration to each of the two elements of marriage, the civil and the religious, and of assigning their control to the appropriate authority, one to the State and the other to the Church, without antagonism and, in fact, by appropriate provisions bringing the two powers into alliance in a common cause. This principle was obeyed in most of the reforms and legislation of the 1700 s.

The Napoleonic Code was the first example of the treatment of marriage as a purely civil act. It did not deny the religious element, but left this, as something quite foreign to civil authority, exclusively to the control of the Church. This is the theory of the present Italian law,[1] although in the interval since the French

---

[1] [Civil Code, art. 93.]

Code, that is in the legislation of the restored governments, canonical rules came to be accepted in varying degrees by the civil powers, always accompanied, however, by provisions which preserved alive and unimpaired the right of the State.

Topic 1. Conditions of Validity

§ 316. **Impediments.** — The conditions necessary for the lawful celebration of marriage were those, the absence of which constituted an impediment. Among the Germanic peoples, as among all people of primitive culture, the theory of impediments was very simple. It had, however, a large development in the canon law, as a continuation and elaboration of its history in the Roman law. Modern civil law, a derivation of medieval law, without returning to the simplicity of antiquity, which would have been impossible, has nevertheless to a notable extent smoothed out the complexity of past legal systems.

In general, impediments were classified as absolute and relative. *Absolute* impediments were those which, so long as present, rendered it impossible to contract marriage with anyone; *relative* were those which raised an obstacle to marriage only between certain persons. Among absolute impediments, besides impotence, were immaturity of age, want of consent by those who had a right to give it, the existence of another matrimonial tie, and religious vows. The relative impediments were reducible to three main categories: those derived from relationship, inequality of station, and crime.

§ 317. **Age.**[1] — The ancient Germans, as Caesar and Tacitus record,[2] customarily prohibited precocious marriages. It was considered shameful for a woman to marry before attaining twenty years; to remain as long as possible in a stage of immaturity was a matter of pride; a suitable proportion in the ages, as in stature and physical vigor, of husband and wife were sought. As such customs were not retained after the invasions, it became necessary that the law should deal with what originally had been left to custom. The first Lombard laws fixed the commencement of legal age in general at twelve years.[3] Subsequently, though changed for many acts, this age was retained for the marriage of females. Any earlier marriage was declared null and the man who contracted

---

[1] *Ante* § 304.
[2] "De bello gallico", VI, 21; "Germania", 20.
[3] *Rothar*, 155.

it was punished as for abduction. In the case of males the age was made thirteen, and no validity was given to a marriage prematurely contracted.[1] The Carlovingian legislation, deploring the serious harm to families, commanded that marriage should not be permited prior to puberty, or, at least, according to the commentators, before eighteen years in the case of males and fourteen in the case of females.[2] Canon law was content with the completion of fourteen and twelve years respectively, and the same limits were retained by many of the subsequent laws. Of this a trace may still be seen in the present Italian Code, according to which twelve years for the woman and fourteen for the man are the earliest ages at which matrimony, by dispensation, is permissible.[3]

§ 318. **Consent.** — Consent freely given was the basis of marriage and, therefore, not only its absence but anything that substantially vitiated it, such as error, fear, or violence, constituted an impediment. Consent was always required, but not always of the same parties. Among the Germanic invaders, the woman was not called upon to give her consent;[4] that of her father, brother or other person exercising the guardianship over her sufficed. This harsh principle was later mitigated. Lombard laws preserved it only in the case of father and brother, punishing any other " mundoald " or guardian who permitted a woman's marriage against her will.[5] The less ancient laws felt called upon to justify this right, even in the case of father and brother, by the presumption that they could never intend anything save the good of their daughter or sister.[6] This idea did not conform with ancient conceptions and opened the way for the law to limit or deprive the father or brother of the right, whenever the presumption was destroyed by contrary proof.

Indeed, a marriage without paternal or fraternal consent, while a cause of punishment for the contracting parties, was certainly not a nullity, since if subsequent consent was obtained, the union, without more, appeared purged of defect.[7]

The Church, always obsequious before the paternal authority, did not at first oppose so great a right over the woman, or even over sons, whom, during minority, their parents might legally promise in marriage, just as they might prepare them for the priesthood. But paternal consent was of itself soon considered insuf-

[1] *Liutprand*, 129.
[2] *Charlemagne*, 140.
[3] Art. 68.
[4] *Ante* § 305.
[5] *Rothar*, 195; *Liutprand*, 12, 119, 120.
[6] *Liutprand*, 12.
[7] *Rothar*, 188, 214.

ficient, so that when given during the minority of those affected, it had to be confirmed by them, just as, when paternal consent was impossible, the consent of the parties could effectively take its place.   Indeed, the maxim of the canon law was that in the free declaration of consent was found the form of the marriage sacrament.   These principles passed into the civil laws.   The Carlovingians and the subsequent emperors accepted them, submitting themselves in this particular entirely to the canons.   The communal statutes of the Middle Ages followed substantially the same course, requiring the consent of relatives, especially the parents, but not in a way to take the place of the consent of the parties themselves.   The former was regarded rather as an element of guarantee of the act to be consummated and as a consequence of the respect due the parents.   It was, therefore, required also in the case of males, where the ancient precept had a more extended application.   On the other hand, there were limitations to the principle, in that marriages were not only valid when contracted without paternal consent, though punished by methods mainly pecuniary, but also in that the necessity of consent ended when the son had reached an age proper for his independence.   These maxims were confirmed and strengthened by the canons of the Council of Trent, which declared that the free consent of the parties was alone necessary to contract marriage; and the same principle has guided subsequent legislation including the existing Italian Code.[1]

§ 319. **Existing Marriage.** — Among the ancient Germanic people, marriage was by custom monogamous, but polygamy was not forbidden and examples of it existed.   The powerful and the rich, especially, practised polygamy and among this class it endured longest.[2]   This, of course, was a right belonging only to the men; for woman, an existing marriage was always an absolute impediment against a second; and by the Lombard laws, not only the woman but also the man who took her, was punished by death.[3]   Conditions changed for the husband as well.   As early as the Lombard Edict, the law had come to be that if a married man took a second wife, the latter lost her estate and the husband had, as was proper, to rejoin his lawful wife; he might not even bring a concubine into the house, for in such case he was fined 500 "solidi" and lost his legal authority over his wife, who was permitted to

[1] Art. 65.
[2] *Caesar*, "De bello gallico", I, 53; *Tacitus*, "Germania", 18.
[3] *Rothar*, 211.

return to her relatives.[1]   Here, again, the Church was active, as
is more clearly seen in the Carlovingian laws.   A capitulary of
Lothar declared that it was unlawful for any one to have two wives
at once, because, as Christ guards the chastity of his Church, so
should the chastity of marriage be preserved.[2]   Thus all traces
of polygamy were eradicated from the early popular customs and
it never reappeared in subsequent legislation.

The period of mourning was considered a continuation of the
marital bond, during which the woman was not permitted to remarry.   From this aspect it was, therefore, one of the matrimonial
impediments.   The period of mourning varied.   Among the
Lombards it was a year, by analogy to the law requiring a year
to pass before a widow might take the veil, unless by leave of the
king.[3]   In fact, Germanic laws, always considered the entry into
monastic life as a marriage.[4]   The reasons why the law prohibited
vows during the first year of widowhood applied equally to marriage; her guardian ("mundoald") profiting by her dejection
due to her recent loss, might induce her to a course which she would
not otherwise have adopted.   This Lombard statute was a faithful
imitation of Justinian's law which forbade a second marriage during
the first year of widowhood, while granting the privilege of peti-
tioning a dispensation from the sovereign.[5]   Other Germanic laws
fixed a year as the period of mourning; and finally the commentators of the Lombard law extended it to marriage, declaring it
applicable when "velare se vel virum suscipere mulier vult."[6]

The Carlovingians had a different rule.   A widow might not
remarry or enter a monastery until a month after her husband's
death, under penalty of the nullity of both these acts and the severe
punishment of her second husband.[7]   So brief a period could not
fulfill its chief aim of removing doubt as to paternity.   Probably
it was intended that the month should serve to provide proof
whether the woman was or was not pregnant and, therefore,
whether the child was the fruit of the first or second union.   Certainly this was the purpose of the later laws, establishing a short
interlude before the second marriage, such as the Pisan "constitu-
tio" of 1271, fixing a six months' period of mourning provided
the widow was not pregnant.   In the present Italian law, the ten

---

[1] *Grimwald*, 6, 7.
[2] "Capitulare italicum", 96, ed. *Padelletti*.
[3] *Liutprand*, 100.   [4] *Id.*, 30.   [5] Novels, XXII, 22.
[6] "Expositio ad Librum papiensum", *Liutprand*, 100, ed. *Boretius*,
M. G. H., "Leges" IV, and *Padelletti*, "Fontes."
[7] *Charlemagne*, 123; *Louis the Pious*, 9.

months' impediment to remarriage, due to mourning, may be shortened by the intervening birth of a child.[1]

§ 320. **Religious Vows.** — This impediment naturally had its origin in ecclesiastical law, from which it was adopted by the civil laws, when the Church's influence had become effective. The Lombard Edict contained very harsh provisions against the nun who escaped in order to marry, and against her accomplices, and in addition held such a marriage void.[2] The later laws were even more subservient to the canons. Although the violation of vows of chastity by monks and nuns had always been punished by the canons, nevertheless, when it came to the validity of their marriage, church law, while reluctant to grant recognition, was for a long time ill-defined. Finally the question was closed by the rigorous prohibition of the Councils of the 1000 s and 1100 s and Gratian's compilation of canons, which in this respect were subsequently followed by the State.

Lastly there was the impediment of religious ordination, concerning which doubt reigned for a long period, even in the Latin Church, which was stricter than the Greek. In general the rules of the Nicean Council were followed, that celibates who had entered the priesthood might not thereafter marry and that those already married were consequently considered widowed. But the marriage of priests was in fact a general practice during the Lombard and Frankish period, and it is known that, during the struggles between Church and Empire a great part of the Italian clergy asserted the right to marry. The stricter doctrine, however, prevailed, and dominated all legislative periods until such problems came to be differently regarded, with quite opposite consequences. So that today neither religious vow nor ordination is any longer an impediment to marriage.

§ 321. **Relationship.** — As relationship might arise from natural ties or be based upon other facts, it was distinguishable as natural and acquired.

Of *natural* relationship the early Germanic peoples made no impediment except as between the nearest kin; but before long the Roman and canon law forced a wider operation of this impediment. The Church especially insisted upon the rule that marriage should not take place between persons having a memory of their common ancestor.[3] But the conversion of the Germanic nations

---

[1] Civil Code, art. 57.   [2] *Liutprand*, 30.
[3] "Corpus Juris Canonici" *Gratian*, "Decretum", part 2, *Causa* XXXV, *quaest.* 2, *cap.* 18.

to this view met with many obstacles and so progressed but slowly. At first marriage was lawful with the fourth generation, but little by little, as the people accepted the faith more formally, the limit was extended until in the 700 s Gregory II required observance of the general rules by all. It must, however, be remembered that the mode of computing the degree of collateral relationship differed in the Germanic and canon law from the Roman law. In the Roman system the degree between relatives was determined by adding the number of generations interposed between each of them and the common ancestor and this is the system used in the present Italian Code.[1] The other method considered only the number of generations between one of the two relatives in question and their common ancestor, giving preference, if the lines were of unequal length, to the more remote of the two. Thus, the seventh degree by the Germanic or canon law might correspond to the fourteenth degree of the Roman system.

Secular law followed the progressive movement of ecclesiastical law. To those whose relationship was an impediment to marriage, Rothar added the mother-in-law, daughter-in-law and the brother's widow,[2] and Liutprand added the wife's sister and the cousin's widow.[3] And since early customs held tenaciously against such legal innovations, Astolf required his magistrates to seek out all persons who were irregularly united and to force them to an immediate separation.[4] Nor were the Carlovingians less zealous. Charlemagne renewed the prohibitions of the canon law; Pepin created commissions composed of " honest men " of each region, who should promptly give notice of all illegal unions; Lothar confirmed Astolf's laws, and so more especially did Henry II, in 1054, with regard to all that the laws of the Church and of his predecessors had established.[5]

During the following period the struggle between the Roman and ecclesiastical method of computing kinship grew more marked. Especially notable was the difference between the romanists of the School of Ravenna and the canonist St. Pietrus Damianus, who wrote his treatise on the subject in refutation of the former. Nevertheless, the Roman law, rejuvenated by the statutes of the mediaeval communes and universally defended by the new jurisprudence, finally triumphed upon the substantial point of establishing the Church's limitation of this impediment at the fourth

[1] Civil Code, art. 51.   [3] *Liutprand*, 32, 33.
[2] *Rothar*, 185.   [4] *Astolf*, 8.
          [5] *Pepin*, 8; *Lothar*, 99; *Henry II*, 4.

Germanic degree, corresponding to the seventh Roman degree. The Council of Trent confirmed this limit and its example was followed by many subsequent systems of legislation. Today this impediment is bound by somewhat stricter limits.[1]

Acquired kinship might be either spiritual or civil. *Spiritual* kinship resulted from baptism and confirmation and existed between the person receiving the sacrament and the person acting as godfather or godmother. It was an impediment of canonical origin, which very soon passed into the civil laws. As early as the Lombard Edict there was confirmation of all that the Council of Rome, of 721, had established in the matter. Marriage with one's godmother, goddaughter, or godfather's daughter was prohibited under penalty of immediate separation and confiscation,[2] and all subsequent laws similarly provided, until the impediment was abandoned in consequence of the Church's loss of exclusive control over marriage law. *Civil* relationship was derived either from adoption, or affinity arising out of marriage between one spouse and the relatives of the other. When resulting from *adoption*, it formed an impediment, as it still does,[3] based on Roman rules. *Affinity* was not an impediment among the early Germanic nations, but it was so considered by the Church, which, by regarding husband and wife as one person, held that each was related to the other's kin as to their own of similar degree. To these principles and their consequences Germanic law soon gave a hearing. The Lombards led the way, placing kindred by affinity among relatives;[4] later laws strengthened these principles, Henry II, in 1054, going so far as to declare affinity by betrothal an impediment to marriage.[5] This extreme was moderated by a return to the precepts of the Roman law. Affinity, by identification with blood relationship, always remained an impediment between those so connected in the direct line, as between one spouse and the relatives in direct line of the other; in the collateral line of relationship by affinity, the rule prevailed that the impediment existed between persons of the nearest degree and generally not beyond the second.

§ 322. **Inequality of Condition.** — As an impediment to marriage inequality of condition might be considered from different points of view: *social, political,* or even *religious.*

---

[1] Civil Code, arts. 58, 59. [The prohibited degrees are: all blood and marriage relations in ascending and descending lines; in collateral lines, brothers and sisters by blood or marriage, uncle and niece, aunt and nephew.]

[2] *Liutprand,* 34.   [3] Civil Code, art. 60.

[4] *Rothar,* 185; *Liutprand,* 32, 33.

[5] "Capitulare italicum", 5.

As to the first, in the Germanic period, the most important difference was that between freemen on the one hand and slaves and " aldii " on the other.[1] Between these two classes marriage was not permitted; their union, when it took place, was either punished or held invalid. But the Church opposed these principles. Marriage being a sacrament, it was bound to hold that validity should not depend upon personal qualities and its efforts were successful in changing the law accordingly. Liutprand tempered the cruelty of Rothar's laws, which pronounced the death penalty upon the slave who married a free woman. If within a year, declared the new law, her family had not executed their blood rights, she, her slave husband, and their children should all enter the service of the king's court, which thus became, instead of a place of punishment, the refuge and guarantee of their permanent union.[2] Since all rights of the fisc were barred if abandoned during sixty years, Rachi decreed that the lapse of a similar period without being subjected to court service would confer permanent liberty upon a free woman, wife of a slave, and upon their children.[3] And it frequently happened that the government's right was abandoned; in fact, Adelchi declared that under these circumstances the wife should not be removed from the house of her husband's master,[4] and finally Lothar abolished the king's right altogether.[5]

The remission from punishment thus obtained did not, however, mean any change in the other consequence of the impediment, namely, the illegality of a marriage between freemen and " aldii " or slaves.[6] But since for the Church such a marriage was regular, the law came to hold it as legal, though not productive of the juridical effects attaching to a perfect union. When slavery came to an end, this impediment (which was not a religious one), was extended to those classes derived from slavery, to the peasants and dependents of all kinds, who continued to be considered socially inferior to the nobles, with whom for that reason they were not always given the civil right of marriage. The nobility disdained to marry persons considered of low birth, and this accorded not only with custom but also with law, which was interested in opposing a degeneration of the noble families through marriages. And this continued to be the law as late as the last years of the 1700 s, not in one region alone, but more or less throughout Italy. The abolition of feudalism and class privileges and the

[1] *Ante* §§ 290, 296.
[2] *Liutprand*, 24.
[3] *Rachi*, 6.

[4] *Adelchi*, 1.
[5] *Lothar*, 75.
[6] *Post* § 330.

proclamation of the equality of all before the law were the causes which led to the disappearance of the impediment based upon diversity of social position.

From *political* inequality might also arise an impediment. During the Germanic period there was no prohibition against marriage between conquerors and conquered; indeed there was an interest in the fusion of the two peoples through marriage. This bar, however, acquired a certain importance during the period of the statutes of the mediaeval cities and of more recent legislation. The communes discouraged the marriage of their women with foreigners or outlaws, in order that no part of their wealth should leave their territories through marriage portions, and that those who had been driven out should acquire no power or relation of importance within their midst. The Sicilian " constitutions " for like reasons, that is, to prevent the acquisition of fiefs within the kingdom by foreigners or enemies, prohibited their marriage with the daughters of nobles without royal consent. This, however, was required only for the marriage of members of the reigning family, and in this form only can a trace of it be found today.

Finally, inequality might arise from a *religious* cause, and this, too, as a consequence of the ecclesiastical laws, produced an obstacle to marriage. From antiquity the marriage of Christian and Jew was prohibited,[1] and this bar was rigorously preserved for a long time, in the statutes of the mediaeval cities and later. All those who were separated from the Church [2] were treated as Jews, though the Church might grant dispensation from the impediment. Today this, as in general all obstacles based upon difference of condition, has disappeared from Italian law.

§ 323. **Crime.** — As an impediment this was unknown to the early Germanic peoples. Indeed the *abduction* or capture of a woman, at least in its legal consequences and in the symbols accompanying certain unions, was preserved as an early form of valid marriage, though the abductor was punished for his violation of the right of the woman's relatives to join in the marriage by their consent and by yielding up their authority over her. *Adultery* was another instance. It was severely punished by ancient customs,[3] and later laws also recognized the husband's right to kill his wife if caught " in flagrante ", and in every case to divorce her; but nothing was said concerning the prohibition of marriage

---

[1] *Cf. Justinian*, Code I, 9, 1, § 6.
[2] *Ante* § 300.
[3] *Tacitus*, "Germania", 19.

between the adulteress and her accomplice. But in this there also came about a change, as usual, through the action of the more civilized elements. During Rothar's reign, the abductor was punished by a maximum fine of nine hundred "solidi", while the woman might leave him and place herself under the protection of a person of her choice, even of the king. If she remained with her abductor until her death, the latter, besides paying the "guidrigild" to her family, had to restore to them whatever the woman had brought with her.[1] These were severe penalties, foreshadowing the idea of impediment, since in a true marriage the woman might not leave her husband, nor was he bound, upon her death, to restore her estate. It was not yet a true impediment, since the abductor could become her lawful husband, if, by pacifying her relatives, he obtained the surrender of authority ("mundium") over her.[2] The impediment appeared in the time of the Carlovingians. It was at first limited to the case of the abduction of a woman already betrothed to another, with the added aggravation that she had consented and that her affianced refused to receive her. The impediment then became absolute and she was forbidden ever to marry. If, however, she had not been an accomplice, she might, even if repudiated by her affianced, marry another. The abductor was subjected to serious corporal and pecuniary penalties.[3] Later the impediment was extended to the abduction of a woman not yet promised in marriage. She had, in every case, to be restored to her relatives, and might marry whomever she pleased, excepting always her paramour, who remained excommunicated and only at the moment of death might out of mercy receive the eucharist.[4]

Such measures clearly show the origin of the motive to make crime an impediment to marriage, and other laws expressly stated that their provisions against abduction were borrowed from the deliberations of the Church Councils,[5] which upon this subject had accepted substantially the Roman theory. But when, especially with the Council of Trent, the principle of the sufficiency of the consent of the parties had become fixed, every abduction, occurring through seduction, ended by marriage, and the impediment remained only in the case where the woman had been taken against her will. It was again the Church that persuaded the temporal

[1] *Rothar*, 186, 187, 191.
[2] *Post* § 325.
[3] *Charlemagne*, 122; *Louis the Pious*, 14; *Lothar*, 84.
[4] *Lothar*, 105; *Louis II*, 3.
[5] *Charlemagne*, 122.

laws not to rest content with the punishment of adulterers, but to prohibit marriage between them. Present day law has limited the impediment of crime to the case of intentional homicide committed or attempted against one of the spouses: between the other spouse and the accomplice marriage is prohibited.[1]

Topic 2. Formalities of Marriage

§ 324. **Betrothal.** — The first act in the celebration of marriage under Germanic law was the betrothal, that is, the solemn promise, mutually made between the person seeking the woman's hand and the person having her under his authority, whereby the latter bound himself to give her in marriage and the former to receive her as his wife. In the history of marriage, the betrothal, which was common to all peoples in the early stages of their culture, represents a step in advance. The first form of marriage must have been by abduction or capture; as customs became somewhat softened, there must have followed a contractual grant of authority over the woman by the person exercising it to the person demanding. Such a transfer was first by purchase and sale. Later it became gratuitous and was externalized by the betrothal, the character of which must consequently reflect the steps by which marriage had formerly been performed.

These steps were indeed of prime necessity; they constituted the legal foundation of marriage with "mundium" or marital authority, and produced, in contrast to the consequences of more progressive laws, a rigorous obligation, for the fulfillment of which all parties to the contract were responsible, under penalties established by law. Furthermore, the essential element was the consent, not of the woman, but of her father or other guardian, that is, of the person possessing the authority to be transferred to the husband. Evidently, therefore, absence of such consent was an absolute impediment to the marriage until new doctrines had substituted for it the consent of the woman.[2] Lastly, in its formalities, the betrothal preserved symbols recalling the earlier bargain and sale.[3] There was the price, which, in antiquity, when real, must consist, unless otherwise stipulated,[4] in the amount of the "guidrigild" or other sum fixed by law.[5] Later it became symbolic,[6]

---

[1] Civil Code, art. 62.
[2] *Ante* § 318.
[3] *Cf.* the "coemptio" of the Roman law.
[4] *Rothar*, 190, 214.
[5] *Liutprand*, 9, 10; *cf.* "Expositio ad Librum papiensum", *Rothar*, 197.
[6] *Cf.* the "aes" in the "mancipatio", applied to the "coemptio."

and as such was valued at a small sum, or even some objects such as skins or horses or the like, and varying, by analogy with the "guidrigild", according to the bride's status. If, however, a price was in fact paid, it served another purpose, namely as a guarantee that the one asking her in marriage would keep his promise. It was, therefore, restored to him on the wedding day, either for his own use or as a provision for the woman. In this way the transfer of the "mundium" over the woman was gratuitous: in fact the "formularies" declared that the husband, on receiving her guardianship, should recompense the "mundoald" with the "launegild" or gift price.[1]

§ 325. **Form of Betrothal.** — The betrothal in antiquity took place before the assembly, just as did alienations of family property; later the presence of all the relatives sufficed. The instrument was executed ("fabula firmata"),[2] promise or actual payment was made of what was to be given to the bride as a dowery ("mefio"), as "faderfio", or as morning-gift ("morgen-gabe");[3] the father, or whoever occupied his place, gave the woman away ("mundium mittere" or "tradere"), by delivering a sword, symbolic of his authority, and a glove, symbolic of the protection due her; the bridegroom gave her the ring by which he pledged and made her his woman ("mundium facere", or "sus-cipere"); and sometimes the betrothed also kissed each other ("osculo interveniente"), thereby marking a still further con-solidation of the pact, not unlike, with regard to its economic consequences, what obtained under the Roman law.[4] When the woman had thus come to belong to her future husband, he left her in the custody of her guardian until the day fixed for the marriage. In the meantime each party gave pledges and sureties to perform their respective promise.[5]

It was precisely in the observance or violation of the promise that may be seen the legal efficacy of the betrothal. It gave rise to an obligation and therefore a right of action against the party violating it.[6] If a breach occurred through the fault of the bride-groom, the father might still hold him to payment of the promised dowery ("mefio");[7] if through the fault of another, who had

[1] *Post* § 500. *Rothar*, 185; *G. Bandini*, "Il costo del mundio maritale sulle ingenue nel diritto longobardo" (Catania, 1891).
[2] *Rothar*, 178.
[3] *Post* §§ 343, 344, 345.
[4] *Justinian*, Code, V, 3, 16.
[5] *Rothar*, 182; *Liutprand*, 30.
[6] *Cf.* "actio ex sponsu" of the Roman law.
[7] *Post* § 343. *Rothar*, 178.

dissuaded the affianced bride, he owed the groom double the "mefio", while to her father, to compensate him for the offence and to placate his enmity, he was bound to pay 40 "solidi" in addition to the price of the "mundium";[1] and lastly to the State his own "guidrigild"; the woman was punished by the loss of her inheritable share from her relatives.[2] If her guardian had consented to the breach, he had to pay the husband double the "mefio", and to the king his own "guidrigild."[3] The Franks confirmed these rules, even increasing their severity, when, to the breach of the betrothal, was added the offense of abduction,[4] and finally, under Lothar, making the breach an impediment to marriage, by an absolute prohibition against taking to wife a woman who had been plighted to another.[5]

There were, however, situations in which one of the betrothed might withdraw from the promise without penalty of any sort. For the man, this occurred when the woman had not been faithful to him, as required of her. She was then punished as an adulteress and the man resumed his freedom and might reclaim all his gifts.[6] This also happened when the woman became the victim of a very serious or permanent infirmity,[7] or when a "faida" — that is a blood feud for the vindication of some grave offense — arose between the two families.[8] On her side, the woman was freed from her contract, if the man allowed two years to elapse from the date of the betrothal without marrying her.[9]

§ 326. **Period of Betrothal.** — The period of two years for the celebration of the marriage existed also in Roman law,[10] which, however, after its earliest period, proclaimed a principle contrary to Germanic law, by recognizing the lawfulness to withdraw at any time from the promise of the betrothal.[11] The Church, on the other hand, supported the Germanic rule; even the betrothal was consecrated; new religious rites were added to the old, and excommunication was added to the ancient penalties.[12] Thus reinforced, the betrothal long retained its efficacy, so that an unjustified violation gave rise to a blood feud ("faida") between the families even as late as the period of the Italian communes, where such events often set the spark to the bloodiest of their civil strifes.

[1] *Rothar*, 190.
[2] *Liutprand*, 119.
[3] *Rothar*, 192; *Liutprand*, 119.
[4] *Ante* § 323.
[5] *Lothar*, 97.
[6] *Rothar*, 179.
[7] *Id.*, 180.
[8] *Liutprand*, 119.
[9] *Rothar*, 178.
[10] *Justinian*, Code, V, 1, 2.
[11] *Id.*, V, 1, 1.
[12] "Corpus Juris Canonici", *Gratian*, "Decretum", *Causa* XXII, *Quaest.* 2, *Cap.* 50.

The doctrine of free consent to marriage was of course damaging to the legal effectiveness of the betrothal. The further the doctrine developed, with the friendly support of the Roman law, the more did betrothal lose in importance, until, when the consent of the parties became the one essential element for the validity of marriage, the betrothal lost all legally coercive effect. It is generally admitted that about the time of the Council of Trent, the betrothal, as had previously happened in Roman law, ceased to bind the parties to marry or to pay the penalties on failure to do so, that is, it ceased to form a legal tie between the contracting parties. This fundamental principle was maintained in subsequent legislation, was incorporated in the codes, and obtains today in Italy.[1]

§ 327. **Celebration of Marriage.** — When the wedding day (" dies votorum ") [2] arrived, the father, or other person having the custody of the woman, solemnly gave her to the husband (" traditio per manum "), in the presence of all the relatives and of friends and witnesses. At the same time he restored to the husband whatever had been given as an earnest for the completion of the marriage, and the bride received the provision made for her by husband and her family,[3] and the gifts of her friends. Great festivities followed ; there was a nuptial banquet ; the bride was accompanied to her new home with ceremonies that recalled the marriage by capture of earlier periods and which were often the occasion of violent affrays ; [4] there was the reception at her husband's house, where over the door hung a sword, by passing under which she gave it to be understood that she commenced her life of marital subjection ; there was the offering of fire and salt, symbolic of the domestic life ; and lastly the entry into the wedding chamber (" conscensio thalami "), whereby the marriage was taken as consummated. In the period of the mediaeval communes, as evidenced by the laws and stories of the time, these Germanic customs were found almost intact and served as means of publicity and as a legal presumption of marriage. On the other hand, in regions where the Roman law dominated, the rules were much simpler, while between the two systems there also took place a confused interchange, giving rise to customs lacking any fixed or determined foundation.

§ 328. **Religious Celebration.** — In these external features of the ceremony the Church did not at first make any change, but

---

[1] Civil Code, arts. 53, 54.   [3] *Post* §§ 343, 344.
[2] *Liutprand*, 3, 103.   [4] *Astolf*, 15.

directed its control to the essential factors.   Nevertheless, the pagan rites were soon christianized, and among the ceremonies accompanying marriage, although neither obligatory nor essential, were added the nuptial benediction and mass for the married couple.   Further steps followed.   In the 1100 s and 1200 s the custom was introduced of giving the bride away, not by her guardian (" mundoald "), but by the priest, who in this way came to have a part in the rites essential to marriage.   The giving of the ring, productive also of important consequences,[1] was then assigned to the minister of the Church.   It even became his duty to see to it that there were no impediments to the marriage and to this end public notice by the Church came into use and was made generally obligatory by the Fourth Lateran Council in 1215.   To the priests was assigned the duty of maintaining a registry of marriages, in order always to have a sure record of them, an office the origin of which goes back to Roman times, with regard to those celebrated in churches.[2]   But these were all external matters that did not deprive the celebration of marriage of its civil character.   They were, however, preparing the way for the great change accomplished by the Council of Trent, when it prescribed that marriages must be celebrated with religious rites, under penalty of absolute nullity.   From that moment the marriage ceremony rested in whole and in its essence on the ecclesiastical rites, through the declaration of consent before the parish priest, who, by the Council's decision, was made the exclusive keeper of the registry. Every other authority remained extraneous, every other formality superfluous, and so disappeared.   From then on no change was made until, in the last years of the 1700 s, marriage came again to be regarded as a secular act, and so to be accomplished before civil magistrates, by formalities, all of them of the simplest nature and consisting in substance of a declaration of consent and a public registration of the act.   The interposition of the State was thus being resolutely affirmed to the total exclusion of the Church. The latter, however, in an effort to harmonize the two interests, religious and civil, was again called to take part by the codes that followed the French domination, and made to coöperate with the State.   Marriage again became a religious rite, but the government, except in the States of the Church, where civil and ecclesiastical authority were one, did not remain a stranger.   In Sardinia a State official periodically examined the parish registries; in Parma and Modena these were required to be deposited in the

---

[1] *Ante* § 325.   [2] *Justinian*, Novels, LXXIV, c. 4.

communal archives; in the Two Sicilies the priest was prohibited from performing the ceremony until presented with a certificate of the registrar of civil status, before whom also the act of betrothal was performed and publication made. In other regions other systems were introduced, having the same aim. These did not, however, solve the problem and today the law has reverted to the system of the French Code, based upon the absolute separation of the two authorities, and dealing with marriage, therefore, solely from the point of view of a civil contract having civil consequences.

CHAPTER IV

IMPERFECT MARRIAGES[1]

§ 329. Causes.
§ 330. Slave Marriages.
§ 331. Morganatic Marriages.

§ 332. Second Marriages.
§ 333. Concubinage.

§ 329. **Causes.** — Alongside the marriage contracted under the conditions and in the manner prescribed by law, and productive of all the legal effects proper to it, were other types of marriage, lacking full efficacy, either because of the status of the contracting parties or because of the absence of necessary formalities.[2] Defects of the former class attached to the imperfect marriages contracted between slaves, morganatic unions and second marriages; defects of the latter class produced concubinage. Such unions, however, were in their nature, true marriages, differing from the others only in that they were juridically imperfect, especially in their consequences. As it was possible to remove the cause of their inferiority, they became, without need of other sanction or any new act, in every respect equivalent to marriages perfectly contracted from the beginning.

§ 330. **Slave Marriages.** — In contrast to the Roman, the Germanic law recognized the capacity of slaves to marry and treated their union as marriage. In the Lombard law the woman married to a slave was held to be his legal wife; infidelity to this marriage was qualified and punished as adultery; no one might with impunity violate the conjugal rights of the slave, not even the master, who, for such an act, suffered the loss of his ownership, in addition to the ordinary penalties; for, according to the legislator, revealing the source of his authority, it is God's law that none shall sin with another's wife.[3] Somewhat later, under the Carlovingians, there came to be applied to marriages between slaves the biblical precept that man shall not put asunder those whom God has joined together.[4] Such marriages differed, then, from others in their civil

---

[1] *Pertile, cit.*, §§ 113, 114; *Salvioli, cit.*, part IV, chaps. 14, 15; *Calisse,* "Diritto ecclesiastico e diritto longobardo", chap. 4.
[2] *Cf.* marriages "sine manu" of the Roman law.
[3] *Liutprand*, 66, 98, 104, 139, 140.
[4] *Charlemagne*, 128.

555

effects; in a word, they lacked the husband's " mundium ", since the parties to the marriage were already, by their status, subject to another "mundium", that of their owner, who could not be forced to accept the creation of another authority injurious to his own rights. The consent of the master was, therefore, necessary to such marriages, and his power, acting as an impediment to the formation of the parental authority, extended also over the children, so that he might, by strict law, at his pleasure, separate the slave's family, had not laws intervened to prevent this in cases where he had consented to the marriage.[1] Other limitations had reference to effects upon the property relations of the marriage.

The condition of the slave was, therefore, by nature so incompatible with the perfect marriage that, for the union to be imperfect, it sufficed for but one of the parties to be slave. It has already been explained that disparity of condition was an impediment to marriage;[2] apart from the penalties which such a marriage might involve, its consequence was that it did not produce the normal legal effects. A free woman who married a slave became a slave, and if both escaped the penalty of death or separation, their union was only servile. If, on the other hand, a free man took a slave woman as wife, civil validity was not accorded the marriage, or legitimacy to their issue. And so it was with unions between the free and half free (" aldii "), and between the half free and slaves.[3] While the slow improvement in the condition of slaves succeeded in bringing about some modifications in the quality of servile marriages, the law remained substantially fixed until the slave class disappeared from society.

§ 331. **Morganatic Marriages.** — Even between free persons there might exist such inequality of social position as to inhibit a marriage productive of full legal effect. This was not true of the Germanic period, when all free men were juridically equal; it became a natural consequence of feudalism, by which even freemen, according as they did or did not possess a fief, were divided into two classes: nobles, *i.e.* feudatories, and non-nobles, *i.e.* merchants, artisans and peasants. Marriage between persons of these dissimilar classes did not, under feudal law, have the effect of rendering the spouses equal, in such wise that the one of inferior station might participate in the rights belonging to the other, such as titles, insignia, offices or feudal lands. These remained closed to the party of inferior status and to the children. To such marriages

[1] *Charlemage*, 128.   [2] *Ante* § 322.
[3] *Rothar*, 216, 217, 221, 222; *Liutprand*, 106.

was, therefore, given the name *morganatic*, derived from the " morgengabe " or morning-gift, which had become a mere allowance to
the wife,[1] since she and her children acquired no rights in the property of the husband and father, except over such part as was settled
upon her at the moment of marriage. Such marriages were said
to be " by the Salic law ", either because they first came into use in
the time of the Franks, or because from their law had come the idea
of excluding part of the family from the paternal estate. They
were called " left-handed " marriages (" dalla mano sinistra "), to
indicate their inferiority to others; and marriages of " disparage-
ment " (" di disparagio "), when the consequences just mentioned
did not result from the agreement (" pacto ") between the spouses,
but from a legislative provision (" lege "). In the latter case there
was an absolute presumption that the union had been between
persons of high and low degree, whereas in the former case such
agreements might be made between persons of equal grade, as, for
example, customarily in second marriages, in order not to impair
the rights of the children of the first.

With the end of feudalism and the assertion of the principle of
social equality, such marriages almost entirely disappeared, a sole
trace remaining in the union of the male members of a reigning
family with women of inferior station.

§ 332. **Second Marriages.** — From certain aspects second marriages might be considered as imperfect, since, especially with
regard to the woman, they were, in Germanic law and in other
legal systems derived from it, tolerated rather than authorized,
regarded always with disfavor and placed, with relation to the first
marriage, always in a position of disadvantage. Ancient Germanic
customs permitted only virgins to marry;[2] the Church saw in a
second marriage reprehensible incontinency;[3] the family regarded
it as a slight to the memory of the deceased, an injury to the family
estate, and so endeavored to prevent it.[4] From all of which arose
a popular sentiment of opposition, so that such unions were a cause
of mockery and nightly brawls, to prevent which, as permanent
causes of disorder, temporal and ecclesiastical laws strove vainly
for centuries. For the law recognized second marriages and forbade the effort to prevent them;[5] nevertheless, as they were surrounded by formalities which had the appearance of penalties, such

---

[1] *Post* § 345.
[2] *Tacitus*, "Germania", 19.
[3] "Corpus Juris Canonici", "Decretum", part 2, *Causa* XXXI, *Quaestio*
1, *Cap.* 9.
[4] *Rothar*, 182.   [5] *Id.*, 182, 183.

as celebration at night, denial of the solemn rites of the Church, absence of an attendance, receiving the ring on a gloved hand, they produced consequences economically disadvantageous. By the Lombard law, a remarried woman lost the life estate left her by her first husband, whether or not he had exacted such a condition; and her second husband, to obtain her guardianship (" mundium "), must pay to the heirs of the first, one-half of the dowry (" mefio "), which the latter had settled upon her.[1] Under the Salic law the marriage of a widow was preceded by a symbolic action in the court of the count or of the royal intendant (" missus "), denoting that only through the law might opposition to such an act be overcome.[2] The husband had to pay the so-called " reipus " (3 " solidi " and 1 " denarius ") to the woman's paternal relatives; or, if none, to her deceased husband's relatives, though they were not her heirs; and in the absence of the latter also, then to the State.   This was not as compensation for the damage which the relatives had suffered by the loss of the wife's inheritance through her new marriage; nor was it a penalty for the stain upon the honor of the family. Had it been so, the payment would have properly been made to those excluded thereby from her inheritance, that is, to her first husband's heirs, especially if she had had children by him.   Rather was it that, among the relatives who exercised no guardianship (" mundium ") over her, or in the State, the woman had to find her defenders against the guardian (" mundoald ") who might have forbid the second marriage; and this defense was compensated by the new husband, whom it principally benefited.   He had also to pay the " achasius ", amounting to one-tenth of the marriage portion (" dos ") received by the first husband, to the heirs of the latter, from whom the woman's guardianship had passed on her second marriage.   The " achasius " thus represented satisfaction for the pecuniary loss sustained by her first husband's family, who on losing the widow lost also her property; and for the moral offense suffered by the slight to the memory of the dead.   It was rightful, therefore, for the first husband's heirs to be in a state of hostility toward the widow, and to pacify them was precisely the aim of the " achasius," " Achasium dedi ", ran the formula, " ut pacem habiam parentum." [3]

These customs, brought into Italy with the Franks and confused with others of the Lombards, had a long life, being still practised

[1] *Rothar*, 182.
[2] "Cartularium longobardicum formularum", 16, ed. *Boretius*, in M. G. H., "Leges" IV and *Padelletti*, "Fontes."
[3] *Rothar*, 199; *Pertz*, in M. G. H., "Leges" II, 3.

in the 1100 s.   During the period of the mediaeval communes, the law did not abandon its dislike to second marriages but imitated the provisions of the last period of the Roman law.   The laws no longer contained dispositions as to the manner of celebrating second marriages, so that all such differences disappeared.   But they did restrict the economic effects by rules intended to protect the interest of the children of the first marriage.   Even the Church withdrew her aversion and cared only for the removal of all danger of injury to the children already born of the first union.   Subsequent legislation followed the canon law and the statutes of the mediaeval communes, which substantially reproduced the Roman principles.   Nor did the Napoleonic Code depart far from this system, as is shown by the rule that to the second spouse may not be left more than is left to the least favored child;[1] and this, repeated in later codes, is found in force in Italy today.[2]

§ 333. Concubinage. — Under Germanic customs concubinage was not what the term meant in Roman law, namely, a union without binding tie or matrimonial intent.   The word, borrowed from Roman sources, signified any union, even matrimonial, which lacked the usual legal consequences, because contracted without the required formalities, and chiefly without payment of the price of the " mundium ", which therefore did not pass to the husband but remained in the guardian belonging to the woman's family. The origin of this kind of marriage is probably related to the ancient marriage by capture, which of course lacked the consent of the person having authority over the woman, and so resulted in an offense to her family and the non-transference of the " mundium " over her.   If the offense was settled by a composition and the guardianship was subsequently acquired by purchase or otherwise, the marriage became legal.   It has already been explained [3] that abduction and absence of the " mundoald's " consent were punishable facts, but not impediments to marriage.   It was a marriage having the status of concubinage, as just defined.   Concubinage, therefore presupposed the non-existence of a lawful wife; it was necessarily monogamic and must be entered into with matrimonial intent.   This explains why the ecclesiastical law of the Middle Ages permitted concubinage; it was regarded, in the Germanic sense, as a true marriage, in all its effects save those depending upon solemn formalities.[4]   Of these, the failure did not consist

[1] Art. 1098.   [2] Ital. Civ. Code, art. 770.   [3] *Ante* § 323.
[4] "Corpus Juris Canonici", *Gratian*, "Decretum", part 2, *Causa* XXXII, *Quaest.* 2, *Cap.* 6.

alone in not having purchased the woman, or in the omission of other Germanic solemnities, but, for the Church, which followed the Roman law, in the fact of having taken the woman without the execution of a formal agreement concerning the marriage portion (" dos "), provision for which was the evidence of the true marriage tie.[1]   On the other hand, reasons were not lacking why the Church should combat such a concubinage, even if, to avoid greater evils, it tolerated it.   The husband, not having marital authority, might find his wife taken from him by the person who preserved a guardianship over her, and this deprived such a union of the guaranty of perfect stability.   Furthermore, marriage being on a higher plane, in order that one might pass to that status, the laws permitted the concubine to be set aside for a lawful wife; and this constituted another cause of uncertainty and disorder.   For these reasons, after seeking to remove the defects by special rules, as, for example, that of encouraging the transformation of the concubine into a lawful wife, the Church finally came to forbid concubinage.   This was a consequence of having declared that the essence of marriage resided solely in the religious rite, whereby it became impossible any longer to distinguish between marriages differing in degree of perfection.   To this end, many " constitutions " of Councils and popes were promulgated, especially when concubinage had degenerated through the vices of the clergy.   But the change was definitely accomplished by the Council of Trent, which prohibited as illegal any union whatsoever outside of lawful marriage.   The civil laws followed these precepts and punished concubinage by various penalties, such as imprisonment, fine, exile, and others.   Among them are worthy of note those established by the statutes of Amadeus VIII, which confirmed the punishment anciently inflicted for adultery [2] and decreed that concubines should be dragged through the most crowded streets and whipped upon their bared shoulders.[3]   And still today the law takes no cognizance of other than matrimonial unions, except to stabilize the position of the children born of them.[4]

[1] *Post* § 347.
[2] *Tacitus*, "Germania", 19.
[3] III, 38, 39.
[4] Civil Code, arts. 179 *et seq.*

Chapter V

THE ARTIFICIAL FAMILY [1]

§ 334. Modes of Formation.   § 336. Adoption.
§ 335. Legitimization.   § 337. Decline of Adoption.

§ 334. **Modes of Formation.** — While the ordinary and legally recognized mode of forming and preserving the family was marriage, accompanied in whole or in part by its legal consequences, nevertheless the law itself provided a means of bringing the family into being artificially when the natural process of procreation failed or was inadequate. There might result children, but if the issue of an unlawful union, they might not be able to secure to the family its desired ends, that is they might be incapable of forming a legally recognized family. Or there might be an absolute failure of issue. In each case, the law came to the rescue: in the first instance by legitimization, in the second by adoption.

§ 335. **Legitimization.** — Children of a union not matrimonial in character, but capable of becoming such, *i.e.* natural children properly speaking, and not those of an adulterous or incestuous union, might be legitimized, that is, received into the legal family, and participate in its rights and duties. By this act, they commenced legally to have the quality of children, and, therefore, the ancient symbols accompanying legitimization expressed this purpose, namely, of evidencing the intent to regard thenceforward the natural as a legitimate child, as by embracing him, or sheltering him under one's cloak, or doing some other similar act. In Lombard law two modes of legitimization existed. The first was to remove from the union, of which the child was issue, the cause making it unlawful, as, for example, to declare the mother free, and hence a true wife, if she were half free (" aldia "), or slave.[2] The second was to recognize the child before the assembly, on condition, however, that any legitimate children which the father already had must have reached majority in order to join in the act and give their consent.[3]

[1] *Pertile, cit.*, §§ 116, 117; *Salvioli, cit.*, part IV, chap. 20; *Schupfer*, "La famiglia presso i longobardi", in "Archivio giuridico", I (1868).
[2] *Rothar*, 222; *Liutprand*, 106.   [3] *Rothar*, 155.

The first method of legitimization was in strict analogy to the
Roman mode " per subsequens matrimonium ", applied to a particular case.   The Roman principle was adopted by the canon law,
which even extended its effects.   Either it considered the marriage
as already existent from the time of birth of the children, who were
thus legitimate and not legitimitized, a distinction of important
practical consequences, since in many respects, especially in matters of inheritance, the status of the latter was inferior to that of
the former; or it caused the subsequent marriage to legitimize
not only the children by a concubine, but also the purely spurious
whom the Roman law excluded, and finally even those of an incestuous union, when, by a papal dispensation, this could be made a
real marriage.

The other mode of legitimization by Germanic law, that by
declaration before the assembly, found a counterpart in another
Roman form, consisting in the intervention of the sovereign authority, evidenced by a royal rescript.   This method was also
found in the canon law, which gave a similar efficacy to the papal
rescript; and in the law of the Empire of the Middle Ages.   There
came also into use the rescript of legitimization granted by the
communes, the imperial vicars, and finally by private individuals,
especially jurists, who were granted this prerogative by the sovereign.   Bartolus of Sassoferato, for example, received it from the
Emperor Charles IV, and instances were to be found as late as the
1700 s.   Legitimization by rescript, however, was less effective
than that by subsequent marriage.   In general its consequence
was not so much to give new rights to the legitimized, as to remove
the stain of birth,[1] unless the rescript itself contained additional
concessions, such as rights of inheritance, admission to feudal
tenures and entails (" fideicommissa "), creations of nobility, and
others, by virtue of which the legitimization was called "complete"
as compared with the less complete form, unproductive of such
effects.   A rescript granting " complete " legitimization had to
emanate directly from the prince.

Alongside the more common forms, were other modes or causes
of legitimization, among which should be mentioned adoption,
entry into a religious order, and declaration before a public official.

In the present law the two fundamental forms of legitimization
have prevailed, that by subsequent marriage and by rescript of
the prince, i.e. royal decree.   The latter may take place only when
it is impossible to legitimize by marriage; when employed, how-

―――――――
[1] Ante § 308.

ever, it produces the same effects as the other form; the natural children acquire, from the date of the decree, all the rights and duties incident to members of a lawful family.[1]

§ 336. **Adoption.** — When procreation failed, the law provided means of forming the family artificially through adoption. This institution has been found among all races of antiquity, for whom the continuance of the family was more important than for modern peoples, because of the religious duties due the dead and because of their as yet imperfect social organization. Thus the Germans used adoption from the most remote times. Since its purpose was to find one who should continue the family, which otherwise would become extinct, the family of the adopted passed into that of the adopting; and since the basis of the family was the patrimony or domestic estate, adoption was merely a transfer also of the estate, together with the name, by means of the " institution " or nomination of an heir. The Germanic adoption was, for these reasons, chiefly a contract affecting a future right of inheritance.[2] It came, therefore, to be described and treated in law as the gift of one's wealth to another. It was conditioned upon a want of issue, for the subsequent birth of children nullified it, entirely if sons were born, and partially if daughters, that is, to the extent to which the family estate passed to females.[3] It was not necessary, however, for the adopting parent to transfer the patrimony to the chosen heir at the time of adoption; entry into possession might be postponed until the parent's death. The former case was the more ancient and was based upon the idea of a gift " inter vivos." [4] The latter more closely resembled in purpose the " donatio causa mortis " (" lidinlaib "), in which the donor retained possession during life. But since he henceforward had a lawful male heir, he could no longer alienate the domestic estate,[5] over which the adopted son had acquired a right. Only in the case of grave necessity, after having first sought the son's aid and been denied it, was it lawful for him to alienate the family property.[6]

The early ceremonies of adoption were symbolic of its purpose. It took place before the popular assembly,[7] for which the court was later substituted,[8] as in the case of all gifts, since, according to the ancient conception of a common ownership of property, the consent of all was necessary to admit a stranger into the possession of what otherwise, upon failure of a legal owner, would have

[1] Civil Code, arts. 196, 198.
[2] *Post* § 388.
[3] *Rothar*, 171.
[4] *Charlemagne*, 92, 105.
[5] *Post* § 375.
[6] *Rothar*, 173.
[7] *Id.*, 172.
[8] *Charlemagne*, 92.

reverted to the community.[1] To transfer the estate the adopting
parent, by the Salic law, threw the " festuca " or wand, the symbol
of the transfer,[2] upon the breast of the adopted; by Lombard law
it was enough to declare one's intention to hold the adopted as a
son. Other ceremonies were employed to give greater publicity
and stability to the act, such as covering the newly adopted with
one's mantle, cutting his hair, giving him arms, placing him upon
the great seat of the family ancestors, kissing him, causing him,
as owner, to receive guests in the house; and yet other acts besides,
varying according to the laws and the condition of the persons.

§ 337. **Decline of Adoption.** — Wherever Roman law governed,
adoption was accomplished by a written act (" chartula adfiliationis "), which avoided the necessity of a contemporaneous transfer of the estate, and assured to the adopted a right over it at the
death of the parent. This was contrary both in form and substance to the Germanic adoption, which, therefore, under the influence of the Roman law, especially at the time of the revival of its
study, was bound to undergo modification in the direction of the
Roman adoption, the more so since the introduction and spread
of the use of wills provided another and simpler means for the
appointment of heirs. This was, in fact, why adoption began to
lose its ancient importance, which was never regained in subsequent systems of law. Feudalism too was unfavorable, because
it did not recognize adoption as a valid title through which to succeed to the fief or acquire nobility. The statutes of the mediaeval
cities generally accepted the Roman theories and like them distinguished adoption proper from " adrogation ", requiring that
adoption take place before a public official, with the participation
and consent of the agnates, unless the assent of the sovereign was
required, which was given personally or by one who had received
authority for the purpose.

This indicates that the act had become infrequent and was no
longer, as among the Germans, necessarily linked with a contract
affecting the future inheritance. Germanic ideas continued naturally, however, to be mingled with the Roman, and by this confusion
may be explained many of the provisions that have passed into the
codes. Some bear the mark of Germanic conceptions, such as
that found in several codes, permitting adoption only by persons
without children; and that of the Sardinian Code, by which the
adopted child was not cut off from all ties with his own family, a
consequence of the fact that ancient adoption was merely a means

---

[1] *Cf.* the "arrogatio" of the Roman law.   [2] *Post* § 440.

of acquiring rights of inheritance from another person, and of creating new ties solely between the two contracting parties and not between one of them and the relatives of the other. These rules are found in the present Italian Code.[1] On the other hand, a Roman derivation may be found for the principle of the present Code that adoption, being productive of a true relation of parent and child, shall be created in imitation of the natural relation, that is, under those conditions by which such a relation might have been established by natural law;[2] that it shall be of advantage to the adopting parent and that the advent of children shall not annul it, but merely place the adopted on the same footing with them.[3]

[1] [Civil Code, art. 212.]   [2] [*Id.*, art. 202.]   [3] [*Id.*, art. 737.]

TITLE II

GOVERNMENT OF THE FAMILY

§ 338. The "Mundium." | § 339. Changes in the "Mundium."

§ 338. **The "Mundium."** — The government of the family in Germanic law centred in the exercise of the "mundium"[1] or authority of the head of the house. The basis of this power, which characterized it at least at its origin, was chiefly ability to bear arms. As common defense was among the most important purposes of the family,[2] whoever was incapable of this might never have the authority of chief, or even a full liberty over his own person. Hence, within the family, the members divided into two classes: on the one hand were those who could be free of the "mundium" exercised by another person ("amundi", "selbmundi"[3]); on the other were those who were always subject to it ("in mundio", "in potestate esse"[4]). The "mundium" was, therefore, a necessary part of the constitution of the family, in whose interest it was mainly exercised for the realization of all the family ends.

From this principle certain consequences followed. First, the "mundium" was not so much a right in him who exercised it (although it appeared to be principally such in the property relations of the family), as a duty, especially the duty of defending those subject to it. In the second place, the "mundium", besides being possible only between persons united by family ties (the slave master exercised ownership not "mundium"[5]), was permanent or temporary, according as the family status of the person admitted or denied the possibility of its being some day dissolved. It was permanent for those who always remained incapable of defending the home by arms. Such were women,[6] who, the law declared, could never be independent;[7] such also were those who,

[1] *Cf.* "Manus" of the Roman law.
[2] *Ante* § 312.
[3] *Cf.* "sui juris."
[4] *Cf.* "alieni juris."
[5] *Liutprand*, 139.
[6] *Cf.* the perpetual guardianship of the woman under Roman law.
[7] *Rothar*, 204, 278.

for any cause, were unfitted for war, and who were therefore relegated to the class of the semi-free. It was temporary, on the other hand, for males fitted to bear arms, who, on reaching majority, became capable of defending themselves. A third consequence of the close relation between the "mundium" and the family constitution was that it extended over all persons forming part of the family, but manifested different qualities according to the particular situation of the individual. There was the "mundium" over the wife (the "manus" in strict sense of the Roman law, to which it is also related etymologically); that over the children ("patria potestas"); and finally that over other relatives ("tutela", "cura"). Of each of these the attributes were necessarily different, though their basis and purpose, as well as their name, were always the same.

§ 339. **Changes in the "Mundium."** — These conceptions had a long life in Italy, no less than the constitution itself of the Germanic family, to which they belonged; and they gained no little strength both from the aristocratic and military nature of feudalism, and from the economic policy of the mediaeval communes. There were, however, two permanent forces, of increasing influence, operating to modify it: the Roman law, with its theories upon the domestic order and woman's position, encouraged in addition by christianity; and the impairment which, with the growth of political power and the extension of its functions, the family, and thereby its head, suffered with respect to many of the powers, characteristic of its ancient constitution, though, in a better organized society, more appropriate to the public authority. This new conception developed from the Middle Ages, when it was evidenced by the institution of the "mundium" exercised by the king, in the absence or inadequacy of the ordinary "mundoald." Later it had a development more far reaching and more conforming to its nature, leading to that right of intervention in the family organization, which, out of public interest, was conferred upon the State, not, as formerly, to substitute the latter for the natural head of the family, but to coöperate with him, assisting him in the exercise of his powers, and restricting his exercise, according to the needs of the particular case.[1]

The whole subject, both in its historical development and its

[1] [See the rôle of the magistrate ("pretore") in the "family council" (Civil Code, art. 251); that of the state attorney and court in the removal of guardians (art. 271); that of the notary and "pretore" in preparing the inventory of the minor's estate (arts. 282 to 287); that of the office of the "pretore" in the guardian's accounts (art. 303).]

consequences, assumed a diversity of aspect according to the objects served; that is, according as it was a question of the family government with respect to the relations between husband and wife, between parents and children, or between other relatives, or finally, with respect to the State.

Chapter VI

RELATIONS OF HUSBAND AND WIFE [1]

§ 340. Marital Authority.

§ 340. **Marital Authority.** — Marriage produced an association over which the husband presided. To produce such a consequence, the marriage had to be perfect, that is, it must possess the "mundium." The so-called "imperfect" marriages [2] could not bring into being the marital authority over the wife. Such authority was, therefore, not a necessary consequence of marriage, since there were true marriages which lacked the "mundium", but resulted from an act accompanying marriage and rendering it perfect, namely, the husband's purchase of the "mundium" from the father or other guardian of the woman. When, chiefly through the Council of Trent, [3] the time came when distinctions between kinds of marriage were abolished and all in substance and effect were reduced to a single type, outside of which marriage did

---

[1] *Pertile, cit.*, §§ 109–113; *Salvioli, cit.*, part IV, chaps. 15, 16, 17; *Schupfer*, "La famiglia", etc., *cit.*, in "Archivio giuridico", I, 139 *et seq.*; *Gaudenzi*, "Le vicende del mundio nei territorii longobardi dell' Italia meridionale", in "Archivio storico prov. napolet.", XIII, vol. I; *Ciccaglione, s.v.* "Alimenti", in "Enciclopedia giuridica"; *Blandini*, "Il costo del mundio maritale", etc., *cit.* (Catania, 1891); *Scaduto*, "Divorzio e cristianesimo in Occidente" (1884); *Del Vecchio*, "Le seconde nozze del coniuge superstite"; *Schulte*, "Histoire du droit", etc., *cit.*, book III, chap. 4, §§ 167–171.
[2] *Ante* § 329.
[3] *Ante* § 315.

not exist, the husband's authority, henceforth inseparable from every marriage, was regarded as a natural consequence of it, and from this conception the law has never since departed.

The marriage association, embracing the whole life of the spouses, controlled their personal as well as their economic relations and it will be well to deal with these separately.

TOPIC 1. PERSONAL RELATIONS

§ 341. Reciprocal Rights and Duties. — The Germanic idea of marriage, higher certainly than that of the Romans before Christianity had influenced their law, placed husband and wife in a relation of mixed rights and duties to one another.

The woman was subordinated to the man. To indicate this condition, her hair was cut on marrying, whence the phrase " esse in capillo ", meaning to be at home and marriageable.

The first duty of the woman was fidelity. Among some peoples not even the husband's death freed her from her promised faith. If she violated it during his life, the penalty was swift and of extraordinary severity. A husband, discovering his wife in adultery, might, according to the ancient custom, drive her with shouts in public disgrace from his house.[1] Nor was his power diminished when laws came to be written; rather did these also give him the right to kill his wife, if caught in her crime; to sell her, beat her, or do what he pleased with her.[2] So he might revenge himself at his pleasure against a wife who plotted against his life. The duty of fidelity was a consequence of marriage and not of the " mundium." Therefore even when the latter was lacking, the husband might always have recourse to the blood feud, and the wife's accomplice must pay him, rather than those having authority over her, the fines which the law decreed for the offense suffered.[3]

The wife was also called upon to be co-worker with her husband in the family interests, and a partner in his joys and misfortunes.[4] Though legally subject to him, she was evidently in fact the companion of her husband, who in turn owed her the duties of protection and fidelity, which found a sanction in the law. The husband who brought a concubine into the home was punished by a severe fine;[5] the wife might always have, indeed she was admonished to have recourse to public authority to denounce a husband who had

[1] *Tacitus*, "Germania", 19.   [3] *Rothar*, 213; *Luitprand*, 121.
[2] *Liutprand*, 122, 139.   [4] *Tacitus, cit.*, 18.
                    [5] *Grimwald*, 6, 8.

failed in conjugal fidelity.[1] A husband who unjustly accused his
wife of adultery as a pretext for separation, paid a fine equal to the
" guidrigild " of her brother, had he killed him;[2] if he killed her
without justification, he paid the maximum fine of 1200 " solidi "
and lost all right to inherit from her.[3] This reciprocity of duties
between spouses was intended not only to place them in an equality
of position, but also and rather to guard through them, as its
representatives, the marriage institution, which was placed above
all individual considerations.   Thus no agreement between them
could free them from their reciprocal ties.[4] The progress thus
gained continued with the Franks, under the constant and direct
inspiration of the canon laws, which, in the husband as head of the
house, and in the wife, saw two persons bound to fidelity by an
oath to God.

The duty of protection obligated the husband to avenge wrongs
done his wife, to recover her compositions and " guidrigild ",[5] but,
at the same time, to answer for her acts and to support her rights
actively or defensively in court.

Principles substantially the same, though modified slightly to
correspond to social conditions, were repeated in the statutes of
the mediaeval communes.   The husband was always looked upon
as the guardian of his wife, who was permanently subordinated to
him and subject always to his right to punish, to kill her for a
flagrant act of adultery, and to be her natural representative.
Furthermore, his authority was constantly justified, more from
the point of view of a right in him, than of benefit to her, as the
motive of a true guardianship should have involved.   Towards
this idea of benefit to the wife, already proper to the Roman law,
Italian legislation did not frankly turn until the period of the codes.
By these, including the actual Civil Code, it was adopted and made
general;   reciprocity of rights and duties was reasserted and the
marital authority was given direction and moderated by juxtapos-
ing the authority of the judge.

Topic 2.   Property Relations

§ 342. **Different Conceptions.** — From antiquity two theories
have shaped the rules governing the property relations of husband
and wife.   By the first, the wife, though not in every respect her
own mistress, had nevertheless a capacity for property rights; by

[1] *Liutprand*, 130.
[2] *Grimwald*, 7.
[3] *Rothar*, 200.
[4] *Liutprand*, 130.
[5] *Rothar*, 201.

the second her property, as part of the family estate, was enjoyed, managed, and represented by her husband.

It may be that, by some of the earliest systems, as in early Roman law, the property right was exclusively in the husband, as a consequence of his power over everything in the home. But generally, at least in less remote times, the right was also recognized in the wife, to whom it came in different ways; among which, during the Germanic period was the " mefio ", " faderfio " and " morgengabe."

§ 343. " Mefio." — The " mefio ", also called " meta ",[1] and in Latin "dos", or better, "donatio propter nuptias", was what the husband according to a custom common to all ancient peoples, including the Germans,[2] gave as a dowery to his wife on the wedding day,[3] rather than what he received from her. At the betrothal, its value and kind were settled (" metam facere "). The ancients did not give feminine gifts, but horses and arms; later money and lands were substituted: and they became so generous, that to avoid abuses, the law had to intervene by fixing maxima, varying according to the condition of the parties, 400 " solidi " for public officials, 300 for nobles, and any less amount for others.[4] The purpose of the " mefio " was to make a settlement upon the wife, so that it differed essentially from the " mundium ", the purpose of which was the acquisition of authority over her. Therefore, while the " mundium " was paid to her guardian (" mundoald "), the " mefio " was paid to the bride herself. There was a point of contact between the two, when, an actual sale of the woman no longer taking place, the " mundium " was not retained by the " mundoald ", but given to the bride herself for her provision.[5] Thus considered, the " mundium " preceded the " mefio ", and may, indeed, have been the origin of the custom of the husband's dowery to his wife, that is, of the " mefio " itself. This, in fact, had the same purpose as the " mundium ", when the latter was transformed into a settlement upon the wife; in antiquity the " mefio " consisted of arms and horses, a fact which makes it probable that it was derived from a gift to men rather than women. That the "mefio" itself was then referred to as a dowery, and that the dowery was proof, even in the canon law, of the perfecting of

---

[1] The word "meta" is said to be derived from "met" or "mieth" (Lat. "munus") and from "veih" (Lat. "pecunia").
[2] *Tacitus*, "Germania", 18.
[3] *Cf.* "donatio ante nuptias" of the Roman law.
[4] *Liutprand*, 89.
[5] *Ante* § 324.

the marriage, is understood on remembering its connection with the "mundium", which, by transferring to the husband the authority over the woman hitherto exercised by another, rendered the marriage effectively perfect.

However this may be, it is certain that whatever was given as " mefio " became the property of the wife.   This is proved by the laws, which, besides requiring payment to the bride,[1] gave her a right to claim it from her husband's heirs as well as her father's in the case where she had returned as a widow to the paternal home and demanded its restoration to her by its separation from the inheritable estate before distribution.[2]   Indeed, the " mefio " belonged to the woman from the date of its promise in the betrothal, so that if, without her fault, the marriage was not consummated, her guardian ("mundoald") nevertheless compelled its payment.[3]   It was only when the woman married without her relatives' consent that she could not, if the heirs refused, obtain payment of the " mefio."   But this was by way of punishment, in that the law did not desire to place her relatives, whom she had offended, under an obligation to aid her in obtaining what might be due her.[4]

§ 344. " Faderfio." — " Faderfio " (" vater ", " vieh ") was the " pecunia patris ", that is, the " father's gift " to his daughter upon her marriage.   It was not a marriage portion (" dos "), but rather a trousseau.   The father was not required to give a marriage portion, because of his duty to conserve the family estate intact, and because such a settlement would be a gratuitous alienation, benefiting another family.   Nor was he required to give the " faderfio ", which was of the nature of a voluntary gift.   And so it remained, although from an early period custom required it [5] — even under the later laws, which continued to designate it a gift.[6]   The " faderfio " was not, however, without interest to the family, since by it the bride came to lose all subsequent claim upon her family's estate.   By an early principle — applied later to the " dos " and continued to a date not long past — when the "faderfio" had been paid by the woman's father or brothers, her family owed her nothing more.[7]   Perhaps anciently the " faderfio " consisted in articles of feminine or household use; but later such gifts were made in lands, though the law never established limits, as in the case of the " mefio ", but always declared that the father should give, as he

[1] *Liutprand*, 89.   [4] *Liutprand*, 114.
[2] *Rothar*, 199.   [5] *Tacitus*, "Germania", 18.
[3] *Id.*, 178.   [6] *Rothar*, 199.
                      [7] *Id.*, 181.

believed in accord with the interests of the family. On this point the law had not yet gone so far as to regulate the action of the head of the family.[1]

The " faderfio ", like the " mefio ", belonged to the woman, so that she had the right to take it from her husband's estate when, as widow, she returned to her father's home. Since the " faderfio " was received from the father, when the married daughter was called as an heir to a share in his estate, such share was computed by returning the " faderfio " to the estate, while the " mefio ", coming from another than the father, was first deducted from the estate.[2]

§ 345. " Morgengabe " or Morning-Gift. — The " morgen-gabe " (" morgen-gabe ", " donum matutinale ") was a gift which the husband, in the presence of the relatives and witnesses, and later by writing,[3] made to the wife the day after the wedding. In antiquity its purpose was to give sanction to the consummated union. By this gift, the husband, who, according to Germanic custom, had the right to repudiate the bride who was not a virgin, made solemn testimony to the contrary, thus forever precluding this danger of severance of the union. Its purpose explains why, in the early period, the " morgengabe " was given only upon the marriage of a virgin; later it was employed also on the marriage of a widow, but by then a change had taken place in the object of the gift, which came to be that of a settlement for the protection of her widowhood. For this it was appropriate, since it became the property of the wife, and since,[4] though at first comprising simple objects, with time and the increase of wealth, it included lands and entire estates, so that the law had to interfere by placing limits to it. The Lombard law provided that in no case might the " mor-gengabe " exceed one fourth of the husband's estate;[5] the Franks limited it to a third;[6] the Beneventine capitularies[7] reduced it to an eighth, and this last proportion was again confirmed in 1560 when the demand was made by the Sicilian Parliament upon Charles V that this proportion should not be exceeded. This is proof that the use of the " morgengabe " long existed in Italy, though without its early characteristics; the form remained but the substance changed. Little by little, through the causes which

---

[1] *Rothar*, 181; *Liutprand*, 102.
[2] *Rothar*, 199.
[3] *Liutprand*, 7.
[4] *Rothar*, 182, 199; *Astolf*, 15.
[5] *Liutprand*, 7.
[6] "Cartularium longobardicum formularum", *cit.*, 1.
[7] *Adelchi*, 3.

were tending to advance society, the Germanic custom was abandoned of repudiating, on the day after the wedding, the bride who was not a virgin, and thus at the same time the reason for the " morgengabe " came to an end.   Nevertheless the institution did not disappear, because a new purpose was substituted and came to receive acceptance in all systems, namely, to assure a proper maintenance for the wife upon her widowhood.   When reduced to this, however, the " morgengabe " did not differ from the " mefio ", which had come to have the same object.   Thus there came about a fusion between them, in which the name " tertia " signified one and " quarta " the other.   Both came to be given on the day of the betrothal; the " morgengabe " was no longer an act of voluntary generosity, but in marriages with the " mundium " was also regularly demanded and gave rise to an action for payment in favor of the woman, even after the death of her husband, and finally in the case where he had never promised the settlement.

§ 346. **Gifts between Husband and Wife.** — In this way, each of the three means by which, under Germanic law, a wife might acquire property, *i.e.* by the " mefio ", " faderfio " and " morgengabe ", lost its particular purpose and was eventually merged with the others into a single institution, tending, in its effects, to repair the difficulties which might result from the absence of the " dos." In this transformation the Roman law had an active part.   In fact, under the name of " donationes propter nuptias ", " sponsalitiae largitates ", " falcidia ", and others in use among the Romans, were found suggested one or the other of the Germanic marriage settlements.   Roman principles themselves were accepted, among others that of forbidding any other form of gift between spouses.   Lombard law declared void any gift by the husband to the wife, other than the " mefio " and the " morgengabe ";[1] and similarly Frankish law, for the " formularies " from which a contrary argument may be drawn,[2] refer also to Roman laws and deal with " donationes mortis causa ", made for the most part in the absence of issue, and often as a mere usufruct or life estate, reciprocally in favor of whichever of the spouses might survive.[3]   They were in other words stipulations for the enrichment of a survivor. The statutes of the mediaeval cities, representing the period of transformation of these Germanic institutions and their infusion

[1] *Liutprand*, 103.
[2] *Pertile, cit.*, III, p. 280, n. 44.
[3] Formularies of *Marcolfo*, II, 7; *Lindebrog*, 50; *Sirmond*, 17; ed. *Zeumer*, M. G. H., "Leges" V.

by Roman elements, preserved and, in fact, re-inforced these principles. Gifts between husband and wife were prohibited, even where they had been allowed by Roman law, with such rigor that no more than a mere right of use was considered to pass with nuptial gifts, including even the wedding ring, whenever they exceeded the most trifling value, which varied with time and place. This severity was later abandoned; even certain gifts came to be permitted, such as the allowance known as " pin money " (" spillatico "), used mostly by the nobles, and the " arrival gift " (" dismontadura "), as the present was called in the Duchy of Friuli, when made to the bride on " dismounting " before her husband's house. And there were others that were similar. But the Roman principle of forbidding gifts was preserved in substance and still figures in the provisions of the existing Italian Code.[1]

§ 347. Marriage Portion (Roman " Dos ").[2] — The ascendancy of Roman law and the resulting transformation of Germanic institutions gave a fresh and general diffusion to the " dos ", or marriage portion.

During the Germanic period the " dos " was preserved among the Roman population, because they retained their own law and because it was an institution greatly favored by the laws of the Church, which found in it a guaranty of the stability and perfection of the marriage. At the close of the Germanic period, including therein the feudal, the " dos " had prevailed over the other analogous Germanic institutions. This had resulted from the break down of the ancient rigidity of the family organization, unfavorable to alienations of the family estate; from the formation of new aggregations of private wealth, derived from trade and industry; from the greater social consideration enjoyed by woman; and chiefly from the new diffusion of Roman law.

Thus, by the legislation of the mediaeval cities, the " dos ", that is, what the wife brought as a marriage portion to her husband to aid in supporting the charges of the home, was generally admitted and governed in large part by the rules of the Roman law, both as to its composition, and as to its enjoyment and eventual restitution. In this, political reasons were certainly not absent,

[1] Art. 1054.

[2] ["La dote" of Italian law, descended from the "dos" of the Roman law, has been translated "marriage portion" in order to avoid possible confusion with the common law estate of "dower." A helpful description of the property relations between husband and wife under modern civil law, with special reference to developments in the 1800 s, will be found in "Continental Legal History Series", vol. XI, "Progress of Continental Law in the 19th Century", pp. 204–218.]

for the Roman " dos ", with its restrictions, was a considerably less dangerous means of alienation of family property from the jurisdiction of the commune than were the Germanic gifts.

The marriage portion of the communal statutes, however Roman in substance, was not yet entirely disassociated from the forms and rules due to Germanic conceptions. It still retained much of the ancient " faderfio." In fact, by the statutes of the mediaeval cities, the marriage portion had always to be harmonized with that other principle affecting the family estate, namely, its preservation to the agnates or males, so that it developed subject to many restrictions. At first, like the " faderfio ", the marriage portion consisted in little more than the trousseau, and never included other than personalty. Then needs grew, and, already in the 1300 s, due to the corruption of customs, the use of marriage portions injurious to the family estate was being condemned.[1] The wife who had been paid the portion was held, as in the case of the " faderfio ", to have received satisfaction of all that she might claim of her family; its receipt excluded her from any other right in the paternal estate ("exclusio propter dotem").[2] But Germanic traces did not disappear at once, as the Roman law continued to gain ascendancy. The serious concern of conserving the family estate always caused the " dos " to be colored by Germanic ideas. There were laws placing a maximum limit to it, as the Germanic law had done in the case of the " mefio " and " morgengabe." In Venice, in 1551, it might not exceed 5000 ducats; at Rome Pius V limited it to 4500 crowns; at Naples, until the first years of the 1800 s, it might at most be 15,000 ducats; and similar rules were found elsewhere. On the other hand, no minimum limit was established and the marriage portion might be reduced to something of little or no value; a principle was generally applied which corresponded to that governing the ancient " faderfio ", according to which the daughter must be content with what the father settled upon her. True, in the special case where the marriage portion was given by another than the father, the law required that it should be *compatible*, but the idea of compatibility was rather vague and did not mean more than that the marriage portion should correspond to the social and financial position of the family. If the woman was placed in a condition not unbefitting, she was deemed to have been provided with a compatible marriage portion and had no further claim. These principles lasted until very

[1] *Dante*, "Paradiso", XV, 104–106.
[2] *Post* § 379.

recent times.[1] On the other hand, however, there were not lacking laws which, to avoid excessive injustice to women, established
methods of computing the suitability of the marriage portion.
Some, from the time of the mediaeval cities, made it determinable
by the " family council " ;[2] others by the magistrate ;[3] but most
fixed its measure as the inalienable portion of her inheritance
(" legittima ").[4] This is explainable not so much as an imitation
of the Roman law, as a consequence of the principle that the settlement of the marriage portion, which excluded the bride from all
later participation in her family's estate, should be in satisfaction
of what was due her from her family, and should, therefore, in its
effects, be equivalent to her inalienable portion of the inheritance,
that is, what the law provided was due to a member of the family.
And even today the woman still has a right to her inalienable share
of the inheritance,[5] no longer because of the correspondence that
existed between it and the " dos ", which is now considered purely
as a gratuity, but because today the woman has gained a position
in the family, with respect to her legal rights, equal in all respects
to that of the male members.

§ 348. " Contrados " or Ante-nuptial Gift. — The diffusion of
the dotal system did not prevent the husband also from making
settlements upon his wife. Favorable to such gifts were the
" mefio " of the Germanic law as well as the " donatio proter nuptias " of the Roman law. A fusion of the two institutions and
laws produced the " contrados." This was its Roman name, but
it was also called *ante-nuptial*, that is, like the " mefio ", given or
promised before marriage at betrothal and operating counterwise
to the " dos ", by which it was generally regulated both as to character and amount. The ante-nuptial settlement might be even
obligatory, whenever the marriage portion was in use in accordance with the Justinian rules.[6] It was so at Milan, Amalfi, Sassari
and other places, though these were not many. As to its amount,
although at first it was left to the husband's pleasure, still it had,
to some extent, to be proportionate to the " dos ", though, certainly, no longer equal to it, as the bride might claim under the
Justinian law. For, economic and political reasons for conserving
the family estate soon induced the legislators of the mediaeval
cities to establish that the " contrados " might amount to but a
portion of the " dos ", a third, a fourth, at most a half, and then,

[1] Regolamenti di Gregorio XVI, § 21 ; [Pope, 1831–1846.]
[2] *Post* § 369.   [3] *Post* § 371.   [4] *Post* § 399.
[5] [Civil Code, art. 805.]
[6] Novels, XCVII, chap. 1.

discarding the idea of proportion, that it might not exceed an inconsiderable sum, fixed by law. Indeed the law even came to a general denial of any legal right to it, admitting it only when the husband offered it voluntarily. Hence the silence of the present Italian Code.

Lastly, there was the widow's portion ("dotarium"[1] or "vidualizio"), not, however, to be confused with "contrados." When the various settlements upon the woman had each its own purpose, the husband was allowed to provide for her widowhood by leaving her the usufruct or life interest in his estate. The Lombard law fixed its magnitude by relation to the number of children and made widowhood a condition though this was not required by the Roman law, unless the testator had so declared.[2] The statutes of the mediaeval cities also limited the wife's right to a life estate in her husband's property, although the system of the "quarta uxoria" came to be more and more generally applied in her favor in imitation of the Roman law, as well as the system of giving her the ownership, in addition to the enjoyment, when there were no children. But as the wishes of the deceased came to have importance through the use of wills, and as the various settlements upon the wife lost their primitive significance, the widow's portion ("dotarium"), properly speaking, came into use, that is, a settlement of property for her widowhood, made at once upon marriage, or even as a stipulation added to the betrothal agreement. It had its origin in the "morgengabe", the purpose of which had changed to that of a provision in case of widowhood.[3] Like the "morgengabe" it was in the beginning due only on the first marriage and was proportioned to the husband's wealth. The use, however, of the "contrados", and of the widow's usufruct or life estate of the Roman law, prevented a general acceptance of the widow's portion ("dotarium") in Italy, or ordinarily of its imposition by law. It did become of general legal acceptance on the other hand in France, and this explains how it assumed the same qualities, after the coming of the Normans, in the southern provinces of Italy. There these qualities were preserved until the period of codification, when the widow's portion again returned to the class of contractual gifts, created for the contingency of survivorship, the law limiting itself, with striking similarity to the Roman rules, to establishing the

---

[1] [English dower evidently resembles the Roman "dotarium" rather than the "dos."]

[2] *Astolf*, 14; *Justinian*, Code, V, 9, 6; 10, 1; Novels, XXII, chap. 32.

[3] *Ante* § 345.

occasions for, and the measure of, the life estate or absolute ownership to which the surviving spouse had a right.

§ 349. " Community of Goods." — The natural reason for
making the possessions of both spouses common property lay in
the propriety of so treating the product of their joint labor and
economy. Upon this reasoning was based the Germanic custom
that, upon dissolution of the marriage, the wife might claim a part
of the gains received by the husband during their joint life, because
she had coöperated in securing them. The Franks called her part
the " tertia collaborationis ", because it amounted to a third.
Christian ideas sanctioned these sentiments as tending to create
the most perfect union and intimacy possible during the married
life. Thus the system of " community of goods " arose and became
more and more general. At first it was regarded merely as a right
of inheritance, given to one spouse over a part of the property of
the other; [1] later it was considered as a right of co-ownership.
Established first by reciprocal agreements, it was later presumed,
unless the contrary was stipulated; ordinarily made to commence
with the marriage, that is, from the date when the marriage was
contracted, it was by local custom postponed until the consummation itself of the marriage, or until husband and wife had lived a
year and a day together, or until the birth of the first son.

Community of property might be of two sorts. One was the
community of acquests, which included all increases of the family
estate while living together, derived from the income from the
property of either or from their labor. Excluded from it, therefore, was both the property belonging to each spouse prior to the
marriage, and that which each acquired subsequently through the
act of a third party. This type was much in use in Sardinia and
Piedmont. But it was difficult, when it came to giving the spouse
his or her share, to determine whether personalty, so susceptible to
deterioration and transfer, should be considered as an acquest, or
as entering the estate for a reason other than that which the system
of " community " presupposed. It was, therefore, determined that,
besides the ascertained acquests, personal property should always
be included in the " community " fund, no matter what the time
or manner of its reception. This was known as *community of
acquests* or of *movables*. The defects of the system were not,
however, wholly eliminated; they might, indeed, be made worse.
It was a period of great commercial and industrial growth, with an
increase not only of the value of personal property, but also of the

[1] *Marcolfo*, "Formularies", II, 7, in M. G. H. ed. *Zeumer*, "Leges", V.

frequency of conversion of landed wealth into personalty. Consequently, by the division of all personalty but not of all realty, an unjust disadvantage was suffered by the spouse, who, through commerce, had accumulated more movable capital than the other. Thus came into use a third class of " community ", called *universal*, because it included all property, regardless of the time or mode of its acquisition. This system found favor among the commercial and industrial bourgeoisie, though to a greater extent outside than within Italy. It was common in Sicily, after the coming of the Normans. In Italy proper, on the other hand, the " community " of *use* was widely practised and was the ordinary system of the statutes of the mediaeval cities. It consisted in the right of the husband to the income from all his wife's property, without exception, and it did not, like the others, threaten the integrity of the estates to the prejudice of the agnates. It, therefore, had the support of the mediaeval communes, with whose economic policy it was in accord ; in fact to such a point that, by their statutory laws, every acquest by the wife belonged to the husband, because presumed to have been made with his money. It was favored also by the aristocracy with whom the preservation of the family estate in the agnates was an essential policy. Furthermore, the " community of use " was the system best fitted to co-exist with the Roman " dos ", or marriage portion, and this was the main reason why the other types of " community ", especially the " universal ", were not well received in Italy, where they were also met by the prohibition against gifts between husband and wife (for which they might be a cover), and against agreements relating to rights of inheritance. From these principles there has not even been a wide departure in the present Code, which allows but one form of " community " : that which gives the *enjoyment* of all the property of the spouses and makes them participate in the *acquests*, whether made jointly or separately, during the existence of the " community " itself.[1]

§ 350. **Husband's Rights.** — All property belonging to the wife, from any of the sources that have been mentioned, was, during marriage, under the control of the husband, as head of the house. This was a result of the marital authority ; and, since such authority did not necessarily accompany all marriages,[2] it was present only in perfect unions.[3] Germanic law declared that the wife was under the " mundium " of her husband, she and all that was hers, even her wedding gifts, for which the husband, who became their

---

[1] Civil Code, arts. 1435, 1436.   [2] *Ante* § 340.   [3] *Ante* § 329.

owner, became answerable through the " launegild." [1]   When later
the natural consequence of marriage was marital authority, the
husband henceforward always had control of his wife's property.

This control manifested itself with diverse qualities.   In the
first place, the husband as the head of the house, administered
everything composing the domestic estate, including, therefore,
the part belonging to the wife.   It has already been seen, when
speaking of the " mefio ", " faderfio " and " morgengabe ", that
the wife had a right to separate the property, coming to her by
those channels, from her husband's estate, with which it was
mingled during his life.   The marriage portion (" dos "), given to
the wife to help meet the expenses of the household, afforded the
husband considerably greater rights than he would have had in
the mere administration of the property, save that he was bound to
restore it, in the cases, and in the manner provided by law and by
the marriage contract.   Over the property settled by an ante-
nuptial agreement (" contrados ", " antefatto "), the wife, during
coverture, had no rights; over the " community of goods " the
husband similarly had the power of administration; and not of
administration merely, but also, as a general rule, of enjoyment
or usufruct of all that belonged to his wife.

On the other hand, since the wife had rights, what belonged to
her was not freely disposable by her husband, but in fact almost
inalienable, though the laws gradually receded from their ancient
rigor,[2] and required only the wife's consent.   This must in every
sense be free and in no way extorted by the husband.   For that
reason her relatives intervened in acts of alienation and formally
demanded of her whether she gave her consent of her own will.[3]
Similarly the husband's consent was necessary to acts of alienation
by the wife.   The reason that this element was necessary to
validity, was at first the assumption of the existence of a right
" in rem " in the husband over the wife's property by virtue of his
marital authority; later the law passed to the theory that the wife
by herself was without capacity or seriousness for matters that
might have grave consequences; and finally the law arrived at
the more logical justification, which is the modern view, that the
husband had supreme authority over all that composed the domestic estate, because to him was entrusted the administration of the
family government.

[1] *Rothar*, 182.   [See *post* § 500.]
[2] *Liutprand*, 22;   *Pepin*, 34;   *Guido*, 8.
[3] *Liutprand*, 22.

To this conception is due the present doctrine of marital authorization, which found place in the French Code as a result of the Germanic traditions, which it borrowed and adopted from the customary law. Marital authorization has never since been abandoned, but merely modified out of consideration for the theory of woman's independence as opposed to the marital authority. The intermediate codes wavered between the two theories, in their provisions governing the property relation of husband and wife. At one extreme was the Austro-Lombard Code, which gave the greatest degree of liberty to the wife; at the other was the papal legislation, under which the wife was in general without capacity.

The present Italian Code has endeavored to reconcile the different tendencies, giving to the husband the right to require and to give authorization, but with regard to the wife, providing that, only for certain acts, those of great consequence, was the authorization required.[1] In no case was it any longer justified by the presumption of incapacity, but by the necessity of giving the head of the house the means of enforcing a single policy in the management of the family property.

It is thus apparent that, in this field, the law's historical development is still in a state of divided doctrines and that rather than adopt a settled solution, it still seeks to reconcile them by opportune compromises.

Topic 3.   Extinguishment of Marital Authority

§ 351. **Modes.** — Since the husband's authority was intended to be in the interests of the family and in protection of the wife, whenever, for abuse, incapacity or other reason, its exercise did not correspond to its purpose, the law intervened as a brake upon it or as a substitute.

It could, then, in the first place, be extinguished by law. This was true from the time of the Lombard laws, especially with regard to the effect upon inheritance, in the case of the husband who had prompted his wife to adultery, or had deserted her without legal cause, or had killed her or in some other manner done her serious injury.[2] It was also true of the Germanic and subsequent laws, in all those instances where the husband had, through civil death, suffered the loss of all his rights.[3]   And of this traces still remain in present Italian law.[4]

[1] [Civil Code, art. 134.]
[2] *Rothar*, 200; *Liutprand*, 130.
[3] *Ante* § 299.
[4] [Civil Code, art. 135.]

But besides by express provision of law, marital authority might be destroyed upon the severing of the marriage union, which was possible under Germanic law.

§ 352. **Divorce.** — Although in conception and purpose marriage was permanent, it was possible, with the Germanic peoples, as it had been with the Romans, to dissolve it. Made in the interest of the family, the head of the house might unmake it, when it did not fulfill its purpose. Similarly to the early period of Roman law, the husband in antiquity had the power to repudiate it, while this right was denied the wife, because she was in all respects dependent upon him. The analogy continued with the appearance of the first laws which, like the first Roman laws, recognized the husband's right and merely restricted its use to certain determined cases in order, out of public interest, to prevent abuses. It was in this guise that divorce appeared in the early Italo-Germanic laws, that is, as a right, given chiefly to the husband, to dissolve the marriage for certain causes, legally recognized as sufficient.

One of these causes, in very remote antiquity, was mutual consent. When the married life had lost its necessary foundation, because, as the Romans said, the " maritalis affectio " had ceased, or when " non caritas secundum Deum, sed discordia regnat ", as the invaders expressed it, it was dissolved by the mutual consent of the spouses themselves, who recognized that they were no longer able to live together. An instrument (" libellum repudii ", " espitola ") was executed with witnesses, which declared the marriage terminated, gave to each freedom to remarry or enter the Church, and provided a penalty, as in any other contract, payable by the party failing to respect it.[1] It is evident that this custom was preserved among the Germanic tribes not only after their entry into the Roman world, but also after their conversion to Christianity.

Another lawful cause for dissolving marriage was serious infirmity. At first, if a wife was childless, the husband was permitted, in accordance with a custom obtaining also among other peoples,[2] to seek an heir by another woman, whom he might bring to the house, without dissolving the marriage. But this practice ceased after conversion to Christianity, and as compensation, the barrenness of the woman and also the impotence of the man were made a legal cause of divorce, provided its existence was proved by trial by ordeal (" judicium dei "). Serious disease, such as leprosy,

---

[1] "Formulae Marculfi", II, 30; *id.*, "Sirmondicae", 19; *id.*, "Andegavensis", 56; in M. G. H. ed. *Zeumer*, "Leges", V.

[2] Genesis, 16, tells how Abram, being without child by his wife Sarai, took Hagar, her handmaid.

might have the same effect, evidence of which may be seen in the fact that the Lombard law required an express provision in order to preserve the husband's rights, in case he fell ill of this disease.[1]

Infidelity was a cause for divorce. With his adulterous wife the husband might do as he willed,[2] but in antiquity the most usual penalty was ignominious repudiation. It was even sometimes sought to make the wife appear guilty, in order to be rid of her, so that a law was adopted that, if the woman proved herself innocent of her husband's charge, he was obliged to swear that he had not accused her with a view to divorce, or be condemned to pay the amount of his own " guidrigild." [3] Repudiation was also permitted the husband if his wife made an attempt upon his life, or refused to follow him to a new domicile, or had in other serious ways failed in her duties. A like right was recognized in the wife, if her husband grossly offended her, as by accusing her falsely of adultery, or by calling her a witch, or bringing another woman into the home.[4]

In other cases it was the law itself that pronounced the divorce, either as a punishment, or because of a supervening impediment to the marriage. As instance of the first, may be recalled the Lombard law allowing the wife to remarry when the husband had absented himself for three years ; [5] in the second case marriage was dissolved when either of the parties had lost the free status enjoyed at the marriage,[6] or had, with the other's consent, taken the religious vow of chastity.

§ 353. Separation. — Dissolution of marriage was contrary to the doctrines of the Church, though it failed to overcome this tenacious custom. It made no headway in the Lombard period, and in that of the Franks it only obtained the concession that spouses who had separated might not contract a new marriage. Thus the principle of the indissolubility of the tie was not wholly compromised, since the possibility of the parties' reunion was still preserved. It was Charlemagne who forbade the separated spouses to enter into new unions, and condemned such transgressors to ecclesiastical and civil penalties.[7] Lothar still more openly espoused the canon law. While forbidding dissolution of the marriage tie, he conceded separation, but only in the case of infidelity, or the intention of both parties, approved by the bishop, to enter a religious life.[8]

[1] *Liutprand*, 122.
[2] *Ante* § 341.
[3] *Grimwald*, 5.
[4] *Rothar*, 196, 187 ; *Grimwald*, 6.

[5] *Ante* § 288.
[6] *Ante* § 322.
[7] *Charlemagne*, 40, 131.
[8] *Lothar*, 95.

This system of compromise between divorce and the absolute permanence of the marriage tie was never abandoned. The early instances of divorce were transformed by the jurists of later periods into cases of separation. Furthermore, divorce was repeatedly and solemnly condemned by the canon law, which governed marriage,[1] while the Council of Trent pronounced anathema against one who should assert the right of divorce even on the ground of adultery. The Protestant Reformation, which replaced marriage upon the basis of a purely civil contract, turned the law more favorably towards divorce in the countries which fell away from the Roman Church. In the Catholic countries, however, nothing was changed, until divorce was introduced by the laws of the French conquerors, to disappear promptly with them. This was followed in Italy by a return to the limited principle of personal separation, which governs the Code today.[2] But the storm of protest, again gathering from the example of the countries where marriage is a civil relation, and from the special conditions of present day society, may before long sweep away the limitation.

[1] *Ante* § 314.   [2] [Civil Code, arts. 148 *et seq.*]

CHAPTER VII

CHILDREN [1]

§ 354.   Paternal Authority.

§ 354.   **Paternal Authority.** — The basis of the father's authority over his children was his power over his whole household; in Germanic terminology, it was the " mundium." [2]   This was not to be understood as exclusively a marital authority, although in perfect analogy to the effect of the " manus " of the Roman law, it might be restricted to refer properly to that one phase of the authority of the head of the house.   In a more general sense the " mundium " was also the paternal authority; and in fact the husband acquired the " mundium " over his wife by a transfer of it from her father, who, therefore, must have had it over his daughter; in the laws, paternal authority was always called " mundium." [3]

In consequence, as the " mundium " did not necessarily accompany marriage, paternal authority was not an attribute of every marriage, but only of those with the " mundium " (as in the " justae nuptiae " of the Roman law), that is, of those productive of the completest possible legal effect.   The authority of the father did not, therefore, result merely from paternity, any more than

---

[1] *Pertile, cit.,* § 115; *Salvioli, cit.,* chap. 18; *Ciccaglione, s.v.* "Alimenti", in "Enciclopedia giuridica"; *Scaduto,* "Consenso nelle nozze", etc. (1885); *Calisse,* "Diritto ecclesiastico e diritto longobardo", chap. 4; *Schulte, cit.,* §§ 172–173.

[2] *Ante* § 338.

[3] *Rothar,* 183, 186, 195, 197, 385; *Liutprand,* 31 etc.

that of the husband followed the simple fact of marriage, so long as marriages were of different grades. It was rather the effect of the legal conditions in the midst of which the natural fact itself occurred.

Partaking of the character of the " mundium ", paternal authority had this further consequence, that, by pure Germanic law, it must be exercised not only solely by the father, who was the head of the house, but also in the interest of the family. It appeared, therefore, more a right than an obligation of the father and in this it accorded with the early Roman law, with this difference, that, while in the Roman law the " patria potestas " possessed strongly the character of a property right belonging to him personally, in Germanic society it was but the consequence of his representation of the family interests, so that he might not exercise it to his own benefit, but for the family needs. As more civilized ideas succeeded to those of the Germanic invaders, paternal authority passed through the same evolution in Italian law that it had experienced in Roman law, in that, without abandoning the principle that it was to safeguard the interests of the family, it grew to be considered not so much an advantage to the father as a right of the child to education and protection.

TOPIC 1. POWERS OVER THE PERSON

§ 355. **Early Paternal Rights.** — The Germanic law of antiquity, with its theory of family tutelage, gave the father absolute power over the persons of his children. No sooner was a child born than it was placed upon the ground and so exhibited to the husband, who, if its legitimacy were doubtful or if it were deformed, or born on an inauspicious day, or if the birth had been accompanied by ill omens, might refuse to recognize it as his child, and, therefore, expose it to die, in accordance with a custom found among all peoples in the early stages of their civilization.[1] There is even evidence that the father might kill the child; in fact an ancient religious tradition forbade the killing of the newborn after it had tasted the sacred food of milk and honey, and this, being a limitation, presupposes a right that could be limited. Some traces of it were discoverable even in the Lombard law, such as the right of the father to kill a daughter married to a slave; also the fact that a father's attempt upon the life of a child was not a sufficient cause to deprive him of the " mundium ",[2] and the legal recognition of

[1] *E.g.* Moses, Cyrus, Paris, Œdipus, Romulus and Remus, etc.
[2] *Rothar*, 195–197.

the father's right to punish, with no parallel regulation of the power. In the last case the justification was the presumption that a father would not abuse his power to the injury of his children, and dated from the period when ancient conceptions had already grown less rude.[1]

While but faint vestiges remained of the right to kill, the other custom of exposing the child to die continued generally in Italy among the invaders. Not even the Church succeeded in extirpating it, but obtained merely that such newborn children should be exposed in a marble receptacle, conveniently located at the church door, rather than in the woods or other deserted places; salt placed near the child indicated that it had not been baptized.

After recognizing and accepting the child, the father was not always thereby obliged to keep it in the family, but might sell it. The Church also opposed this, but again to little effect. It was only able to limit the right to cases of extreme necessity and to make the father's right of redemption always an implied condition of the sale. Under these circumstances the sale of children was still permitted by the capitularies of Charles the Bald, in the 800 s;[2] it was still practised in the 1000 s, especially in Calabria, where certain of the most renowned of the fairs profited by it.

Finally, if he kept the child, the father might place him in any status of life that he thought most advantageous to the family. The daughters he might promise in marriage at any age and to any person, provided free.[3] Whether boys or girls, he might destine them for a religious life. By the Lombard law, the punishment of a nun who broke the vow was equally severe, whether made by herself or her father;[4] and the documents of the Germanic period are full of instances of children dedicated from infancy to the monastery. The Church was not so opposed to this as to other excessive instances of the paternal power; indeed it favored it, declaring that children were bound by the vows made for them by their parents. It was not until later, when the legal theory of consent was more strictly applied, that the paternal will, as in marriage,[5] had also, in the case of the religious life, to be ratified by the child on reaching the age of capacity. With this stage the exercise of the paternal authority had gained a different quality from hitherto.

§ 356. **Later Character of Paternal Authority.** — This change of character began with the 1100 s and its subsequent development

[1] *Liutprand*, 120.
[2] *Boretius*, "Capitularien in Langobardenreich" (1864), year A.D. 864, chap. 34.
[3] *Rothar*, 195; *Liutprand*, 12. [4] *Liutprand*, 30. [5] *Ante* § 318.

was influenced by the rediffusion of Roman principles. Paternal authority became a duty, imposed upon the father, to protect, maintain and educate his offspring. This conception had, indeed, existed in the past, since, in addition to his manifold rights he was under a duty to represent his child, defend him, wage a blood feud for him and answer for his acts. All this, however, was not the effect of rights in the child himself, but of the father's obligation to protect the family interests, in the persons and acts of his children. When this interest counseled otherwise, the children, of themselves, might presume to no rights, but remained within the authority of the father, who might kill, expose, sell, or send them from the house in any other way. Soon, however, he was forced to recognize certain rights in the children as opposed to himself, whence there arose a modification of his personal relations to them. He might no longer rid himself of his legitimate offspring, but was bound to recognize, support, and educate them; his right of punishment, become rather a duty of correction, was limited to acts of simple discipline, and in the graver matters had to be completed by the intervention of the public authority; the paternal consent was still required in the more important acts in the child's life, but as a protection and to furnish needed assistance; it could, therefore, be replaced by the public authority and ceased with the presumption that the child no longer required assistance.

It was with qualities such as these that the paternal authority made its appearance in the first statutes of the mediaeval cities. According to them, however, it might be exercised by the grandfather or mother in place of the father. During minority paternal consent was required for marriage, even of males, and the commune aided the father in punishing the disobedient son. But on this point also uniformity was not found in the statutes; conflict between differing principles had not disappeared and particular provisions conformed now to one, now to another. Thus alongside a permanent paternal power, reflection of the Roman law, was found the temporary form, derived from the Germanic system;[1] in one locality legal capacity was denied children, elsewhere even contracts between father and child were possible; here a joint responsibility of members of the family was maintained, there the legal personality of each was distinct; everywhere, in fact, different conclusions were reached, according to the theory from which they set out.

This diversity disappeared little by little as greater solidity of legal standards took the place of the uncertainty of the transitional

[1] *Post* § 359.

period from old to new.   The result was a system which became well defined in the period of the codes, and which drew upon both preceding systems, yet had an existence and character of its own, wherein all elements were combined.   Family interest is now represented in the measures conceded to the paternal authority to maintain order; the right of the parents, with the recognized legal duty of the children to honor and respect them,[1] forms the moral basis of the " patria potestas " itself; the right of the children to support, education and protection is the source of the various attributes of the father's personal relations to them.

Topic 2.   Property Relations

§ 357. " Peculium "; Separate Property. — The Germanic conception of the ownership of property by the family, gave the father merely its management and use, and as the family interests were personified in him so long as he lived, no right in relation to them might be exercised by any other than himself.   Whatever a child acquired belonged to the family and, therefore, to the father; the child had no power to alienate, and if he did so, the father might reclaim the objects; he might not obligate himself to a performance unless his father consented, nor bring or defend a suit affecting the family property, save through the father's representation; and for like reason a child might not ordinarily claim from his father an assignment of a part of the patrimony.   For Germanic law did not possess the Roman institution of the " peculium " or son's separate estate.   It has been thought that a trace was observable in the Lombard laws, where it was said that the son should share with his brothers what he had gained in war, and that he might retain all that he had gained by service at court.[2]   Certainly in this provision there is a clear correspondence to the Roman distinction between the " peculium castrense ", and " peculium quasi castrense "; and it is certain that in the expressions used there was a concordance between Lombard and Roman law.[3]   But the difference in substance was such that it cannot be said that the Lombard law was dealing with a " peculium."   There, the assumption was that the father was dead, while the " peculium " rested upon the fact of the father's existence.   Furthermore, while by Roman law the " peculium castrense " belonged exclusively to him who gained it, by Lombard law it was divided with the brothers who remained

[1] Civil Code, art. 220.
[2] *Rothar,*.167.
[3] *Cf. Justinian,* Institutes, II, 12 and Code, XII, 28, 1.

at home, since they too met the family obligations by providing the needs of the members away at war.

On the other hand, while the representation of domestic interests, which the father exercised, excluded the children from immediate rights over the family estate, the fact that the estate, so far as title was concerned, belonged to the family and not the father, meant that the children possessed a kind of co-ownership in it with the father himself, and that their right remained merely in suspension before the dominant authority of the latter.[1] It followed that the father might do nothing in any way injurious to the rights of the children, who, therefore, on acquiring legal capacity upon majority, might intervene by withholding consent to acts harmful to their rights, such as the legitimization of natural children,[2] or the alienation of family property.[3]

These usages continued for a very long period, and even under the statutes of the mediaeval cities the children joined with their father in acts affecting the patrimony. But during the same period these statutes were welcoming other principles. Thus, the whole Roman theory of the "peculium" was developed, in such wise as again to be considered as "castrense" or "quasi castrense", as "perfectitium" or "adventitium", with all the effects produced by each form under Roman law — that is, in the first two cases, of being the absolute property of the son and so disposable at his pleasure; and ordinarily in the last two cases of giving the management and use to the father; while there was added, by interpretation and extension, all that the Glossators and later jurists were able to construct upon the Roman basis. But in substance the Roman doctrines were never again abandoned, and thus, in the property relations between father and child, the law came to distinguish the estates of each. The family estate belonged to the father, and in its disposition he was free, save for the interference of the State, which placed legal checks upon him, lest he should improvidently waste it. Other property might belong exclusively to the children, by whatever title acquired, and over this, with a few exceptions, the father ordinarily had the right of management and use.

TOPIC 3. EXTINGUISHMENT OF PATERNAL AUTHORITY

§ 358. **Modes.** — In contrast to the permanent "mundium" exercised over the woman, that over males was temporary.[4] The

---

[1] *Cf.* the "sui heredes" of the Roman law. [3] *Rothar*, 125.
[2] *Ante* § 335. [4] *Ante* § 338.

woman also might leave the paternal " mundium ", but as this occurred upon marriage, it did not bring a release from authority, but only a transfer from the father's to the husband's.   Males, on the other hand, became their own masters, when the paternal authority was extinguished and they ceased to be minors or to occupy any other status demanding the continuation of protection over them.   The presumption that they were able, without harm to the family, to provide for themselves, was in general the cause of extinguishing the paternal authority.   Such a condition might show itself in different ways: by the natural development of capacity in the son, measured by his age; or by the father's desire, evidenced by emancipation; or by some cause, preventing a continuance of the paternal authority by the father over the son, and determined by law.

§ 359. **Age.** — The attainment of a certain age was the most common, since a natural reason why all need of protection should cease and with it the power instituted for that purpose, namely the paternal authority.   In Roman law this did not happen, because the " patria potestas " was considered as a right akin to " dominium ", inhering in the father, so that he could not be deprived of it by an accidental or extraneous fact, such as the completion of a certain number of years.   If the voluntary act of the father, or, in exceptional cases, the law, did not dissolve it, the Roman paternal authority was permanent.   Some have thought the same was true in Germanic law,[1] but this opinion is untenable.   In the first place, on reaching the age suitable to bear arms, which marked the attainment of majority,[2] the reason and justification of the paternal " mundium ", namely the need of defence, disappeared.   In the second place, the continuation of the paternal authority is contradicted by the fact, consistently proved by the laws and documents, that the son, on reaching the age of majority, took part in the government of the family along with his father, so that the latter, for certain acts, had need of his son's express consent, which would be inconceivable if the authority of the one were still exerted over the other.   Nor is it an argument to the contrary, that the sons continued to form a part, morally and economically, of the father's family, since this was perfectly possible after the extinction of the paternal authority, as conceived by Germanic law.   With it ceased merely the legal necessity of paternal protection and representation, but not the legal tie between father and son.   Indeed the family bond was strengthened because in the son the father

[1] *Salvioli, cit.,* p. 339.   [2] *Ante* § 304.

acquired a companion in the representation and direction of the home.

Notwithstanding the contrary efforts of the statutes of the mediaeval cities, so servile to Roman theories, modern legal systems have accepted the Germanic principle that, upon attaining an age determined by law, the son was freed from the paternal authority.[1]

§ 360. **Emancipation.** — A father's will to free his son from his authority might be evidenced in two ways : either by an act giving rise to a presumption, or by express declaration.

Such a presumption arose when the father placed the son in a position of itself requiring independence of action and personal responsibility. The example may be cited of the emancipation called " juris germanici ", because peculiar to Germanic law, or " per separatam œconomiam ", because of the fact that gave rise to it, namely, that the son became " sui juris " through the establishment of a separate household, distinct from the father's and with his consent. Marriage was by some laws, as by modern law,[2] another cause of emancipation, based upon the presumed will of the father, who had given his consent. Other laws required that the marriage should be accompanied by the establishment of a separate home. As commerce developed, the exercise of a trade by the son with his father's consent, was still another cause of presumed emancipation. This was the policy of the mediaeval communes, which desired to develop and safeguard commerce.

More common, however, was the emancipation by express declaration. We do not know what special rites were used in the very early Germanic law, save that they were a gift of arms before the assembled people. The traces of a triple symbolic manumission, dating from antiquity, were evidently of Roman origin, and this mode was in fact practised in Italy. With feudalism there evolved the new bond of fealty,[3] which could not co-exist with paternal authority, and so became a cause of the latter's dissolution. Consequently one mode of emancipation was to give the son in " commendation " to the king or other seignior. Later, especially in the statutes of the mediaeval cities, there was a return to the Justinian emancipation, by a declaration by the father before a magistrate or notary, with additional provisions, however, that the father might not emancipate his son before a certain age, four-

[1] [Italian Civil Code, art. 323, fixes the normal age of majority at 21 years.]
[2] Civil Code, arts. 1052, 1386.
[3] *Ante* § 26.

teen, eighteen, twenty, or other, varying with the time and place, and that such an emancipation must be published by means of bans, cried through the streets, or by inscription in the communal registers.   This rule, never later abandoned, led to emancipation as regulated in the law of today.[1]

By emancipation according to the Germanic conception, there did not result the loss of the rights derived from the paternal relationship, especially those of inheritance; nor might father or son thus be exempt from the reciprocal duties of aid and support. The sole important consequence was the son's personal independence and, therefore, the recognition of his capacity to take part in the government of the family.   With this conception modern law accords, limiting the effect of emancipation to capacity for acts of so-called simple administration.[2]

§ 361. **By Provision of Law.** — The interference of the law in severing the paternal authority had its origin in public policy, that is, the prevention of its exercise to the injury of the child, or its incompatibility with greater duties incumbent upon the child.

In the former instance, the law might declare the father unworthy to continue in authority over his son.   In antiquity the law did not have this power, since it did not penetrate the home in order to control the internal life of the family.   Among the Lombards the father's power was also above the law, which declared, however, that in so leaving it, it presumed that he would not abuse it to the injury of his children.   Contrary proof, destroying the presumption, might authorize the law to supervise the father in the exercise of his power.   The way was thus opened; and in fact, from the period of the Franks, but especially under the communal governments of the Middle Ages, when there occurred a considerable concentration of political power, the authority over the child was withdrawn by a legal judgment of " unworthiness " (" indegnità ") against the father, whenever he maltreated the person of the child, dissipated his fortune, was outlawed, condemned to the loss of civil rights,[3] or persisted in adhering to another faith after the conversion of his son to Christianity.[4]

The second reason for the extinction of the paternal authority was that it should not be allowed to conflict with major public interests.   This occurred, in evident analogy to the Roman rule, whenever the son was elevated to any important office, entered the army, was invested with a fief, or received holy orders.   The duties

[1] Civil Code, art. 311.
[2] Civil Code, art. 317.
[3] *Ante* § 299.
[4] *Ante* § 300.

proper to the new status were irreconcilable with, and so effected a liberation from, those other duties which resulted from subjection to the paternal authority.

Its loss through "unworthiness" ("indegnità") still exists in the case of the penal condemnation of the parent [1] or of abuse of the power.[2] On the other hand, loss through appointment to public office is no longer recognized, since for such office the age of majority is a requisite and this wholly terminates the paternal authority.

TOPIC 4. ILLEGITIMATE CHILDREN

§ 362. **Early Status.** — As legitimacy was the basis of the paternal authority, children born of irregular unions were not under the power of the father, but were dependent upon whoever had authority over the mother.[3] The relation, therefore, between such children and their father necessarily differed from that described with regard to legitimate offspring.

By Germanic law illegitimate children were divided into two classes, *natural* and *unlawful*, according as their recognition was or was not possible.[4] Their condition was very different, in that the unlawful, that is, the adulterous, incestuous and spurious, could not be legitimized [5] and so were denied all family rights. Natural children, on the other hand, born of unions which might become perfect marriages, belonged to the paternal branch, even before being legitimized, although their status was naturally inferior to that of legitimate children. This is clearly shown in inheritance from the father, in which natural children were expressly made to share by the law, even in competition with legitimate children, though with less rights; [6] also in the fact that they were made to share, though in the same inferior proportion, in the recovery of the compositions to which the family was entitled, and to participate in the price of the " mundium " of a sister, because along with the rights went the family duties of vengeance and common defense.[7]

§ 363. **Later Status.** — The condition of natural children later changed to their disadvantage. To this feudal law contributed, in that it denied consent to inheritance of the fief except by legitimate children.[8] Nor was the canon law indifferent, with its constant aim to purify marriage and to set it off from other unions,

[1] [Penal Code, art. 22.]
[2] [Civil Code, art. 233.]
[3] *Liutprand,* 126.
[4] *Ante* § 335.

[5] *Liutprand,* 105; *Arechi,* 8.
[6] *Post* § 375.
[7] *Rothar,* 161, 162.
[8] *Post* § 384.

which it opposed not only in themselves but also in their consequences. Children born outside the perfect marriage were more and more considered as strangers to the family; they steadily lost the rights conceded them by Germanic laws and so gradually approached the position of children who were not recognizable. Hence the disfavor with which they were treated by the legislation of the mediaeval cities. Furthermore the communes were in accord with the Church in combating in every possible way the concubinage practised by the clergy, whose children, and with them, consequently, all illegitimate children, were placed in the worst possible condition, in order to root out the causes of their being. They came almost to be placed outside the law; they were excluded from public office; they might not inherit from their father except in the most insignificant measure; they were prohibited from benefiting through entails ("fideicommissa");[1] they were stamped with the stigma of infamy which they could not remove except by a modification of their status; they were placed, for want of paternal authority, under that of the State, and more often under that of the feudal lord, who gravely abused the right.

What remained to the natural child was the right always to support, which the law also conceded to those in the most unfavorable condition, born of adulterous or incestuous unions, as an obligation due by the father during his life, and binding also upon his heirs. This right was related to another conceded by the law, that of inquiry into paternity, in order that the father might be forced to fulfill his duties also towards his illegitimate children. The means adopted was the trial by ordeal, with the test of red-hot iron, to be undergone by the one asserting his filiation to a particular person. The canon law, and on its example also the civil law, admitted other modes of investigation of the paternity of the supposed father, such as reputation, the oath of the mother, the testimony of others, and like means. From these methods there necessarily arose abuses having very serious possibilities and such as to injure the good order and interests of the family. To prevent these the law began to show that dislike of research into paternity which led to its prohibition in the codes.[2] But the question is not yet at rest; the scientist and the legislative reformer maintain that research of paternity should be allowed, and the possibility of abuse removed by appropriate provisions, since it is at the abuse and not the principle itself that the present prohibition is aimed.

[1] *Post* §§ 385–387.   [2] [Civil Code, art. 189.]

CHAPTER VIII

GUARDIANSHIP

TOPIC 1. GUARDIANSHIP BY THIRD PERSONS ("TUTELA")

§ 364. **Ancient Form.** — When by death or other cause paternal authority ceased before the child had attained capacity to govern itself, its protection was assumed by the remaining members of the family, in order to guard, in the person of the minor, the interest of the family (that is, the minor's own interests), of which they were the representatives.[1] As in the early Roman law, Germanic guardianship appeared more as a right than as a duty; as the Roman law gave its exercise collectively to the agnates, so in Germanic law it was given to all members of the family, because all were jointly bound by the duty of defence and all participated equally in the family interests. A very late trace of this may be seen in the powers of interference given to neighbors, even by the statutes of the mediaeval cities, with respect to the mutual interests of families and of their contiguous lands, in which tradition harked back to the time when, on the distribution of the family domain, the nearest neighbors were doubtless relatives.

When relationship began to disintegrate, when it no longer remained united in a single family, the latter's representatives were the nearest relatives only, who, consequently, were always called to the guardianship of the children.[2] But the substitution of a single guardian for the various members of the family, exercising their right in common, came about through the influence of the Roman law, as is shown by the use of the term " tutor ", which, as the office gradually came to be conferred upon a single person, was substituted for the Germanic word " mundoald." The Latin

---

[1] *Rothar*, 188, 265; *Liutprand*, 14.   [2] *Liutprand*, 74, 75.

form was not yet found in the Lombard laws, but it may be discovered in the Carlovingian laws, which were more subject to the action of the Roman law.[1]

Guardianship by a "tutor" possessed different attributes, according as it was exercised over a male or female. Over the latter it was perpetual, and gave rise, in the "mundoald", to important rights over her property, person and acts. Until she emerged from this position, under the influence of more advanced ideas,[2] she was held to be without civil capacity. In the case of males, on the contrary, it ceased with their minority, or with the disappearance of any other cause which had placed them under a guardianship.

The direct aim of the guardian was the tutelage of the family interests; he assumed the complete representation of his ward, acting in the latter's name, but by himself, and not merely intervening to provide the ward, as under Roman law, with the authority needed to complete his imperfect capacity. Representation, thus broadly conceived, really permitted the guardian none but administrative acts, since otherwise serious damage might be done the interests of a ward, totally excluded from the management of his affairs. Indeed, in the early law, none might sue a minor, until Liutprand, to repair the damage which might thus be done to others, gave them the right, while reaffirming the principle of representation by the guardian.[3] Similarly, any alienation of the minor's estate was forbidden,[4] and contrary provisions allowing it, were all exceptions, governing special cases, such as that permitting, to the extent necessary but not beyond, a conveyance for the purpose of marriage, to pay the father's debts, to make a religious gift when on the point of death, or to save the minor from hunger in time of want.[5] Furthermore, the guardian, who acted alone and who, in his ward's interests was protecting merely those of the family, had no other obligation towards his charge than to provide for his needs, according to his family's station. Beyond that, the guardian enjoyed the use of all the ward's property, and need render no account. The ward's best protection was the incapacity of his guardian to perform more than acts of ordinary administration. Later came the right of the ward himself, on reaching majority, if these limits had been exceeded, to demand restoration of his original estate. If, for

---

[1] *Lothar*, 60; *Pepin*, 5.   [3] *Liutprand*, 75; *Lothar*, 60.
[2] *Ante* § 305.   [4] *Liutprand*, 99.
                    [5] *Id.*, 19, 24, 117, 149.

example, the guardian had alienated lands without advantage to his ward, the latter might recover them, without obligation to compensate the purchaser ;[1] or if he had suffered in court through improper representation by the guardian, the latter personally owed him compensation ;[2] and finally in acts of any importance the law controlled the guardian's authority by that of the judge or of members of the family.[3]

§ 365. **Modern Form.** — The character of guardianship by others than the parents (" tutela ") altered as the influence of the Roman law grew. In analogy to its history under that system, it ceased to be a right of the agnates and became a public office, directly in the interest of the person subject to it. An institution affecting public interests, proper for State concern and directed exclusively to the advantage of the minor, such had guardianship already become under the laws of the mediaeval communes, which also had borrowed from the Roman law the consequences of this new principle. Thus the different classes of guardians came again into being. In the 1200 s the testamentary guardianship (" tutela testamentaria ") was revived, which had been unknown to the Germanic invaders of Italy, among whom the use of wills did not exist,[4] and for whom guardianship was a right connected with inheritance. A father, on dying, might, however, recommend his child to any one having his confidence, and from this originated the " tutela pacticia " or " contractual " guardianship of the Middle Ages, wherein the guardian was designated by an agreement between the father and the person of his choice. The judicial appointment of guardians developed along with the idea that the State might interfere in the government of the family, to maintain good order within it. Faint signs of this existed in the Lombard period, in those cases where the king ordered his magistrate to aid the minor.[5] But in the Carlovingian period, with the strengthening of the State and a somewhat greater understanding of the Roman guardianship, the judicial form became well developed. Public authority reached the point of itself appointing a guardian, whenever, by refusal or other cause, none existed.[6] Feudalism continued this system and gave rise to abuses, for, like all others, that of naming the guardian became a seigniorial right, exercised for profit; testamentary guardianship was opposed and judicial appointments, thus artificially rendered necessary, required the payment of money, if they were not sold to the highest bidder.

[1] *Liutprand.* 58.   [3] *Post* § 370.   [5] *Post* § 370.
[2] *Id.*, 75.   [4] *Post* § 388.   [6] *Pepin*, 5.

Under the mediaeval communes, however, the institution was perfected and, with an eye single to the interest of the wards, a special magistracy was created, in order to provide all with the guardian they might require. Whoever nominated the guardian remained his surety; the guardian might be removed; he was again bound to render an account, and he was again circumscribed by the guarantees formerly established by the Roman law.

But along with all these Roman traits, this form of guardianship ("tutela") retained many principles from the Germanic law, from which it derived new qualities. The Roman notion of the "auctoritatis interpositio" was never renewed, even by the Glossators, who, accustomed to the new conditions, saw in the guardian merely the representative and administrator of the ward's affairs. This explains why this Roman idea was never adopted even by the codes. Moreover, guardianship was not yet always and exclusively considered a public office. Traces still endured of the profit which the guardian drew from it, if no longer in the form of a general right of use, at least of a right to appropriate a proportion of the income. So deep-rooted were these vestiges that the last, as for example, those in Sardinia, were abolished only on the introduction of the codes; and even some codes, such as the Austrian, indirectly confirmed them, by providing compensation for the guardian.

The new attributes were those which guardianship, during transformation, acquired through the interposition of public authority. The State not only emerged from the impotency which marked it during the Germanic period, but even exceeded the limits of power which Roman law had assigned to it. The magistrate no longer waited a petition for the appointment of a guardian, but acted of his own motion. He not only extended his authority over his appointee, but also over the legal and the testamentary guardian; and when he did not have the power of nomination he assumed that of confirmation and exacted an oath and surety. Among the legal guardians were the mother and the grandparents, who were never again excluded; every guardian was subordinated to the "family council",[1] to whom he had to account, not only at the end of his trust but annually. Other similar rules were laid down, which are still preserved in present Italian law,[2] among such being the important right of intervention by public authority.

Thus the doctrines of the Italian law of guardianship have been

[1] *Post* § 369. [2] Civil Code, art. 303.

derived from various sources, the Roman law, Germanic principles, and the improvements introduced by the mediaeval communes and legal science.   Each has left well recognizable marks without, however, destroying the unity and harmony of the institution.

TOPIC 2.   INSTITUTIONS OF THE NATURE OF GUARDIANSHIP

§ 366. Protection of the Wife by Relatives. — The large authority of the husband and heirs over the woman in Germanic society and the possible danger of its abuse, especially by the heirs, had from antiquity turned the law towards a provision of defense to be furnished her from another direction than that whence the danger arose.   She always had a right of recourse to the king against an abuse of power by her " mundoald " ;[1] but she was not always in a position to exercise it.   Her most natural and sure defenders were her own relatives, her cognates or blood kin, who were ready to run to her aid, not only at her call but whenever she might be in danger.   When her husband wished to punish her, her relatives must have a voice in the judgment, as happened in the domestic court of the ancient Roman family ; when accused by her husband, it was her relatives' duty to vindicate her in court, by oath or judicial duel ;[2] if the husband, for abuse of authority, was condemned to a composition, part at least belonged to the injured wife's relatives ;[3] it was her relatives who took her back when her husband's heirs mal-treated her ; in fact, it was said that the " reipus " was payable to them by one who married the widow, because it was they who overcame the opposition of the heirs of the first husband.[4]   When the husband conveyed away property belonging to her, her relatives, were present at the act to demand of her if her consent had been given voluntarily or had been forced from her by her husband.[5]   These rules, especially the last, still continued during the period of the mediaeval communes, and only began to disappear when the active intervention of the law placed well defined limits to the marital power, and subjected it to the supervision of the court.

§ 367. Feudal Guardianship. — The guardianship (called " ballaggium ") of an orphan child of feudal parents, differed from ordinary guardianship because to the enjoyment of the feudal property was attached the obligation of services, especially military, which became the duty of the guardian since the minor could

[1] *Rothar*, 182.   [3] *Id.*, 187.
[2] *Id.*, 202.   [4] *Ante* § 332.
[5] *Liutprand*, 22.

not yet perform them. Two consequences followed: first, the guardian must be qualified to perform the feudal services; second, he enjoyed, as in the ordinary guardianship of antiquity, all the profits of the property, as compensation for the services, and owed the ward merely support and education. The right of naming the guardian naturally belonged to the lord of the ward's fief, who was interested not only in the performance of the services but also in the education of his vassal. The lord might, therefore, during the vassal's minority, take possession of the fief himself without entrusting it to a special guardian. But this was no longer possible when fiefs became very numerous; and the appointment of a special guardian became even more necessary, when the lord of all fiefs again became effectively the sovereign, who thus was enabled to make of the appointment a regalia, a prerogative of majesty, as was, in fact, declared by Frederick II. It was then better regulated. Its exercise had to be authorized by the sovereign, who might grant it to a stranger, though he more often gave it to relatives, not excluding those who were entitled to it under the ordinary civil laws, or even women who in that case satisfied the requirement of military service through representatives. The guardian lost the right to appropriate all the profits of the fief; he was allowed to expend only the costs of the guardianship itself and was required to account.[1] In this the guardianship of the feudal law kept drawing closer to that of the civil law and finally became confused with it, when fiefs lost their political importance and when military service was no longer a necessary attribute. With this change sovereigns abandoned the right which they had at first jealously exercised.

§ 368. "Cura" or Guardianship Solely of the Estate. — In Germanic law the two forms of guardianship, the "cura" and the "tutela", were not distinct. All who for any cause needed protection were placed under the guardianship or "mundium" of whoever exercised authority within the family. The basis of such guardianship was in every case to provide not so much for the interests of the ward as for those of the family and the guardian. The revival of the "cura" in Italian law was due to Roman influence, and in fact grew out of the idea that protection should be given the interests of persons not themselves in a position to provide it, though not in a condition to require true guardianship ("tutela"). Such persons were the infirm, physically or men-

[1] "Constitutionis regni Siciliae", III, 30.

tally,[1] and those who would injure themselves by their extrava-
gance, unless the law prevented by its " interdict " and declared
them without capacity.

§ 369. **Family Council.** — When the duties of guardianship
(" tutela ") were concentrated in a single person, the others who
had hitherto had a part in them [2] were not deprived of all share
in the family government. The guardian assumed all the active
functions, as representative and administrator. But the others
preserved something of their ancient position by joining with
him, for counsel and deliberation, in the more serious affairs.
From the combination of the two systems, the Roman with a
single guardian and the Germanic with its guardianship entrusted
to all the relatives, was derived the institution of the " family
council " which was adopted throughout subsequent Italian law.
The first examples were found in the Lombard laws. The council of relatives had to consent to the marriage of the women of the
family; all her relatives had the right to punish a woman who had
compromised the family honor; in any cause in which a minor was
interested, the judge, on deciding, must have before him the
minor's nearest relatives.[3] But the greatest and most orderly
development was given to this institution by the statutes of the
mediaeval cities. Most of these required that deliberation upon
matters of grave concern to minors should be taken by their relatives, in varying number, for the most part two or four, as many
maternal as paternal, or, if there was none, by the same number
of neighbors or friends, who consulted under the direction of the
magistrate. The number of matters upon which the family council was consulted continued to increase in proportion as the law
assumed greater supervisory powers in this direction. Besides
the early functions of providing for the interests of the ward in
important transactions, in litigation, in the partition and alienation
of property, the council extended its jurisdiction over his education, the preparation of the inventory of his estate, the invest-
ment of his property, and finally over the choice and supervision
of the guardian (" tutor "), the receipt and approval of accounts,
and removal. In this way, while the executive side was left
to the guardian, the substantial responsibilities of guardianship
passed to the family council, which, as a domestic magistracy,
preserves these qualities in the present Italian law.[4]

[1] *Ante* § 306.
[2] *Ante* § 364.
[3] *Rothar*, 188, 189, 221; *Liutprand*, 75, 144.
[4] [Civil Code, arts. 249 to 263.]

Chapter IX

RELATIONS BETWEEN FAMILY AND STATE

§ 370. Early History. | § 371. Later History.

§ 370. **Early History.** — When the State had gained consciousness of its rights and at the same time power to exercise them, it
was to its interest that the family, to which it owed its origin and
on which it was founded, should be well regulated. It thus came
to take a part, through its officials, in this control, and this gave
rise to reciprocal relations.

Political interference increased as the rigidity of the family ties
and the power of the head of the house diminished. Before the
State had been formed, the family existed, strongly organized, as
a State in itself. Law, in its earlier stages, halted upon the family
threshold; beyond the father was supreme; when it was in a
position to dominate, it long showed itself uncertain and moved
only step by step. The Lombard laws did not yet dare to punish
a father who exercised his authority in such a way as would have
constituted an abuse and punishable in any other " mundoald."
The reason was found in the respect for paternal authority,
although subsequently, with the weakening of the ancient theories
of family organization, legal justification was sought in the presumption that a father would not abuse his authority. This shows
that the State felt that paternal authority was no longer an absolute bar to its interference in the family régime, whenever there
was need. The authority of the sovereign was henceforth recognized as supreme over all other authorities, and, in the internal
affairs of his State, his character as principal defender [1] led him to
turn his concern towards those persons within the family who
were without defense. He declared that he would provide a
guardian for those who, on the refusal of their agnates, found
themselves without one.[2] The protective function, continuing
to develop, later caused the interests of those in need of defense
to be regarded, even by the sovereign, as a duty rather than as a
right, and this principle was applied not only to those who lacked

[1] *Ante* § 29.   [2] *Pepin,* 5.

protection but also to those who were damaged by its abusive exercise in the hands of persons to whom they were subject.

The guardianship of women was the first to claim the attention of the State, as one which, by its permanency and the very position of woman, might lead to misuse more serious than that over minors.   In fact, the first Lombard laws contained provisions for the protection of women against the arbitrary power of the " mundoald ",[1] while those applicable to minors belonged to a subsequent period.   These latter required that, when a distribution was to be made of an estate in which a minor had an interest, when his property was to be conveyed, when summoned to justice, or when the minor had to pay debts left by his father, — in all such cases a judge, that is, a public official, authorized for this by the king, should intervene, to prevent any danger of damage to the ward's interests.[2]   In these laws certainly neither Roman nor church influence was absent.   Proof may be had in the very words of the law, where it was always declared, in perfect correspondence with words of the canon and Roman law, that the king should choose a godfearing person, and that this royal representative should render his decisions according to justice, finding compensation in what God would render him of good or evil, according to his labors.[3]   In this direction the law continued during the Carlovingian period, with a still greater expansion of the rôle of the State, due to the growing authority of the Church, or to the fact that the revived Empire was an institution of great social protection.   Indeed the Carlovingians not only confirmed the Lombard laws but added others.   The principle was laid down that guardianship (" tutela ") must be directed toward the interests of the person subject to it, not of the person exercising it ; that the king should furnish a " godfearing " guardian to those who were without one; that cases of minors and widows should be the first to be heard in the courts; that guardians should be subject to constant supervision; that it was the bishop's duty to examine their accounts; that it fell to the king to recall them to their duty when they strayed from it.[4]

371. Later History. — With the rise of feudalism, however, these salutary ideas changed.   The duty to provide a guardian for those who had none became a right which was turned to gainful ends, while feudal guardianship, the chief concern of which

---

[1] *Rothar*, 182, 193, 197 ; *Liutprand*, 30, 100, 129.
[2] *Liutprand*, 19, 74, 75, 149.
[3] *Cf. Justinian*, Code, I, 4, 26, § 1.
[4] *Pepin*, 5; *Louis the Pious*, 8; *Lothar*, 102, 106.

was the seignior's interests,[1] gave fresh strength to the ancient theory that the scope of guardianship was not the sole interests of the ward. Under the communal regulations of the Middle Ages, however, when Roman influence was strong and opposition to feudal law great, there was a return to the principle of placing the interests of the minor foremost, and of directing the interference of the State solely to this end. Hence the numerous provisions in the communal statutes covering the proper conduct of the guardian, his appointment and responsibility, the review of his accounts, his removal, the definition of incapacities for the office, and finally the re-incorporation of the subject into public law, so that its regulation might not be set aside by private agreement and so that it should always receive the supervision of public authority. For these needs a special magistracy was created; the " Procurators of St. Mark "[2] at Venice, the wards' " Elders " or " Just Men "[3] at Florence, the office of " Controller of Minors "[4] at Siena, and similar elsewhere. But they did not relieve the head magistrate, podestà or other, from a like obligation; in his oath of office he bound himself also to protect the rights of widows and orphans, and of this custom examples were still extant in the 1300 s. If necessary, the magistrates themselves undertook the guardianship, and this practice continued in Tuscany up to 1767, when Grand Duke Peter Leopold abolished it and limited the judge to appointive and supervisory powers.

In general all laws, subsequent to the statutes of the mediaeval communes, preserved in substance the principles underlying State interference in the interests of the family. These same principles are still today the basis of the State's tutorial authority, exercised by a magistrate ("pretore"), who takes part in the "family council", convoking and presiding over it ;[5] or by the State's attorney (" procuratore del re "), who receives the petitions of persons interested in the proper exercise of the guardianship ;[6] or finally by the courts, which approve the decisions of the family council in matters of special importance.[7]

[1] *Ante* § 364.
[2] "Procuratori di San Marco."
[3] The "Savi" or "Razionali dei pupilli."
[4] "Ufficio del sindacato dei minori."
[5] [Civil Code, art. 251.]
[6] [*Id.*, art. 255.]
[7] [*Id.*, art. 260.]

PART III

DECEDENTS' ESTATES

PART III

DECEDENTS' ESTATES [1]

§ 372. General Character. | § 373. Later Character.

§ 372. General Character. — As the ancient Germanic law spread throughout Italy, two systems of inheritance, essentially different, confronted each other, the Germanic and the Roman. The causes of their diversity were chiefly two: the special organization of the Germanic family, which aimed to accomplish certain objects, chief being the preservation of the family; [2] and the status of landed property, closely linked to the family, and not yet completely liberated from the condition of collective ownership.

Interest in preserving the family had made the system of inheritance by agnates prevail, and it gained in importance in proportion as common village ownership narrowed to family ownership, and as property itself gained in economic importance. Property had to be preserved within the family, that is, to those who remained in it and were in a position to perpetuate it in their persons and names. In other words, inheritance must be through the males, and females were excluded with greater or less strictness according to time and place.

But the law of male succession would have been vain and but a delusion to family interest, if the father had had the power to dispose of the domestic estate at will. This power, therefore, was not given him; his heirs were such by compulsion, and were determined by their positions within the family. The idea was expressed by the saying that heirs were born and not made, since they were given by nature or by God. A first consequence of this was that wills were impossible. An heir was such by his own right; the death of the father was merely the fact through which the right commenced to operate; an heir, therefore, could neither be made nor disinherited. Furthermore it would be improper to speak of an inheritance determined by law, either in the Roman or

[1] [Part III, §§ 372–400 is a translation of *Calisse*, Part III, §§ 87–115.]
[2] *Ante* § 312.

611

modern sense, since that would presume or infer a possible contrasting intent on the part of the decedent. The Germanic succession was invariably a family succession, a necessary consequence of status within the family. The heir, unless he severed the ties binding him to his family, might not renounce his inheritance; denial of an inheritance was equivalent to a repudiation of one's own family; whence the disfavor accompanying such acts throughout the Middle Ages. For the same reason, no act by the heir was necessary to accept the inheritance, which passed to him by law. The idea of an unclaimed estate was wholly unknown. True, by ancient customs, the heir was admitted to the deceased's estate with solemn formalities, banquets, sacrifices, witnesses. But these had no reference to the acquisition of the right; they were largely of religious significance, and furthermore were connected with the entry into possession, which was always effected by public and external formalities, however much it was the natural consequence of the pre-existing right.

Such being the character of the heir in Germanic law, all the subtleties of the Roman law, arising for the most part from the fact that inheritance was regarded from the point of view of the deceased, were unknown to the Germanic system, which looked to the survivor. It did not distinguish between heirs of the whole (" a titolo universale ") and heirs of specific parts (" a titolo singolare "), since all were heirs who shared in the estate; there was no prohibition against agreements affecting successions, since the subject matter was a right already fixed. There was even no legal obligation to pay the decedent's debts, that is, there was no conception of the continuation of the personality of the deceased in the heir. Later such independence in the heirs was no longer found in the laws, which required the payment of the debts of the predecessor in possession.[1] But in two important respects traces remained in the Lombard laws of the contrary principle. When by failure of kin the succession devolved upon the State, it did not pay the deceased's debts;[2] when the heirs were called upon to pay the debts, their liability was limited to the extent of the inherited estate, and the property which they had acquired in any other way remained exempt.[3] In other words, the Germanic system came naturally to the same result as the Roman system had reached exceptionally through the expedient of the " inventory."

[1] *Rothar*, 365, 385; *Liutprand*, 16, 18, 19; *Arechi*, 10.
[2] *Rothar*, 223, 231.   [3] *Liutprand*, 17, 57.

§ 373. **Later Character.** — The rules of the Roman law, to a large extent contrary, but favored by the Church, were naturally certain to influence and modify the Germanic law, although in no other field of the law did this influence penetrate so little or produce less effect.

The most important effect was the acceptance of testamentary succession by the Germanic peoples, hitherto absolutely unknown to their law. But the fundamental Germanic principles of the conservation of the family estate, the total or partial exclusion of women, and the others already mentioned, were not thereby abandoned. Rather did the Roman population accept them also, and out of the fusion of the two systems, which gave rise to the most diverse combinations, there developed a law substantially uniform for all Italy. The testament was everywhere accepted, but it was also everywhere surrounded by limitations of a Germanic character, and agnation still remained the first and fundamental basis of inheritance. Other Roman principles, which came into honor in the schools of jurisprudence, instead of receiving a genuine application, served as habiliments, refinements, a more rationalized exercise of the Germanic principles, which remained the foundation of the system.

For this system to change radically and for Roman doctrines in consequence to be restored to their purity, new social tendencies, away from those of the Middle Ages, were needed. This change came only with the new age, and with the aid of all those resources which made the doctrine of equality prevail throughout civil life. The legislator, ignoring thereby distinctions of sex, primogeniture, origin or kinds of property, was led to treat all members of the family alike, having regard only to natural ties, without, however, denying to the head of the family a reasonable power to dispose of his property.

TITLE I

INTESTATE SUCCESSION [1]

§ 374. The Germanic System. — Contrary to the Roman law, which, from the time of the Twelve Tables, had regulated testamentary succession, the Germanic law knew only legal or intestate succession, meaning by that term a devolution in way depending upon the will, expressed or presumed, of the decedent. As the estate belonged to the family, only those members in a position to continue its existence and defend its dignity, should or could be heirs.

Several persons might fulfill this condition, standing however in diverse relationship to one another, so that it was necessary to adopt some system whereby they would be chosen for the inheritance. What this was is disputed. It is certain, however, that one of the prevailing systems in Germanic law was that known under the name of " graduated-lineal " (" lineare-graduale "). Its elements were two: the line and the degree. The line, called also family, was the whole number of descendants of the decedent or other person under consideration. Thus, there was more than one line. The first was that of the decedent himself, composed, that is, of his children and their descendants; the second was that to which the deceased belonged by origin, that is, his father's, and included, therefore, his brothers and their descendants; the third started with the grandfather of the deceased, and counted also uncles and their descendants; that is, the children of the grandfather, and their issue, were a part of it. And thus the system might be continued backward through generations, at each remove embracing a more far reaching circle of relatives, up to the point at which kinship was considered by law to cease. This seems to be the system indicated by Tacitus: " Si liberi non sunt, proximus gradus in possessione, fratres, patrui, avunculi ": [2] first of all children (first line); next, upon their failure, brothers (second line); if no brothers, then uncles (third line), and so on, as just

---

[1] *Pertile, cit.*, §§ 120–132; *Salvioli, cit.*, part IV, chaps. 33, 35; *Schröder*, "Lehrbuch der deutschen Rechtsgeschichte", §§ 11, 38, 61; *Schulte, cit.*, bk. III, chap. 5.
[2] "Germania", 20.

described. Nor were the relatives specified by Tacitus meant to be considered as individuals, but as groups with their descendants. Otherwise, it would have resulted that a deceased who was survived by descendants but not by immediate issue — by grandchildren, for example — would have had as his heirs his kin belonging to another line, such as his brothers or uncles, instead of those forming his own line or family proper. It is true that representation was not recognized in Germanic succession.[1] But this rule applied only when reckoning by degree, and not by line; that is, it meant that among those composing the same line, no one could be reckoned as taking the place of one who had predeceased, and the nearer degree excluded the more remote; it did not mean that the estate passed to another line, so long as there existed representatives of the deceased's own line or of a nearer line, however far down they might be in that line. For line was not to be confused with degree. Degree was something within the line and concerned solely the propinquity of kin, according to the number of generations intervening, whether computed according to the Roman system or the system proper to the Germanic peoples and followed by the canonists.[2]

Whether the choice of heirs was regulated in this manner by the Lombard law is uncertain. The fundamental law of Rothar lends itself to other interpretations. From early times, the subject has been one of endless dispute.[3] Rothar's law declared that " parens parenti per gradum et parentillam heres succedat." [4] It would seem that the two elements, degree and line (" parentilla "), of the system first described, are here clearly expressed, and that this system, therefore, belonged also to the Lombards. But then it may be argued that Rothar was speaking of the propinquity of the degree only (" per gradum "), and that the added words " per parentillam " indicated that succession by degree was possible, so far as the chain of relationship was recognized, according to the words immediately preceding in the law itself: " Omnis parentilla usque in septimum genuculum nometur." The first opinion, however, seems preferable. Even the Roman law, throughout its various periods, never considered the degree independently of the classes of those called to inherit, but always both in combination.[5] And if degree alone is to be considered in

---

[1] *Post* § 376.　　　　　　　　　　　　　　[2] *Ante* § 321.

[3] "Expositio" to *Rothar*, 153: "Huius legis semper fuit, est et erit inter causidicos contentio."

[4] *Rothar*, 153.

[5] *Justinian*, Novels, CXVIII, CXXVII.

Rothar's law, it must be understood, and in fact was understood,[1] not to refer to descendants, for it is inadmissible that Germanic law could prefer any other relative, no matter how close, to the deceased's own descendants, by whom the name and family were perpetuated.

Other proof of the general diffusion, and, therefore, of the more probable application of the " graduated-lineal " system also by the Lombards, is that it was reproduced in the statutes of the mediaeval cities, which termed the lines " columns " (" colon-nelli "), and which continued to govern until the domination and general acceptance of the Justinian system, with which the present Italian Code substantially agrees.[2]

---

[1] *Cf. Salvioli, cit.*, § 248.   [2] Civil Code, arts. 736 *et seq.*

Chapter X

NORMAL DEVOLUTION

Topic 1. Agnates

§ 375. Descendants.
§ 376. Representation.

§ 377. Ascendants and Collaterals.

Topic 2. Women

§ 378. Early Position.

§ 379. Later Position.

Topic 3. Other Lines of Devolution

§ 380. Husband and Wife.
§ 381. Escheat.

§ 382. Religious Orders.

Topic 1. Agnates

§ 375. **Descendants.** — The children of the deceased were preferred above all others as the legal and necessary heirs.[1] But, since this right came to them by reason of their position in the family, and their ability to fulfill its various purposes, the family had to be legally constituted and the children legitimate, that is, subject to the paternal " mundium ", in order to possess in their own right the perfect status of heirs, preferred above all others. Not, indeed, that only such participated in the inheritance, for the law also admitted the illegitimate children, but in a very different measure, and under different standards. In antiquity, probably all illegitimates were excluded; later such exclusion was maintained only against those born of unlawful unions,[2] while others, that is, natural children, were by the Lombard laws expressly granted participation in the paternal estate. These laws provided that if one died, leaving both legitimate and natural children, the latter together were entitled to one-half of what each of the former received. If, for example, there were two legitimate children, each took two-fifths of the estate, and the half of such share, or one-fifth, was divided amongst the natural children, without regard to number.[3] If among the legitimate there was a daughter but no sons, the inheritance was divided into three parts, of which one went to the daughter, one to the natural children, and one to the nearest agnate kin. If there were more than one daughter, to-

---

[1] *Ante* § 372.   [2] *Liutprand,* 34; *ante* § 362.   [3] *Rothar,* 154.

gether they took a half, and the other half was divided, two-thirds to the natural children and one-third to the nearest relatives. Lacking legitimate children and near relatives, the State took their portion, so that the natural children never took the entire inheritance from their father.[1]

In subsequent legislation and especially in the statutes of the mediaeval communes, the principle of preferring legitimate males was not changed,[2] but the condition of the illegitimate children was made worse.[3]   Even the interpreters of the Lombard law sought to discover a rule of exclusion, basing their theory on laws subsequent to those of Rothar.[4]   But the statutes of the mediaeval cities were expressly hostile, some wholly excluding illegitimates from inheriting from their father, others preferring the most distant relatives, including women, and yet others (the most numerous) assigning them, as against the other heirs, a portion always rather less than that granted by the Lombard law, and sometimes not amounting to more than a mere right to maintenance. It should be observed, however, that as the tie between the deceased and his legitimate heirs grew more distant, the portion allotted to the natural children increased, until, with the total failure of the former, they received the whole.   Uniformity of rule was not yet attained.   The general principles that natural children always shared in smaller portions than the legitimate heirs, that their part increased with the distance of the relationship between the legitimate heirs and the deceased, and that they took the whole estate upon failure of the latter — these formed the basis underlying the great variety found in the laws; and they have been substantially reproduced in the present Italian Code.[5]

§ 376. **Representation.** — As to the other descendants, Germanic law was ignorant of the principle of representation, by which persons, who would not otherwise inherit, do so by stepping into the rights of those who have died prior to the devolution of the estate.   Within a particular line, therefore, the nearer relative excluded the more remote, although the latter could be admitted if the former, whose heir he was, had predeceased him.   Uncles, for example, excluded nephews from competing in the inheritance of a decedent who was father of the former and grandfather of the latter.[6]   This rule may have been a result of the ancient manner

---

[1] *Id.*, 158, 160.   [2] *Ante* § 373.   [3] *Ante* § 363.
[4] *Líutprand*, 1; "Expositio" to *Rothar*, 161, § 1.
[5] Arts. 744, 745, 747.
[6] "Formulae Marculfi", II, 10; *id.* "Sirmondicae", 22; *id.*, "Lindebrogianae", 55, in M. G. H., ed. *Zeumer*, "Leges", V.

of looking upon the succession. The property belonged to the family, and, upon the death of the head of the house, it was to be taken in charge by whoever was in the best position to represent the family, apart from any consideration of individual interests. The nearest relatives received the estate, because at the moment they represented the family, without inquiry whether, had it not been for the predecease of one who would have been their co-heir, other relatives would have found themselves in the same position.

This principle was soon overcome by the opposite doctrine of the Roman law. Some of the first modifications to Rothar's laws were due to the thought that it was against natural justice that, should one die, while one's father still governed the family, one's children should lose the inheritance they would otherwise have received. So it was provided that the descendants of children who predeceased their father should share with the surviving children, but not to a greater extent than the part which would have belonged to their father.[1] Thus the principle of representation entered the Lombard laws, and little by little was extended to other persons not at first considered, and to other laws. The celebrated duel may be recalled, fought at the command of Otto I, between the champions and adversaries of this right of representation in Germany, in which the former were victorious, so that henceforth the principle was generally recognized,[2] while the growing diffusion of the Roman law destroyed the traces of the earlier contrary rule.

§ 377. **Ascendants and Collaterals.** — The Germanic laws made no mention of ascendants as heirs. Rather than from any *a priori* reason, this silence must have been the result of the great difficulty presented by the situation itself, wherein the child would have to be freed from the " mundium " or guardianship of a living father, and have in addition, as it was called, an " œconomia separata ", a situation foreign to the ancient family.[3] But in this matter also the influence of the Roman law was soon felt, and after the 900 s the ascendants were expressly taken into consideration by the Lombard jurists, who gave them a position of preference over all relatives other than descendants. But this same acceptance of Roman rules brought ascendants, in the call to inherit, into line with the nearest collaterals of the deceased. The latter, the brothers, had already been admitted in preference to all other

---

[1] *Grimwald,* 5.
[2] *Pertz,* in M. G. H., "Scriptores", III, p. 440.
[3] *Ante* § 360.

collaterals by the Lombard law;[1] after them the inheritance passed from one relative to another, according to the system of lines and degrees which has been described, or simply of proximity of degree,[2] always holding firmly to the principle of preference for males and exclusion of females and their descendants, not only when the two sexes were in the same degree of relationship toward the decedent, but even when the males were more distant, though within the degree admitted by the law.

The statutes of the mediaeval communes extended to collaterals the principle of representation which Germanic law had accepted only in favor of ascendants.

And further, during the same period, the principle "paterna paternis, materna maternis" was applied wherever collaterals inherited. This meant that the decedent's property was divided into two classes, according as it had been derived by inheritance from the father or the mother. Relatives on the father's side were called to inherit the former, relatives on the mother's side the latter. This was the "jus recadentiae" or "jus revolutionis", which was retained by the laws of the intermediate period and adopted by the French Code,[3] but not by the Italian, which, along with the privilege of agnates, abolishes all other causes giving rise to difference of treatment among those who, by natural ties and the demands of justice, are in a parity of relation to the decedent.[4]

TOPIC 2. WOMEN

§ 378. **Early Position.** — The general principle that females were postponed to males, was not applied with equal rigor by all Germanic laws. Some admitted them to share in the personal property only, such as that alone which the head of the house might dispose of, when land was held in common or had not yet wholly emerged from that state.[5] Others, less strict, excluded women from the property forming the family substance, inherited from ancestors and transmissible solely to the males within the family proper, but admitted them to all that had entered the deceased's estate by other channels.[6] Still others, the most severe of all, provided that a woman had no right save to her trousseau (" corredo "), given her on marriage, or to a suitable maintenance so long as she remained unmarried in the paternal home. Such were

---

[1] *Liutprand*, 17, 18.
[2] *Rothar*, 153.
[3] [French Civil Code, art. 732.]
[4] [Ital. Civil Code, arts. 722, 736.]
[5] *Post* § 408.
[6] *Post* § 410.

the Lombard laws.[1]   And this exclusion of women, a consequence of the family structure, must also have operated, in the earliest period, in the absence of descendants, with regard to the other agnates, no matter how distant from the decedent.

However, a change soon took place.   When there were no male descendants, women were called by all systems to share in the inheritance, in proportion depending upon the degree of their relationship and upon the position of the males with whom they competed.   Precise rules were formulated by the Lombard law. When the decedent was without sons but left a daughter, the latter had a right to a third; if more than one daughter, they shared together one-half of the estate; the remainder in both cases went to the nearest male relatives, and if none, to the State.[2]   Later this limitation was also withdrawn, and the laws of Liutprand established that, whenever there were no sons, the daughters should inherit the entire paternal estate, except what had been received in the form of " guidrigild " or composition, which always went to the male relatives, having been derived from the right of private revenge, for which women were unfitted.[3]   Nor was any difference made in this rule between unmarried and married women; all shared equally, except that whatever had been received on marriage as " faderfio "[4] was charged against her in the computation.[5]

Attention next turned to other female relatives of the decedent. The Lombard laws were silent as to a mother, and the jurists interpreted this as excluding her since, in the female line, the reasons for ignoring ascendants were even more serious.[6]   On the other hand, the Lombard laws early took cognizance of the decedent's sisters. The reason was that the brother's "mundium" enjoyed in general the same efficacy as the father's,[7] and, therefore, the sister's position was not regarded as differing greatly from the daughter's. For the most part, they were treated alike.   In fact, in the early period they were called to share with the daughters in one-half of the estate, whenever, for want of legitimate male descendants, this was admissible;[8] and when later, under the same facts, the daughters' rights were extended to the whole estate, the same

---

[1] *Rothar*, 181; *Liutprand*, 102.
[2] *Rothar*, 158, 159.
[3] *Liutprand*, 1, 13.
[4] *Ante* § 344.
[5] *Rothar*, 199; *Liutprand*, 2.
[6] *Ante* § 377.
[7] *Rothar*, 181, 195–197; *Liutprand*, 5, 12, 31.
[8] *Rothar*, 160.

rights enured to sisters, though a distinction was made between the unmarried and the married. If the decedent left no children at all, both classes succeeded equally; but if daughters survived, only the unmarried sisters shared with them.[1] Finally attention turned to those sisters of the deceased's father who remained unmarried at home, and they too, if there were neither sons nor daughters, were admitted with the deceased's sisters to a division of the inheritance.[2]

As to the inheritance of the woman's estate, it regularly devolved upon whoever had the "mundoald's" power over her.[3] The law looked to this relationship alone, so that not only the male relatives who did not possess it, but also the female, who could not, were invariably excluded from the woman's estate. But here also the rule was moderated. First the law considered the case in which, as a punishment, the "mundoald" had lost his right to inherit from his female ward; her children were then admitted as heirs.[4] Later the children were always preferred above all others.[5] Sisters were also considered; and it was provided that, where one of several sisters died unmarried, her surviving sisters, both unmarried and married, should be her heirs and no concession was made in favor of the "mundoald" beyond the measure of his right of representation through the "mundium", that is, beyond the value of his authority over her.[6] These were isolated rules, surrounded by many limitations, always interpreted in the strictest possible manner, introduced into the law, not in execution of any general design of reform in the laws of succession, but, case by case, to remedy some defect in the existing system.[7] Nevertheless these changes sufficed to improve the rules of Germanic succession and furthermore to give rise to the sentiment that even women had rights, to violate which was unjust.[8]

§ 379. **Later Position.** — This sentiment, however, did not triumph in the laws for many centuries to come. Feudalism and the policies of the mediaeval communes were no less damaging to the recognition of the rights of women than the organization of the Germanic family. The mediaeval statutes excluded the woman from succeeding to the family estate, out of favor to the agnates ("propter masculos"), or because of what she had previously

---

[1] *Liutprand*, 3, 4.
[2] *Astolf*, 10.
[3] *Rothar*, 188, 215; *Liutprand*, 145.
[4] *Rothar*, 200; *Liutprand*, 130.
[5] *Henry I*, 1.   [6] *Liutprand*, 14.   [7] *Id.*, 145, art. 10.
[8] "Formulae Marculfi", *cit.*, II, 12: "Impia inter nos consuetudo tenetur ut de terra paterna sorores . . . portionem non habeant."

received by way of a marriage portion ("propter dotem"), but also to prevent any diminution of the wealth or power of the commune, through marriage with an outsider ("propter nuptias extra territorium"). For these reasons the desire to favor the agnates resulted in applying to the devolution from women (to whom the "mundoald" could no longer succeed, as guardianship over women more and more lost ground) the same principles regulating inheritance from males, by which males were always preferred. Thus, although such rigor was not general, the rule was sometimes pushed to the point of depriving the daughters of their mother's estate, in order to give it to her husband's sons by a former marriage. These principles were not substantially abrogated until modern times. During the course of the intermediate period of legislation, they were merely moderated, whenever and wherever they appeared too rigid. But to any mitigation was opposed the interest of the agnate family, who fought with weapons furnished by the law itself. One of these was the trust-entail ("fideicommissum");[1] another was the practice of making the woman, on receiving her marriage portion, waive whatever right she might have in the family estate. Such waivers were valid under the Germanic system, which permitted contracts affecting inheritance,[2] and later laws upheld them, even those, as late as the second constitution of the Cisalpine Republic, which for the rest destroyed the ancient system. This, however, was not generally abolished until the end of the 1700 s, under the fire of the new principles of equality, which today inspire all systems of law.

Topic 3. Other Lines of Devolution

§ 380. **Husband and Wife.** — Through the "mundium", or marital authority, the husband acquired the property of his deceased wife,[3] in such wise that all other rights yielded to his. Even when Liutprand permitted sisters to inherit from a deceased sister, he made an exception if the deceased sister was married, because in that case her husband would be her natural heir;[4] so also, where a deceased woman left children, they could only inherit if the father (her husband), because of abuse of his powers, had been deprived of the marital authority, to which the right of succession inhered.[5] If, therefore, the marriage was without "mundium", the husband, neither in his own right, nor through his children,

---

[1] *Post* § 385.   [2] *Ante* § 372.   [3] *Ante* § 350.   [4] *Ante* § 378.
[5] *Rothar*, 200; *Liutprand*, 130.

had any claim over his deceased wife's estate.   In such a case her relatives who retained the "mundium" inherited all; and the same was true when the husband had lost the "mundium" and no issue was born of the marriage.

After the Lombard period the husband's right was limited. The Frankish laws gave the father only the usufruct or life enjoyment of his wife's property, the title passing to the children; if there were no children, the father received the estate; but a part only, for her relatives shared with him.   These were substantially the principles adopted by Henry I, when, in 1019, he ruled that the husband should be his wife's heir, provided there were no children.[1]   By implication the children were thus preferred to the husband in the inheritance of the maternal estate; in other words, in the children the husband encountered a limitation to his status as heir of his wife, unknown to the Lombards.

In the statutes of the mediaeval communes no uniform principle prevailed; a mass of differing rules was in force.   Some followed the laws of Henry I, preferring the children to the husband; others, on the other hand, gave the latter precedence, in accord with the early Lombard law; others followed the Frankish rule, granting the husband either the use or absolute ownership of his wife's property, but always in varying measure.   Sometimes it was of her whole estate, sometimes only of the marriage portion ("dos"), and in the latter case calculated, sometimes according to the number of children, sometimes by reference to what the husband had given as a dowery ("contrados"), or as a widow's allowance ("vidualizio").[2]   All this, furthermore, was subject to the condition, rarely broken, that the marriage was perfectly regular, and that this fact had been demonstrated by proof of the solemnities accompanying the celebration, and of cohabitation for at least a year.

The wife's position with reference to her husband was different. In the Germanic period the law gave her no right save to the settlements known as the "mefio" and "morgengabe", made by her husband or required of him by law.[3]   These belonged to her, so that if she left the marital home she might take them with her, or later claim them, when called to share in the distribution of the estate in which they had accumulated.[4]   And now that these settlements were never lacking, the laws gave the widow no invariable right of inheritance from her husband.   When they did rec-

[1] "Capitulare italicum", Henry I, 1, ed. *Padelletti*, "Fontes."
[2] *Ante* § 348.   [3] *Ante* § 345.   [4] *Ante* § 378.

ognize her, it was to reëstablish legally the very settlements which the husband had failed to make. The widow's "tertia collaborationis " of the Frankish law was based upon a different principle, namely, to compensate her for her industry, which, like the husband's, had increased the family income.[1]

Similar principles were found in the statutes of the mediaeval communes, save that under them, due to the resurgence of the Roman law, the latter's rules were imitated in regulating inheritance between husband and wife as in other matters. Besides the " quarta uxoria " to the widow, the basis of this succession was principally the " bonorum possessio unde vir et uxor ", by which, in the absence of relatives, the surviving was made the heir of the predeceasing spouse. This was in fact accepted by the legislation of the communes and continued, substantially unchanged, throughout all the subsequent history of Italian law.

§ 381. **Escheat.** — The fisc, that is the patrimony of the State, called by Germanic law " curtis regia " or " publicum ", and confused with that of the prince,[2] acquired the estates of individuals under various circumstances, in addition to confiscation, which was of frequent occurrence.

One such instance was when the property of the deceased was without an owner, for lack of persons having capacity to inherit, so that, there being no other heirs, the State inherited.[3]

This might result in two ways: either there were no relatives within the most remote degree of legally recognized relationship, or such relatives had been denied capacity to succeed, as a punishment for misconduct.[4] In both cases the State was subrogated to the rights of heirs who were lacking or had been declared " unworthy." Both situations might arise with respect to the whole estate upon entire failure of relatives capable of inheriting, or with respect to part only of the estate, whenever one class of relatives entitled to share failed while others existed. The latter's share was not increased by failure of the former; the State became a co-heir. For example, the estate being divisible among daughters, natural children and agnates,[5] if the last were lacking, the State shared with the daughters and the natural children.[6]

There were also persons to whose estates the State had a right to succeed, because of some quality inseparable from their condition. The king, who was considered as their patron, inherited

---

[1] *Ante* § 349.
[2] *Ante* § 36.
[3] *Rothar,* 223.

[4] *Id.,* 158–160.
[5] *Ante* § 375.
[6] *Rothar,* 163; *Liutprand,* 17, 18.

from freedmen (" liberti "), manumitted in a way to sever all ties with their former patron, if they died without children.[1] The same was true of illegitimate children, since they too were under a public guardianship (" tutela "). It was this right, on failure of legitimate issue, that the feudal law called bastardage (" bastardaggium "). Public guardianship was exercised also over foreigners, and the State, therefore, had a right to inherit from them also. The Lombard law limited this right to the case of the foreigner who died leaving no legitimate children ; [2] but other laws, *e.g.* those of the Franks, did not distinguish, but made the fisc the heir of all foreigners, and so the law continued so long as the right of " albinaggium " endured.[3]

§ 382. **Religious Orders.** — From the time of the Roman law [4] churches and religious orders inherited from their clergy and members. This principle, confirmed by the canons, passed into Germanic law, and was, throughout the Middle Ages, a source of great enrichment of ecclesiastical domains. In many places the bishop had the right to succeed to property left without an owner, to claim from the heirs a portion of the estate, called the " mortuarium ", to inherit the property of Jews placed under his jurisdiction,[5] or of persons condemned by ecclesiastical law. Rights also belonged to asylums for the poor, hospitals, and other religious bodies, in manner and measure varying under different systems of law, and of these rights traces have survived to recent times. The practice can still be remembered when a notary, on drawing a will, was obliged to ask the testator if he wished to benefit the Church or some charitable institution of his neighborhood and to note the testator's answer in the will.

[1] *Rothar*, 224; *Liutprand*, 77.
[2] *Rothar*, 367.
[3] *Ante* § 298.
[4] *Justinian*, Code, I, 2, 20; Novels CXXXI, c. 13.
[5] *Ante* § 301.

Chapter XI

SPECIAL SYSTEMS OF DEVOLUTION

Topic 1. Feudal Succession

§ 383. General Character.	§ 384. Particularities of Feudal Succession.

Topic 2. "Fideicommissa" (Trust-Entailed Estates)

§ 385. General Character.	§ 387. History Since A.D. 1500.
§ 386. Particularities.	

Topic 1. Feudal Succession

§ 383. **General Character.** — Property subject to feudal bonds, even when the fief was considered as a simple patrimonial right, possessed so special a character that it required, with respect to inheritance, as to other matters, a body of rules different from those applied to the ordinary case.

The inheritance of a fief affected not only the tenant and his family but also the grantor, that is, the seignior, whose rights remained unaltered, notwithstanding the change of persons produced by succession; this evidently, therefore, required a regulation differing from the ordinary. Furthermore in the grant of a fief, as in any gift, the grantor might impose as many conditions as he chose, and so fix a special order of descent. Consequently, in establishing the heirs to the fief, regard had to be paid to the grant rather than to the rules of the common law. Around these grants grew up such a variety of special customs that it is impossible to do more than describe their general character.

It is also to be remembered that to the possession of the fief was united an obligation to perform certain services, demanding special qualifications, so that persons could not inherit unless they were competent in these respects. The obligation of military service, for example, produced, by strict law, the incapacity of women, of those physically disabled, and of the clergy, to whom the canon law forbid the use of arms. And finally, it should not be forgotten that, as a rule, the possession of a fief created nobility, and, therefore, another special condition of feudal inheritance was that the

627

heir was or might be noble.   Illegitimate children, those born of
morganatic marriages, Jews, heretics, convicts, and all who were
barred from the noble class were excluded in the devolution of
feudal property.

For these reasons, that is, the rights of the seignior, the stipulations in the grant, the qualification for feudal service, and the
nobility inhering in the fief, the rules governing the inheritance of
fiefs drew away from the common law and acquired a particular
character of their own.

§ 384. **Particularities of Feudal Succession.** — This special
quality was mainly seen in three features, if we restrict ourselves
solely to general qualities.

The first was the exclusion of many persons admissible to ordinary succession.   Thus, if the fief was " pazionato ", *i.e.* constituted, with regard to its inheritance, with the formula " tibi et
filiis ", then, of all the persons who might be heirs of the deceased
generally, none was considered so of the fief who did not possess the
quality of descendant.   And of these again all did not have capacity to inherit.   Thus, illegitimate descendants might not inherit,
since the descent had to be by lawful marriage ; nor might adopted
children, since the element of legality had to unite with that of
blood descent ; and so of morganatic children, since they did not
take the noble status of their father ; and of legitimatized children,
because the stigma of their origin could not be removed.[1]   Exceptions to these rules might of course find place in the intent of the
grantor of the fief, as when, for instance, the fief was " hereditary ",
that is, granted by the general formula " tibi et heredibus ", in
which case it was transmissible not only to descendants but to
collaterals and all others designated by law as allodial heirs.   But
here too a restriction arose in view of the conditions necessary for
the possession of a fief.   Ascendants were excluded,[2] as also ecclesiastics [3] and females, in the absence of a stipulation to the contrary.
Such pacts were not rare, and might even be implied from the fact
either of a grant having been made to a woman, or of acquiescence
in her tenure.   Thus the custom gained force that upon failure of
the masculine line, the female should inherit.   The same was true of
ecclesiastics.   The fief in such cases remained obligated to the usual
services, among them military service, which the possessors performed through substitutes, placed over the vassals for this special
purpose.   However, it was not rare to see women and ecclesiastics
themselves take arms and follow their seignior in the field.

[1] "Libri feudorum", II, 26.   [2] *Id.*, II, 50.   [3] *Id.*, II, 26.

A second quality of feudal succession was that ordinarily it might not be divided among several heirs. In this respect fiefs were divided into those " jure langobardorum " and those " jure francorum." In the former, when several persons stood in equal degree to inherit, according to the ordinary rules, division among all was admitted " per capita " or " per stirpes ", as circumstances required. By Frankish law, on the other hand, the fief was not divisible, and so was not partitioned among all the heirs of the last tenant, but was given to the eldest, *viz.* the firstborn, if the inheritance passed to males, and if to females, to the eldest unmarried, these being preferred to married daughters. This rule was first made general in Naples and Sicily, through the Norman conquest, and then spread elsewhere. And Italian laws, until the last years of the 1700 s, generally sanctioned the indivisibility of feudal property, because it provided a better guarantee of the rights of the seignior, who could more easily obtain performance when they devolved upon a single person, and means were not lacking to satisfy them.

Lastly, feudal devolution produced certain obligations peculiar to the heir. Like, indeed, every new possessor by whatsoever title, he was bound to ask and obtain a new investiture of the fief ; he had also to give the oath of fealty and pay the lord a sum, called " laudemium ", from " laudare ", that is, to commend, referring to the approval of the new feudatory by the seignior, and called also "relief", from " relevare ", to " take up " the fief, which otherwise would have lapsed to the overlord. This practice, the purpose of which was the recognition of the seignior's right, by a payment for the renewal of the feudal grant, was derived from custom. The law of 1037 of the Salic king, Conrad, declared that it was the custom of " valvasors " to offer arms and horses to their seigniors, and that this custom he extended to minor feudatories, for whose advantage the law was intended.[1] Nevertheless, it only gradually became generalized and, in so doing, was transformed into a money payment, variously determined, but usually either corresponding to a fraction, a fortieth or a twentieth of the value of the fief, or to its yield for a fixed period, as for a year or a half year. Examples existed, however, of fixed sums, as in the Sicilian " constitutions ", whereby the " laudemium " might in no case exceed the value of ten ounces of gold.[2]

[1] [*Calisse*, "Storia del diritto Italiano", "Diritto Publico", p. 200, much abridged at § 38, *ante.*]
[2] "Constitutiones regni Siciliae", III, 22.

TOPIC 2.   "FIDEICOMMISSA" (TRUST-ENTAILED ESTATES) [1]

§ 385. General Character. — In the case of the "fideicommissa" (trust-entailed estates), it is also true that the special features of the succession resulted from the peculiarities of their creation. These were determined by the purpose of the "fideicommissum", which was the maintenance of the family in the assured possession of the ancestral estate, by protecting it as well against the possessor himself, with whose own property it was not confused, as against those who would have taken it from the agnates. Against its possessor the property subject to the "fideicommissum" was protected by impressing upon it a perpetual inalienability and indivisibility; against one who might withdraw from the agnate line, protection was afforded by a preëstablished system of succession, by which it descended within a determined family. Inalienability, indivisibility, family link, preëstablished order of succession — these were the characteristics of the "fideicommissum", which evolved little by little and reached its full development in the 1500 s.

The qualities of the trust-entail depended upon its act of creation. This might be a will, whereby the whole or part of the estate was affected by the "fideicommissum"; or it might be a contract, either controlling the future succession, or constituting a family agreement, or an added stipulation in a gift, or other mode. It determined the particular type of the entail, *i.e.* perpetual or precarious, absolute or conditional, special or general, and so on. But these particularities might not be inconsistent with the qualities, already described, which constituted its very essence and from which consequently flowed the rules for its governance, among which were those relating to its succession.

[1] [The "fideicommissum" or precatory disposition by will of the Roman law was indeed a "trust." Intended as a mode of circumventing the restrictions of the strict law as to legatees, they were at first invalid and later came to have obligatory force in Roman equitable jurisdiction. The "fideicommissum" of the Middle Ages, while the descendant of the Roman institution, attained an immense extension through feudalism, since it served to check the gradual subdivision of lands among heirs and to preserve the estates of the nobles intact through generations. Whereas it originated in Roman law as an entreaty addressed to a person of confidence to see that a third person should benefit who was incapable of taking in strict law, it became, under feudalism a gift, testamentary or inter vivos, to an immediate donee to be enjoyed for a period and passed on intact to a second designated donee whose rights might be subjected to the same conditions, and so on through generations. It is these feudal "fideicommissa" which are here studied by *Calisse*, and the Translator has preferred to call them trust-entails rather than trusts, since he feels that they more nearly approach the conditional fee of the English common law than the "use" or "trust" that developed in English equitable jurisdiction.]

§ 386. **Particularities.** — From inalienability arose the consequence that the person called to succeed to the " fideicommissum " might in no manner lose or see his right diminished, since it belonged to him, not through his predecessor in possession, but through him who first created the " fideicommissum " (" ex pacto fundatoris ", " ex providentia majorum "). Consequently, a renunciation of the inheritance by one who should have preceded did not injure the right of the one called subsequently to inherit; nor could one be made to answer for the acts of an immediate predecessor, with respect to the " fideicommissum ", since it was bound to be transferred subject only to those conditions which its founder had established.

Indivisibility and limitation to a determined family excluded many persons who would ordinarily have had capacity to inherit. Being indivisible, but one member of the family obtained its possession; since it could not leave the family, those members who withdrew were ineligible. Thus females and younger sons had no rights. As compensation, however, they might have assured them from the income a marriage portion or provision, that is an " apanage ", consisting of a right of maintenance within the family or of suitable means of maintenance elsewhere. No sum was fixed for the apanage, and this consequently gave rise to questions, for the solution of which different standards were adopted. The laws of Victor Amadeus II left the determination of the sum to the Senate; at Naples it was provided that the right of cadets should consist in the usufruct or enjoyment of the undisposable portion of the estate (" legittima "),[1] calculated according to the rules of the Roman law. The legal nature of the apanage was variously described according to the point of view from which it was regarded. It was a personal right of the holder, extinguished by his death and not passing to his heirs; in him who bore the burden, it was an obligation to certain and periodic performances; as a charge upon the " fideicommissum ", it was a right " in rem ", in the nature of the " jura in re aliena."

As the order of inheritance was fixed at the time of the creation of the " fideicommissum ", regard was necessary, as in the case of the fief, to the constituent act, rather than to the rules of the common law, in determining the line of devolution. The possible combinations were various. By the rule of the " maggiorasco ", the relative nearest in degree of the last possessor was called to inherit, regardless of line;[2] if several were of the same degree, the

[1] *Post* §:399.   [2] *Ante* § 374.

eldest was preferred.   Where, however, the line and not proximity
of degree was made the basis, so that the succession must pass to
the descendants of the first possessor, and among them to the
eldest, even though not the nearest relative of the last possessor,
the rule was called the "seniorasco" or "seniorato."   The
"juniorasco" was the reverse of that last described: here the
youngest of the family was called to succeed.   This last system
was perhaps the result of ancient Germanic traditions of the
nomadic period, when sons, as they reached a suitable age, left
their father's house in search of new homes, so that only the
youngest remained in the paternal household at his father's death
and became his heir, the others, having already received their
share on departing.   But of all the systems the commonest was
always that of primogeniture.   The inheritance passed from first-
born to first-born among the descendants of the first possessor.
If the first-born predeceased his father without leaving issue, the
right passed to the possessor's other sons, of whom the eldest was
always preferred.   If he had no other sons, the eldest brother
inherited; brothers failing, the uncle was called; and so on,
passing, according to the lineal system, from one line or family to
the other, preferring the relative nearest in degree to the last
possessor, and, among those of equal degree, the eldest.   Those
newly called to succeed transmitted the "fideicommissum" to
their own first-born, who was always in the line of descent from
the first possessor.   If the direct line of descent failed entirely,
the same transfer was made from the line of the first possessor as
was made in the case of subsequent possessors — the "fideicommissum" was given to that descendant of the brother, uncle
or other relative of the first possessor, who would actually have
been in a position to take, if, from the beginning, the "fideicommissum" had been given to his line of descent.

§ 387.   **History Since 1500.** — With the 1500 s, "fideicommissa"
spread rapidly.   Besides being a means of preventing the disper-
sion of the family property, they enjoyed the favor of the laws;
to own one was the ambition of all who aspired to nobility, or who
merely wished to preserve what their labor had accumulated.
All, therefore, who had something to dispose of, though but little,
had recourse to the creation of "fideicommissa", so that, by the
end of the 1600 s, the greater part of landed property was thus
entailed.

Then disadvantages appeared.   A great amount of land was
withdrawn from commerce; agricultural improvement was dis-

couraged, since the possessor had no other interest than to extract the greatest profit at the least expense, without concern for its future impoverishment. Credit was limited, because such lands could not be used as security, save with respect to their income, which also bore the burden of the marriage portion, the apanage, and the expenses of administration and maintenance. To pay the debts accumulated against them, the "fideicommissa" were often placed under the administration of the courts; they created unfair differences of condition among members of the same family, damaging not only to the family itself, but also to society.

It was not long, therefore, before a movement against trust-entails manifested itself. In France the Encyclopaedists, in Italy, the economists opened the attack, and the effect was soon felt in legislative reforms. At first limitations were put upon the spread of such estates. The right to create "fideicommissa" was denied to all save the nobility by Victor Amadeus II, Francis III of Modena, Francis of Lorraine and the Code of the Two Sicilies. By the Piedmontese and Modenese laws, the Tuscan law of June 22, 1747, and the papal "motu proprio" of 1834, they were permitted only to apply to lands or to property similarly treated, such as a collection of paintings or objects of special value. The period of inalienability was limited; that is, the law forbade a perpetual entail, the property becoming again free after a certain number of transfers, four, for example, according to the Piedmontese laws, two according to those enacted by Maria Theresa. From limitation the law next passed to prohibition. Peter Leopold, Grand Duke of Tuscany, was the first, by his legislation of 1782 and 1789, to order the unshackling of all existing "fideicommissa" and to prohibit the creation of new ones, thereby anticipating the French Revolution,[1] which made the abolition general. The Cisalpine Republic dissolved all entails in 1797, and this movement, effective in 1798 in Piedmont, Naples and Rome and extended also in 1806 to Venetia, became common to all parts of Italy occupied by French arms. But the abolition was but temporary, for the French Empire restored the "fideicommissa" as a means of rewarding those faithful to it and of creating a nobility attached to it; and after the Empire, the "fideicom-

[1] [Decree Nov. 14, 1792. It was natural for the French Revolution to abolish feudal entails of this sort. The prohibition was renewed in the Napoleonic Code, Art. 896, where they are called "substitutions." Napoleon himself, by Decree, March 30, 1806, and "Senatus-consulte", Aug. 14, 1806, restored the "majorat", which was simply a "fideicommissum" stipulating descent through the eldest male child. The future creation of "majorats" was prohibited by the law of May 12, 1835.]

missum " returned to favor in the laws of all the restored Italian governments.   Not, however, without an effort to correct evils. To this end, not only were the limitations of the period prior to abolition retained, but fresh ones were enacted.   Some required sovereign consent to the creation of trust-entails ; others restricted them to lands and houses of not less than a certain value, as for example 15,000 crowns by Pius VII's decree of 1816; while yet other appropriate limitations were laid upon them.

Thus did this institution descend to the period of the present Code, which, obedient to economic interests and the principle of equality, abolished it in every possible form.[1]

[1] Art. 899.   [It is here called "sostituzione fedecommessaria", all "substitutions" not being prohibited.]

TITLE II

TESTATE SUCCESSION [1]

CHAPTER XII

INTESTABLE PERIOD

§ 388. Germanic Law.
§ 389. Adoption; Gifts in View of Death.

§ 390. Contracts Affecting Inheritance.

§ 388. **Germanic Law.** — The organization of the family and the link which bound its property to it deprived the head of the house of any power to alienate even the smallest part of the patrimony. In antiquity the Germanic peoples, therefore, could not dispose by will;[2] their laws did not recognize the will until they yielded to the contrary principles of the Roman law, which had the support of the Church. Intestability was complete, not only in that there were no true dispositions by last will, but also in that the same end could not be obtained by other means, as by a "donatio mortis causa", which was of testamentary character, *i.e.* unilateral and revocable. Adoption, too, was really a contract affecting a future inheritance and therefore transferred the estate to the person whom the owner, by the adoption, designated.[3] But it differed altogether from the will, or "donatio mortis causa." Its purpose was to procure an heir for the family, and hence flowed two important consequences, which could not possibly have found acceptance in testamentary dispositions. The first was that there must be no issue, or that none must survive; the second was that freedom of the party disposing ended with the very act of adoption, for the adopted, placed in the position of a true child, became as such the lawful heir, rendering the transfer of the estate irrevocable.[4] The will, on the other hand, was by nature essentially revocable; the survival of children was no obstacle, save that the will might not impair the rights which the law assured them.

---

[1] *Pertile, cit.,* §§ 121–128; *Salvioli, cit.,* part IV, chaps. 34–36.
[2] *Tacitus,* "Germania."
[3] *Ante* § 336.
[4] *Charlemagne,* 78.

§ 389. **Adoption; Gifts in View of Death.** — Little by little, however, the character of contracts affecting inheritance, through adoption, changed, and they became more like the " donatio mortis causa " of the Roman law.   The reasons of this later development were the example of the Roman population, who continued to employ the will; the desire, encouraged by ecclesiastical exhortation, to dispose of a small part of the family estate; the advantage of avoiding a total exclusion of women, and of having at hand a means of rewarding the more deserving children; the growing sense of individual proprietorship, accompanied by a weakening of the ancient family ties.   Under these influences the adoption of an heir did not fail to acquire new qualities.   Failure of children came to be no longer necessary; it was enough that their legal rights should be preserved, because the purpose was no longer to supply the want of an heir, but rather to make specific gifts independently of the existence of the heir.   Such acts, which constantly and more closely approximated the " donatio mortis causa ", were then deprived of their irrevocable nature.   The person, in whose favor the disposition had been made, did not become owner from the termination of the arrangement; the transferor remained proprietor until the fulfillment of the condition, that is, until his death.   With this change the ancient formalities of the act disappeared, especially those of publicity and of the gift of the " launegild ", or compensation to the donor.[1]   These innovations were at first opposed; in fact a law of Charlemagne prohibited a second alienation of something already appropriated to another, that is, he imposed irrevocability upon such donations.[2] But all opposition proving ineffectual, the new gifts resumed their development and became genuine gifts in view of death (" donationes post obitum "), according to the fundamental principles of the Roman law.

§ 390. **Contracts Affecting Inheritance.** — Thus transformed, the ancient contract affecting inheritance prepared the way for the will.   This object once gained, however, the earlier contract did not disappear, but continued alongside the will, employed for special purposes and forming a third means, besides the testament and the provisions of the law, by which title passed to an heir.   The contract over a future succession, for example, was long made use of by two or even more families, who, as it were, by a fiction, regarded each other as brothers and created each other reciprocal heirs, so that when one died out, the surviving

[1] *Rothar,* 174.   [2] *Liutprand,* 73.

family succeeded.   Contracts over future successions, of varying nature and scope, might be concluded between husband and wife, either as part of the marriage act itself, or otherwise.   The renunciation by a woman, on receipt of her marriage portion, of all right in the family estate was also a contract affecting inheritance, made for the benefit of the brothers or other male relatives.   Such agreements, of which examples might be multiplied, held strictly to Germanic principles, especially that of irrevocability, both because based on the ancient Germanic law, and also because the will, now of general use, became the means employed to dispose of one's property, while reserving the power to alter the disposition.   A difficulty, however, arose when these contracts, acceptable because suited to social conditions, had to be reconciled with the principles of the Roman law, to which it was customary to seek justification for everything.   By some jurists they were considered as gifts " mortis causa " and were subjected to all the regulations governing them.   But their character was repugnant to this theory since they retained their irrevocability.   Other jurists then thought to assimilate them to gifts " inter vivos ", in order to justify their irrevocability; but this theory was then inconsistent with the continuance of ownership in the donor   until   death. In the search for theories intermediate between these two, recourse was had to subtleties, distinctions and presumptions, but always without success, since the reason of the contract affecting inheritance was to be found elsewhere than in Roman law.   It should have been sought in their historical origin, the ancient Germanic laws and customs; in their social cause, namely, the advantages which families, especially noble, derived from them; in their political cause, that is the favor shown them by the State, which gained in the solidity of its own institutions by reinforcing and investing with privileges the nobility, which was its support and its arm.   Today these causes have all lost their significance, due to the modern principles governing society and the State.   Thus the law has been able to turn again to Roman principles, which did not recognize compacts over future successions.

CHAPTER XIII

THE WILL

TOPIC 1.   HISTORICAL DEVELOPMENT

§ 391. **Early Period.** — To the Germanic adoption of the will, two factors, then at work civilizing society, contributed. The influence of the Roman law must have been very great, to judge alone from the daily example which the Roman population gave of the use of wills, and from the evident concordance between the first Lombard laws concerning wills and the Roman laws upon the same subject.[1] But greater still was the influence of the Church, which, in its own interests, directly urged acceptance of the will upon the Germanic legislators. This is proved especially by the fact that the earliest laws did not use the word " testamentum ", but substituted others indicating a " disposition for the good of the soul ", " pro anima judicare." [2] Still better is it shown by the fact that the first wills might only be of gifts for spiritual benefits, for the law at first granted the right of testamentary disposal only when limited to this purpose and as an exception to the general rule. To dispose of his property, a Lombard had to appear before the assembly and there make a declaration to that effect, as in the case of adoption; [3] but when he desired to bestow a gift for the

---

[1] *Cf. Justinian*, Digest, XVIII, 1, 2; Code, I, 2, 1; V, 22, 8; VI, 23, 29, with *Liutprand*, 6.
[2] *Liutprand*, 6, 65.   [3] *Post* § 395.

safety of his soul, he might do so, though disabled because of sickness to perform that formality.[1]   A Lombard woman's heir was her " mundoald "; nevertheless she could dispose of one-third of her property as a gift for her spiritual welfare.[2]   A minor might not alien his property for any cause; but as an exception, when in danger of death, he was permitted to do so, if to a religious use.[3] The legal character of such dispositions was always that of gifts " mortis causa ", so that they were always called donations by the laws, and death was the condition of their taking effect.[4]   They ran a danger, however, from another source, namely, the opposition of the heirs, who, though their rights might not be invaded by last will dispositions,[5] opposed them as the cause and means of taking from the family a portion, though small, of the estate.   The law, therefore, had to intervene and sanction the concession, expressly requiring the legal heirs to carry out the dispositions which the dying man pleased to make, provided they did not exceed legal limits.[6]

But these limits, when once wills had been accepted, came easily to be transcended, because of the rapid diffusion of wills themselves, especially in Italy, where they had never been abandoned by the Roman population.   From legacies for religious uses they little by little extended to other purposes.   By the end of the Lombard period, a father might, by last will, settle upon an unmarried daughter a part of his property, variable according to the number of his sons.[7]   He was then allowed to reward the most commendable of his sons, by leaving him a share of his estate over and above the undisposable or legal portion to which all had a right.[8]   This provision was next extended in favor of daughters.[9] A right was similarly recognized in the husband to will to his widow the use of a part of his property, proportioned to the number of their children.[10]   Masters obtained the right to free their slaves by last will.[11]   Thus fresh uses of the will were constantly made, as its facility and convenience became better understood.

§ 392. **Later Period.** — The will finally attained its real perfection in the period of the revived study of the Roman law, the

[1] *Liutprand*, 6; *Arechi*, 14.
[2] *Liutprand*, 101.
[3] *Id.*, 19.
[4] *Id.*, Formulary, 102, in M. G. H. ed. *Boretius*, "Leges" IV and *Padelletti*, "Fontes."
[5] *Liutprand*, 65, 101.
[6] *Astolf*, 12, 16.
[7] *Liutprand*, 102.
[8] *Id.*, 112.

[9] *Astolf*, 13.
[10] *Id.*, 14.
[11] *Id.*, 12.

principles of which were again applied. But the impress of Germanic theories, in the midst of which it had developed, was not wholly lost. Traces remained, especially in the limitations by which, in greater or less degree, according to time and place, the statutes of the mediaeval communes circumscribed the testator's powers.

These limitations referred in the first place to the *kind of property* disposable. According to many statutes, the distinction was still made between property inherited and property acquired by one's own effort.[1] Over the former, as property intended to be retained within the family, testamentary power was either absolutely denied, when there were descendants, or was permitted over a part only, at most a half or third, if there were no descendants.

Secondly, there were limitations as to the *persons* who might make a will. Apart from the mentally unsound, those who had suffered civil death, and those prevented by legal or physical impediment, there were still others who, though having capacity, were nevertheless limited in the exercise of their right. Such were persons whose property, for lack of legal heirs, would escheat to the State, represented by king, baron or commune, as for example, illegitimates, " coloni ", vassals and others, around whom were thrown as many testamentary restrictions as possible, in order that the expectancy of the State might not be defeated. The same was true of women, who were not permitted to impair the rights of husband, father, children and other relatives; their consent or ratification was, therefore, required by some mediaeval communes for her will to be valid. Even the husband's right of disposition in favor of his wife was considerably restricted, in order not to damage the children; by some mediaeval city statutes he might leave her nothing absolutely and a life estate in but a part.

Finally, there were limitations as to the *object* benefited by and the *mode* of executing the will. There were not lacking statutes of the mediaeval communes that recognized the will only if employed for a special purpose, as a legacy to a religious use, the appointment of a guardian for children, and the like. These marked a step back towards its primitive condition. Other city statutes held the will valid only for a definite period, and required that it be made public before the great council of the city, much as when, in its relation to adoption, it had to be made before the public assembly.

[1] *Post* § 410.

The abandonment of these different limitations, which came about here and there and by degrees, resulted in the general perfecting of the will. But, no matter how many rights might be given to the testator, those of the family have not been forgotten. Today the laws still aim to protect with vigor the rights of the family from the possible abuse of individual desires.[1]

Topic 2.   Character of the Will

§ 393. **Roman and Germanic Contrasted.** — The will, as accepted by Germanic laws, differed substantially from that of the Roman law. The first and necessary purpose of the Roman will was the establishment of the heir; the Germanic peoples, on the other hand, firm in their principle that the heir could not be designated by others but was such in his own right,[2] used the will for the purpose filled by the Roman codicil, that is, to bequeath legacies of a part of the estate to different ends. It was, indeed, for this sole object that the will was understood and accepted, namely to provide for one's own spiritual welfare by a disposition of a part of one's estate. Strictly speaking, therefore, the Germanic will was merely a direction as to legacies.

From this variance of conception sprang those special qualities which gave to the mediaeval will a physiognomy of its own, different from the Roman, from which it was derived. The Roman principle " nemo pro parte testatus pro parte intestatus decedere potest ", no longer had any basis, since the will could be but the disposal of a legacy as a charge upon the heir, and not the establishment of an heir. The heir existed independently of the will, and those named in it might not be the heirs. Hence there could be several wills, even of different dates, without the last revoking the earlier, provided they did not contain inconsistent provisions with regard to the same object. It was also possible for several persons to join in making a will, by a single act, when they desired to place some charge upon the inheritance of property owned in common. Thus, contemporaneous with the testamentary succession to an estate, existed a succession fixed by law; there was, in other words, a succession both with respect to that portion of the patrimony withdrawn by law from the testator's disposal, and also with respect to the balance, of which he might dispose. Any unbestowed portion of the latter did not swell the shares of those

---

[1] [See the subject of the disposable portion of a testamentary succession, Civil Code, Book III, sec. IV., and *post* § 399.]

[2] *Ante* § 372.

named in the will, but of the legal heirs, since those named in the will had the quality of specific legatees.   External proof of this is seen in the fact that the number of testamentary witnesses was not always seven, as required by Roman law, but sometimes only five, which was the number stipulated by the Roman law for the codicil, the nature of which had been reproduced in the Germanic will.

§ 394. **Later Development.** — This character, peculiar to wills of the Germanic period by reason of their historical origin and purpose, was not without great influence upon their regulation in subsequent periods.   It was still observable in the statutes of the mediaeval cities, although to a greater extent mingled with Roman principles, which were constantly gaining strength.   Later laws brought order into the confusion of differing principles, but did not wholly abandon those developed by the special conditions of the will during the Germanic period.   Indeed, some of these survive in Italian law today.   Most important among them is the rejection of the Roman maxim that one may not die partially testate and partially intestate; whence the consequences, still operative, that one may make a partial will, that several wills may co-exist without annulling one another, that testate and intestate succession to the same estate may exist together, and other similar possibilities.[1]

TOPIC 3.   FORM OF WILLS

§ 395. **Early Requirements.** — The will, so far as known to the Germanic peoples, having derived from the contract of adoption,[2] of which it retained some features, at first also assumed the latter's form.   It had to be made before the assembly, " per gairethinx ", especially because, by such solemnity and publicity, the legal heirs had a guarantee that their rights would not be threatened.   The courts were later substituted for the assembly.[3]   The will consisted in an act of tradition,[4] " per chartam ", " per festucam ", or otherwise, by which the right over the object in question was transmitted to the person in whose favor the disposition was made. The testator had therefore to appear in person before the assembly; deathbed wills were not valid, and the requirement of the testator's health was added to those of solemn form and publicity.

This system was combated by the Church.   It proclaimed the principle that, if the testator's intent was clear, it might not be impugned for lack or insufficiency of external formalities; so also it maintained that the means of obtaining a spiritual benefit

[1] Civil Code, arts. 720, 759, 920.   [3] *Charlemagne*, 92.
[2] *Ante* § 390.   [4] *Post* § 440.

should not be removed at the very moment of greatest need, that is, on the approach of death. The contentions of the Church were strengthened by the example of the simplicity of Roman testamentary forms, in daily use by the native Italian population. Thus it was not difficult for the Church to obtain its designs. Gifts or legacies to the Church did not require solemn formalities,[1] and the first deathbed wills were permitted as exceptions, for the very purpose of benefiting ecclesiastical interests.[2] But the same concessions were not validated at once for all wills, which, throughout the Germanic period, approached but gradually towards Roman simplicity.

§ 396. **Kinds of Wills.** — By the time of the mediaeval communes, the form of the will had completely developed. Their statutes show various kinds of wills, depending upon their form. There was the " public " or " judicial " will, made before a public official in the presence of a certain number of witnesses. The public official was then, as now, generally a notary, but he might be a judge or other person clothed with public authority. Here was seen the continued effort of the Church, which, to render wills simpler and easier, authorized the priest, attending the sick, to receive the will with full legal effect. Wills were " secret ", on the other hand, when written by the testator himself and deposited with a notary or other public official. In the mediaeval communes this form of will might be legally left for custody in the sacristy of any religious congregation, or appropriate files were kept for the purpose in the court house or other designated place. " Holographic " wills were also secret, but they differed from the latter in that they were not deposited with a public official. In this form of will no formality was required, but the statutes of the mediaeval communes required, as a guarantee, that it be judicially established after the testator's death. Finally, there was the " nuncupative " or " oral " will. The testator expressed his desires to witnesses, whose number was not fixed, but varied at times according to the value of the property disposed of. In Venice, for example, two witnesses sufficed if the value did not exceed one hundred ducats, while three were required for a greater sum. The witnesses themselves had as a rule to reduce the intent of the testator to writing, not to give it effect, but to establish proof of it in case the witnesses were unavailable. This writing, like every other private memorandum, was generally called a " breviarium ", or in some places, as in Naples, " gesta." The last term recalls

[1] *Liutprand*, 73.   [2] *Ante* § 391.

the "insinuatio" of the Roman wills in the "gesta municipalia", that is, their registration in the city archives. It is certain that the custom of registration had been maintained and it appeared as the rule under the communal statutes, which required it especially in the case of the "nuncupative" will, because of the greater danger of destruction, alteration, or attack. There were many other precautions. In some localities its use was permitted only when another form was impossible; in others, a magistrate had to establish its regularity; elsewhere, those who founded rights upon it were obliged to swear to its truth. Thus everywhere the same objects were sought by various measures.

All these testamentary forms and precautions, elaborated at length by court decisions, are, in substantial part, those of modern Italian law.[1]

TOPIC 4.   EXECUTORS

§ 397. **Germanic Origin.** — The testamentary executor was a novelty to the Roman law and originated as a necessary consequence of the will, as it developed under Germanic law. In antiquity, in the period, that is, when the will did not exist, something like them can be recognized in those persons through whom a means was found to supply the lack of all testamentary power. Whoever wished to dispose of an object so that it would not pass to his legal heirs, transferred it in the manner usual to acts "inter vivos", that is, by tradition, either before the assembly or in court, to a person having his confidence called "electus", "manus fidelis", "salmann", "gisel", who, having thus acquired ownership, delivered it, after the donor's death, within a year according to the Salic law, or within some other determined period, to the person designated by the deceased.[2] With the introduction of the will, such intermediaries or representatives of the deceased's intent continued to exist, but changed their purpose and character, since the will henceforth met the need which they had at first fulfilled. As the will need make no mention of the heir, and as the legal heir might find himself actuated by his own interest to oppose the purposes of the deceased, it was necessary to guarantee their execution by setting up a defender other than the heir. Such a champion was found in the fiduciary, already employed before the will existed; with this difference, however, that, because of the

---

[1] [Italian Civil Code recognizes two ordinary forms of wills; (1) holographic and (2) public and secret ("per atto di notaio"), arts. 774–788; and certain forms used in cases of specified emergencies, among them the nuncupative will, arts. 789–803.]

[2] *Cf.* "emptor familiae" in the "testamentum per aes et libram."

will, it was no longer necessary to convey the property by tradition " inter vivos ", to be in turn delivered to others; it now sufficed to declare him charged with the execution of the purposes expressed in the will. So, too, it was no longer necessary to determine the objects upon which the will operated; it was enough to indicate in general the purpose to which a part of the estate was to be devoted, such as the expenditure of a certain sum in religious offices, in alms, or in the founding of a charity, or the like. To give effect to such purposes was the office of the executor, who, therefore, in Lombard Law, was called " dispensator."

In the Carlovingian period, their use became more common and the institution received confirmation in the laws. It was provided that if the executor died before having carried out the deceased's will, it was the duty of the royal intendant (" missus dominicus ") and of the bishop of the diocese, within a month, to give the vacant property to an object beneficial to the State. It was also provided that when, in obedience to the testator's intent, the executor alienated the whole of the patrimony, manumitting, for example, all his slaves, although the decedent's daughter survived, she had a right, as opposed to the executor, to retain a third of her father's property for herself, in accordance with the Lombard Edict.[1] In these laws, as in the documents of the Frankish period, such executors were called " erogatores "; the act of charging the executor and the obligation itself were called " elemosina "; and to execute, that is, to distribute the property in accordance with the decedent's intent, was called " dispensare." The peculiarity of the executor of the Frankish period was that his appointment still preserved, in form, the requirements for the ancient " electi " or " salmannen ", that is, the transmission of the ownership of the objects to the executor by the testator himself.[2] Of this there is proof in the laws, and the documents of the period show that the practice was very frequent. This was true only of those who lived under Frankish law; for those governed by Lombard law it was not necessary. Thus came into existence two classes of testamentary executors; those having possession of the property to be bestowed, and those invested with a simple duty to distribute. The first, employed by the Franks, had a direct right in the property itself, transmissible to his heirs, upon whom also rested the obligation of carrying out the will of the testator. In the second, in use by the Lombards, the obligation was personal and was extinguished by death, having merely the quality of an agency.

[1] *Pepin*, 31, 32; *cf. Liutprand*, 65.   [2] *Liutprand*, 65.

§ 398. Development During and Subsequent to the Mediaeval Communes. — In the statutes of the mediaeval communes and other contemporaneous and subsequent laws, testamentary executors were preserved under the name of " commissarii ", " fidei-commissarii ", " distributores ", and finally by the name which was to prevail, " executores ultimae voluntatis." It was in the period, opened by the communal statutes, and mainly through the decisions of the courts, that all those rules were being formulated and precautions laid down that were to make of the testamentary executor a special and important institution.

A special aim was to insure that executors should be faithful and earnest interpreters of the decedent's will. They were therefore required, within a definite time, to declare whether they accepted or refused the charge; to make an inventory of all that came into their possession; to complete their duties within a fixed period. They were placed under the supervision of the courts; and it was no longer lawful, as it had been, to give authority to the executor to dispose of the deceased's property according to his own pleasure, or in the manner in which he claimed the deceased had confided to him, since there was lacking the desired guarantee of perfect correspondence between the testator's intent and the executor's acts.

The codes also recognized the executor and preserved the numerous peculiarities of the office resulting from its historical origin. Not only are many of the rules already mentioned still observed, but traces also remain of its ancient Germanic qualities. While, on the one hand, present law regards the obligation of the executor as that of an agent, as did the Lombards, although an agency of a special kind, since, while ordinary agency terminates with the death of the principal, this begins at that moment; on the other hand, it is admitted that possession of the property may be given to the executor, according to Frankish custom. This, however, is only true of personal property, because, after its historical reason had been lost, such possession was made justifiable on the grounds of a custodianship against the danger of removal. Also, it may endure only for one year, as in the Salic law, a rule which passed from French customary law into the Napoleonic Code,[1] and thence by imitation into the Italian Code.[2]

[1] [Civil Code, art. 1031. Testamentary executors originated in France in the region of customary law. They are well defined in the collections of customs; see *Beaumanoir*, "Coutumes de Beauvoisis", chap. XII, and *Cailemer's* essay in "Select Essays in Anglo-American Legal History."]
[2] [Ital. Civil Code, arts. 903–911; as to the year's duration of office especially art. 908.]

CHAPTER XIV

RIGHTS OF THE FAMILY AGAINST THE WILL

§ 399. Legally Disposable and Undisposable Portions ("Legittima").

§ 400. "Unworthiness"; Disinheritance.

§ 399. **Legally Disposable and Undisposable Portions ("Legittima").** —The reservation of a portion of the family estate to the legal heir, by withholding it from unrestricted disposal to others, would not have been conceivable in ancient Germanic law, according to which the right of inheritance was inseparably linked to the family, and there could be no right to set up a stranger as heir, or to disinherit the person so designated by virtue of his position in the family.   But when the will came into general use, less and less respect was paid to the rights of the family.   Recalling its ancient co-ownership, it resisted the threatening danger of the will and secured the rule that it was not only possible, but even necessary, that a portion of the estate should be beyond the testator's free disposal, that is, that what had been characteristic of the whole family estate should be preserved at least with regard to a part. To this end the "legitima pars bonorum" of the Roman law of wills presented a ready and appropriate means.   Together with the will it was taken over by Germanic law, which, moreover, as in the case of the will, while following the Roman conception, imparted special qualities to it.   The laws provided that, if there were sons, the father might dispose only of such portion as would be his if an even division of the estate were made between each of his sons and himself; in the case of daughters, the father's power was limited to two-thirds or a half, according as there was one or more than one daughter.[1]   Though unlike in application, this recalled the third and half of the Justinian "legitima"[2] with this difference, that, while the Roman law determined the part which might not be taken from the legal heir, the Germanic law fixed the portion at the testator's disposal.   The Germanic rule, therefore, not only was more favorable to the heir, but maintained the prin-

[1] *Rothar*, 158, 159; *Liutprand*, 65, 113; *Pepin*, 32.
[2] Novels, XVIII.

ciple that disposability was the exception, and that the general rule remained that the estate belonged to the family.

These limitations were not always and everywhere accepted. During the Germanic period there was still evidence in Italy of the practice of reckoning the " legittima " as a fourth of the estate, corresponding to the Roman " falcidia ", of which it also in fact preserved the name. During the Middle Ages came the usual diversity of communal legislation. Among the statutes, together with the Lombard rule that the " legittima " or disposable portion was the share belonging to each, upon a division of the estate amongst all, including the father (testator), was also found the rule that the portion was a half or a third, and also a rule which left its magnitude to the father's pleasure, provided that he did not wholly neglect his children. Furthermore the children were treated differently according to sex. Daughters were usually given, as their legal portion, only what their father would consider an appropriate marriage portion.[1]   Sex was also of consequence with respect to the person against whom the right to the legal portion or "legittima " was asserted, since this was a different and larger measure (" statutory portion ") in the case of estates left by female than of those left by male relatives.

Distinctions and differences of this sort disappeared little by little as the legal standards became more uniform and the principle prevailed of equal treatment for all occupying the same position in the family. Present day differences in the legally undisposable quotas, still determined externally as in the Roman and mediaeval periods, are referable solely to diversities of kinship between the deceased and the persons claiming the right.[2]   Between persons of the same degree all difference has disappeared.

§ 400. " Unworthiness "; Disinheritance. — The right to deprive the heir of the part of the family estate belonging to him was irreconcilable with the ancient line of succession, bound to the family.[3]   Disinheritance was, therefore, forbidden.[4]   However, since the heir must have capacity for the various purposes of the family organization, the right of inheritance was taken from the relative whose conduct made him unworthy of the family. To bring about a loss of the right to inherit, such conduct had to be defined by law, and might not be left to individual caprice. In other words, while it was not possible to be disinherited, it was possible to be declared legally " unworthy " to inherit.

[1] *Ante* § 347.
[2] Ital. Civil Code, arts. 805–807.
[3] *Ante* § 372.
[4] *Rothar*, 168.

The right of succession was denied to a son who used violence against a father, striking him or otherwise injuring him;[1] to a brother or other relation who killed or attempted to kill the person of whom he was heir;[2] to a daughter who disobeyed her father, especially by breaking a betrothal concluded by him, or by marrying a slave;[3] to a husband who killed, defamed, or was guilty of other serious offense against his wife.[4] The decisions of the courts extended these laws to similar instances,[5] so that, little by little, in place of the express provision of the law, was substituted the donor's intent, especially when confirmed by the use of the will and by the weakening of the ancient family constitution. In other words disinheritance now came to take the place of " unworthiness " (" indegnità "). Not that the law renounced the right to threaten the loss of the inheritance in certain cases. Without mentioning such persons as convicts, foreigners, priests, and others to whom capacity to inherit was wholly or partially denied, this disability was preserved by the imperial " constitutions ", the statutes of the mediaeval cities and subsequent laws, where cases of " unworthiness " were still to be found. Often these instances were analogous to those of the Germanic period, as where a child married in a way to bring disgrace upon the family ; sometimes there were new examples, as thwarting the expression or execution of the deceased's last will. But alongside these legal provisions there came to be set up the declaration of the testator, who took upon himself the right to pronounce the forfeiture of the inheritance. The father who for any reason considered himself injured by his child, the head of the family who thought one of its members unworthy to remain within the group, might punish such a person, sending him away, and disinheriting him. It was a grave responsibility, not sufficiently controlled by law, and so the source of very great abuses. To avoid these, modern Italian law,[6] following the French Code,[7] returned to the Germanic notion of legally determined causes of " unworthiness." Nevertheless, as a compromise between the two theories, regard is paid to the desires of the testator, who is not permitted to inflict such punishment himself, but is given the power to negative the effect of the law's penalty by rehabilitating the person who has suffered it.[8]

[1] *Rothar,* 169.
[2] *Id.,* 163; *Liutprand,* 17.
[3] *Rothar,* 221; *Liutprand,* 5, 119.
[4] *Rothar,* 196, 197, 200; *Liutprand,* 130.
[5] "Expositio" to *Rothar,* 169, § 3.
[6] [Civil Code, arts. 725–728.]
[7] [Civil Code, art. 727.]   [8] Ital. Civil Code, art. 726.

PART IV
PROPERTY RIGHTS

PART IV

PROPERTY RIGHTS [1]

§ 401. Early Rights in Personal | § 402. Later Rights in Land.
       Property.

§ **401. Early Rights in Personal Property.** — More than all others, a person's right over things receives and preserves the impress of the conditions of the period in which it develops. It has, therefore, progressed contemporaneously and parallel with civilization. Elevating, with civilization, the condition of the individual and of society, improving also the conception and forms of man's title to things, private rights are made to harmonize with social interests, and both gain more effective instrumentalities and greater guarantees. This truth is proved by the fact that, among all peoples, the two extremes of the course, covered by the history of property rights, correspond to those of the road along which each people has traveled towards civilization. When the social institutions of a people are in their infancy, property, if recognized in all its applications, appears in the rudimentary form of ownership in common. Little by little, as the organization of a people advances, the property right also acquires greater perfection, evidenced chiefly by the throwing off of ancient restrictions, the assigning of greater definition to its qualities, and the tendency to concentrate the right in the individual. When, finally, a people attains mature development, property has also run its evolution and appears principally as a private right.

Such was its course in the history of Italian law. In its Germanic origins property was collective. Nomadic life, supported chiefly by pastoral pursuits, hunting and war, permitted of no other form of ownership of land than one in common. But it was no obstacle to the ownership of movable property or personalty. The carts in which the people lived, for they had no houses; the flocks and fruits that nourished them; their clothes and utensils; their arms for the chase, war and defense, — these were the things of which they chiefly felt the need and over which, because also easily

<hr>

[1] [Part IV, §§ 401–473 is a translation of *Calisse*, part IV, §§ 116–188.]

acquired and defended, the right of ownership first developed. Thus it was true that in antiquity movable property had greater importance than land, and over personalty the first legal regulations came into being with respect to use, acquisition and defense. These regulations always remained distinct from those relating to land, since the former necessarily represented the poverty and simplicity of a primitive state of law, while the latter, belonging to a period when law had progressed, received a more perfect ordering.

§ 402. **Later Rights in Land.** — The supremacy of personal property was not of long duration. When ownership of land had been recognized, that of movables lost in esteem. The winning of permanent homes; the distribution of conquered lands; the pursuit of agriculture on an increasing scale; interest in the preservation of the family; the linking up of public office and of rights and duties to tenure; feudalism, which imparted a political character to land: — these were factors contributing to increase the importance of landed, and consequently to debase that of movable property. But the latter could not remain neglected when industry and commerce made it an abundant source of social wealth. A movement in its favor reawakened. The first sign was the military laws of the Lombards, which placed movable and landed wealth on an equality with respect to the obligations attaching to it,[1] a movement which received its greatest development in the time of the mediaeval communes. But the contrary notion continued to prevail to such a point that, in order to give full legal sanction to rights over personalty, they were likened to rights in land. This fiction had been foreshadowed in the Roman law, which regarded as immovables things which, by nature movable, yet formed an integral part of an immovable object. Such were trees in the ground and the stones of a house. But in the Middle Ages, for the reasons already outlined, this conception had a considerably wider application. The appurtenances, viz. movables appropriated to the service of land, were assimilated to it; later, independent of any such relation, a like consideration was accorded to commercial capital and finally to contractual rights, although in themselves incorporeal, whenever secured by land, *e.g.* rents and tithes, or whenever they produced a determined and perpetual return, such as feudal rights to office, the public debt and the like. The Glossators, canonists, and jurists of a

---

[1] *Ante* § 64. [See in full *Calisse*, "Storia", etc., vol. II, "Diritto Publico", § 162, p. 291.]

later period continued this tendency, so that two classes of immovables came to be recognized: those that were such by nature and those declared such by law.

All these conceptions have passed into modern Italian law, which reflects the Germanic law much more in respect to personalty than to realty, wherein Roman principles have prevailed.[1]

[1] Ital. Civil Code, arts. 413, 415.

TITLE I

PROPERTY IN LAND [1]

CHAPTER XV

COLLECTIVE OWNERSHIP

§ 403. Tribal and Family Ownership.

§ 403. **Tribal and Family Ownership.** — The first form of ownership was, as has been said, collective, that is, common to all members of a determined social group. Such ownership, however, was in the individual, and not in the association, considered as a juristic person, possessed of rights and conceding them to its component members. It was a title by co-ownership, residing " pro indiviso " in the aggregate of members, who used the property together and for their common advantage. Thus a juridical explanation is furnished for the frequent partitions of the common lands among all in equal parts and by lot.

Freedom from the restrictions of such co-ownership was always the goal towards which the historical and legal development of property was directed. And it succeeded, slowly, laboriously, not in one leap but step by step, passing from title over large to title

---

[1] *Pertile, cit.*, part II, §§ 133–148; *Salvioli, cit.*, part I, chap. 6; part IV, sec. III; *B. di Vesme e Fossati*, "Vicende della proprietà fondiaria in Italia" in "Atti dell' Accademia di Scienze in Torino" (1836); *Schupfer*, "L'Allodio" in "Digesto Italiano"; *Gaudenzi*, "Sulla proprietà in Italia nella prima metà del medio evo" (1884); *Calisse*, "La proprietà territoriale nelle provincie romane secondo i documenti dei secoli VIII, IX, X (Rome, 1886); *Laveleye*, "La Propriété et ses formes primitives" (1877); *Fustel de Coulanges*, "Recherches sur quelques problèmes d'histoire" (1885); *Brunner*, "Deutsche Rechtsgeschichte", § 10.

over more limited areas, until it was finally possible to concentrate ownership in the individual. Co-ownership on the largest scale was that of the whole people, and was termed tribal or village; co-ownership of a family was the most restricted and formed the intermediate link between ownership common to all and individual ownership.

TOPIC 1. TRIBAL OWNERSHIP

§ 404. **Its Reasons.** — The impermanency of homes in ancient Germanic life prevented the formation of a man's interest for the land where he camped, which would lead to the expenditure of labor on it, or the desire to possess it by an exclusive ownership, or transmit it to heirs, all factors which form the basis of private property. From the lands of others the Germanic peoples sought only the provisions necessary for the time of their sojourn, and, for this, ownership was not needed and would not have been possible, in the absence of the element of permanent possession.[1] But since the land upon which the tribe settled, even though temporarily, had to be cultivated by the members, used for their habitations and other needs, and defended against external attack, the tribe was, and alone could be, the owner. There were other secondary reasons why individual ownership did not exist. On becoming agricultural the people did not lose their love of arms, of which they continued to have need for defense against other roving tribes; furthermore, when private estates came into being, no great differences of fortune arose, either to cause oppression by the rich or revolt by the poor.[2]

Of such ancient title to land there is explicit proof in the early writers,[3] as well as traces surviving in later laws and even in the language, which, it is to be observed, lacked in antiquity any word for ownership as subsequently conceived. The many words later adopted to this end represented so many successive stages, through which property passed and in correspondence with which it developed.[4]

§ 405. **Stages of Development.** — Different stages or periods may be distinguished in the development of ownership, while still in the collective state, corresponding to the stages through which the civilization of the people passed.

The first must have been that of complete community, whereby

---

[1] *Caesar*, "De bello gallico", VI, 22.
[2] *Ibid.*
[3] *Ibid.*; *Tacitus*, "Germania", 26; *Horace*, "Odes", III, 24.
[4] *Post* § 410.

even the products of labor were put at the common disposal. Caesar testifies to this among the Suevi, when he says that those who remained at home to cultivate the fields provided both for themselves and those who were away warring, and that the agricultural and military duty alternated year by year.[1] Traces of this early period were found in later years, especially in certain military laws, which provided that those who remained at home, either because exempt or because they did not own the quantity of land required for military service, should contribute to the expense of arming and maintaining those who went to war.[2]

From this first period ownership passed to a second, during which there was the beginning of individual right, if not as yet in the land itself, at least in the products obtained from it by labor. The land was annually distributed to the families and each retained the products for its own needs. Such distributions were made in equal parts, by the magistrates, in such wise that neither the domination by some nor the discontent of others should arise.[3]

But the time came when all persons were no longer equal and a diversity of condition among individuals gave rise to diversity in the distribution of the lands.[4] This change, indicative of progress, was a consequence of another change that had taken place in Germanic society. The tribes had arrived in their migrations at the Empire's boundaries; there they met a resistance that checked their advance, and yet they could not retrace their steps, for other tribes had occupied the regions behind them. There arose of necessity a greater permanency of sojourn, that gave an impulse to agriculture and that love of ownership according to which power is measured by the quantity of land controlled.[5]

Finally, the confines of the Empire were broken through, and the tribes, inundating the provinces, obtained the land which they had so long been seeking. As was their custom they took possession of the conquered territory, and distributed it among all. But this time there was to be no restitution, because they were not again to abandon their homes. As these lands remained firmly held by those to whom they had been distributed, public ownership, at least as to them, ceased, and private ownership evolved from it as a necessary consequence.

---

[1] *Caesar*, "De bello gallico", IV, 1.
[2] *Ante* § 64. [See *Calisse*, "Storia", etc., vol. II, "Diritto Publico", § 162, p. 292.]
[3] *Caesar*, "De bello gallico", VI, 22.
[4] *Tacitus*, "Germania", 26.
[5] *Id.*, 17, 26, 46.

§ 406. **Late Traces of Collective Ownership.** — It was not possible, however, at one stroke, to efface all the consequences of a condition of such long duration, that is, of ownership common to the tribe or village. Even as to the lands distributed, the remembrance remained that they had once belonged to all. And this remembrance found application in the title of the king, that is the State, as the supreme owner of all the land, with the consequent power to place restrictions on the rights which individuals had obtained over it;[1] and in the maintenance over the distributed lands of certain rights of common enjoyment. But the most striking trace of collective ownership is found in those lands which, particularly because unfitted to individual cultivation, were left in common, and which, still possessing this status, have in part so descended to the present day.

During the Germanic period such lands were given various names. Besides commons, they were called "fiwaida", that is, intended for pasture.[2] The lands used for this purpose remained longest in common, there being no need for individual labor upon them. They were also called "vicinage" lands, because all the inhabitants of a "vicus" or village were its co-owners and thereby had rights over it. The name also of "march" ("marca") was preserved, although more so beyond the Alps than in Italy. "Vicini", "commarcani", "consortes" were the users of these common lands, still preserved amidst those that had fallen under the dominion of the individual. Their right, which was principally to pasture cattle, take wood, hunt or the like, was based upon the legal character of the co-ownership, which, as stated, was simply a condominium in each separate member composing the community. To enjoy such rights it was, therefore, necessary in the first place to belong to the community by origin or admission. The latter was possible by the consent of the others, or by peaceful residence for a certain period, or by grant of the king, the universal owner. Similar principles were followed later, in the time of the mediaeval communes, with regard to foreigners who wished to share in the rights peculiar to citizens. It was also necessary to own land in the community, and so later, when the Italian municipality was revived, the landed proprietors always remained the true "cives optimo jure." The reason lay in the fact that all the original co-owners of the collective property received their portion on division and this portion came thus to indicate those who had been members

---

[1] *Post* § 417.
[2] *Cf.* "bona compascua" of the Romans.

of the community and so preserved rights over such of its land as still remained in common. Not to be an owner was evidence, on the other hand, of not having belonged, at least as a free man, to the community, and, therefore, of not having corresponding rights. When ownership of land acquired this significance, the rights just mentioned came to be regarded as inhering to the land itself, which was not deprived of them when it passed from one owner to another. Indeed, the documents are numerous in which either the rights in the commons were considered as a necessary appurtenance to the ownership of the land described, or acquisition of land in a given commune was said to carry with it the right to participate in all benefits enjoyed by the members of the commune.

§ 407. **Easements.** — The common lands were constantly restricted within narrower limits, both in point of extent and of enjoyment, by the steady growth of private ownership. Forbidden or proclaimed lands ("terre difese", "terre bandite"), that is, closed to common use, constantly increased, in order to encourage the development of individual ownership, and they also received the protection of the law.[1] In the Carlovingian period a sensible weakening of the rights of "commarcani" and of the bonds of their union was already noticeable. They suffered still more under feudalism. Not only did the usurpations of the seignior diminish the communal lands, but the idea itself of co-ownership, as then conceived, was destroyed. For, in the feudalized communities, equality of condition among the inhabitants disappeared; the seignior was superposed over all; he held, as his own, rights that were formerly common, so that their exercise assumed the character of a grant from him, which was not always gratuitous, but indeed for the most part linked to compensatory obligations of various kinds. There was no substantial change under the régime of the mediaeval cities. These won from the feudal lords, against whom they had battled, some lands that formerly belonged to their citizens, who thus re-acquired their use, without the need of further grant, by virtue of their mere status as members of the commune: "ex jure civitatis" or "ex jure civico", as they said. Hence the name "civic uses", given to the rights of the citizens, prevailed over all other names, such as "participation", "commonalty", "rights of use" and the like, found in various regions of Italy. The legal character of the rights was variously defined. The personality assumed by the commune had not caused a revival of the ancient idea of an undivided co-ownership in all those com-

[1] *Liutprand*, 151.

posing the community. The municipality, as a legal entity, was now the owner of the common property; to the citizens was granted only its enjoyment, provided their status was that required by the city's statutes, and this right, variously considered at first, later took the character of an inalienable easement (" servitù ") over others' lands. As such it was treated by the jurists and by their labors the conception was perfected and perpetuated to the present day.

For even now, although within rather narrow limits and soon destined to disappear, traces of communal lands remain as a last reminder of the ancient collective state of ownership. They are seen in two types of cases. First, there are the lands still withdrawn from private ownership, principally because of their nature, rendering them unfit for intensive cultivation. They remain open to all, for such uses as nature itself or ancient customs have destined them. As examples, may be mentioned the high pasture lands of the Apennines, those on the " Sila " range in Calabria and the plains or " Tavoliere " of Apulia. The second form, under which are still preserved traces of early common ownership of land, is found in the easements of pasture, wood, seed or other right over another's land, existent today in various regions of Italy.

Motives, especially of an economic nature, have encouraged the law to oppose both forms of common ownership, in order to relieve the land, so far as possible, of impediments to its marketability. This policy began in the 1700 s. Lands held in common were the subject of attack by many laws, always restrictive in nature. Some gave the title to the users;[1] some required the lands to be sold,[2] some gave them out on leases,[3] some granted them to the communes for lease by the latter;[4] by others they devolved upon the State.[5] Lands were affranchised of rights conceded by others than the owner. In 1778 Grand Duke Leopold II made this reform in Tuscany; the French government imitated him in Naples in 1806; and today it has been applied more widely by a series of laws, such as those of 1865 for Sardinia, of 1859 and 1882 for Venetia, and those which in the last of the 1800 s were ordered to be put in execution in the former papal provinces.

Thus did individualism grow in strength, while about it, with all

[1] Those of Ferdinand IV of Naples in 1783, 1787, 1792; in Piedmont, 1820; in Sardinia, 1839.
[2] Piedmont, 1720, 1750.
[3] Ferdinand IV of Naples, 1806, 1816; Piedmont and Sardinia.
[4] Venice, 1806.
[5] The pasture land of the Sila mountains of Calabria, 1876, 1880.

their consequences, were drawn limitations, intended to check the abuse of the rights conceded, so that public interests should not suffer.

TOPIC 2. FAMILY OWNERSHIP

§ 408. Its Consequences. — In the early Germanic State distributions of land, even when periodic, were made not to individuals but to families,[1] and they created no right of ownership. When, with the abandonment of migratory life and of constant change of lands, there was a beginning of private property, it was first an ownership by the family of the lands temporarily occupied. At the time of the Germanic invasions of Italy, this form of title, intermediate between ownership in common by all and individual ownership, was at the height of its development, for just at that time, with the making of permanent settlements, the last distributions of land took place. The apportioned lands took commonly the name "fara", meaning the "gens", line or generation, *i.e.*, the family whose property it became. It is still recognizable in the place-names of many rural districts and communes of Italy. When it had thus become family property, it constituted the family estate, inalienable and transmissible to the heirs alone, for the members of the family had but the enjoyment and management of the common patrimony; they formed but an association of users of the land, under the management of the head of the house; they were co-owners, but bound by family interests,[2] which the patrimony was intended to serve.

From this several consequences followed. Since all were co-owners, if a division of the family property took place during the life of the father, who had no greater rights than his children, the division had to be in equal parts.[3] Hence the "portiones", of which each member became master, but which still remained bound to the family, if only by the reciprocal rights of expectancy over the inheritance.

In the second place, no member of the family might dispose of his property. It might well happen that an alienation, at least partial, of the patrimony was necessary in the interests of the family. But for this three conditions were requisite. The first was that a price had to be paid, so that there was a transformation for family needs but not a true diminution of the estate. The second was that all members then composing the family should

---

[1] *Caesar,* "De bello gallico", VI, 22.   [3] *Ante* § 312.
[2] *Cf. Justinian,* Novels, Valent. III, tit. 3, a. 439.

join by giving their consent to the alienation. The last condition was that the alienation should be made to relatives in preference to any other person.

A third and important consequence of the quality of the family title was that succession determined by law was alone recognized.[1] Since the father might not alienate, neither was he permitted to will the property; his children were the obligatory heirs to the family rights and he might do no act, such as adopt or legitimize, which would injure those rights or which was not in accord with the safeguards and the limits established by law.[2]

§ 409. **Conflict Between Family and Individual Rights.** — To family ownership and the restrictions of various nature to which the family estate was consequently subjected, was opposed the principle of individualism, which never could have developed, had it not, at least in part, deprived the family of its ancient right. There were influences favorable to individual ownership, such as the example of the conquered Romans, who were freer in the enjoyment of their property than their conquerors; there was the Roman law itself, in which individual property had reached a maximum development; the Church, in order to facilitate conveyances to its own benefit, encouraged the freeing of property from its ancient impedimenta; trade was increasing; in a word, civilization was progressing and with it advanced also the law of property. Thus, despite the older principles, the individual step by step acquired the right of alienation and of conveyance by a will. It was a right at first surrounded by many limitations, but its recognition sufficed to shake the institution of family ownership to its foundations.

Family ownership, however, set up a vigorous resistance, through the continuous opposition of the legal heirs to the acts of their ancestor, by which at least a part of the domestic fortune was removed from the ownership of the house. Every means was tried to elude the intention of the deceased. The extension of the deceased's obligation to the heirs, the threat of penalties, the fact that the disposition had been made by conveyance " inter vivos ", availed nothing. But the law intervened in favor of the liberty of the individual, requiring the children and other heirs-at-law rigorously to respect the acts of their predecessor, and to see to the exact execution of all his dispositions.[3]

Thus aided by the law, individual ownership triumphed over that of the family, though not without leaving enduring traces throughout subsequent periods. In place of the legal family group

[1] *Ante* § 372. [2] *Ante* §§ 335, 336. [3] *Astolf*, 12, 16.

were substituted voluntary fraternities or associations (" consortiones "), composed of members, held together by traditions and an
interest in preventing the destruction of the family estate by the
process of subdivision.   Even the laws record instances of brothers
who by agreement elected to remain co-owners ; [1] the documents
furnish frequent evidence of community of ownership established
among relatives or neighbors, for better opportunity to work or
to meet more easily the charges upon the land.   And traditions of
this form of ownership have not yet wholly vanished, for it is usual
in the country districts for the family not to dissolve upon the
death of the father, but to continue united under the direction of
the eldest brother.   Ancient unity still preserved traces also in the
provisions of the law relative to " family property."   It was a very
frequent rule of the statutes of the mediaeval cities to require the
consent of the relatives to conveyances ; the latters' right in such
alienations to be preferred as purchasers to strangers was long
maintained, as also their right to redeem the property conveyed,
if an offer had not first been made to them ; [2] the limitations upon
testamentary powers,[3] the exclusion of women from inheritance [4]
were but consequences of the ancient co-ownership of the family.

[1] *Rothar,* 167.   [2] *Post* § 422.   [3] *Ante* § 392.   [4] *Ante* § 373.

Chapter XVI

INDIVIDUAL OWNERSHIP

§ 410. "Allodium."

Topic 1. Physical Aspect

§ 411. "Mansus" or Dwelling. | § 412. Disappearance of the "Mansus."

Topic 2. Economic Aspect

§ 413. Concentration of Wealth. | § 414. Land Values.

Topic 3. Legal Aspect

§ 415. Roman and Germanic Theories. | § 416. Social and Individual Interests in Property.

§ 410. **"Allodium."**—"Allodium" was the name given to property held by an individual. The word is said to be derived from the prefix "an", a particle having a separative sense, and the root, "lod" or "lot", meaning lot or portion. The term thus indicated in its primitive significance the part detached from the common property and given to the individual, that is to say, the "sors" which fell to each on the division of lands. This portion became the patrimony of the family, who imparted to it its quality of enforced preservation and transmission to the heirs. This was the portion which was transmitted and acquired by inheritance, and therefore, in a secondary sense, "allodium" was equivalent to "hereditas", to legal succession. But not the whole family estate had this same quality, for there was a portion which, having been acquired by the personal labor of the individual, belonged to him exclusively, free from any family obligations.[1] There were thus formed two categories of property, distinguished by their origin, from which their special qualities derived. Into one fell the things that were proper to the individual ("bona ex adquisitio", "ex labore", "propria", "conquista", "comparata"); into the other fell those proper to the family ("bona ex jure parentum", "sortes", "terrae aviaticae"), to which was appropriately preserved the name of "allodium." Both had in common the fundamental quality of being full and free, unburdened of any

[1] *Rothar*, 167; *Liutprand*, 57.

665

rights vesting in strangers. And since, with the creation of benefices, a title which was neither full nor free grew up and was widely
distributed, the word "allodium", in its last and proper significa-
tion, came to denote ownership exempt from any claim beyond
that of the family, in contrast with the "benefice", signifying
ownership by grant from another and subject to obligations exacted
as compensation for the grant.

Benefices attained the widest possible diffusion, while allodial
property remained scarce. When later the bonds of the benefices
were severed and liberty was restored to the land, social conditions
had been reached, very different from those among which the
"allodium" had arisen. The name was not revived, however,
especially since the decline of the benefice deprived the latter of its
true conception, and since other and more appropriate names were
offered by the Roman law, under whose influence the new ownership was being regulated.

Individual ownership, with respect also to its history, may be
examined from three points of view : — physical constitution, economic status, and the legal theories to which it has given rise.

TOPIC 1.   PHYSICAL CONSTITUTION

§ 411. " Mansus " or Dwelling. — When they first came to
belong to the individual, lands had a uniform constitution, founded
on the system of the " mansi." The word is derived from " ma-
nere" and indicated the land upon which a family was established,
had fixed its abode, in contrast to other lands held temporarily, to
be abandoned or restored to another. The " mansus " was, therefore, in origin merely the " sors ", that is, properly speaking, the
" allodium." Arising, as such, either from the distribution of
lands or from the equal partition, among individuals, of property
held in common,[1] it came into being subject to an invariable measure, that is, one common to all " mansi." There is additional
proof of this in the military laws of Charlemagne, which, with the
purpose of bringing the obligations of military service into perfect
correspondence and proportion with the ownership of land, established that there should be one soldier in the army for every four
" mansi " of land,[2] and this presupposed that the " mansi " were
all equal, as otherwise the result would have been contrary to the
intention.

[1] *Ante* § 408.
[2] [*Calisse*, "Storia del diritto d'Italia", vol. II, "Diritto publico ", § 163
p. 293, much abbreviated in translation *ante* § 64.]

Their extent, however, cannot be determined with certainty; nor were they always in the laws and documents calculated in like manner. Even the measures employed differed widely, but they may be grouped according to certain general standards. Either they were reckoned by *area*, using perches, squares, feet, cords, paces, palms and like units; or by the amount of *work* that could be performed upon land in a given time, in which case yokes, ploughs, oxen, turns, a day's work, etc., were employed; or by a sowing, in terms of bushels, sixths, quarters, gallons; and finally by *value*, as by " solidi ", " denarii " and sometimes by heads of cattle.

The composition of the " mansus " is better known. Two parts are distinguishable, one held directly by the owner, the other assigned by various titles to the " coloni." The former was the " res domnicatae ", or owner's part; the latter the " res perti-nentes", or dependencies. To the "res domnicatae" belonged, above all, the owner's house, called " casa " or " sala domnicata " or " sundrialis ", because " sundrium " (*cf.* " sonder ") indicated property separate from that enjoyed in common; it was also called " domus culta ", from the extent and state of its cultivation, and more commonly " curtis " or " hoba " (*cf.* " hof "), being enclosed and defended. This part was held in special protection by the laws. " Hoberos ", or " curtis ruptura ", that is, breaking into such a house, was a special crime in Lombard law, and severely punished;[1] even a public official might not enter without the owner's consent, if the latter promised to perform there the service for which the other demanded entrance. Around the house were the lands occupied by the owner and, therefore, also a part of the " res domnicatae." Marked trees or stones fixed in the ground indicated the bounds, to which the law gave special protection.[2]

Beyond this central part extended the lands forming the dependency. These were woods, vineyards, meadows, fields sown in wheat or other grains, granted out by contracts of emphyteusis lease or " livello ", with stipulations calling for rents and the most varied kinds of services, to slaves, " aldii ", " coloni ", free lease holders and as many others as made up the diversified peasant population.[3] From the condition of the occupants the lands themselves derived their quality, so that there were lands and houses designated as those of slaves, " aldii ", freemen or " coloni ", according to the status of the possessor. And depending upon that status, the lands, and thereby their possessors, were bound by dif-

---

[1] *Rothar*, 34, 380.   [2] *Id.* 236, 241.   [3] *Ante* § 40.

ferent obligations with respect to rents or service towards the owner. Sometimes these obligations were appropriate to freemen, who held the lands solely by contract; or again they were appropriate to persons occupying a dependent status, as " aldii " or slaves.

§ 412. **Disappearance of the " Mansus."** — The physical constitution of the " mansi " did not remain long unchanged. Several causes coöperated to alter the physical aspect of landed property. The partitions taking place within families brought the first disintegration, for the voluntary family associations (" consortiones ") did not always suffice to maintain unity. To partitions were added alienations, to which the law vainly tried to oppose obstacles,[1] and by which persons stranger to the family secured entrance upon the " mansi " and still further dismembered them. The diffusion of benefices also contributed, by destroying in great measure independent ownership, and concentrating property in the hands of the few rich. Evident too was the spirit of revolt. Spreading to bands of peasants, wherever successful, it destroyed the ties binding them to the owners of the lands on which they worked.

Of the parcelling of the lands into " mansi " and of the ancient relation between their constituent parts, a trace long remained (besides that of place names) in the fact that many estates continued to have rights of common, and in the fact that such estates were not considered as integral in themselves but as parts of a vaster estate at one time a unit; they were in fact measured by the " uncia ", that is, by fractions of the ancient unity represented by the " as."

Thus came about the commingling of all landed property, which passed down into subsequent periods despoiled of all regularity and uniformity of composition.

TOPIC 2. ECONOMIC ASPECT

§ 413. **Concentration of Wealth.** — The distributions of land which followed the Germanic invasions of Italy were not economically harmful. The great estates or " latifundia " were broken up, the number of landed proprietors increased, a certain equality of fortune was established among them, and life and labor on the fields increased. But this favorable condition did not long endure. Two great tendencies to mortmain were forming and everywhere

[1] *Charles the Bald*, Edict. pist., c., 30.

spreading their influence. One was the Church, which, by the gifts of the faithful and many other sources of title, was accumulating estates, the magnitude of which it would be difficult to conceive today. The other was the State, which, through the theories of ancient co-ownership, had opened many channels by which to reclaim private property. The evil grew with feudalism. Amidst the usurpations of the seigniors and the grants of land made to them by those needing protection, small ownership disappeared and the new " latifundium " or great estate, that took its place, was strengthened also by the numerous rights added by the fief.

Once the inequality and disproportion of estates had become established, no effective remedy followed to remove them. The mediaeval communes, by shaking off the fief and liberating the rural population, created a great number of small land owners, but could not prevent the continued flow of property into great aggregations of wealth. The peasants did not again lose their liberty, but because of their poverty they soon lost all real exercise of it. On the other hand, mortmain increased and the number of the families of the nobility increased; the additions to such estates were the more easy and dangerous in that, while channels existed for property to enter a patrimony, there were few or none by which it left, in view of the inalienability of ecclesiastical property, the exclusion of women from inheritance, the restrictions of fiefs and trust-entails (" fideicommissa "), and the favor of the laws which shared in the pride of the nobility in retaining the estate intact and in perpetuity within the family.

The consequences of these conditions are still seen, especially in the disuse of vast estates, removed from the force and clash of opposing interests. But today all those ancient fetters have fallen away that caused such conditions in the past, so that these lands may look forward to great improvement in the future.

§ 414. **Land Values.** — As to the value of land, it is clear that it was not what might be expected. In general there was but little wealth; in the Germanic period sales of land for a small sum of money or a few head of cattle were frequent. Of this economic fact several causes may be named. In the first place, there was the condition of the land. Long abandoned, overrun by so many invaders, the theatre of so many wars, very sparsely populated, it must have promised but little return at great expense of labor to those who first resumed cultivation. When its condition had improved, and values for that reason might have increased, there arose other causes of depression, all centering in the incumbrances which it carried.   Agnate limitations, trust-entails ("fideicommissa"), preëmption, preference, apanage; feudal incumbrances of rent, service, tithes, devolution, and reliefs; legal restrictions fixing crops, creating monopolies in the sale of products, regulating military service and the conscription of labor; community easements of pasture, way and wood — all these, to which were added uncertainty of title in the absence of land records and the danger of disturbance of possession by lawless feudal barons, continued to depress land below its natural value.

The mediaeval cities took measures to change these conditions. Agriculture was stimulated by the grant of aids, in the form of exemption from taxes for certain labors judged important, the recognition of title in those who tilled abandoned land, pardon for outlaws who settled on land as " coloni "; effort was made to increase the agricultural population, by forbidding emigration and favoring immigration.   The liberation of the land from its fetters was facilitated by combating the abuses of the powerful and by moderating the restrictive laws and the easements enjoyed over the lands of others.   There followed a general improvement in the condition of land; the mediaeval communes themselves undertook cultivation, the study of agriculture was encouraged, registries and land records were introduced and improved, by which it became possible at once and without danger of fraud to know the condition of the title.

Such remedies, it is certain, had their good effect, but they did not remove all the economically injurious conditions, because the causes which had produced them remained, namely, mortmain, privileges, the bonds of agnation.   Not until our own times have these causes been completely removed.

TOPIC 3.   LEGAL ASPECT OF OWNERSHIP

§ 415. **Roman and Germanic Theories.** — The theory of individual ownership, as held by Germanic law and also in subsequent periods, had peculiarities of its own distinguishing it from the Roman conception, which is that of the present day.   By the Roman and modern systems ownership is the " plena in re potestas ", the right to do what one wishes with one's own, provided that it is not a use prohibited by law.   It is, therefore, a right single in conception and absolute, in that one is either owner in this sense or one is not.   In Germanic law, on the other hand, ownership lent itself to modifications; its conception was broader, less rigid, and, therefore, capable of different modes. Juridically ownership varied according to the *object* over which it was exercised; ownership of land, for example, differed from that of personalty, both in origin and in the powers conferred, both in the manner of asserting and of defending the right. Secondly, Germanic ownership varied according to the *subject* or person exercising it. Land possessed by slaves produced servile obligations; that belonging to free men created conditions of freedom; the " res domnicatae ", because of the master of the " mansus ", gave rise to rights, while the dependent lands (" pertinentes "), because possessed by the " coloni ", gave rise to duties. And lastly ownership varied also with respect to its *scope*, that is, to the greater or less number of rights which it conferred upon the owner. Thus the ownership of feudal land bestowed even sovereign political rights; ecclesiastical ownership produced exemption from public obligations; simple allodial title merely gave the rights of a free man.

Furthermore, ownership by the Roman law extended to the whole of an object. Ownership in a part only of a single object was not conceivable; hence two principles: that co-ownership " in solido " by several persons was inadmissible; that it was not possible that the owner of the principal object should not also be owner of the accessory. The Germanic law differed, being less rigid in this respect. The right of the owner need not extend over the whole object. For example, one might be the owner of the soil, but not of the crops growing on it; one might own the house, and not the land on which it was built. Later the law returned to the unity of the Roman conception and to its consequences. But the Germanic notion of ownership endured for a long time. Its transformation took place in those statutory provisions of the mediaeval communes which, by forced purchases and sales between owners, tended to reintegrate ownership in all its parts and to bring the law into line with nature, the accessory combining with the principal from which it derived its existence.

§ 416. **Social and Individual Interests in Property.** — It is no less interesting to observe that, in the Germanic period, political elements entered into the conception of ownership, which thus came to find a place in public law. By the distributions of land, ownership had acquired a singular connection with the status of the free man. Given as a reward for victory, it was distinctive of the warrior, the conqueror, the man possessing complete freedom, who, besides a continuous and evident proof of his liberty, had in his property also a guarantee of his status. And it was a liberty not

671

only personal, but political.   Hence the political character infused
into ownership.   This increased when ownership was made a condition of military service, which in turn was a condition for complete enjoyment of all the rights of a free man.[1]   It increased still
more when, with the growth of immunities or special charters of
privilege, landed property became the subject of the rights composing the immunities and conferred their enjoyment upon the owner.[2]
Consequently public law, the boundary between which and private
law was not clearly defined, considered property as its field, altering its true nature by raising it to a political institution.   Such it
really became under feudalism.   Then came a reaction, brought
about as much through the Roman law, which had again become
a matter of common knowledge, as by the political interests of the
mediaeval communes.   The middle class of the cities, engaged in
commerce and the professions and aroused against the feudal
nobility, rich in lands, effected a revolution whereby the enjoyment of rights, especially political, were no longer considered a consequence of ownership but of the personal qualities determining
the individual's status.   This change did not, however, occur
suddenly, leaving no mark of the ancient order.   Traces even
remained in the statutes of the communes themselves, where the
State was still seen guarding its direct interests in property, and
where property was still a qualification for certain offices and the
source of certain rights.   But by that time the contrary principle
had been advanced and was bound to bear fruit.   Property continued to withdraw within its natural bounds and the concentration of its function was completed when, with the destruction of
all relation of dependency or cause between the rights proper
to a man and those accidentally due to the possession of property,
all obstacles were removed to a fresh and complete acceptance of
the more exact ideas of the Roman law.

Finally, it should be observed that, from the time when the
ownership of land became concentrated in the individual, it continued to have a close bearing upon social interests.   The predominance of the social factor had but recently disappeared with
collective ownership, and hence not only the memory but also
numerous and firm traces remained.   While Roman ownership, like
that of modern law, was absolute, in the sense that it did not tolerate
another's participation, but brought the benefit of it solely to the

---

[1] *Ante* § 64.   [See in full *Calisse*, "Storia", etc., vol. II, "Diritto publico", §§ 161, 162, p. 288 *et seq.*]
[2] *Ante* § 27.

owner, mediaeval ownership, on the other hand, did not exclude at least a partial recognition of social interests.   It did not claim that, because the property was concentrated in the power of one individual, all others were excluded from every enjoyment which it was capable of providing.   The social factor was not excluded from the conception of ownership; and this was a gain, for it did not appear as an institution hostile to social interest, and was therefore not combated, as at a later period, when individual interest gained an exaggerated ascendancy.   Individualism still controls today, but the need of reconciling it with the common good is again felt and is preparing to impart a new direction to the law.

CHAPTER XVII

LIMITATIONS TO THE RIGHT OF OWNERSHIP

TOPIC 1. LIMITATIONS UPON ITS EXERCISE

TOPIC 2. EXTINGUISHMENT OF OWNERSHIP

TOPIC 1. LIMITATIONS UPON ITS EXERCISE

§ 417. **Classes of Limitations.** — From the part reserved to society in the enjoyment of private property, from the political interests attaching to it, and from what remained of the ancient community of ownership by State or family, were derived the many limitations with which individual ownership was surrounded. These formed one of the most characteristic qualities of ownership during the Germanic period, but in subsequent periods they fell away in large part, little by little as the right of the individual was made more absolute and exclusive.

The right to restrict individual conduct, in order to keep it in harmony with the social good, was exercised by the State, as representative of all the various interests needing such limitations and because endowed with the necessary means to enforce them. Thus in the State, and hence in the sovereign, a supreme title was recognized over all property. This of itself was a grave encroachment upon the dominion of the individual; but it produced still graver as a consequence of the powers which might be derived from it, to the injury of the rights of others. From the point of view of their effects, these powers were distinguishable into two categories. Some produced limitations to the exercise of the property right, in such wise that the owner could not derive all its benefits or dispose

674

of it in all the ways otherwise possible; others, on the other hand, by restricting the property right to the point where it ceased to exist, were a cause of the extinguishment of individual ownership.

§ 418. **Origin of the Regalia.** — Individual ownership suffered first of all the limitation of not extending, in whole or in part, to certain classes of property which, by nature or the purpose to which they were destined, were better preserved outside of exclusive private control. These fell into the public dominion, with the result, however, that while in Roman law their use remained in this case common to all, in Germanic law, and in general in all the systems of law preceding the present, it was also withdrawn from the individual, and was consolidated under the dominion assumed over it by the State. The reason was that the State, especially in matters relating to property, was not clearly distinguished from the person of the ruler, who, therefore, used to his own benefit what in reality belonged solely to the State. Thus over the things withdrawn from private control were created the regalia or royal prerogatives.[1] Of these the king made monopolies and derived a profit from them, either using them directly or demanding a compensation for their concession.

In the Germanic period, the regalia consisted of waters, forests, mines and pastures. Waters that were declared public were not the subject of private ownership. There was lacking, however, the Roman doctrine that, for such a declaration, there must be a corresponding possibility of use for the public benefit, which the exercise of a private right would either destroy or hinder. As the Germanic king, on the other hand, possessed many courses and expanses of water not directly of common utility, so also, when they were such, he was not responsive to their natural purposes, but prohibited their use or made a profit from them by concessions to private individuals for a compensation. This royal proprietorship is better explained, therefore, as a survival of collective ownership and the " dominium eminens " which resulted from it in favor of the State.[2] Similar regalia existed in woodlands, and these had no qualities that excluded them from private ownership. The explanation is that as private property came into being, wooded land in large part remained in common ownership, either to continue the common benefit of drawing wood, fodder and game from them, or because their reduction to cultivation was not necessary, in view of the abundance of other lands, and would not have been profitable because of the great labor required. Remaining com-

[1] *Ante* § 61.   [2] *Ante* § 406.

mon property, the woodlands were considered to belong to the State, representing the rights of the community, and through the State they were considered to belong to the king. In this way he became their owner, and when he had become such, the rights of others were more and more restricted. They were called "forests" (from the Latin "foras", meaning outside), that is, outside common use; or they were called "closed" or "protected" lands, because enclosed and forbidden to entrance; or proclaimed or "banned" lands, because anyone violating the royal prohibition was placed under the ban.[1]

The waters and woods thus became royal domain, and private individuals were required to abstain from any use of them. They might not fish or hunt, open canals for irrigation, construct mills, bridges or docks, lead animals upon it, cut wood, etc.[2] All these uses were reserved to the sovereign, who, therefore, retained custodians ("valdemanni", "valdatores") on the closed lands; or the use of the land was given to such as paid a price for it ("erbaticum", "grandaticum", "legnaticum", "venaticum"), or had received a special concession from the king.

In the same way the regalia in mines and pastures must have arisen. In the Germanic period the subsoil belonged to the State, for, as private ownership grew out of limitations upon ownership in common, it was restricted to what was necessary, and the owner needed only the surface of the soil. In fact it was not unusual to find it stated that his dominion did not extend below the roots of his trees or the furrows of his plough. Moreover, the Germanic invaders of Italy encountered no principles that were contrary to this state of things, because the Ostrogoths had not only accepted Roman principles, but had even gone further, attributing to the State a right over all precious minerals found in the earth.[3] In no other way can the origin of the regalia or monopoly in mines be explained. The excavations from the silver mines, made in the 900 s by Otto I in Germany, will not suffice as an explanation, since these localities were not private property, and even prior to that the right had existed in the State. True, in the Germanic period, this right was little used, but that was because the mining industries were then but little, if at all, developed. Otto I may, in this sense, have contributed to render the regalia profitable, by giving an impulse to turn them to their intended use.

[1] *Ante* §§ 29, 50.
[2] *Rothar*, 319, 320; *Charlemagne*, 71.
[3] *Cassiodorus*, "Variae," *cit.*, IV, 34; VI, 8.

On the other hand, there was a very general use of the regalia in pasture land, considered as a fiscal right exercisable over others' property. The use of the common lands was generally for pasturage,[1] which thus constituted a right of all members of the community. But when the lands which had belonged to all passed into the ownership of the State (" terrae publicae ", " pascua publica "), a compensation was exacted for the use of the pastures (" erbaticum ", " pensionaticum ", " fida "), except in the case of a special royal concession. This payment thus became a royal right. And since the king might, and in fact did, by the bestowal of offices, gifts and other titles, make concessions of public lands to private persons, these had to support the burden of the pasturage rights, which he was not bound to convey along with the land, but might reserve as a profit to himself; or he might assign them to a third person, who thus acquired a right over the lands of the first grantee; or finally he might convey the pasturage rights to the grantee of the land, who, as representative of the king, came in this way to enjoy the same privilege. Such transfers, originating from the king, might also be repeated with respect to other persons, whose land, once held in common, had fallen into private ownership.

§ 419. **Regalia under the Communes.** — As happened in the case of all the regalia, so of waters, woods, mines and pastures, the seigniors made themselves masters during the feudal period, substituting their own authority for that of the sovereign. Abuses resulted. The first was that these regalia were transformed into rights of a private character, though founded upon reasons of public law, in such wise that they became attached to the feudal estates and could not thereafter be separated from them, even when the fief ceased to have a political character. Another abuse was that their number so increased that they became injurious to private ownership; for as fiefs multiplied, these rights multiplied, each seignior desiring as many as possible for himself. Thus the instances of forbidden uses of waters increased. Woodlands especially became in large part seigniorial " forests ", in spite of resistance of the laws;[2] hunting became the privilege of the lord; the pasture lands were all his and their use had to be paid for; on every hand other innumerable restrictions to ownership arose.

During the period of the mediaeval communes many of these fell away. Over their own territory the communes were the heirs of the feudatories and from them acquired the rights first yielded up

[1] *Ante* § 406.
[2] *Louis the Pious*, 49; *Honorius*, III, Capit. of the year 1282.

by the State. The Peace of Constance expressly enumerated, among the rights recognized in the communes, those of woods, pastures and rivers, which earlier, at the Diet of Roncaglia, the Emperor had himself attempted to claim.[1]

Under the communes all these rights were turned to other purposes. In general they were no longer used for the sole purpose of profit but with a view to social good; the more so as Roman doctrines were re-accepted, which were not adapted to support those of the regalia, in their Germanic significance.

The first consequence was the removal of many prohibitions. It again came to be lawful for all to draw water for irrigation, to hunt, to build mills, to mine, etc. But the State, that is, the commune, did not abandon all rights. Not only were some reserved for State revenue, as, for example, the right of pasture, but over all it asserted its authority, subjecting them to such regulations as seemed necessary to keep them in accord with public interests. It was then that emerged that tendency, still dominant, to limit the exercise of private ownership, so that it might not harm the rights of society. For the use of water, rules were laid down which were beneficial to agriculture, industry, and hygiene. The same was done for pasture land, for its preservation and the prevention of any disorder that might arise out of its common use. Provisions were also made for the woodlands, with regard to cutting, pasturing and especially hunting. The last was limited, for the public benefit, both as to method and season, and to this end was subjected to the requirement of licenses containing the restrictions held necessary in the general interest, to prevent the extinction of the animals, damage to other persons' property, and danger to public security.

§ 420. **Subsequent History of Regalia.** — By these efforts, initiated by the mediaeval communes, an end was certainly not made of all the abuses that might arise from the undue interference of the State in what should more naturally be exclusively objects of private ownership. The States succeeding the mediaeval communes even increased the regalia. Waters were incorporated in the public domain, even though they were without public utility and ran through private lands, so that, in some districts, as, for example, Venetia during the 1500 s, private ownership of water ceased to exist, and its use always required public authorization. Over wooded land not only were powers of various kinds maintained, but the State asserted the right to appropriate all standing timber

---

[1] *Ante* § 77.

which might be of public value, though belonging to private lands. For this purpose special magistrates were instituted, who could inflict fines for contraventions and prevent abandonment or private benefit. In Venetia, for example, all oak trees were reserved for the State arsenal; in Piedmont elm trees were reserved for the needs of the artillery; other reservations existed in Tuscany. And so everywhere, over a long period, such systems, more or less generally accepted, came down from the 1400 s to the first years of the 1800 s. The reservation of the right to mine also continued to be considered a State prerogative. The alum mines, discovered in Roman territory in the 1400 s, were famous for the profits which enabled the Papal Curia to maintain constant and vigorous war against the Turks. Finally, pasture rights, exercised over others' lands in the name of the State, continued also to return a public revenue. But this right assumed more and more a private character and passed by successive stages into private ownership.

The economic reforms of the 1700 s were directed to this problem of the limitations upon the exercise of private ownership. Peter Leopold, Grand Duke of Tuscany, went farthest in these efforts. Prohibitions relating to woodlands and waters ceased; hunting and fishing were again declared the natural rights of all; all might excavate for minerals, with the sole limitation that the right of the owner should be respected, if upon another's land, in which case the latter's consent was necessary and the conditions of the consent had to be performed. Against the private right of pasturage on another's land the State itself intervened, holding the right inseparable from the ownership of the land itself and providing the owner with means, therefore, of emancipating his land and consolidating the two rights.

The effects of these reforms continued. There were, of course, many and repeated attempts at reaction, traces of which are found in the codes, which contain provisions that still reflect the conception of the regalia, as, for example, in the matter of public waters, which are defined as rivers and torrents,[1] and in the matter of mines, to exploit which governmental authorization is required.[2] Notwithstanding the reforms, there has been no abandonment, but indeed a strengthening of the policy, negative rather than otherwise, of surrounding the exercise of ownership with limitations preventive of injury to public interests.

[1] Present Ital. Civil Code, art. 427.
[2] [Law, Nov. 20, 1859.]

§ 421. **Prescribed Uses of Property under the Mediaeval Communes.** — The system of restricting the exercise of the right of property for the benefit of the public did not stop at preventing harmful uses by the owner, but went farther and imposed uses which were, or were thought to be, for the public good and desirable.

This movement had its greatest development in the statutes of the mediaeval cities, which, to further now one and now another public interest, obliged owners to use their property as the laws prescribed. Such provisions were minute and numerous and varied according to local conditions. Some aimed to encourage agriculture. They required an owner to cultivate annually a determined area, or to plant a certain number of trees of a designated kind; they fixed the date of the beginning and the end of the harvests, of the grape gathering, and other important labors; they established regulations between the owners of land and the " coloni " as to labor, compensation, discharge and all other relations. Other communal statutes aimed to encourage industries. Land, therefore, had to be planted in products required for some industry, such as mulberries for silk manufacture, hemp for fabrics, large timber for building and naval construction, and so on. To this end were directed the prescriptions for the upkeep of wooded lands, regulating the cutting and replacement of trees; also the provisions forbidding the cutting of unripe fruit; requiring the cultivation of special products, such as rice, subject to certain regulations; prescribing the steeping of flax beyond a certain distance from habitations; and many others. Much thought was also given to maintaining an abundance of public supplies. This would not have been possible without coercive measures, since frequent hostility and the multiplication of political divisions made it important that each commune should be self sufficient. Exportation was, therefore, prohibited unless there was a superabundance, a fact to be determined by public officials. Wholesale marketing was prohibited until a retail market had been held for a period, varying according to the quality of the product; the policy of price fixing was general; still other provisions were taken to avoid the occurrence of want in the cities.

In subsequent periods the State did not maintain so direct a control over private property, nor would it have been necessary, when political and economic conditions had wholly changed. Nevertheless, wherever it appeared helpful, the laws throughout Italy retained down to recent times their close hold upon the use of private property; and these provisions have been continued in special laws, which aim today to co-ordinate private rights and public interest.

§ 422. **Limitations upon Alienation; Pre-emption, Redemption.** — Lastly, a restriction might be placed on alienation. Inalienability arose by law; it was sometimes absolute, but more often relative.

In the former case, it prevented any alienation whatsoever of the land. In Roman times, the property of the " curiales ", over which the government had accumulated so many liens, was inalienable without license;[1] later, the " sortes ", that is the lands distributed to the Germanic invaders, were inalienable, because this property was the guarantee of the status of a freeman and of the performance of his obligations to the State, and because the family had an hereditary right to it. Family interests, supported by the State, made trust-entails ("fideicommissa") inalienable.[2] So also were the lands upon which rested certain obligations, the performance of which was a matter of public concern, such as the lands of the churches and other religious organizations.

Relative inalienability was more frequent. It forbade the owner to transfer his right to certain determined persons, as, for example, in the Middle Ages, to those who by privilege or for any other personal reason, were not subject to the burdens of the commune. Or it obligated him to convey, if at all, to certain preferred persons. In the person enjoying it, this was called the right of " prelation " (" prelazione ") or " pre-emption " (" preemzione "), and gave rise, if his preference had not been recognized, to a corresponding right of redemption (" retratto " or " riscatto "), assuring its execution. It was known by other names at different times and places. In the southern provinces it was commonly called " jus congrui ", and also, by association with Roman institutions, " jus prothimiseos "; in Corsica it was known as " avocatio "; in Venetia as " recupera "; and by yet other names elsewhere.[3]

§ 423. **Kinds of Redemption** (" Retratto "). — The legal basis of the right of redemption varied according to its kind. First and most important was that " jure sanguinis ", *i.e.*, founded on the right which relatives enjoyed, as a consequence of ancient family co-ownership,[4] to intervene in a conveyance of family property by one of their members, and to authorize it by their personal consent.

---

[1] *Ante* § 6.   [2] *Ante* § 385.
[3] *Tamassia*, "Il diritto de prelazione e l'espropriazione forzata negli statuti dei comuni italiani" (Bologna, 1885).
[4] *Ante* § 409.

If their consent had not been asked, the relatives might require that the land be returned to the family; if it had been asked but not given, the relatives might prevent one of their number selling his property, only by offering to meet the need actuating the alienation, taking in compensation the property in question.

The Lombard law was clear. The adoptive father might not sell his property over which his adopted son had a right; but if, in extremity, he turned to the son, asking his aid in return for the preservation of his estate, and did not receive it, he was free to sell his property as and to whom he pleased.[1] The owner was bound to proceed similarly with all who had any right of succession, even though remote, over the object to be conveyed, that is with all agnates. This was due to the right of preference (" prelazione ") or of redemption (" retratto "), called " familial " or " noble ", by reason of its origin.

There was a second kind, " jure contiguitatis loci ", *i.e.* by right of vicinage, so called because, besides the relatives, the neighbors also of the landowner thereby obtained a similar right. It took its origin in the Roman fiscal laws and in the conditions thereby laid upon land owners in the last years of the Empire. The system which made one person responsible for another, with regard to debts owed the State, was applied as widely as possible. When several worked a piece of land in association, they were held jointly liable for taxes. Such associations or societies came to be formed also by the laws, and especially after the so-called " adjectio " or obligation cast upon owners to take over adjacent lands — abandoned because of sterility, excessive burdens, or other reasons — in order that the State should not lose its desired income. It was, therefore, to the interest of all to have as associations or as single contiguous neighbors such individuals as would give assurance that they would not desert the land or fail to perform the obligations inhering to it. And thus arose the right to see that persons, concerning whom such assurance was not possible, should not come into the vicinage. To this end there was need of a right in neighbors to be preferred to outsiders in the acquisition of vicinage lands. While it cannot be denied that such a condition attaching to ownership influenced the formation of the right of preference among neighbors, nevertheless all Germanic influence should not be excluded from the history of this kind of redemption. Suffice to observe that, on the division of a family estate, neighbors took the place of relatives, for relatives must have

[1] *Rothar*, 173.

been the first neighbors; and that, therefore, many of the obligations between relatives, derived from family solidarity, were transferred to neighbors, *e.g.* common responsibility for a crime committed by an unknown person in the vicinage; mutual suretyship;
labor in common, for which they formed themselves into societies,
as in antiquity; reciprocal duty of testifying in court; and other
like duties.[1] Thus neighbors acquired rights, formerly belonging
to the family, and of these one was this very right of preference,
exercised among each other on the occasion of conveyances.   To
this the laws were favorable, in order to prevent the dismemberment of lands forming together the " corpus " of an estate.   It has
already been noted that Charles the Bald, to prevent the destruction of the " mansi ",[2] permitted their sale only among those living
within them, that is, among neighbors; and the Church had already
similarly disposed with regard to its estates, in order that they
should not lose their unity.

A third class of redemption was that by right of citizenship,
justified, that is, " jure civitatis."   By it the citizens, in last resort
represented by the commune, were preferred over foreigners.   To
the Roman elements, whereby the citizens might all be held as
contiguous owners within the communal territory, and to the
Germanic elements, maintaining among the inhabitants of the
commune traces of ancient village ownership in common, was
added, to form this third type of redemption, the political interest
of the Italian commune.   Because of its small territory and almost
constant hostility towards adjacent territories, the commune dared
not permit lands within its boundaries to pass to strangers who, if
not unfriendly, at least had no interest in its prosperity.   It was,
therefore, during the mediaeval communes that this as well as the
other rights of relatives and neighbors attained their greatest
importance.   For, not only did the statutory legislation of the
communes fuse together the various principles to form the true
redemption (" retratto ") of Italian law, but also the emancipation
of the individual from his ancient family bonds and the growth in
the number of land owners, due to the wealth acquired by the
citizens and the liberation of the peasantry, made conveyances far
more frequent, and the need more imperative that the law should
intervene to prevent resulting harm.

§ 424. **Exercise of Redemption.** — The exercise of the right of
preference or of redemption was subject to certain conditions, referring chiefly to the persons who could claim it and to time and price.

[1] *Rothar*, 146, *Liutprand*, 55 .   [2] *Ante* § 412.

As to persons, first in order of preference came relatives, and among them originally and generally came the one who would have had the right to inherit the property conveyed, that is, the nearest agnate.   But as family ties weakened and the purpose of redemption became the prevention of injurious dismemberment of estates, there were included among the relatives also those merely of the same blood, and preference was determined by proximity of degree, according to canonical computation.   There were some special rules.   One was that of the " jus recadentiae ", applied also to inheritance, by which the right belonged to the relative in the line through which the property to be conveyed had been derived. The other was formed by a combination of the " jus sanguinis " and the " jus contiguitatis ", and gave the preference to the relative who was also an adjacent owner, and, if several relatives were such, to the one having the largest contiguous boundary.

If there were no relatives, or if they did not wish to, or could not, exercise their right of redemption, it next fell to the neighbors, first the co-owners, if there were any, then to the largest contiguous owners and after them to the other neighbors.   Finally came the inhabitants of the commune.

Additional rules were established as to the time of exercise.   It could not be permitted that the transferee of the land should remain perpetually threatened with the exercise of others' rights of redemption; it must be exerted within a given time or lost.   The periods varied very much, from a few months, or a year and a day, with gradual increase up to thirty years, that is, the ordinary prescriptive period.   The shorter terms, however, were commonest. Whatever it might be, the time did not always and necessarily run from the date of the alienation, but from notice of it, received when no impediment existed to the exercise of the right.   Hence the further rule, that the transfer of land must be made public, through notarial or judicial notice, and more often by " stride ", that is, by a crier through the public streets.   When this was done in a legal manner, no exception to the conveyance might be raised, if the right to redeem was not claimed within the time fixed.

Finally, there were conditions of price.   This was usually made the same as the price for which the land, over which the right of pre-emption was asserted, could have been sold or actually had been sold; and in the latter case the expenses of the purchase had to be added.   This rule, too, suffered exceptions.   Some of the statutes of the mediaeval cities provided that those having the right of pre-emption might exercise it for a less price than would be demanded of a stranger, while others on the contrary increased it by a given percentage, proportioned to the degree of relationship.

§ 425. **Limitations; Abolition of Redemption.** — From the exercise of the right of redemption several inconveniences might arise, principal among which was the uncertainty of a grantee's title, at least for a while; another was that ownership was not left free to the extent that public interest demanded. It was not long, therefore, before an opposing tendency showed itself. At first this took the form of limitations, to serve as guarantees against abuses. The right of redemption might in fact be exercised out of malice, with an intent to injure. The law, therefore, required an oath that it was exercised for one's own benefit, and not for the account of a third person; the property redeemed might not be reconveyed within a fixed time. Redemption might furthermore result in the owner's loss of all freedom of action with respect to his property, with consequent damage; or on the other hand it might produce an excessive accumulation of property in one individual. To prevent this, certain kinds of property were exempt from the claim of preference, which was frequently limited solely to property inherited from ancestors; exempt also was the property settled as a marriage portion, given by gift or exchange, or left by will, or conveyed in settlement of a dispute. Thus redemption came to be limited to the cases of sales and of transactions, almost of the nature of sales, such as the lien of the hypotec or the contract of emphyteusis.

Nevertheless, however limited, the right continued, though the reasons of its existence had disappeared. The laws preserved it during the 1700 s, *e.g.* those of Piedmont of 1770, those of Francis III of Este, and Italian legislation generally until the introduction of French laws. Some attempts to abolish or reduce it, however, had been made. In 1571, Pope Pius V withdrew it from neighbors and co-tenants, but it was restored in 1574 by Gregory XIII; in 1751, the Grand Duke of Tuscany, Francis of Lorraine, prohibited it between co-tenants, and his son, Leopold, attempted its abolition. But, as already stated, abolition came about through the French laws between 1798 and 1808, step by step, as French domination extended over Italy. The legislation of the restored governments sought, as they did in the case of many other institutions, to breathe new life into what remained of the right of redemption; but today all traces of it have been erased from the Civil Code.

TOPIC 2.   EXTINGUISHMENT OF OWNERSHIP

§ 426. **Power of the State.** — Not only might ownership suffer limitations of exercise, in the various manners just described, but its very existence might also be affected. For the State, for the reasons already mentioned,[1] could decree its extinction in relation to certain objects or persons.

Confiscation was one of these powers. It deprived of ownership not only the person condemned for a crime of his own doing, but also his heirs or others who were innocent of wrongdoing. In the Germanic period confiscation was rather common, especially as a penalty for crimes of disloyalty to the State.

Another example was succession by the State or escheat which, in the Germanic period, was not limited to cases where the deceased left no relatives, but was claimed by the State even in competition with them, so that at least a part of the estate was taken from them. If, for example, a decedent left legitimate daughters and natural sons, but no agnates, the share of the last, that is, one-third, fell to the State.[2] Like confiscation, escheat came to be of more and more restricted application, as the doctrine of the State's right over private property weakened; today the former has lost all importance, being limited to objects which are themselves a contravention of the law; while the latter is only exercised when the decedent's property lacks an owner because of a failure of kin.

The power of the State to terminate ownership for reasons of public policy manifested itself in the fullest manner where it appropriated to itself the entire property, either by destruction of the title, as happened in the suppression of mortmain, or by contracting with the owner, as in the case of expropriation.

§ 427. **Mortmain.** — The properties of the Church, because of their vast extent and inalienability, provided the best example of mortmain. The patrimony of the Church had many constant sources of aggrandizement. Inheritance by members of religious orders, endowments for pious uses, the gifts of the faithful, were, throughout the Middle Ages, very copious springs of wealth for the Church. On the other hand, every outlet was closed to its loss, when once acquired. The inalienability of ecclesiastical property, early recognized by the Roman, and later sustained by canon law, was confirmed by that of the Germanic invaders, by the statutes of the mediaeval communes, and by subsequent Italian legislation, almost down to the present time.

[1] *Ante* § 417.   [2] *Rothar*, 158.

At first the increase of ecclesiastical estates was a benefit rather than a harm. In the hands of religious institutions, uncultivated lands were ploughed; with the abundance of land, the scanty population was not conscious that large areas were being withdrawn from trade and credit; by placing one's property in the name of the Church a sure defense was found from the attacks of the powerful; ecclesiastical property had a task of public charity to perform, for by law or the intent of the donor the support of schools, hospitals, the poor, sacred edifices, and travelers' hospices was a charge upon the rents of the Church. Such benefits were lost, however, so soon as the concentration of property in the clergy passed beyond reasonable bounds and social conditions so changed that the causes disappeared which had made the Church's patrimony a public benefit. There was danger that all individual property would vanish, drawn into the vast vortex of ecclesiastical mortmain. The resulting damage was becoming evident to all. The State suffered; it could make but an impoverished and weak front against the Church; through immunities or charters of privilege it lost, over a great portion of its territories, the taxes and services which private owners had paid. Society was damaged, because the vast ecclesiastical domains on the one hand were an obstacle to the emancipation of the rustic serfs, needed for their cultivation, and on the other hand, by their excessive enrichment, caused the corruption and deviation of the clergy from their proper duties. Public economy also suffered: ecclesiastical mortmain dried up very fruitful sources of national wealth, by closing vast estates to the use of credit and to commercial circulation, and by discouraging agriculture and industry over immense areas, whose owner no longer felt the stimulus of self interest and need.

Society tolerated these evils until it came to a clear recognition of them and so long as it lacked the power to remove them. These once gained, it initiated that movement, based upon the sovereign right of the State, which eventually led to the suppression of ecclesiastical mortmain.

§ 428. **Suppression of Mortmain.** — In the Germanic laws, this movement was not yet evident. There were but a few provisions, aimed to prevent gross abuses, such as the often repeated prohibition against benefiting the Church to the injury of heirs. It was in the time of the mediaeval communes that an opposing tendency manifested itself, directed also for political reasons against the rich clergy, as allies of the Empire. Here and there ardent reformers, such as Arnold of Brescia, raised a voice to lead the clergy back to apostolic poverty, while the communes felt it important that neither person nor property should be legally exempt from the support of the public expenses. These at once set out to suppress mortmain. They forbade the acquisition of lands by citizens who did not participate in the common obligations towards the State, and thus checked the increase of the Church's patrimony. A similar ordinance was enacted by Roger for the Kingdom of Sicily; before him Frederick II, with the same intent, by the constitution of 1231, which became the basis of all subsequent legislation on the subject in southern Italy, decreed that land could not, under any title, be transferred to a religious order, save on condition that it should be sold within a year.[1] This rule was adopted in the statutes of the mediaeval cities — by Modena in 1327 and by the Venetian Republic — which required that not only the lands given outright to religious bodies, but also those charged with any rent or other right in their favor, should be sold by them. These rules, extended later to all territory subject to the Republic, were a cause of that serious disagreement with the Holy See for which the names of Sarpi and Pope Paul IV are remembered.

These laws prevented the growth of mortmain, but did not destroy it where it already existed. But such an attack soon took form. First it aimed to subject such land to the ordinary burdens, even to a special tax, called mortmain tax, consisting of part of the value of the land, payable every so many years, as the price of a license from the sovereign to the ecclesiastical institution to hold property. It was a radical step; if the sovereign refused the license, the title of the order would no longer receive legal recognition. On the other hand, there were not lacking laws that, by way of reaction, favored ecclesiastical estates. Thus the constitution of Frederick II was abolished by the Angevins; in Sicily, without express repeal, it fell into disuse; there was no question of such laws in the States of the Church; nor were the foreign governments, Spain and Austria, opposed to mortmain, though they received petitions and protests, such as that of the city of Naples to Charles VI, in 1712, and by the Sicilian Parliaments to Charles III (Charles VII of Naples), in 1738.

We thus see how, though undertaken so long ago, the struggle against ecclesiastical mortmain was not victorious until modern times. In the 1700 s, urged on by the Encyclopaedists and economists, who demanded its suppression, there were also reforms touching the principles governing ecclesiastical property. The

[1] *Scaduto*, "Stato e Chiesa nelle due Sicilie" (Palermo, 1887), chap. 4.

method pursued, however, was to seek peace with the Church through mutual concessions; and in fact, from the middle to the end of the 1700 s nothing was done affecting Church property except by concordat with the Holy See.[1] But the question was abruptly settled by the French Constituent Assembly, which, in 1789, declared all lands held in mortmain to be the property of the nation, and this declaration acquired legal force in Italy, as the French conquest proceeded. The restored governments re-established mortmain and it again flourished; but these lands returned to the State, when the laws now in force decreed the suppression of the religious orders.[2]

§ 429. **Right of Eminent Domain.** — The principle that public interests must take precedence over private has been the constant basis of the recognized right of the State to expropriate, that is, take over the ownership of private property. The elements of this principle that have varied have been the manner of conceiving public interest and the means of exercising the right.

In the Germanic period the interest of the public was confused with that of the prince. As a consequence of the regalia or royal prerogatives, attributed to him by reason of the supreme dominion which he held over all his territory, the prince might take possession of private property whenever he deemed it useful, without the necessity of compensating the owner, for the latter had only such right of ownership as the sovereign, personifying the State, had conceded and preserved to him. The occupation of the conquered lands and their ensuing distribution among the invaders, without indemnity to the despoiled, was a true expropriation, under the law of the conquering State. The same should be said of the frequent conversions of Church property by sovereigns, to satisfy State needs; and so also of the conversions of private property, judging from the recitals frequently recurring in the documents of the period, according to which the vendor declared that he assumed no guarantee concerning any action by the State, with respect to the land sold.

With such standards as these regulating expropriation throughout the Germanic period, abuses were certain to, and in fact did, arise. They increased under feudalism, when the purposes and interests of the seigniors were substituted for those of the State, as a consequence of the transfer to them of many, if not all, sovereign rights.

[1] With Naples, 1741, 1769, 1776; Sicily, 1771; Tuscany, 1751, 1769; Genoa, 1761; Modena, 1763, 1767; Parma, 1764, 1774; Lucca, 1764; Lombardy, 1767; Venice, 1767, etc.
[2] [Together with the conversion of their property in 1867.]

The succeeding communes continued to make large use of the right of expropriation, which they needed for their manifold interests. But at the same time they began to establish the two fundamental conditions of justifiable expropriation, viz. public utility and compensation of the individual. In the statutes of the mediaeval cities are enumerated the principal grounds for the expropriation of private property. For the most part they were the opening of streets and drains, the construction of walls and river embankments, in short, works of real public interest. The rule as to compensation, which was also formulated, provided that it should be due in every case and that the amount should be fixed by agreement between the interested individual and the public authority, or, if necessary, by arbitrators.

These rules were never after abandoned. Not that abuses ceased, or that authors were lacking to defend in the sovereign prince, as representing the State, the continuation, as regalia, of the right of eminent domain over all his territory and hence his right to expropriate without true public interest and without compensation to the owner. But abuses were fewer as the law's authority grew firmer. Opposed to those who defended the regalia, appeared other authors, less subservient to royalty, who advanced the doctrine that not even the sovereign might be permitted to injure others, and that, therefore, public interest on the one hand and the right to compensation on the other must always accompany expropriation. This period, which extended from the first Glossators to the 1600 s, represented, in substance, a time of conflict in the subject between Germanic principles and the more moderate and just doctrines, derived from the Roman law and supported by the canon law, which were accepted by the governments as they progressed towards a new civilization. From this conflict finally emerged the well defined theory of the right of eminent domain, which recognizes the right in the sovereign authority of the State, founds it upon a recognized social interest, and accompanies it always with compensation to the owner.

§ 430. **Special Forms of Eminent Domain.** — A peculiarity worthy of note in the history of expropriation by right of eminent domain is that there developed an instance in which the public advantage was concealed under a private interest and public authority intervened only as intermediary between the private owners who desired to utilize the right. This form of expropriation, called " enlargement " ("ingrossazione "), " increment " ("incremento "), " straightening " (" drizatio "), was very common in the period of the mediaeval communes. It might arise in several ways. If a lot was too small to provide residence for " coloni " or return fair compensation for the cost of cultivation, and at the same time was enclosed within a large estate or located along its boundary, the owner of the latter had the right to force the smaller owner to convey his land to him by sale or exchange, and incorporate it in his own lands, which were thus " enlarged " or " straightened." Hence the names given to this particular kind of expropriation. Or the owner of the land might not be the owner of the surface soil,[1] so that the crops belonged to the latter. In this case also the former had the right to require that what was by nature accessory should be sold to him in order to add it to the principal object of ownership. If a private individual desired to construct a great palace in the city, he might by law force the owners of the neighboring houses to sell to him, to the extent necessary for his own construction. In all these examples it is apparent that the public interest was found either in the embellishment of the city, the encouragement of agriculture, or the liberation of land from some encumbrance. But along with these motives there was the private interest, which was indeed the immediate cause of the expropriation.

In the period of the mediaeval communes expropriation for the purpose of " enlargement " reached its greatest development. But it was retained also in the legislation of the governments that followed and even in the 1700 s it was found in the laws of Modena, Lucca and elsewhere. It disappeared, however, along with so many other traces of the earlier period, when the French Revolution ushered in a new era, and has found no place in the present law.

Modern legislation has perfected the theory of the right of eminent domain, exercised for a common benefit. It has risen above special instances to form an institution regulated by special rules, based always upon public utility and the right of compensation.[2]

[1] *Ante* § 415.   [2] [Civil Code, arts. 438, 2076–2092.]

CHAPTER XVIII

MODES OF ACQUIRING PROPERTY

§ 431. **Contact of Germanic and Roman Law.** — While it may not be said that the ancient Germanic peoples took no notice of the modes by which title is acquired, for such a statement would contradict the known facts of the Germanic period, it is nevertheless true that they were not acquainted with all modes, and did not make them the object of special legal rules until their law came in contact with Roman law.   In fact the first Germanic laws concerning modes of acquisition were inspired by Roman ideas, which either modified the ancient customs, as, for example, the excessive freedom to hunt, or accepted principles not before known, as in the case of title by accession.   Thus, in this field of law also, is to be found a mingling of both elements, Roman and Germanic. It is, furthermore, to be observed that what the Germanic invaders received from the Roman law was particularly those modes of acquisition which were shown, or at least revealed to them by the Romans; while of their own they preserved mostly those first known to the Germanic peoples, and of these chiefly the modes that had received legal form in antiquity, and only to a less degree those which, existing in popular custom, were systematized later as they developed under the influence of the Roman law.

692

And it should not be forgotten that the modes of acquisition peculiar to the Germanic period were as much the consequence of the history of the origin of ownership itself as of the elements entering into its conception.[1] The clarification of this conception, especially under the action of Roman law, had the same effect upon the modes of acquisition, as upon all phases of the law of property: considerations not properly germane were gradually abandoned and, by a fresh address to Roman precepts, the uniform and perfected rules of modern law were attained.

Topic 1. Occupation

§ 432. **Personal Property.** — As individual ownership of movable objects was recognized from antiquity,[2] and as such objects, when abandoned, might, therefore, be considered as without an owner, the Germanic law, like the Roman law, admitted of their acquisition by occupation. It was something that did not even need statement, and if the law made mention of it, it was due to the example of the Roman law. Indeed not only did their law faithfully reflect the idea, namely, that an ownerless object belonged by the law of nature to whoever first gained possession of it, but this was repeated in a phraseology almost identical to that of the corresponding Roman rule.[3]

Occupation of movable objects might take place in various ways. The most natural was that of the chase, a right open to all free men without need of confirmatory laws. These but indicated limitations, derived from those factual considerations which negatived an existing absence of ownership of the animal in question. If the animal bore any indication whatsoever of another's ownership, because subject to control, as in the case of falcons, hunting dogs, and in general the tamer animals; or because intended for a purpose, e.g. a definite labor or a domestic use, as was true of domestic animals; or because bearing a wound received within twenty-four hours, or because still pursued or in a snare; or if the trees in which the birds nested were marked; or if the woods or other place of chase had been declared a " forest ",[4] — if any of these facts or signs were present, they indicated that the animal was not without an owner and so might not be taken by the hunter. Such were the provisions of the Lombard laws.[5] Later, however, as

[1] *Ante* § 416.
[2] *Ante* § 401.
[3] *Cf. Rothar*, 319, and *Justinian*, Digest, II, 1, 1, § 12.
[4] *Ante* § 417.   [5] *Rothar*, 309–321.

already seen, the right of chase was more and more limited,[1] until it became regalia of the State or feudal lord. But when it was restored as a common right, substantially these same limitations came again into force, so that, except for certain applications due to the special conditions of the period, they did not differ from the rules of the Roman law and of present day legislation.

Another mode of occupation of movable objects was *discovery*, that is, the finding of an object without an owner. This too might happen in various ways. As to *treasure-trove* the rules of Germanic law differed from those of the Roman law. Among the Germanic peoples the right of the land-owner might not extend to the subsoil.[2] Until individual ownership arose, this remained the property of the State. To the State, therefore, belonged treasure-trove and by way of compensation a portion was given to the discoverer, though nothing was given to the proprietor of the land, whereas the last, under Roman law, had the major right. The Roman principle of giving a portion to the owner of the land began to be recognized again in the period of the Carlovingians, by a law which awarded one-third to the religious order on whose lands it had been found.[3] Roman influence was even clearer in the Books of the Fiefs ("Libri feudorum"), where a distinction was made between a treasure found by chance and that found as a result of special search. In the former case it was divided with the finder; in the latter it was awarded entirely to the owner of the soil, and to the State, if discovered upon the public domain.[4] The different combinations of rights possible between the three parties, State, finder and land-owner, gave rise to the variations in subsequent systems. Some held to Germanic law, preferring the State, until the exaggerated notion was reached that all invariably belonged to the State, as was decreed by William II in the Kingdom of Sicily;[5] other rules leaned to the Roman law, as those of Charles II of Anjou, who limited the right of the State to such treasure as was found upon the public lands, and provided that in other cases it should be divided between the finder and the land-owner. These Roman rules are found today in the present Italian Code.[6]

Another sort of discovery was that relating to *mislaid* objects. These were not presumed to be ownerless until knowledge or a

---

[1] *Ante* § 419.   [2] *Ante* § 415.
[3] "Capitula Italica", c. 5, ed. *Boretius*, "Capitularien in Langobardenreich", (1864), I, 215.
[4] "Libri feudorum", II, 56; *cf. Justinian*, Code, "De rev. div.", 1, 2, § 39.
[5] "Constitutiones regni Siciliae", III, 31.
[6] Art. 714.

presumption arose that their proprietor intended to abandon them, and so long as the formalities required by law to establish this had not been fulfilled, no title by occupation could be gained. This principle has remained constant through all periods; the differences observable have pertained to the formalities and means applied by the law to obtain a knowledge whether the objects were really without an owner. Germanic law held that one who found an object on a public way, or an animal on his land, might not appropriate it, but should deposit it with the judge and have it publicly cried four or five times in the square before the church, while the people were assembled there, so that the owner might have notice and recover it if mislaid involuntarily. If none claimed it, title passed to the finder.[1] Similar rules obtained in the mediaeval communes, which required that notice of objects found should be published in the court house or church, and that the finder, on failure to do so, should suffer a penalty; and like rules were adopted in all subsequent laws.[2]

The property of *shipwrecked* persons, found either in the sea or cast upon the shore, received special treatment. Because of the special status occupied in antiquity by the foreigner who had not received the king's protection, as was in fact the case of one shipwrecked, his property was considered ownerless and therefore fell to the first person who took possession of it. But this barbarous law, after a long struggle, disappeared from civilized society.[3] Similarly special rules governed property occupied in war, *i.e.* the war prize or "preda bellica." Here Germanic and Roman law agreed. Under neither did the enemy possess rights, and as conquered territory became the property of the victorious State, so the movable property of the vanquished belonged to whoever first made himself master of it. A particular application of this was made by the mediaeval communes in the matter of "reprisals."[4] Whoever obtained the right of reprisal might seize the property of the person against whom the right had been granted. But little by little, and especially with the formation of treaties and the rise of international law, belligerent occupation, as a mode of acquisition, disappeared, and no mention of it is made in the law of the present day.

§ 433. **Real Property.** — Germanic law did not admit of an individual's gaining title by occupation of immovable property, especially land, because it did not admit the possibility of its being

[1] *Rothar*, 260, 343, 347.
[2] Ital. Civil Code, arts. 915–918.
[3] *Ante* § 298.
[4] *Ante* § 47.

without an owner. The supreme title of the State brought the
lands which had not yet come under individual ownership, or which
had been abandoned, within the proprietorship of the sovereign,
and they therefore could not be an object of occupation by another. Land could be acquired by occupation, but by the State,
by right of conquest, and not otherwise. Such was the basis upon
which the Germanic State acquired its Italian territories, which
were then divided among its members. For distribution by the
State, that is, concession by the sovereign prince, was the sole title
by which occupied lands could become the object of individual
ownership. Because of the great quantity of abandoned land, it
might happen that a family, or more often a monastery, would
establish itself there and cultivate it. This was a beginning by
which title might be acquired, but it was not of itself a perfect
title. An essential element in this case also was the concession by
the sovereign, which was not in fact difficult to obtain and which,
by legalizing the pre-existing occupation on the basis of the labor
expended, became the origin of many ecclesiastical estates. The
ploughing of uncultivated lands was even more encouraged in the
time of the mediaeval communes, and was a basis of acquiring
ownership, though always through a grant from the State and not
by the sole fact of occupation. The latter mode was further hindered by the ancient doctrine that vacant lands were regalia, so
that they could not be considered as ownerless. Of this traces
long remained and reappeared in the codes. In the present Civil
Code there is no sign of it,[1] and it may be truly said that, in the
present system of property, there are no lands without owner
within the territory of the State. The discoverer of unknown
lands may become their owner by occupation, when facts are
additionally present indicative of their reduction to possession.

TOPIC 2. ACCESSION [2]

§ 434. **Kinds.** — The rule of the Roman law that a thing which
was accessory to another should, in respect to ownership, follow
the principal object, *i.e.* the object from which it received its special
utility, was but partly accepted by Germanic law, and that little

---

[1] Art. 711. [This Article does not specifically mention land; but on
the contrary cites wild animals and fish, treasure, and abandoned personal
property. Inasmuch as the condition laid down for occupation (viz., that
the thing is not, but may become the object of ownership) is as applicable to land as to personalty, the Article is considered to apply to land.
Giorgi, "La dottrina delle persone giuridiche", II, 49.]

[2] *G. Blandini*, "L'accessione nel diritto longobardo", in "Archivio
giuridico", vol. XLVI, nos. 4, 5.

solely as a consequence of Roman influence. The reasons were many: the supreme title of the State, which penetrated wherever individual right had not become effective and complete; consideration for labor expended which it did not seem just to leave without compensation; the possibility of distinct rights over different parts of the same object. As a consequence the Roman rules governing accession were modified by other and different Germanic principles to form a mixed theory, in force in the subsequent periods, and of which some traces are found in the present Italian Code.

Three kinds of accession are to be noted, according to the three ways in which the accessory might be united to the principal object. It might be the natural product of the latter; a natural, though external, force might have united them; or the voluntary act of man might have brought them together.

§ 435. **Fruits.** — The first of these cases was that of acquisition, by accession, of the *fruits* of a thing, whether the products of land, the young of animals, or, by extension, so-called " civil " or pecuniary fruits ("fructus civiles"). The principle was one of natural reason, but it might, nevertheless, give rise to doubts and contrary solutions, when a continuity of ownership was lacking in the same person, that is, when there was a change of ownership intermediate between the expenditure of the labor necessary for the production of the fruits and their production itself. In Roman, as in modern law, the question was of easy solution, as no right other than that of the actual owner was recognized. Whoever was owner of the thing at the moment of the maturity of its fruits, acquired these also, subject to any contrary agreement that had been made at the time of the transfer of title. Such was not, however, the Germanic rule, which, out of consideration for the labor expended, awarded the fruits to the person whose efforts had produced them. But the solution of the question of ownership in such cases would raise difficulties and dangers, if always left to the decision of the interested parties. There thus came to be established a fixed point, a day of the year, up to which, according to custom, the more important labor of the fields should be completed. If owner of the land up to that date, he who had performed the labor had the right later to gather the fruits. By the statutes of the mediaeval communes the termination of this period was made the first of March. Whoever, therefore, conveyed his land on the first of that month had a right to the whole year's fruits, since presumed to have performed the labor essential to their production. This was a serious consequence that might also be the cause of hardships, to remove which the rule was moderated. In some places the date after which the fruits fell to the first possessor was postponed, for example to June first; elsewhere two dates were fixed, according to which an owner, who conveyed before the first, could make no claim to the crops; one who surrendered the land between the two dates had a right to the fruits that ripened up to the second; if the conveyance was subsequent to the second date, the grantor might harvest all the crops for the agricultural year, which generally ended at vintage time. There were also examples, such as the Modenese laws, which applied the Roman rule as to "civil" or pecuniary fruits, and divided also natural fruits between the two owners, in proportion to the time that each had been in possession during the year.

All this was intended to give to labor a proportionate compensation out of the fruits which it had produced. But there was no longer need of so complete a system on the revival of the Roman rule, which is in fact that of the present Italian Code,[1] namely that the natural fruits are acquired by the person who is owner of the land at the moment of their separation.

§ 436. **Fluvial Accession.** — The second case of accession, in which a natural force produced a union of two objects, was that known as fluvial. The earliest Germanic law was silent on this type and left it to be governed by the Roman rule that the accessory followed the principal. But when, with the exception of very small water courses between private lands, the regalia were extended over rivers, torrents and other water courses of any importance,[2] and when all the profits that could be derived from these waters belonged to the sovereign, there came also to belong to him all the land that formed in them by accession. Rules different from the Roman law were thus necessary. An islet formed in running water, a river-bed left dry, an alluvial increment to the shore, all were property over which riparian owners had no right, since they belonged to the sovereign. The Roman rule, in all respects opposed to this, at a later period attracted jurists and legislators, who revived its theories after the Germanic period had passed. All traces of the older régime, however, did not disappear; indeed they may even be found in the present Italian Code. If on the one hand this has followed the Roman law and rejected the novelties of the French Code,[3] adopted by several of the subse-

---

[1] Art. 480.
[2] *Ante* § 420.
[3] [French Civil Code, original art. 563, modified by the Law of April 8, 1898, art. 37; Ital. Civil Code, arts. 454, 461.]

quent Italian codes, according to which an abandoned river-bed is divided, by way of compensation, between the owners on whose land the new channel has formed; on the other hand it has departed from the Roman theory in some cases, preferring the Germanic tradition, as, for example, in the rule that an island formed in a navigable stream belongs to the State, subject solely to an obligation to compensate the riparian owner if the island has been formed by a sudden separation of the soil from his shore.[1]

§ 437. Accession by Labor. — Lastly, accession might result from a man's labor. In this also the Germanic law possessed rules unknown to the Romans, due to the consideration paid to labor, which gave rise to the feeling that it should not go uncompensated, and to the possibility that the different parts of a single object might have different owners. The consequences may be illustrated in separate instances. The Roman " aedificium ", as in modern Italian law,[2] became the property of the owner of the soil upon which it was built, subject to reimbursement for the value, or cost, or the recovery of damages by the owner of the materials used in the construction. In Germanic law, on the other hand, unity of house and land in point of ownership was not necessary. It is true that a law declared that whoever built on another's land lost house and labor,[3] but the purpose of this provision was penal, in that it presumed the bad faith of the builder. The law, by its purpose, declared in fact that everyone must know what does not belong to him; " Omnes scire debent quod suum non est." The words were borrowed from an analogous Roman law, referring to the case of bad faith, and subjecting those to whom it applied to an action for theft (" actio furti ").[4] Otherwise, if one were to lose both his labor and the thing which he had in good faith constructed, the Germanic law would, against its own principles, have been not only unjust but indeed severer than the Roman law, which gave to the person constructing in good faith both a right to reimbursement for the value lost and the cost sustained and also possession of the construction until his right had been satisfied. And if the narrower interpretation of those who supported the contrary opinion, i.e. the limitation of Rothar's law to the case of bad faith, had arisen in later Italian practice, as is specifically declared in the " Expositio " to the Lombard Edict, and in

[1] Ital. Civil Code, arts. 457, 461.
[2] [Civil Code, art. 452.]
[3] *Rothar*, 151.
[4] *Justinian*, Code, VIII, 4, 11; Institutes, II, 1, § 30.

the commentaries of Albert and Ariprand,[1] it would have meant that the legists, altering the principles of the Edict, had departed from Roman law, at the very time they were seeking instead to introduce it into the Edict.   As to the practical consequences of the Lombard law, grave difficulties could not arise, once the Germanic principle was recognized that there was no necessary accession as between the soil and the construction built upon it, since each might belong to different owners.   The principle received an important application with regard to the improvements made by the " colonus ", the vassal or any other having mere possession. Since such improvements might not belong by accession to the land owner, the builder, on giving up possession, was given the right either to remove them or to recover compensation.[2]   The same was true of the products of cultivation, *i.e.* crops or emblements.   What had been planted or sown belonged by Roman law to the owner of the soil, who was bound to compensate the person who had set them out in good faith.   In Germanic law, on the other hand, except where the fruits were taken away as a punishment of one whose labor had been performed in bad faith,[3] what was above ground might belong to a person distinct from the owner of the land.   Examples were not rare of the sale of land, excepting the crops, because these did not belong to the vendor; or of the sale of crops without the land.   Such principles had a long life, and were found also in the statutory law of the mediaeval communes, though this often exhibited a purpose to return to the principles of the Roman law.   These statutes indeed contained some provisions destructive of the consequences of the Germanic doctrine, such, for example, as the rule permitting the owner of the soil to force the owner of the plants upon it to sell them to him.[4] The Roman rules, restored to honor, are those which have been adopted by the present law of this subject.[5]

TOPIC 3.   PRESCRIPTION

§ 438.   **Rise of Germanic Prescription.** — Among the Germanic tribes continuous possession, during a certain time and under certain conditions, did not have the same effect that it had among the

[1] [See the description of these sources in "Continental Legal History Series", Vol. I, "General Survey", pp. 98, 102, translated from *Calisse* "Fonti".]

[2] "Libri feudorum", II, 28.

[3] *Rothar*, 354.

[4] *Ante* § 430.

[5] [Ital. Civil Code, art. 444].

Romans, namely, of extinguishing a right in one person ("prae-scriptio") and giving rise to a new corresponding right in another ("usucapio"). The reason is found in the history of Germanic property rights. The customs of these people, when their life was nomadic, did not permit of a prolonged possession; and if it did, no presumption thereupon arose that ownership accompanied it, since individual ownership was as yet unknown. But later when they made permanent homes and felt the influence of the Roman law, possession among them also gained an efficacy that it at first lacked, beginning, as was natural to the condition of the people, first in the customs, and then passing into the laws. Paul the Deacon tells how Lopichi, his ancestor, returning to Italy after a long absence, was prevented from recovering possession of his family property, by those who had held it " longa et diuturna pos-sessione." [1] The laws were stubbornly resisted, and when they were forced to adopt the principles of prescription, they did so in a way not to reproduce those of the Roman law, but to relate them to others of Germanic origin. This is seen both in the conditions required for prescription, and in the various instances where it was recognized.

§ 439. Conditions. — What was retained as essential to pre-scription was not opposed to what had already been laid down by Roman law. Difference, however, there was, in that while Roman law only in some cases required the concurrence of all the requi-sites of prescription, Germanic law, less inclined to the principle, demanded the presence of all in every case. Thus, it not only insisted that possession should have certain qualities, as in Roman law, namely, that it should be uninterrupted, peaceful and notori-ous,[2] and that the period should run in favor of the possessor from the day when it was possible for the true owner to assert his rights,[3] but it also exacted in every case, contrary to Roman law, both " bona fides " [4] and a " justus titulus ", that is, capable of transfer-ring the property.[5] And even when there was a concurrence of all these, the resulting prescription did not have the effect of usu-capion, *i.e.* the acquisition of a right, but was merely extinctive, robbing the original title of defense against the person who had prescripted it: as the law frankly said,[6] to punish neglect of his interests, as in the case of one who had negligently allowed the time to run within which an action might be brought.

[1] *Paulus Diaconus*, "Historia gentis Longobardorum", c. 23.
[2] *Rothar*, 227; *Liutprand*, 54, 78.
[3] *Rothar*, 227.
[4] *Id.*, 228; *Lothar*, 31.
[5] *Rothar*, 227; *Adelchi*, 5.
[6] *Adelchi*, 5.

Germanic law had in these principles an ally in the canon law. It confirmed the rule that good faith was always a necessary element, and even departed farther from the Roman law by requiring that there should be good faith not only at the moment of acquiring possession but throughout its whole term. This was as much to restrain frequent and violent usurpations as because of the fact that prescription, made applicable to all objects, was possible in a greater number of instances than in Roman law. Similarly it demanded that the title by which possession was taken should be just, that is, capable of transferring ownership (" dominium "). Various papal constitutions placed this point beyond all doubt or discussion. With this as a basis, it is easy to understand how such conceptions, derived from Germanic law and supported by the Church, though not conforming to Roman doctrine, were bound to be adopted by later Italian legislators and were, in fact, found in the statutes of the mediaeval communes, in the laws of the succeeding governments, and also in several codes. They are not, however, found in the present Italian Civil Code, which, following the French example, returned to Roman principles, requiring neither a just title nor good faith, but solely a " lawful " possession, in the case of the thirty-year prescription.[1]

§ 440. **Kinds.** — Since all cases of prescription required the same elements under Germanic law and its effect was everywhere extinctive and not acquisitive of rights, differences of kind could exist, apart from the origin of each, only in the period necessary to accomplish the prescription. In this particular there were some that were peculiar to the Germanic peoples, such chiefly as that of a year and a day. In Roman law may be found something analogous, in the usucapion of movable property, which in the early period of the law was perfected in a year; and in fact movable objects were the first over which the Germanic peoples recognized individual ownership, and, therefore, they were first capable of prescription. Furthermore, the limitation of the earliest prescription to one year must also be explained by the fact that residence in one place did not last longer than this, and that, therefore, the possession of land would not exceed that term, when the Germanic tribes did not as yet have fixed homes. One year, besides, brought a peremptory end to the right of action, if allowed to run unavailingly, since in every district as many courts were to be held during the year as the law established for the disposal of all matters. These various facts are probably all related in origin and all may

[1] Ital. Civil Code, arts. 686, 702, 2135; [French Civil Code, art. 2262.]

have contributed to fix the term of the earliest Germanic prescription at one completed year, that is, a year and a day. This naturally gave way to other periods, but for a long time it left very numerous traces,[1] some of which may be seen today.[2]

The longer prescriptive periods were due to Roman influence and passed into Germanic law little by little, not without resistance and consequent modification. First appeared that of five years, in the Edict of Rothar. It had, however, a special character, in that possession, to have prescriptive effect, had to be supported either by oath, when it came to proof of the " justus titulus " upon which the possession was based, as against the claimant who contested it; or by judicial duel, when, without reference to any title in particular, the " lawfulness " of the possession was questioned.[3] Hence, this quinquennial possession was rather a means of facilitating proof of one's own right: without oath or duel, that is, without judicial proof, it was insufficient to defend the possession, a notion contrary to true prescription. But, on the other hand, it gave to these forms of proof the effect, which they would not otherwise have had, of silencing a claimant who had other means of proving his right. The germ of prescription was, therefore, present, although mixed with foreign elements. To purge it of these was the work of later laws. Grimwald made a beginning. He repeated Rothar's provisions but declared that the duel was no longer necessary and that the oath alone sufficed, when possession had continued not five but thirty years.[4] Liutprand completed the change, holding that continuous possession during thirty years of itself defeated all proof of contrary title, without any need of support by oath or duel.[5] Thus the Roman prescription of thirty years was adopted, though, as has already been said, it exerted its force by extinguishing rather than by creating a new corresponding right.

There were special forms of prescription in the Germanic laws requiring terms even longer than thirty years. There was that requiring thirty-one years, due probably to a union of the one year prescription of the Germanic peoples and the trentennial of

[1] Examples in *Rothar*, 221, 361; *Adelchi*, 5; *Louis the Pious*, 16; "Libri feudorum", II, 24; 26, § 14; 52, § 3; 55, § 2; "Corpus Juris Canonici", *Gratian*, "Decretum", Part 2, *Causa* XX, *Quaest.* 2, *Cap.* 2; in the statutes of the mediaeval cities and subsequent legislation, *see Pertile, cit.*, I, p. 267; III, 62, 299, 369; IV, 38, 173, 232, 284; *Schupfer*, "Allodio", etc., *cit.*, p. 125–129, etc.
[2] Ital. Civil Code, arts. 694, 906.
[3] *Rothar*, 227, 228.
[4] *Grimwald*, 4.
[5] *Liutprand*, 54; *Astolf*, 18; *Arechi*, 15; *Louis the Pious*, 55.

the Romans; forty years were required for the prescription of inherited property against relatives,[1] and it was the period in force against churches, with the exception, introduced by Lombard law [2] but repealed by the Carlovingians,[3] that thirty years sufficed against the churches, when the possessor was a Lombard, whose rights a like period of occupancy by another would suffice to destroy.   There was also the sixty years' term against the State; [4] and lastly, though unmentioned by the Germanic laws, there was the prescription " ab immemorabile " of Roman origin, for Justinian, in defending the Church estates, had established that prescription had not run against them until the expiration of a hundred years.   This the Church of Rome maintained to its own advantage, and it was later extended by Frederick II to the property of the State and by the statutes of the mediaeval cities to the property of the commune.

In the meantime Roman principles were again gaining force and general acceptance in the courts.   Just as these principles continued to remove the characteristics imparted to prescription by Germanic law, so they also caused the disappearance of the types that did not conform to them.   Although there still remained in the statutes of the mediaeval republics a great variety of prescriptive terms — five, fifteen, twenty, twenty-five, twenty-nine, thirty, thirty-one, forty years, and even longer — nevertheless there was already a tendency towards uniformity and a preference for the trentennial period, which, confirmed by the laws of subsequent periods, governs today uncontested in Italian law.

TOPIC 4.   DELIVERY OF POSSESSION (TRADITION)

§ 441. **Its Character.** — This mode of acquisition differed from the others already described, chiefly in that it was not accomplished independently of another person, but presupposed the derivation of the right by one person from another, from him who yielded it and by him who received it.   It was, in other words, a mode of acquiring ownership having its foundation in contract.   Contract alone would not suffice, for, like the Roman law, Germanic law did not possess the conception, prevailing today, that ownership could be transferred by mere agreement.   The contract, or other juristic act, was the source of the obligation to bring about a passage of

---

[1] *Liutprand*, 70.
[2] *Astolf*, 18.
[3] *Pepin*, 6, 27; *Louis the Pious*, 53; *Lothar*, 21, 22, 24.
[4] *Liutprand*, 78.

ownership from one person to another; but in order to bring about such a passage, an external act, consequent upon the contract, was necessary, and this act was tradition or delivery of possession ("traditio"). Without it, the law declared, there was no stability in acquired rights.[1] In its substantial sense, therefore, tradition was simply the formality, consequent upon an antecedent obligation, founded upon a title sufficient to pass ownership, by means of which one person yielded and another received the ownership of a particular thing. The transfer by virtue of the contract, however, reached only to the right; while for a transfer of the possession, tradition by itself, in its pure sense, was insufficient; the person who had divested himself of the right had also effectively to relinquish the object of the right, and this had unreservedly to pass into the possession of the other, to whom the corresponding right had already been assigned. It was furthermore necessary that the act, antecedently consummated between the parties, should acquire, by its material manifestation, a finality also with respect to third persons; especially since, if the party, to whom the tradition had been made, had not acquired the effective possession of the object, he ran the danger of seeing his right rendered nugatory through prescription. Now, to secure this completed result, which was a consequence of the tradition but not included in it, a subsequent act of investiture was necessary, by which the passage of ownership was perfected in all its effects.

§ 442. **Forms.** — In antiquity, tradition had to be made publicly before the assembly of freemen, for the same reasons that demanded this method in adoption and all other solemn acts involving alienations of property.[2] Subsequently, as happened in Roman law in the case of the will, it was enough that the act should be performed before witnesses, varying in number according to the value of the object whose ownership was conveyed. Nevertheless, for a long time traces of the earlier publicity were preserved, as proved by documents recording instances of the delivery of possession made in public at market places, festivals and other occasions of public gathering. Tradition need not be made to the alienee personally; it might be made to his representative;[3] nor was it necessary to make a physical delivery of the object itself, since, while this was possible in the case of movable objects, in

[1] *Rothar*, 183; *cf. Justinian*, Code, II, 3, 20.
[2] *Ante* § 336.
[3] "Chartularium longobardicum formularum", 2, ed. *Boretius*, M. G. H., IV, and *Padelletti*, "Fontes."

the case of immovables only symbols could be used; in these are found the peculiarity of Germanic tradition.

The purpose of the symbolic forms was to clothe the right with a material proof, or to give it voice, as it were, in order that all might understand and that no doubt should remain as to the nature and effect of the act being performed.   The more primitive a civilization, the more is law bound by formalism, which supplies the incapacity for abstract conception.   Many indeed were the formalities of the Germanic law of Italy, long and tenaciously preserved, in spite of the example of the simplicity of Roman juridical acts.   And because the transfer of property was among the acts of major importance, it was, to a greater degree than others, accompanied by symbols and rites.

The symbols were of two kinds: natural, when related in nature to the object which they represented, e.g. a clod of earth for land, branches of trees for woods, stones for houses, water for streams, etc.; conventional, on the other hand, when the representative quality of the symbols arose by understanding between the parties, e.g. extending the hand to indicate the yielding up of one's own right; the glove as the symbol of guarantee;[1] the "festuca" or small staff, denoting power, called "festuca notata", when marked to serve as a memorandum; the lance and arrow, signifying liberty and dominion, used principally among the Lombards, who called the solemn transmission of ownership "gairethinx", because made with a "gaira" (lance) before the "thinx" (assembly).   The "charta" was also a conventional symbol that became very common among the Lombards, doubtless through the influence of the Roman law.[2]   The "charta", however, was not the "pergamena" or parchment on which the document was written, or the document itself, which was called "notitia" and which at best might have value as a means of proof.   The "charta" was rather the symbol, completing the transmission of the right and consisting of the "pergamena" itself, after the "notitia" had been written on it and when used to effect the delivery of possession.   This act, which gave to the "pergamena" a value that it lacked by itself, changed its name to "charta."   Thus the formula ran: "Trade per hanc pergamenam chartam venditionis."[3]

So much for the symbols themselves.   The manner of carrying out the tradition varied with different laws.   Among the Lombards there was a question and answer.   After the written act had

---

[1] *Rothar*, 182, 183.   [2] *Post* § 480.
[3] "Chartularium longobardicum formularum", *cit.*, 1.

been read, a person, expert in the laws, asked the transferor: "Do you assent?" ("Approvi?") and he replied, "I assent" ("Approvo"). Then: "Make, therefore, tradition to the acquirer." And the tradition, that is, the delivery of the symbol, ordinarily the "charta", was made ("traditio ad proprium"). The parchment was then delivered to the notary to be inscribed ("traditio ad scribendum"). "Touch it", the witnesses were told, and, when they had done so, the notary, taking it, signed it and redelivered it, saying, "Here it is, I have completed it and I deliver it." [1]

In other laws the ceremonies were more complex. The Franks required the alienor to lay the "charta" upon the ground and to place upon it a quantity of symbolic objects, — the knife, the "festuca", the glove, the lump of earth, a branch, the inkhorn; then to take it up and deliver it, first to the alienee, in order that he should thereby acquire the right, then to the notary, in order that it should be inscribed or that it should merely be sanctioned by his signature and those of the witnesses.

§ 443. **Investiture.** — Tradition had to be completed by *investiture*.[2] The name indicated the putting into possession, giving vestment or external perfection to the transmitted right. It had to be performed by the person who had conveyed the right, that is, by the person making tradition or his representative, with words expressing his intent to abandon ("exire", "exitum facere") the object aliened. If the person making tradition failed in this duty, the acquirer might lawfully take possession upon his own authority or by decree of the magistrate. The acquirer himself, or his legal representative, must receive the investiture and perform the acts indicative of his effective taking of possession. Among the Romans, even in the Germanic period, a simple declaration accompanying the act of tradition sufficed for this: but the Germans used many formalities, not only because of the scope of their symbolic forms, but also in order to give the greatest publicity to the act, the more so since for the Germanic peoples the possession was given no less weight than the right itself which was its basis.[3] In substance the idea contained in all the formalities of investiture was to demonstrate the exercise of the acquired right: *e.g.* to receive guests in the house to which ownership had been acquired, to light a fire there, to draw water, open the doors, uproot plants, cut branches, guide the plough through a short furrow, take a tile from the roof, or do some similar act —

[1] "Chartularium longobardicum formularium", *cit.*, 1.
[2] *Ante* § 441.   [3] *Post* § 468.

all in the presence of witnesses and of the persons, if any, who had a concern in the land acquired. The Lombards had simpler rites, and the Roman law could not have seemed strange to them. For them investiture was satisfied by the delivery of a stick, the giving of the document, the solemn entry upon the land.

As tradition without investiture would not have transferred possession, so investiture without tradition would have given possession but not ownership. And, in fact, when possession only was to be transferred, as happened, for example, in the grant of benefices, the ownership of which remained in the grantor, tradition was not made, but only investiture. For a perfect contractual transfer of property, therefore, three elements were necessary: first, title to the thing acquired; second, "tradition", for the transfer of the right; and lastly, investiture, for the transfer of possession.

§ 444. **Confusion of Tradition and Investiture.** — These elements did not continue clearly distinguished from one another. In later periods especially, one was confused with another and there resulted a transformation of both. This change must now be considered.

Tradition and investiture finally became one act. For this the way was early prepared for several reasons. The two acts had substantially the same purpose, namely, to complete a single act, the transfer of the property. There were ceremonies common to both, such as the delivery of the "charta", or of the stick; and they were besides so closely related in cause and effect, that they could be considered as phases of a single rather than of two acts. It should be added that, under feudal institutions, investiture rendered true tradition almost needless, since the transfer of lands was generally limited strictly to possession, so that during the feudal period tradition itself, when it took place, was called investiture. Still further, the interest of the contracting parties themselves tended to bring about the fusion, not only to save time and expense, but also to remove the danger that tradition might remain without investiture, to the possible injury of the right of the transferee by prescription. It is true that the acquirer himself had means of taking possession if the alienor did not invest him; but by death, absence, or other cause it might happen that the act of taking possession was lacking, so that it was safer that this should be understood, without more, as effected by the same act that accomplished tradition. From the two acts there thus resulted one, having the names and forms of either indiscriminately, and uniting the purpose of each.

From this union came about the suppression of an act, the special purpose of which was the transfer of the possession of an object, of which the ownership had already been transferred. In this there lay the beginning of a new conception, destined later to prevail, namely that, for the complete transmission of ownership, it was not necessary physically to transmit the object itself; it should be enough that there was the formal expression of intent contained in the single and united act of tradition and investiture, the latter no longer real but symbolic. True, this act did not as yet consist so much in the expression of consent as in the rites and formulae which still marked, although symbolically, the fact, once real, of the delivery of the object and of the yielding up of possession. But as the legal ideas, at first symbolized by external formalities, became more solidly fixed, and as Roman theories that avoided all suggestion of materiality came to be applied,[1] the external formalities themselves were bound little by little to lose importance and finally to fall into disuse. They remained only in the solemnity of certain phrases, intended to recall the ancient symbols. Thus deprived of all importance and significance, they were preserved almost up to the present time in notarial formulae, which, however, tended constantly towards greater simplicity. Of substance, therefore, there remained in the act only the declaration of yielding and receiving the right of ownership, determined by the contract and upon the conditions therein established. From that point it was easy to pass to the principle, accepted by the Italian Code, though subject to numerous exceptions,[2] that, for the transfer of the right, the mere declaration of intent was enough, since nothing else of a material sort was contained in the act.

§ 445. **Measures of Publicity.** — If modern Italian law has departed from the Germanic system, it has, nevertheless, remained faithful to the principle that publicity must be given to the act of transferring ownership. Since, with the abandonment of the ancient formalities of tradition and investiture, the act consummated between the immediate parties had lost all notoriety for third persons, recourse was necessary to other means to attain the same end. The need began to be felt and to be met so soon as the early character of tradition began to change. For this reason and also because of the then importance of the right of preemption in sales,[3] the statutes of the mediaeval communes saw to it that acts translative of ownership had a maximum of publicity,

---

[1] *Cf.* "traditio brevi manu" and "constitutum possessorium."
[2] Arts. 1125, 1162, 1448.   [3] *Ante* § 423.

and they, therefore, required such acts to be performed before magistrates, or proclaimed before the public council, or announced by the public criers of bans through the streets. Later came the registration or transcription of the act in public books of record established for the purpose. Venice possessed such a system, called the "notatorio", and gradually extended these records throughout her jurisdiction; in the 1500 s they were found in Sicily, where perhaps the memory of the Roman system of registration ("insinuationes") had not disappeared; in Neapolitan territory, King Robert decreed that a register of the status of ownership should be open to the public in the principal church of each district, but for the purpose of determining questions of boundary rather than of making known transfers of title from one person to another. During the 1500 s the Neapolitan Parliament several times demanded registers for the latter purpose, but without success. During the same century they were found in northern Italy, for example at Aosta; in Florence it was attempted by private initiative in the 1300 s, but abandoned because of the difficulties encountered. It is today the system of the Italian Code, which, as to third parties, denies the validity of transfers, unless transcribed in registries established for the purpose.[1]

[1] Art. 1932.

CHAPTER XIX

DEFENSE OF PROPERTY RIGHTS

§ 446. In General.

TOPIC 1. RECOVERY OF MOVABLE PROPERTY

§ 447. Germanic Period. | § 448. Later History.

TOPIC 2. RECOVERY OF LAND

§ 449. Influence of Germanic Law. | § 450. Period of the Mediaeval Communes.

§ 446. **In General.** — The power to defend the things that one owns against molestation by others is a necessary consequence of the right of property itself and is, therefore, recognized by all legal systems. For such defense what was required, in substance and, therefore, in general, was a demonstration of the existence of the right, carried to a point where it could no longer be legally controverted. This was accomplished by presenting a title of original acquisition, belonging either to the actual owner himself or to the person from whom the right was derived; or by making good the lack of title through prescription or other fact of equal efficacy. This demonstration acquired outwardly certain forms, differing according to the period and the people. It had special qualities in Germanic law, to which the various Roman actions were unknown; and within Germanic law itself it differed according as the proof concerned personalty or realty.

TOPIC 1. RECOVERY OF MOVABLE PROPERTY

§ 447. **Germanic Period.** — To re-acquire movable objects Germanic law did not possess a special action. One who had lost such property might seek the restoration of his right by a personal action or one derived from the crime, according as one or the other was required by the circumstances of fact by which the owner had been deprived of his property. Cases had, therefore, to be distinguished. When the owner had voluntarily given up possession of something and wished to recover it, as in the case of a loan, or where the recipient was unable to restore the object, because he had been robbed of it or had aliened or lost it in some other way,

711

the owner could not follow the object itself in the hands of its possessor, but was limited to a personal action against the person to whom he had given it, who alone could be constrained to pay damages. The third party possessor was responsible only to him to whom the thing had been given by its owner. If, therefore, the third party possessor had acquired it by a title which could not be disturbed, as by a sale, he might retain the object without fear of being legally molested, in spite of the fact that the sale had been by one without right.[1] If, on the other hand, the owner had lost possession against his will, as when the object had been stolen, or had been mislaid and the finder had not given the requisite publicity,[2] his action was then aimed at a true recovery of the object, though it had a penal character, in that it arose from the illegal act by which he had been dispossessed.

This action required several conditions and formalities. In the first place, it belonged to the owner. It was true that it might also be brought by one who had received the chattel from its true owner and had lost it; but such person, by the fact of reception, had to be considered himself as owner; because toward his original owner nothing was owed save damages, and therefore, if the party to whom the latter had delivered the object recovered it, he held it for himself and if he failed, the loss fell upon him alone. In the second place, certain formalities had to be performed. The claimant had to set on foot a search for the lost object; to this end he organized his relatives, friends and servants into a search party, and they were given special protection by the law.[3] If the object was found, the claimant could himself take possession of it, whenever the act, by which it had been lost, could still be considered flagrant, as, for instance, before the end of the third night since its commission. If not flagrant, the claimant, placing his hand upon the object and declaring his right, left the possession in him who then had it, who thereupon became its responsible custodian, and was required, upon the date fixed, to present it at trial. If stolen in the interval, the custodian had to swear to his innocence; if lost through the latter's negligence, he had to restore its equivalent.[4]

If, at trial, the party summoned, on whom rested the burden of proof,[5] failed to establish his right to the object in dispute, he had to restore it and pay a fine in addition, unless he could show his

[1] *Liutprand*, 131.   [2] *Ante* § 432.   [3] *Rothar*, 208.
[4] *Id.* 232 and "Expositio", §§ 3, 343; *Charlemagne*, 129; cf. *Justinian*, Code, VIII, 37, 4.
[5] *Ante* § 55.

good faith.[1] But he could extricate himself from the suit by lay-
ing an accusation against the person from whom he had received
the litigated object. This was called " intertiare ", or " in tertiam
manum mittere ", that is, placing the burden upon a third party.
Hence arose the name of " interziazione " (interpleader by a third
party) given to the action itself. The third party thus accused was
obliged to appear in court and, if he failed to prove the falsity of
the fact averred against him, was required to take the place of the
first defendant and establish his right as against the plaintiff or
denounce still another party as the one from whom he had acquired
possession. If he could do neither, he was ordered to restore the
object and to pay all damages, both to the owner and to the first
defendant. It was, therefore, possible that the trial might not end
even with this party, but that the burden might pass to still another, who thus found himself in the same situation as his predecessor summoned. In this way, passing responsibility from one to
another, a person was finally reached who could neither refer it
beyond nor justify himself, and at that point the litigation ended
with the victory of the claimant. Or, it might reach the point at
which the defendant's right was established and then the plaintiff
lost, and for his temerity was punished by a fine.

§ 448. **Later History.** — This sort of action for the recovery of
personalty did not come down beyond the Germanic period, properly speaking. A law of Otto I, as early as the 900 s, placed limitations upon it by establishing that the charging of new defendants
might not go beyond three, that is, that not more than three guar-
antors of the possession transferred might be summoned ; and that
not even one might be called, that is, the defendant might not
force an interpleader (" interziazione "), when the party whom he
proposed to bring into the action resided at a distance of more than
three counts' districts away.[2] In the 1000 s the Lombard " formularies " of the Pavian School declared this form of procedure
already antiquated and superseded by the " actio ad exhibendum "
of the Roman law.[3] Traces, however, remained in various places,
as in Sardinia, where it was still found in the 1300 s, and some may
even still be seen in certain provisions of the present Italian Code.
The Code, in fact, announces the principle that in the case of movable objects possession is equivalent to title, and, in accord with this

---

[1] *Rothar*, 232, 222; "Expositio" §§ 4, 5.
[2] *Otto I*, 1, 7, in ed. *Pertz*, M. G. H., "Leges", II.
[3] *Rothar*, "Formulary", 231, 232, "Tota haec altercatio poene nichil
valet, debet enim esse ut legitur in romana lege"; in M. G. H. "Leges",
VI, ed. *Boretius*, and in *Padelletti*, "Fontes."

principle, the same distinction is implicitly made that was found in Germanic law, between the owner's loss of possession by his own act and by the act of another.   In the former case, in perfect analogy to Germanic procedure, no action is admitted against the third possessor, provided he received the object in good faith; in the latter, the action lies against any one who has the object and is in a position to restore it.[1]

TOPIC 2.   RECOVERY OF LAND

§ 449. **Influence of Germanic Law.** — For the recovery of immovable property, Germanic law had special formalities, very analogous to the ancient "actio sacramenti" of the Roman law. The litigants, that is, the claimant and the possessor, went to the disputed land with the judge and witnesses; they took a part of it — a clod, a handful of earth or a twig — and gave it to a third person, who on a day fixed should present it to the court, before which, by mutual guarantees, that is by gage ("wadia"),[2] the parties bound themselves to appear and to produce proof of their respective claims.

The most usual mode of proof in the case of land was to call into the suit the person from whom possession had been received, to defend it against the plaintiff.

Such was the Lombard law.   On the other hand, if the defendant was Roman, he would not need to call the person from whom he had derived possession, in order to substitute him in the action.[3] The reason for the difference was that in Roman law the author of the act, constituting the cause of the plaintiff's claim against the defendant, was always responsible, provided he had been brought in by a summons to appear ("litis denuntiatio"); but in Germanic law he would not be responsible if the defendant went on with the action in his own name.   Hence the latter's interest in calling upon the author of his possession, in order to have recourse against him in case of an unfavorable judgment; hence also the obligation of the author of the title himself to intervene as guarantor of the right which he had transferred.   And this obligation was in fact always expressed in acts of alienation.   It might happen, however, that the obligation could not be fulfilled, because of the death or absence of the guarantor, or of the excessive

---

[1] Civil Code, arts. 707, 708.   [2] *Post* § 479.

[3] *Rothar*, "Formulary", *cit.*, 234, "Langobardus semper dat auctorem et numquam stat loco auctoris; romanus semper stat loco auctoris, et numquam dat auctorem."

inconvenience, due to distance, expense, or other difficulty. Equivalent remedies began to be sought, which appeared, first, as exceptions to the rule requiring the summoning of the grantor, but which later became themselves the general rules governing the action.

The first was the law already mentioned,[1] which established that, whenever possession had lasted five years, it was no longer necessary to call the author of the contested right; it was enough for the defendant himself to prove this fact by judicial duel or oath.[2] Then followed express stipulations, by which the transferor of the right bound himself to guarantee it, even though not called upon in the action. At first, this was done in special cases, as a provision, for example, against the transferor's absence; then it became the general rule. In consequence, the defendant, who had to protect himself against the claimant's action, had need of other means to substitute for the absence of his grantor, by which he might establish his own title. These means came to be the documents which attested the title to his right and which, therefore, were delivered to the grantee at the time of the alienation, for his use in defending the land acquired. If this assignment could not be made, the grantor promised to present the documents of title himself, whenever needed. To establish proof, the documents produced had to date back to a point at which, through prescription, original acquisition, or other "just cause", the defendant's right could not be contested on any other grounds. The deeds had furthermore to be legal, that is, satisfy all the conditions of validity. Between two or more repugnant deeds, the earliest in date prevailed; if any question arose as to them, recourse was had to other proof to remove the doubt or to determine the right independently of them. Among the kinds of proof was that by witnesses and that by oath, given with proper sacramental guarantees, both varying in number according to the importance of the litigation. The supreme proof was the "judicium dei", determined by duel. Rothar had already required this to perfect the efficacy of quinquennial possession; but the duel attained its greatest importance as judicial proof by the laws of Otto I, who commanded its use in almost all those cases that first required proof by oath, intending thereby to restrain the too frequent practice of perjury.[3]

When proof had been concluded, judgment, according to the " personal law " of the defendant, or of the land in question, if there was such a law, recognized and gave sanction to the right of

[1] *Ante* § 440.   [2] *Rothar*, 227, 228.   [3] *Otto I*, 1, 2.

the victor. If the plaintiff, the vanquished or the judge himself restored possession of the land by the formality of investiture.[1] Restitution was the full extent of the defendant's liability, if he had acted in good faith; but if otherwise, he was bound to restore also the fruits gathered, and he might also be subject to a penalty, when the disturbance of the plaintiff's right had been of the nature of a crime.[2]

§ 450. **Period of the Mediaeval Communes.** — During the period of the mediaeval communes, owners formed associations or corporations, called " regole ", with the object of watching over and defending their properties. On members' lands were placed wardens, called " gastaldi ", " saltarii ", and " fideiussores " — names derived from analogous Germanic institutions — whose duty was to watch all that happened on these properties, promptly accuse those who in any way disturbed their lawful enjoyment, and gather and present evidence to the court. This was necessitated by the still disturbed state of society, still subject, especially in rural districts, to feudalism and to the uncertainties of the law during the transition from the Germanic period. But when the State had attained a more perfect organization and authority, and when law had gained a surer direction through the revival of Roman principles, the reasons for these associations (" regole ") disappeared, and with them their consequences and the institutions themselves. Property in all its forms received effective protection by the actions of the Roman law, among which the principal was the " rei vindicatio ", which thus came again to form, as it does today, the fundamental remedy in the system of defenses.[3]

[1] *Ante* § 443.
[2] *Rothar*, 354, 355, 356.
[3] [Ital. Civil Code, arts. 439, 708, 709, 1513.]

TITLE II

RIGHTS OVER THE PROPERTY OF ANOTHER

§ 451. Beneficial or "Use" and | § 452. Later General Develop-
     Bare or "Direct" Title. | ment.

§ 451. Beneficial or " Use " and Bare or " Direct " Title. — The idea of ownership made its appearance in Germanic law with certain characteristics distinguishing it from the Roman conception, and the same was true of rights over the property of another. Roman law considered these from the point of view of the uses to which a thing could be put, while ownership remained in the same person; Germanic law, on the other hand, regarded the uses themselves as rights of ownership, conceived of as existing in a part of the thing itself, for it was possible to look upon ownership as embracing less than the whole and, therefore, divisible into its constituent elements, residing in more than one person.[1] There are in fact examples, like the obligatory easement for flowage of water over another's land (" acquedotto coattivo ")[2] which, though later qualified as easements, were early conceived merely as rights to a material part of another's land, so that an expropriation of the part came to be deemed necessary in order to constitute the right.

Furthermore, the Germans considered the subject matter itself, especially land, as itself possessed of rights and bound by obligations.[3] Hence, while its ownership resided in another, certain rights could be created with reference to it, of a special quality, in that they did not consist, as was usual in rights over another's property, in the uses to which the land might be put, but in some act. The land, through its revenues, assured its performance, and, in the person of the owner, designated the party obligated. Such was the character of all those rights over another's property, termed " charges " (" oneri reali ").[4]

During the Germanic period, therefore, the theory of rights over another's property tended in substance to divide ownership between the one having the object and the one rightfully deriving some use

[1] *Ante* § 415.   [2] *Post* § 465.   [3] *Ante* § 416.   [4] *Post* § 461.

from it; to consider both, that is, as united in a co-ownership. But when the light of science was directed upon these rights, the dominion of one was seen to be very different from that of the other. In the former it consisted in the power to draw from the thing all possible uses, without limitation, save that of not injuring the right of another; in the latter it consisted in enjoying that use alone which was the object of the right. To distinguish each of these sorts of title, it was desirable to apply a special name, and one was borrowed from Roman law. There had been in the Roman law, in contrast to the " actiones directae ", those called "utiles", the latter employed in cases which arose by analogy to those for which the former had been expressly introduced. " Utiles " were, therefore, actions given to those having rights over another's property, by analogy to the " direct " actions, permitted solely to the owner of the thing. Then, by a transfer of the names of such actions to the rights themselves which they respectively protected, and by a continuance of the conception of both rights as a " dominium ", there began with the Glossators the application of the term beneficial or " use title " (" dominium utilis "), to designate that of the person having a right (especially emphyteusis) over another's land; and of the term bare or " direct title " (" dominium directum "), to designate that of the true owner.

Such distinctions and names met with favor, in that they were accepted by all jurists and legislators, and have been perpetuated through subsequent periods down to our own times, when science and legislation have deprived them of all value, as the product of a doctrine founded upon error, however it may be interpreted. In the first place the doctrine is irreconcilable with the principles of Roman law, which never admitted such a division of ownership (" dominium ") in the " jura in re aliena ", as these words themselves indicate, and as Donellus, Cujas and other jurists long ago pointed out, although without result in practice. And secondly, the error of the division is demonstrated by the consequences to which it leads. If one having merely a limited right over an object is an owner, the other, as co-owner, may not convey it without the consent of the former, who, with equal privilege, may consolidate in himself the two rights of " dominium " and himself alienate the land. However, even those who asserted the division did not admit these logical consequences, but in fact held that the right of alienation was recognized solely in the " direct title ", denying it to the beneficial title, as also the power to unite the other's ownership to his own.

718

Today the theory has been abandoned and Italian law has returned to the Roman system.

§ 452. **Later General Development.** — There was a richer variety of rights over another's property in the Middle Ages than there had been under the Roman law. New forms of uses were found to which the property of others might be put, and these were subjected to rules hitherto unknown.

The causes of this larger development were various. The lingering traces of collective ownership contributed much, since all the resulting limitations to ownership were in substance merely rights over the property of others, and the distinctive quality of these rights was that for the most part they belonged to the field of public law. But with time and the passing of such rights from king to public officials, churches, and feudatories, they also entered private estates, and differed from other property rights of a private nature solely in the peculiarity of their origin. Furthermore the conditions of society favored the rise and multiplication of such rights. There was the fief, an institution unknown to Roman law, which gave to the vassals, who formed a large element of society, rights, also of the class of the beneficial or " use title ", over the property of the seignior. Because of the need of protection in a turbulent time, or of the desire to enjoy the " immunities " or special privileges conceded to the seigniors, there was also a general tendency to divest oneself of ownership, in order to receive the property back by concession, whose stipulations gave rise to new rights over the same property as often as there were fresh transfers. Nor were economic conditions unfavorable. Uncultivated land abounded; the concentration of property in the religious orders constantly increased; while capital with which to turn the land to profit was scarce. No better means of securing a benefit from it existed than to grant concessions, which while reserving ownership, yielded up certain uses, which were in fact rights " in rem " over another's property.

Along with this development, there came about an interchange of features among such rights, which thus lost in clearness of definition. Some gained a wider extension during the Middle Ages than under Roman law, as, for example, emphyteusis;[1] others were formed by such a mixture of elements that they were classified now in one, now in another category of rights, and always with a show of reason, as for example in the case of charges on land.[2] Some, however, lost their proper and early features and

[1] *Post* § 453.   [2] *Post* § 461.

diminished in importance, as was generally true of easements properly speaking.[1]

These facts, namely, the diversity of fundamental ideas, and the expansion, with its consequences, of rights over another's property during the Middle Ages, make up, with their various interrelations and modifications, the history of this form of property.

[1] *Post* § 465.

CHAPTER XX

EMPHYTEUSIS

TOPIC 1. GENERAL CHARACTER

§ 453. **Early History.** — The origin of *emphyteusis* goes back to a late period of the Roman Empire. The Emperor Zeno, resolving the question whether the contract by which this right came into being should be regarded as one of purchase and sale or of lease, with both of which it had features in common, declared it to be a special contract, differing from both, and called it emphyteusis, expressing by this Greek word its object, which was to improve uncultivated and waste lands.[1] Indeed it could not be confused with purchase and sale in that there was no transfer of ownership; nor with lease, since emphyteusis was always for a very long term, might be perpetual and contained many more rights than simple lease. It was a genuine right " in rem " over the land of another, for the purpose of its improvement, accompanied by full rights of enjoyment and subject to an annual payment to the owner. The system was used as an experiment in Roman times for the special purpose of bringing under cultivation lands belonging to the State, communal lands, and the " latifundia."

In the Middle Ages, for reasons already given,[2] and because of its great use by the Church, the inalienability of whose vast domains provided no better means of placing them under cultivation,

---

[1] *Justinian*, Code, IV, 66.   [2] *Ante* § 450.

emphyteusis underwent a tremendous development, to the advantage of agriculture and the well-being of the population. It did not, however, retain its original purity, but was transformed by the changed conditions and new needs of society. First, in the Germanic period, there was some slackening of its rigid Roman character. Now losing some one of its requisites, now adding others not previously possessed, emphyteusis came to be assimilated to its many related contracts from which arose rights over another's property. Neatness in conception of single institutions, like the subtleties of legal distinctions in general, was not within the grasp or application of the Germanic mind.

The second and most important change in emphyteusis came about through feudalism. To maintain its distinction from emphyteusis, the fief had its own peculiar quality as a political institution; but viewed as property the likeness between the two was great. It is easy to see the analogy between the condition of the vassal and of the emphyteuta, between feudal services and emphyteutic rent, between the rights of the feudal lord on the one hand and the "laudemium", or the right of redemption ("retratto"), and others belonging to the owner, on the other. Thus when the political yielded to the patrimonial character of the fief, it was subjected by the jurists to the regulations governing emphyteusis. But the latter was not immune to feudal contact, for in time it acquired principles and features whose origin and justification can only be discovered in feudal institutions.

§ 454. **Later History.** — The consequences of this transformation are evident in every feature of emphyteusis. Above all, the rights of the owner or grantor felt the effects of feudalism. Those already known to the Roman law remained but acquired feudal names. Thus the Justinian "quinquagesima", to which the owner was entitled when the emphyteuta aliened the land, was called "laudemium"; redemption ("retratto") was the name given to his right of preference over all other purchasers; and investiture the concession of the emphyteutic land. Other rights arose in favor of the owner, not formerly enjoyed, such as that of a periodic renewal of the emphyteusis during its term, every five, ten or fifteen years, in analogy to feudal investitures. Similar changes might be noted with regard to the things which might be the subject of emphyteusis. At first limited to land, in conformity with its original purpose, it later extended to other immovable property, especially houses, and finally, as in the case of the fief, it came to embrace also rights to money payments, rents, tithes and divers services. And so of the kinds of emphyteusis. Contrary to the Roman principle of free alienability of the emphyteusis, it became surrounded by restrictions and stipulations corresponding to those attaching to the fief, especially in relation to its inheritance. There was the "stipulatory" emphyteusis ("pazionata"), the inheritance of which was given preferably or exclusively to males; and other "pacts" were inserted by which, as happened in the trust-entails ("fideicommissa"),[1] the persons called to succeed were designated at the creation of the emphyteusis and the emphyteuta was powerless to disturb their right. In this way, emphyteutic property became inalienable, was withdrawn from commerce and finally lost its original purpose, which was to restore the land to labor and productiveness. As a result, instead of beneficial as at first, emphyteusis became injurious. During subsequent periods it was critically resisted, not with a view to destroy it, but to restore it, purged of the foreign accumulations that had fastened upon it.

TOPIC 2. RELATION TO ANALOGOUS CONTRACTS

§ 455. **Differences.** — As emphyteusis drew away from its original character, it lost its distinctive features and was confused with other forms of assignments of immovable property with which it had some element in common, chief among such elements being the transfer of possession and enjoyment of a thing, whose title was retained in another. When, however, their nature is analyzed, certain inherent differences are discovered between emphyteusis and the other estates which it resembled. While the perpetual lease ("affitto perpetuo") bore an apparent likeness to emphyteusis, there was a difference in purpose, in that in the former the owner did not aim to improve the land and did not impose upon the lessee obligations of good husbandry, but was satisfied to assure to himself, through the rent, an unalterable and perpetual return. In the grant reserving a rent charge ("concessione a censo"), in spite of an external similarity with emphyteusis, a note of difference is observable in that in the rent charge the right of ownership passed to the grantee, while in the emphyteusis, under both Roman and Germanic theories, it remained in the grantor. The lease ("locazione") was very similar to emphyteusis, especially when joined with the right of the lessee to alienate and transfer his interest. But it was distinct in respect to its

---

[1] *Ante* § 385.

term, which never exceeded twenty-nine years. It was renewable,
but in that case, during the succeeding terms it was called emphyteusis, the name lease being limited to the first term. From the
feudal grant, even when considered solely as a private right, emphyteusis differed in historical origin and in the peculiarity of certain
services, which were not due in the latter and which were retained
in the former, through derivation from the feudal contract.
Finally there was the usufruct (" usufrutto ") or estate for years,
distinct from emphyteusis in purpose, in that it was for the exclusive benefit of the grantee; the right was, therefore, limited to a
determined person and lacked the free power of disposal; it was
also either wholly lacking a provision for rent, or the rent was such
as to exclude any idea of profit to the grantor, for when a rent was
paid its only purpose was to interrupt the running of a prescriptive
term. Difference of purpose also marked emphyteusis from the
benefice. This, considered independently of the fief, was limited
almost entirely to the ecclesiastical form, which exacted from the
beneficiary a service, requiring special personal qualities, reserved
as the reason for the benefice, rather than as compensation for it.
And furthermore the benefice gave no right of alienation. The
cropper tenant's contract (" colonia parziaria ") differed in the
peculiarity of the obligation, which consisted in giving the owner
half of the soil's products. The lease with fractional reversion
(" contratto porzionario ") was a preparatory step to emphyteusis; for it provided that the land should first be brought to the
desired state of cultivation by the grantee, who should then return
a part to the owner, entirely free from any claim, while retaining
another part as compensation for his labor upon the basis of an
emphyteusis.

§ 456. "Livellum". — Among all the grants of emphyteutic
character, the contract of "livellum" assumed the greatest importance during the Middle Ages. The word, derived from the
Latin "libellus", in its primitive significance indicated merely
the request for a grant of land, accorded by the owner, and
restricted by such stipulations as the latter believed best suited to
advance his interests. "Livellum" was, therefore, synonymous
with "precarium", a word expressive of the idea of the prayer or
demand contained in the "libellus", the purpose of which was to
obtain the grant of the land; it was also synonymous with "praes-
taria", the name given to the effect of the prayer itself, that is,
the bestowal or concession of the land. It did not differ, therefore, in this aspect from the Roman "precarium", so-called be-

cause the land " precibus petentis conceditur." But it resembled it in another more substantial way than in name. The Roman " precarium " was analogous to the mediaeval " livellum " and may be considered as its historical antecedent in that in neither case was the grantor bound by those rules that grew up around the emphyteusis or other nominate contracts. He might stipulate in the grant, as in an act of pure generosity, any condition pleasing to him.[1] It was precisely in respect to this greater freedom of action of the owner that lay the difference in the special rules governing emphyteusis and " livellum." The two contracts were indeed considerably confused, though each at least preserved its fundamental character. For the " livellum " there was the rule, inapplicable to emphyteusis, that the grant should not extend beyond twenty-nine years;[2] the tenant of the " livellum ", unlike the emphyteuta, might not without special consent alienate his interest in the land; the obligation to renew, which was not native to the emphyteusis, was required every so often in the " livellum." But, because of the already mentioned departure from the pure conception of emphyteusis, an interchange of qualities took place between it and the " livellum ", which led to their fusion, when the obligation of renewal was imposed upon the emphyteuta and the right of alienation was given to the tenant of the " livellum ", upon notice to the owner. Furthermore, as happened in the emphyteusis, feudal principles were gradually introduced into the " livellum ", especially in the matter of its inheritance, which was modelled on feudal succession, both as to the persons called to succeed and to those excluded. This growing confusion with emphyteusis was the greatest possible benefit to the tenant of the " livellum ", for it still happened, and not infrequently, that the " livellum ", under the force of feudal oppression, developed in another direction and became confused with those grants of land of servile character, thus transforming the tenants into " coloni ", very similar in condition to serfs of the glebe. As the " livellum " thus became confused with emphyteusis or transformed into a contract constitutive of serfdom, it lost, in the 1100 s and 1200 s, the character of an autonomous contract, and its name alone remained, having a wider application, denoting generically all the various titles, more or less akin to emphyteusis, by which a right " in rem " over another's property was created.

[1] [Calisse, "Storia del diritto Italiano", vol. II, "Diritto publico", § 77, p. 121 et seq., much abridged in this translation, ante § 25.]
[2] "Chartularium Longabardicum formularum". 7, in M. G. H. "Leges", IV, ed. Boretius, and in Padelletti, "Fontes."

TOPIC 3. EXERCISE OF EMPHYTEUTIC RIGHTS

§ 457. **Term.** — The first condition of exercise referred to time, or duration of the right over another's property. On this point there was great diversity in the Middle Ages, from the perpetuity of the Roman emphyteusis to the short terms proper to the simple lease, due to the historical differences of origin from the many contracts by which emphyteutic rights might be created. In the Middle Ages perpetual grants were rare, and such examples as are recorded were for the most part, though under the guise of a petty rent or service, in reality gifts. Grants for a term of many generations were rare, but those through three generations were frequent. They were called " tertii generis ", or " in tribus personis ", where the successive possessors need not in fact be descended one from another, and the three transfers might be made to persons in no wise related. Beyond the third possessor the right was extinguished and the land, relieved of the burden, reverted to the owner and grantor. Not infrequently the term was for life, especially when a religious order was a party, for in order to compensate one who made a gift of land, the order would reconvey its possession and enjoyment, together with that of additional land, to the donor for life. While, among grants for a determinate number of years, there were not lacking some for forty years and even one hundred years, the commonest examples were for twenty-nine years. This term was fixed in the interest of the grantor so that he need not fear the running of the prescriptive period, and it was principally used in the " livellum ", properly so called.[1] This did not mean that on the completion of the twenty-ninth year the land had necessarily to be surrendered; indeed it was usually stipulated that, either with or without compensation to the grantor, the assignment might be periodically renewed; and thus, through a continued series of renewals every twenty-nine years, it acquired a perpetual character. Though less frequent, there were other terms of less than twenty-nine years, as for example ten, eight, six, and even five or three years. These were really instances of true leases, by which the tenant in possession, a person generally poor and of a rank making him dependent upon the owner, cultivated and drew support from the land, under the direct surveillance of the owner himself or his representative.

[1] *Cf.* Ital. Civil Code, art. 1563. [The owner-grantor may demand recognition of his title from the emphyteuta every twenty-nine years. This safeguards the owner against the running of the thirty years' prescriptive period: art. 2135.]

§ 458. **Rental.** — The second element to examine is the rental, concerning which again diversity reigned. A money payment was always used, but its extension, until it became the rule, belonged to the period subsequent to that in which emphyteutic and allied rights were created almost exclusively for the encouragement of agriculture. In the years following shortly upon the Germanic invasions land was not as yet capable of returning an adequate compensation for the labor required for cultivation;[1] the farmer could not, therefore, be presumed able to pay a fixed pecuniary return, a rent (" census ") properly so called. It was preferable to fix the return as a proportion of the products, variously calculated. Sometimes it was a proportion of the harvest, a half for example, as in the " mezzeria "; sometimes it was independent of the amount of the harvest itself, as a certain weight of grain, wine, or the like; or it was proportioned to the labor to be performed, small when the land was first broken and increasing little by little as the production became more bountiful. Under a system of this sort no return of any sort need be exacted, if the owner considered the improvement obtained a sufficient compensation. But Church influence contributed to render some return usual in all cases, since it was permitted neither to alien its property nor even to grant out the use without compensation. Nevertheless, rentals without any real pecuniary value proportionate to the use of the land were not infrequent, *e.g.* a " denarius ", some small object, a trifling offering in products, a ceremonial candle, or the like. The exaction of such rentals was merely intended to protect the owner against prescription, or to conceal, by this change of legal character, a gratuitous alienation, otherwise impossible.

Alongside the rent, other obligations, in the nature of special services due the owner, might be required of the possessor of another's land. For the most part, these services took the form of labor, differing in quality and quantity according to the condition of the persons upon whom they were imposed. The very poor and those upon whom the owner's authority weighed, were bound to labor upon the latter's lands whenever he had need, subject solely to the reservation of a few free days to work the land which they themselves held. In the case of the less dependent, the contract fixed the number of days owed the master and the quality of work that might be required of them; for others still better situated, the obligation was fixed at some special service, such as the carry-

[1] *Ante* § 414.

ing of his goods, gathering his harvests, providing him with lodging, all evidently derived from the feudal relation.

Besides obtaining some general assurances, as against conveying the interest to persons of too powerful a station or to the religious orders, since it was difficult to enforce claims against such recalcitrant grantees because of their power or privileges, the owner, to secure performance of his various rights, had also certain direct means created either by law or by agreement, such as the exaction of double rent when payment was in arrear, or a stipulated fine, or the penalty of forfeiture for failure of performance, a measure that still continues to be the chief protection allowed the owner.[1]

TOPIC 4.   LATER HISTORY

§ 459.   **To the Period of Codification.** — When, by the accumulation of attributes proper to the fief,[2] emphyteusis had lost its ancient economic purpose of encouraging agriculture, it became the target of legislative reform.   Beginning with the period of the mediaeval communes and continuing to the present period, this aimed to eliminate the extraneous elements gathered in its long historical course, and to restore it to the pure conception of the Roman law, subject to the modifications necessary to make it conform to new social conditions.

Whenever the communes incorporated within their domain land over which the feudal owner had constituted emphyteutic estates, they robbed these of the political character which the fief had impressed upon them, did away with the purely personal services, relieved them also from the duties based upon simple homage, and preserved only the natural attributes of this private right.   They also strove to better the conditions of the tenants themselves of such lands, by enacting laws that rendered less burdensome the terms of their tenure; their possession was better secured by requiring the owner to renew the grant upon payment of a small compensation; the nearest relatives were called to inherit the estate, so as to reduce the instances of forfeiture; forfeiture for default of rent was changed to an agreed penalty; testate inheritance of the emphyteutic estate was permitted; and other similar provisions were introduced.   As a result, emphyteusis, restored to usefulness, gained a new vigor, even the feudal seigniors favoring it, since, by stipulating conditions, they succeeded in preserving rights which they otherwise would have lost with the abolition of the fief.

[1] [Ital. Civil Code, art. 1565].   [2] *Ante* § 453.

The result meant, on the other hand, the perpetuation of certain influences that prevented a complete divorce between emphyteusis and the fief. Subsequent legislation, therefore, continued the attack from this point. In some localities emphyteusis was prohibited, as in Modena in the 1300 s; elsewhere the power to affranchise the emphyteutic estate was conceded, as by Francis II of Este in the 1700 s, but more especially was provision taken in Tuscany by the so-called " Leopoldine " lease system. Grand Duke Leopold aimed to improve the condition of the tenant cultivators of others' lands, not so much for their personal benefit as for the improvement of the property itself. Towards this the principal provisions of his sytem were directed. Every cause of fear on the part of the emphyteuta was removed, by binding the owner to renew, forbidding an increase of the rental, and limiting the causes of forfeiture. The emphyteuta himself was given a greater interest in good cultivation, by subventions in the form of advances to meet payments and to furnish animals and implements; by admitting him as well as the owner to share in the increment due to the improvement of the land; by abolishing the requirement of the owner's consent to alienation and of the latter's right of preference; finally by enabling the emphyteuta to become the owner of the land by a method of affranchisement.

§ 460. **Since Codification.** — When the period of codification came, emphyteusis, including therein all other related rights, faced the new law in a double aspect. On one hand, it appeared as an institution to be attacked as a cover to feudal relics; on the other hand, it was favored as a means for the economic improvement of land, and above all of the peasant population. According as one or the other of these two aspects gained ascendancy, emphyteusis was rejected or accepted by the codes. The French Code rejected it; the Italian systems accepted it, while divesting it of its feudal qualities and restoring it completely to pure Roman conceptions; and these were again forsaken by the present Italian Civil Code. While this Code has abandoned the mediaeval doctrine of " direct " and beneficial or " use " title,[1] it has not only refused to despoil the emphyteuta of the right of ownership which he gained under that doctrine, but it has rendered his ownership complete, vesting this exclusively in him (in derogation of its theory of ownership [2]), and leaving to him who used to be recognized as owner only the right of rent. It follows that emphyteusis is transmitted by the ordinary modes of inheritance; that the emphy-

---

[1] *Ante* § 451.   [2] Civil Code, art. 436.

teuta, become owner, may always affranchise his property from the rent; and that he may sell it without the consent of the owner of the rent; that he need not pay the latter the "laudemium" or fine for renewal, or perform any act indicative of ownership in the grantor.

Chapter XXI

CHARGES UPON LAND

§ 461. Distinctions. — By a charge upon property ("onere reale") is meant the obligation to perform some definite act, the burden of which rests in such wise that the land appears as the passive subject of the obligation and the owner merely the intermediary through whom the performance in question is discharged for the benefit of the party enjoying the right.

This sort of property right, unknown to the Romans, originated in the Middle Ages, out of the special conditions of the period. That personal credit counted little and no good system of guaranteeing credit had been developed; that land alone had a serious economic value and that it might itself be the subject of rights and obligations, — such were the conditions that gave rise to charges upon land. By linking a new right to the land, in such wise as to separate it from the person of the land-owner, was the best, nay the only guarantee, then possible. The idea approximated the notion of the easement ("servitù") of Roman and modern Italian law, so that, in the past, legal science and practice treated charges upon land as easements and sought to subject them to rules belonging to the latter. But an external analogy should not lead us to forget the inherent and wide difference between the two institutions. The land charge was not a right, like an easement, exercised over another's land; rather it produced a right to take a definite something from the land, and thereby from its owner. Hence the other essential difference, that while in the easement the owner of the servient tenement could not be obligated to the performance of any act, but only to abstain or allow another to act, the owner of land impressed with the charge was, on the other hand, bound to fulfil the obligation to the owner of the right.

From this point of view, *i.e.* of the duty incumbent upon the possessor of the land, charges were analogous to obligations. The owner of the land was always under duty to make the determined payments, irrespective of what the land might produce; to him the owner of the right always looked for performance, and so found himself in the position of a promissee. But the likeness was also more apparent than real. To the conceptions underlying obligations many rules essential to land charges were repugnant, such as that the duty to perform ceased or was reduced upon the total or partial destruction of the property encumbered with the charge; that possession of the property was a necessary condition of liability, which, therefore, ceased with its loss; that the succeeding possessor was liable for what his predecessor should have paid, but did not. In view of this, it should again be remarked that charges upon land possessed qualities that related them to both species of rights — easements and obligations — but that they are not to be confused wholly with either.

§ 462. **Influence of the Roman Law.** — This difference was not well understood by the jurists of the time of the return to the study of Roman law. They customarily sought to relate everything to the principles of that system, and, when they failed to find charges upon land, at least in the sphere of private law, they thought to discover in public law a correspondence in the " munera patrimonialia " [1] of public law. To fit them to Roman rules, they considered charges upon land now as obligations, now as easements, now as hypothecary liens, according to the importance given to one or another of their qualities, and there naturally resulted, in science and practice, a confusion and contradiction of principles and rules.

For charges upon land should be considered as a distinct class of rights.

The causes that gave rise to them were such as to show that they were not to be confused in any wise with easements or obligations, within whose limitations it was not possible to restrict them. Land charges might indeed have a reference to public law, since, in relation to the State, they included the land taxes; the duty to military service, measured by land ownership; as well as the various obligations, proportioned to the value of the land, to contribute to certain public works, *e.g.* the construction of roads, ditches, bridges, and the like. In its relation to the fief, the land charge was to be considered as including all those services which the vassal owed to his overlord solely by virtue of his land. But apart from public law, in which the origin and purpose of land charges were different, though their nature remained substantially the same, within the

---

[1] [*Ante* § 27, much abbreviated from *Calisse*, "Storia del diritto Italiano", vol. II, "Diritto publico", § 83, p. 134.]

field of private law the causes from which they were derived were varied and isolated.   One source was the transformation of a relationship, hitherto of public law, into one of a private nature, as happened in the case of many feudal rights, which became purely property rights.   Charges might also arise by act of law, as in the case of apanages, secured to younger sons upon the " fideicommissa " or trust-entails.   And lastly there was the voluntary act of the individual, expressed by will or contract.   This last was the commonest of all sources of charges.

§ 463.   **Rent Charges (" Censi ").** — Charges upon land created by contract were principally of the class known as rent charges (" censi ").   These were of two sorts and were given names corresponding to their nature, *i.e.* by purchase (" costitutivi "), and by reservation (" reservativi ").   A rent by purchase, called also by delivery (" consegnativus "), arose when, by a contract, called an " annuity purchase " (" compra di annue entrate "), there was laid upon certain land, by payment of a capital sum, a charge consisting of the periodic payment, from the revenues of the land itself, of a determined rent to the beneficiary under the contract.   " Reserved " rents had the same purpose as those by purchase, but, being created by the conveyance of the land instead of the payment of a capital sum, they arose from the reservation of a rent, charged upon the land, by the grantor, either for his own or for another's benefit, as for example a life annuity or widow's provision.   Whether by purchase or reservation, the rent was perpetual and the obligation, inhering to the land, ran from one possessor to another.   But at the same time, the land suffered no harm, so far as freedom of transfer was concerned, from the fact that the obligation was inalienable; nor did it give a right to demand the repayment of the principal sum, though, on the debtor's side, it was at all times (" quandocumque ") redeemable, hence also the name " quandocumque ", in the papal bulls, given to the contract out of which it arose.

The condition that the principal could not be reclaimed distinguished rent charges from loans at interest, secured on another's land.   Since it could not be legally maintained that they were a cover for the charging of interest (they were at first condemned for this reason by the canon law), and since they were an evident benefit to agriculture as a means of finding the capital needed for its development, without embarassing the marketability, or dangerously burdening the productivity of the land, the laws favored them, including even the papal legislation, which, indeed, by the bulls of Pope Martin V in 1425, Nicholas V in 1452, Clement VII in 1592, and Pius V in 1569, played an important part in their history. Not only did the laws approve the creation of such rents, but they also established the relation between the capital and the rent by determining to what interests in the capital the rent should correspond. Upon this point, however, there was always a lack of uniformity, varying according to the places, times and persons involved.

In the present Italian Civil Code, the rent by purchase is called " simple rent " or " censo " and that by reservation is called " land rent " (" rendita fondiaria ").

But besides the name, their legal nature has also changed. The "censo" is now considered as a right "in personam," save that it is secured upon land.[1]

§ 464. **Tithes.** — Amongst tithes, which were also land charges, must be distinguished those based upon ownership of the land in one person and possession in another, and those due the Church by canon law. The former were called " feudal " or " lay " tithes (" decime feudale ", " decime laicali ") ; but when they were due to the Church by reason of a right of possession of the land granted by the Church, they were given the special name of " nones ", because estimated on the capital remaining after payment of the " sacramental " tithe, *i.e.* on nine-tenths of the entire capital, so that the two tithes were to each other in the proportion of 9 to 10.

The tithes due the Church by canon law, called " ecclesiastical " or " sacramental " tithes, were of a different order. Their origin was the divine precept, known from biblical times and confirmed by the patristic writers and Church laws. They were an act of homage to God, and of gratitude for fructifying man's labor. The produce of man's efforts was thus reached by the ecclesiastical laws, and only indirectly the land, as the necessary source of the products themselves. Hence arose certain differences which distinguished these tithes from land charges.[2] The temporal laws did not at first make tithes the object of any special provisions. Among the Lombards, tithes were always in use, but they were voluntary offerings, as they had also been in an earlier period by the Church's canons. Charlemagne first made them obligatory ; his son, Louis, reënacted his ordinance, and Lothar introduced into his laws from the canons the prohibition against the payment to one church of the tithes belonging to another, and the imposition

---

[1] Civil Code, arts. 1778 *et seq.*   [2] *Pertile, cit.*, IV, p. 419.

of special penalties against those who sought to escape payment.[1] This favorable attitude was also shown by other rulers, such as the Norman princes, and in some places went so far as to subject State lands to the burden of the Church tithes.

Reaction was not slow to manifest itself.   During the mediaeval communes economic and political reasons opposed the development of tithes.   It was not desired that this enrichment should come to the clergy, whose privileges freed them from the common obligations towards the State; and on the other hand it was desired, so far as possible, to free the land from burdens.   The State ceased to pay tithes; the creation of new tithes, on land not already subject, was forbidden; and there next appeared that tendency toward abolition, which began to be effective under the reforms of the 1700 s, which progressed far under French legislation; and reached completion in the last laws on the subject in Italy.[2]

[1] *Charlemagne*, 60; *Louis the Pious*, 47; *Lothar*, 43.
[2] [Laws from 1860 to 1887.]

CHAPTER XXII

OTHER KINDS OF PROPERTY RIGHTS

§ 465. Easements ("Servitù"). | § 467. Later History of Hypothec.
§ 466. Pledge and Hypothec. |

§ 465. **Easements** (" **Servitù** "). — The perfection of the Roman rules upon the subject of servitudes, rules which, restored to honor at the time of the revival of the Roman law, form substantially the provisions of the present Italian Code, was unknown to Germanic law. Not that the latter did not possess the easement; it had in fact many such rights, because of the limitations of various kinds to which private ownership was subjected. But they were not governed by uniform rules; they appeared rather as quasi servitudes, as special provisions of the law.

Among them may be recalled the right of pasture. Exercised over common or public lands, it constituted a "civic use" or regalia;[1] exercised over private property, it was of the character of a servitude. There was an ancient provision, derived from early custom, that travelers might not be hindered from halting and pasturing their beasts upon unenclosed lands, provided it was not harvest time.[2] This use continued in subsequent periods, and that this right of pasture was not only found in the statutes of the mediaeval communes but maintained unchanged to a still later date, is shown by the hostility it met from land-owners, the Sicilian barons for example, against whom in 1458 the Parliament demanded relief, because they prevented the pasturage on their lands of cattle, moving from place to place. On the other hand, as lands, formerly public, passed into private hands, carrying with them the servitude of pasture,[3] this right became vaguer; and when it had thus, without distinction of origin, been rendered wholly private in character, it fell under the reforms instituted to unshackle property from its ancient encumbrances. The same should be said of those other rights, which, once peculiar to the "march" or border lands, having passed into private ownership or been created in other ways, assumed the aspect of servitudes, because in their exercise it became lawful to enter upon another's

[1] *Ante* § 418.   [2] *Rothar*, 358.   [3] *Ante* § 418.

land and take from it some determined utility.   Thus it happened with the right *to hunt*, according to which, except at the time of the ripening of the crops, it was lawful, under the statutes of the mediaeval communes, not only to enter upon the land, but also to cut stakes and branches and so on, without other consequence than that of paying the damage to the owner who complained.   Another basis for entering upon another's land was the right *to gather wood*, limited, however, to what was fallen, or dead though standing. So to a right of *passage*, if necessary, another's property must remain subject; and here certainly the analogous servitudes of Roman law were influential; in fact it is in the legislation of the mediaeval cities that this easement is found well developed and regulated.   So also in the right to take needed *water* or to drain it from one's land or use it in other ways.   In this connection an important instance was the obligatory easement of flowage or of *aqueduct* (" acquedotto coattivo "), consisting in the right to construct a canal across another's land, to draw off water from a river or other natural source, to the place where consumed or where necessary to some industry.   Germanic law held this to be a case of expropriation, because, for the reasons stated,[1] before attaining the conception of a true servitude, it regarded the person having the right of aqueduct as the owner of the strip of land necessary to it, which the owner of the land traversed was, therefore, obliged to sell to him.   When, in the period of the mediaeval communes, agriculture and industry developed, increasing the need of irrigation and water supply, the laws still further favored the use of another's land to these purposes.

Private individuals, to obtain the greatest benefit at the least cost, used to form associations to execute the work at common expense and enjoy the profits together, according to regulations established among themselves.   Thus originated the "water companies" (" consorzi per le acque ").   The idea of expropriation continued firmly intrenched, however, and was not abandoned until a later period, certainly with a resulting improvement in scientific theory and practical utility.   Expropriation was no longer deemed necessary, since it might damage both parties and hinder the very purposes desired.   In imitation of the Roman law, the idea of the servitude was preferred, by which, without conveying any part of the land, the owner declared himself bound to give a passage to the water to whoever had a right to it for agricultural, industrial or domestic uses.[2]

[1] *Ante* § 451.   [2] Civil Code, art. 598.

§ 466. Pledge and Hypothec. — In early Germanic, as in early Roman law, no distinction was made between pledge and hypothec. The conceptions corresponding precisely to each of these institutions had not yet developed; there was but a single and as yet imperfect form of security, by means of a right over the debtor's property.

Traces of the time when it was lawful to execute one's own justice and when the pledge was, therefore, appropriated on the creditor's own authority, were numerous and tenacious in Lombard law, and have certainly given their character to the development of all guarantees in the form of rights " in rem." Indeed, in Lombard laws especially were cases found of permissible private seizure,[1] in which the debtor either redeemed the object distrained by performing his obligation, or the creditor, after a certain time, became its owner. But the consequences of the ancient customs are also seen in the regulations by which the pledge was surrounded. Possession of the object, even if immovable, did not remain, as in the Roman hypothec, in the debtor; the creditor took possession in conformity with the primitive Germanic pledge.[2] That the documents sometimes show the debtor retaining possession, does not contradict the rule, because in those instances he remained in possession by permission and in the name of the creditor, as his "colonus" or tenant, or by other similar title, promising to give the creditor part of the crops and to watch well over the land. Hence, if the creditor had, as ordinarily happened, possession of the thing, he had a right to all that it produced, as though such a pledge was always accompanied by a contract of "anticresis"; as though there inhered, by its very nature, a stipulation for forfeiture ("patto commissorio"[3]), i.e. an understanding that the creditor, if not paid, should retain the ownership of the thing. Both of these privileges, which in Roman law had to be expressly stipulated, followed as consequences of the character of the Germanic pledge. This might, therefore, be considered as an alienation, subject to condition precedent, that is, producing no transfer of ownership until violation of the obligation guaranteed by the pledge.

Other consequences of the ancient nature of the Germanic pledge may also be seen in the preference shown by the laws to movable property as the subject of pledge and in the exemption of at least some forms of immovable property, when disproportionate

---

[1] *Rothar*, 245, 246; *Liutprand*, 41. [2] *Liutprand*, 58.
[3] [Roman "lex commissoria".]

damage would result to the debtor by the manner of exercising the right;[1] also in the continuing right of the creditor to demand the discharge of the obligation, even after he had made the pledged property his own,[2] since that fact did not extinguish the obligation but was merely a means of compelling satisfaction, by forcing the debtor to redeem.[3]

The Roman law, with different principles, contributed to the gradual modification of these Germanic characteristics. Its influence was soon seen in the Roman name of " fiducia ", given to the pledge in Germanic laws. In antiquity the word referred to the agreement to reconvey, accompanying the assignment of the pledge, by which the property passed; it was then extended to the contract itself, the right arising from it, and the thing covered by it. From the Roman " fiducia ", however, the Germanic pledge differed, in that, while in the latter there was a transfer of possession, there was none of ownership, which remained, at least until the happening of the condition precedent, in the debtor, who was therefore expressly referred to by the laws as owner.[4] Secondly, Roman influence is apparent in the fact that the Lombard laws began to have some notion of their own of the hypothec, even though remote. The debtor was forbidden to alienate the property which he had made the guarantee of his obligation.[5] Evidently the law referred to the case in which the debtor remained in possession, a clear derivation from the Roman hypothec. This was, however, imperfectly imitated, for the effectiveness of the right did not consist, as the true hypothec would have provided, in the exercise of a right of property in the creditor, but in the limitation of the debtor's power of disposal, a fact which likened it more to the Germanic pledge. It was, therefore, a combination of the two elements and this was the character of the law so long as the Germanic principles had force.

§ 467. **Later History of Hypothec.** — In the subsequent periods Roman law triumphed. It had a powerful ally in the canon law, which in its condemnation of the exaction of interest, opposed the Germanic pledge because, through the contract of " antichresis " and the stipulation of forfeiture (" patto commissorio "), the payment of interest was not only possible but necessary. The laws of the mediaeval communes also retained some Germanic traces,

---

[1] *Rothar*, 252.
[2] *Liutprand*, 108 and "Formularies", *cit.*, 108 *et seq.*, 147.
[3] *Post* § 497.
[4] *Rothar*, 252; *Liutprand*, 110.
[5] *Liutprand*, 67.

as in the case of security distrainable by the creditor without legal process, permitted by agreement between the parties in the case of animals caught damaging another's land, and in other cases also, among which may be recalled that of reprisals, although these had properly passed into the domain of public law.[1]   Except for these cases, the statutes of the communes forbade the use of private force and succeeded, by a constantly wider acceptance of Roman principles, in reconstructing the hypothec in accord with them. In this way it came to regain its own true character, definitely distinct from the pledge properly speaking, which was left for the use of movable property only.

Succeeding laws never again turned backward along the road but sought to bring every opportune improvement to the hypothec. The agreement of forfeiture (" patto commissorio ") was abolished, and the land subject to the hypothec was required to be sold, the debtor receiving so much of the price as remained after satisfying his creditor ; the creditor was forbidden to sell the property himself privately ; he was required to secure public authorization and to proceed by public auction.   Above all, to safeguard purchasers of the land, publication of hypothecs replaced the ancient secrecy, through the creation of public registries in which they had to be recorded.[2]

[1] *Ante* § 49.
[2] [Civil Code, arts. 1964–2127.]

Title III

POSSESSION [1]

Topic 1. Conception and History

§ 468. Under Germanic Law. | § 470. New Theories.
§ 469. Changes in Early Concep-
        tion.

Topic 2. Protection of Possession

§ 471. Rise of Possessory Actions. | § 473. Protection from Disturb-
§ 472. Recovery   of   Possession | ance ("Manutenzione").
        ("Reintegrazione").

Topic 1. Conception and History

§ 468. **Under Germanic Law.** — The precise distinction, made in Roman and in present Italian law, between possession and ownership, was unknown to the Germanic peoples. In the fact of possessing an object they did not see the possibility of the disunion of the right of possession, much less of a right that might be opposed to it. In other words, they had not reached the stage of conceiving the *fact of enjoyment* of an object (" jus possessionis ") as separate from the *right to enjoy* it (" jus possidendi "). This was because, in the first place, their juristic acumen had not developed so far as to be able to consider a fact independently of the right on which it was founded, and to treat each with appropriate rules. But other causes contributed, connected with the social conditions of the Germanic tribes and the historical origin of the property right among them. The more backward the general state of a culture, the greater the importance of external forms, *i.e.* the material manifestations of any right or of any principle.[2] The fact of possession, visible to all, was, therefore, held of greater consideration than its juridical basis, which could be made evident only through possession and of which possession, therefore, furnished the presumption. As a result the right over things was usually treated in the Germanic laws from the standpoint of possession. And it should be added that, when property had not yet become a subject of individual right and when, on a basis of use and labor, the lands occu-

[1] *Pertile, cit.*, §§ 135, 136; *Salvioli, cit.*, IV., chap. 31.   [2] *Ante* § 443.

741

pied in common came to be distributed among individuals,[1] the only right possible in the individual was that of possession. Beyond this no right went; more than this it was impossible to give or guarantee. Hence when, in consequence of the greater stability acquired by possession, individual ownership emerged, it was natural that it should appear in the closest union with possession, indeed, that it should be in a sense dependent upon it, possession being always its indicia and the reason for its presumption, and never something separate from, much less opposed to, ownership.

Here resided the fundamental difference from the Roman law, which made of possession a self-sustaining juridical institution, without the necessity of union with the right to possess, and so independently regulated and protected. Furthermore, the Germanic notion of possession had a wider extension than the Roman permitted. By the latter, to have legal effect, possession had to satisfy certain conditions, among which the chief was the intention to hold the object for one's self (" animus possidendi "), and by which it was restricted to but a few instances. In Germanic law, on the other hand, this intention was unnecessary and possession embraced what the Romans called simple detention. As the owner was possessor, so also was one who held the object in the name of another, as the " colonus ", who must necessarily have lacked the " animus possidendi." From all this arose yet another difference from Roman possession, namely, that in Germanic law there was no protection given to mere possession, as such; there was no exclusively possessory process.

This Germanic possession was technically called " gewere ", a word which contained as well the idea of the taking of possession and the right to it, as of its guarantee and protection. In translation it seems to have corresponded to the word " vestitura ", used especially in the documents of the Frankish period and preserved also later, though then restricted solely to the significance of introduction into possession. The word " seisin " (" saisina ") was also found, and in this, etymologically at least, the dominant idea was the fact of having taken possession.

§ 469. **Changes in Early Conceptions.** — Possession long preserved its Germanic character in Italy; not, however, without early manifesting the germ of future change, due to the constantly greater stability of ownership, whereby the latter's relation to possession was clarified and possession became more amenable to Roman theories.

---

[1] *Ante* § 405.

First, then, possession began to receive protection in and for itself. This meant that it began to be considered independently of the right that supported it or conflicted with it. But this occurred in instances and modes that were quite exceptional. The disturbance of possession began to be punished whenever the disturber could not prove that he had the "jus possidendi"; and the punishment was a fine.[1] This was hardly an indication of the new tendency. It did not evidence a desire to remove the disturbance of possession, because for that it was expressly required, according to the early theory, that the possessor should have the right of possession and that the disturber should be punished only when he failed to prove that he had that right. Rather did the indication of a new tendency lie in the fact that the disturbance of possession, whenever punished, was treated as an act wrongful in itself, without regard to the consequences arising from the reparation of the injured right. Reparation certainly existed and consisted principally in the restoration of the object to its former possessor. But restitution did not result by virtue of a possessory remedy, which went no further than the punishment of the wrongdoer, but arose from the fact that the original possessor was presumed to have the right of possession, since his despoiler was unable to prove that such a right was his. So true was this that it has been thought that restitution of the object was imposed only later upon the wrongful taker by a law of King Guido.[2] But this can not be sustained, either in the light of what has already been said regarding the character of Germanic possession, or of Guido's law itself. This had reference to the case where a third party had acquired the object from one who had in turn taken it from the possessor, and provided that, upon conviction of the wrongful intent, such third person should pay the fine and also make restitution; because otherwise it might have been said that restitution was not due from the third party, but from the one who had received a price for the object, which he had taken from its lawful possessor.

In these various laws, however, and in those also of the Carlovingians, which inflicted payment of the royal ban upon whoever disturbed another's possession without magisterial authority,[3] the penal conception was always dominant. The purpose was to punish recklessness and the use of private force, to guarantee social order; in that way possession came indirectly to be guaranteed. But its civil importance was not yet recognized, and pro-

[1] *Liutprand*, 148.   [2] *Pertile, cit.*, IV, p. 170, note 4.   [3] *Pepin*, 23.

tection was provided only if, in its disturbance, there had appeared the element of crime.   This meant that possession had not yet arrived where it was considered as a juristic fact wholly independent of the right to possess.

§ 470. **New Theories.** — So we come to the period of the revived Roman law.   But in the matter of possession it did not bear the same good fruit as in other fields.   Legal practice, formed upon Germanic traditions, did not harmonize with legal science, which had turned toward Roman ideas.   The attempted reconciliation resulted in a serious confusion of principles, which has ever since encumbered the law of possession.   The principal cause of this was the multiplicity of the Germanic forms of possession.   On the one hand, to many situations which, under the Roman law, would not have been considered juridical possession, were carried over rules which were applied to cases, by nature different, which admitted such possession; on the other hand, there were forced, into the nomenclature and classification of the Romans, Germanic institutions which did not fit, while Roman theories were strained to explain what were consequences of Germanic principles.   For these reasons the revival of the Roman law did not resuscitate the pure Roman theory of possession.   Vigorous Germanic traits clung to it and some are still found in the present Italian Code, where the term "possession" no longer has the technical and restricted sense given to it by the Romans, but is vague; so vague, indeed, that, contrary to Roman principles, incorporeal things, such as the enjoyment of rights, may also be objects of possession.[1]

In the midst of the confusion, nevertheless, a few theories prevailed and remained fundamental.   Such was the Roman doctrine that possession should be legally recognized and protected for its own sake; such also, on the other hand, was the Germanic principle, accepted and extended by the canon law, that possession was possible not only over corporeal objects, but also over all those rights whose exercise was capable of being disturbed.[2]   Thus, there was the possession of tithes, custom rights, benefices, public offices, family position, personal status, and of yet other rights.

TOPIC 2. PROTECTION OF POSSESSION

§ 471. **Rise of Possessory Actions.** — As a consequence of this reconstruction of the attributes of possession, there arose its pro-

[1] Civil Code, art. 685: ["Possession is the detention of a thing or the enjoyment of a right, which one has either in himself or through another who detains the object or exercises the right in the former's name".]
[2] *Cf.* "juris quasi possessio."

tection, no longer indirect and penal in character, but by civil process. The possessor was admitted to proof of his right, his " jus possessionis ", by oath alone, and so repelled contrary proof, which his adversary might have presented, according to the rule of Germanic procedure, according to which advantage did not lie in being absolved from proof, but in the privilege of presenting it.[1] This defense of possession was generally conceded in the statutes of the mediaeval communes, but the introduction of genuine civil possessory actions was due in large part to the canon law, and also to the precedent of the Roman " interdicts ", although between them and the new possessory actions there were substantial differences.

In general the aim of the protection of possession was twofold — recovery of lost possession and immunity from disturbance. To these two purposes corresponded special possessory actions.

§ 472. **Recovery of Possession** (" **Reintegrazione** "). — To accomplish the first of these purposes, for which Roman law had the " interdicta recuperandae possessionis ", there was the " actio spolii " or action of " reintegration " (" reintegrazione "). It was a maxim of the canon law that, whenever a bishop, by violence or any other illegal method, was expelled from his see, there should be, before the reception of any charge, before any examination by a judge or initiation of process, a restoration of his violated possession, under pain of nullity of the procedure. There was, that is, a defensive plea to the proposed action, by which the criminal charge was suspended until the situation had been restored to its original state through the action of the judge himself. The fundamental canon on this point began with the word " redintegranda ",[2] from which was derived the name " reintegration ", which this possessory action still preserves.[3]

In canon law, however, in the sense just mentioned, this was not an action but a defensive plea. Nor was it a true possessory remedy, so far as it presupposed the assertion of a contrary claim, and was applied to cases which involved an accusation against the person who had suffered dispossession, and in which a final decision was not at once manifest. But by the interpretation of the jurists and the extension given it in practice, it became a true possessory remedy, was adopted by the civil laws, and as such was no longer a plea but an action, begun at the instance of the

---

[1] *Ante* § 55.
[2] " Redintegranda sunt omnia expoliatis vel eiectis episcopis " . . . " Corpus Juris Canonici ", *Gratian*, " Decretum ", *Causa*, III, *Quaest.* 1, c. 3.
[3] Civil Code, arts. 695–697.

dispossessed, to recover the object lost. This "actio spolii" had an analogy, therefore, to the "interdictum unde vi" of the Roman law, but differed in the more extended use that it gained. This extension took place in respect to parties, since it could also be brought against third possessors, who, in Roman law, were not liable except to the extent of an unjust enrichment; in respect to time, which was not limited to a year, as in the Roman interdict; in respect to the objects recoverable, because while the "interdictum unde vi" was limited to immovable property, the "actio spolii" was extended to embrace also movables; and finally, in respect to the mode of the dispossession, in that violence was not necessary, any act sufficing which had unjustly deprived of possession. On the other hand, while its penal character made it resemble the Germanic defense of possession, the "actio spolii" diverged yet further from it, in that it was in essence a preliminary process, whereas the Germanic law awaited the outcome of the litigation, which it aimed to render unfavorable to the disturber of possession,[1] by punishing his unjust act.

Obstacles to the development of the "actio spolii" were not lacking, not only because of its difference from Roman law, which led to resistance by one party of jurists, but also because the great extension of its use produced difficulties. Efforts were therefore made to place restrictions about it. Such, for example, was the very important limitation of Pope Innocent III, prohibiting the use of the "actio spolii" against a third possessor, unless the latter had known that the party from whom he received the object, had taken possession of it by violence to another's damage; and even in this case there could not be demanded of him more than the restoration of the thing itself.

Nevertheless, the "actio spolii" continued to have wide application and in its subsequent development an inversion of its two elements took place. In place of the penal element, aiming under the Germanic theory at the punishment of the disturber of possession, succeeded the civil element, which sought to recover the object, conformably to Roman principles; and this latter function has remained the characteristic of this action. Such it descended to the present Italian Code, where it was again surrounded by Roman rules, abandoned during the intermediate period. By these it may be brought only against the author of the dispossession, which must have been accomplished "vi aut clam" (violently or covertly), within the year prior to the institution of the suit.

[1] *Ante* § 467.

§ 473. Protection from Disturbance ("Manutenzione"). —
For the second object, that of maintaining one's peaceful possession,
accomplished under the Roman law by the interdicts "retinendae
possessionis", the Middle Ages provided possessory processes.
In contrast to the "actio spolii", these processes required that the
possession should have been lawful ("legittimo"), though the
lapse of a fixed period, such as a year and a day, in accordance with
the Germanic law of prescription, sufficed to render it so.[1]

The purpose of the possessory process ("giudizio possessorio")
was to determine to whom belonged the legal possession of an object
over which a controversy had arisen, followed by a condemnation
to pay the damages arising from the fact of disturbance, and a
determination of the rôle which each of the contending parties, as
possessor (defendant) or claimant (plaintiff), should sustain in the
action to determine the ownership ("giudizio petitorio"). To
decide all this required a long procedure, and so arose the necessity
of finding another remedy to determine with whom possession
should remain during the pendency and until the final decision of
the suit. A solution external to the process itself was first tried,
by giving to the magistrate power to sequestrate or deposit the
litigated object with some suitable person. But this expedient
might produce other difficulties, give rise to arbitrary acts, injure
the lawful possessor, and, therefore, complicate, indeed bring the
suit to naught. This administrative act was, therefore, made a
procedural act, that is, a preliminary process, to be accomplished
in the briefest possible time, before arriving at the ordinary possessory process. This latter also, being preliminary to still another
process, called the "petitory" which decided the right of ownership, called for a concise procedure (though it was not such in
fact) which was, therefore, termed "summary"; hence the·
new preliminary process, which required much more expeditious
formalities, was referred to as "most summary." This last
process did not aim to pass in a final manner upon the possession,
but merely to give it to one of the parties, to avoid violence or
disturbance during the course of the litigation. The judge's
decision was, therefore, interlocutory, having effect only during
the pendency of the litigation. But the decision in the ordinary
"summary" possessory process was definitive unless annulled by
a contrary judgment in the subsequent "petitory" process which
finally determined the title.

This dual possessory procedure was adopted by the laws, by

[1] *Ante* § 440.

court practice, and even by some of the earlier codes. Today there is only the action called " manutenzione del possesso ", that is of " retention of possession ", a name derived from the " most summary " part of the possessory process. Because of its purpose, it is still referred to as " mandatum de manutenendo ", and recalls also another rule of mediaeval law which required that possession, to receive protection, should have become lawful by having been continuous during a year.[1]

[1] *Ante* § 440.

PART V
OBLIGATIONS

PART V

OBLIGATIONS [1]

§ 474. General Formative Influences. — The three elements that have given life to every part of Italian Law — Roman civilization, Germanic tradition and Christian morality — are found united in the history of obligations. In their origin and as they stand today, each has contributed in an essential manner.

Roman law has undoubtedly played the dominant rôle in the present doctrine of obligations. But the principles derived from Germanic law and the Church are very important, for to them are due the most radical and useful innovations, distinguishing present Italian from Roman obligations.

The domination of Roman law was assured from the Germanic period. Few, simple, and without system were the obligations of the Germanic invaders, chiefly for the reason that the conditions of their society permitted of but little trade and almost no credit. They knew, therefore, no complete theory of obligations save through the Romans, whose legal principles they had no great difficulty in adopting, because the Roman law of obligation had attained to such a point of perfection that even new combinations of ideas and interests found suitable place in their rules; and because obligations compose that branch of law which, more successfully than any other, can separate itself from the special conditions in which a nation lives; for, being almost exclusively the product of man's will, it lacks that close relation to his condition that characterizes other departments of law, such as property or family.

Nevertheless, on contact with Germanic society, even the Roman law of obligations did not remain immune from some modification. The invaders left an impress of their mode of conceiving rights, revealing, with important consequences, the ancient practice of taking justice into one's own hands; they contributed the Germanic tendency to the use of formalities as the vestments of their legal conceptions; [2] and most important of all, they left traces

---

[1] [Sections 474–503 are a translation of *Calisse*, Part V, final §§ 189–219.]

[2] *Ante* § 442.

751

of the Germanic notion of obligations, in which more importance was given to the objective element of property than to its subjective or personal element.   For the Germanic principles were not only retained alongside the Roman, wherever they could be reconciled, throughout the whole period of Germanic legal ascendancy; subsequently, when legal science had restored Roman law to a commanding position in the field of obligations, the Germanic principles that had not been abandoned, were even confirmed, as possessing elements by which the Roman law could better shape itself to all the needs, especially commercial, of the new society.

Society also drew upon the material that was developing about the field of obligations under the inspiration of the canon law.   At first this resulted in confusion between what properly belonged to morals and to law.   But with time, there were drawn from the moral element important legal consequences, which are evident today in many ways, but especially in the force given to the idea of equity, and also, in part at least, in placing the element of pure intent before the old formalism, to which the canon law was opposed.

Title I

GENERAL CHARACTER [1]

§ 475. **Spheres of Roman, Germanic and Canonical Influences.** — The mingling of these elements is shown throughout the whole course of the history of obligations. But it becomes more evident and richer in consequences in a general view of the character of obligations, than in the particular rules governing any one contract. Such a general view, with special reference to the source of the law itself, may be conveniently considered with relation, first to the formation of obligations, second to the modes of securing their performance, and finally to the manner of their extinguishment.

Chapter XXIII

FORMATION OF OBLIGATIONS

Topic 1. Sources

Topic 1. Sources

§ 476. **Early History.** — The sources of obligations have been substantially the same in all ages. They derived either from the act of the individual or the command of law. The importance and the interrelation of those sources, however, have changed with the period, now one, now the other predominating, the same consequences being traceable at times to one and at times to the other source. In the early stages of Italian legal history, law was a very rare source of obligations, because its field was as limited

[1] *Pertile, cit.,* §§ 149–155; *Salvioli, cit.,* IV, chaps. 37–39; *Schupfer,* "Singrafe e Chirografi", in "Revista italiana delle scienze giuridiche", VII (1889).

as the sphere left to the individual was vast; yet vaster was the sphere wherein developed family life. Conversely, therefore, the act of the individual was a very abundant source. Here a distinction must be made. The unlawful was a more prevalent source of obligations than the lawful act; that is to say obligations derived more frequently, according to the language of the Roman law, from " delicts " and " quasi-delicts ", than from contracts and quasi-contracts. The reason was twofold. It lay first in the character which every unlawful act possessed for the Germans. It was always considered from the side of its material consequences, that is, of the damage caused to another, and so was regarded as an offence for which that other sought his own redress, first by armed revenge and later by pecuniary compositions.[1] Every unlawful act, therefore, gave rise in its author to an obligation to make amends, just as the right to recover them arose in the victim. In other words, a debit and credit right arose and an obligation was formed. The second reason was that, in ancient Germanic society, contracts, as a source of obligations, had the very scantiest development, because of the conditions themselves of that society. In this they did not differ from every primitive civilization. The development of contracts is linked with the development of individual activity, and this latter was very limited among the Germanic peoples, because the individual had little power or interest to create a novel legal relationship. As to his power, it must be remembered that the individual had little freedom of action, outside those institutions of which, by birth or profession, he found himself a part; the family especially concentrated in itself the forces which, in more progressive times, belong to the individual. If, on the one hand, the State abandoned to others certain functions which properly belonged to it, on the other, and especially through the doctrines of common family ownership, it invaded the field of individual activity. And this was limited by still other bonds which easily developed in the then state of society. Such were the placing of the warrior youth under the command of some valiant prince;[2] the tendency of the weak to seek the protection of the strong; and all those reciprocal personal relationships from which feudalism finally derived and which were certainly not favorable to the development of contracts. Incentive, no less than power, to contract was limited. The impulse of trade was almost entirely lacking; grazing of cattle and agriculture were the occupations to which the Germanic peoples, in time of

[1] *Ante* §§ 46, 47.   [2] *Ante* § 30.

peace, were almost exclusively devoted. Personal credit, indispensable to obligations, was almost unknown, because not the individual, but the family, was the subject of rights, and because the family had its own estate which furnished it an income and which it might not alien or even diminish.[1] Thus no need of contracts was felt, except of the very simplest, required by daily life, *e.g.* the exchange of products, the acquisition of animals or implements of labor, and in general contracts of exchange or purchase and sale limited to personal property. Such contracts were not capable of producing true obligations. They did not create such juridical consequences as held the two contracting parties in the relation of promisee and promisor for any length of time, since they were executed contemporaneously with their making; and the theories had not yet developed as to responsibility supervening after the act, by reason of an eviction, the discovery of latent defects, or other similar cause. Then, too, the personal element, upon which obligations are founded, was wholly subordinate to the economic element, for nothing was in view save the material and immediate advantage which each party saw in the action to which he was thus induced. Consideration of the person as yet had no importance.

§ 477. **Transitional Period.** — After the Germanic invaders, by their conquest of Italy, had come in contact with the Roman population, their law of obligations underwent a sudden expansion and development. Those originating in unlawful acts decreased, because the State, to the gradual exclusion of the individual, took an ever greater part in the repression of crime and in punitive justice in general.[2] There was an increase, on the other hand, of that class which arose by law, especially since many of those rights which were the natural consequences of the early common ownership of property found, in legislation, a refuge and protection against the dissolution of the ancient ties. There were thus obligations based upon a condition of fact, even transitory, such as being in possession of certain land, especially due to the Germanic idea that lands were capable, as though having a law of their own, of being the subject of legal rights and duties. Finally contracts as a source of obligations increased, and henceforward were destined to be the most copious source.

The causes which had held contracts within the narrowest limits gave way to others which were to have the opposite effect. With

[1] *Ante* § 312.
[2] *Ante* § 47.

the emergence of private ownership, individual activity shook itself free from its ancient restrictions; commerce and industry increased, opening up a vast and productive field for contracts. Naturally this did not happen immediately and completely. The transition from the old to the new conditions was accomplished slowly, in step with civilization, and the various causes leading to greater contractual activity developed with the same slow pace; the more so since traces of ancient communism, whether of the social group or of the family, still remained alive and capable of sensibly limiting the individual's power. To this should be added the fact that the institutions then forming in society, such as the benefice, vassalage and finally the fief, were not such as to permit the individual to move freely within the sphere of his individual will. This condition of things was faithfully represented in the Lombard, Frankish and feudal laws, in which may be read the slow development of the liberty of the individual over himself and his property. During this period, therefore, it may more correctly be said that the seeds were being sown and fertilized, which, under more favorable conditions, were to bear fruit.

§ 478. **Period of the Revival of Roman Law.** — More propitious conditions came with the rise of the mediaeval communes. Political and social conditions generally were leading men to cast off their ancient bonds, and to find in the State an encouragement and protection for the exercise of their activities. Commerce expanded to a degree never before known and credit became its principal basis; contracts multiplied, and some were of new form, inasmuch as the conversion of land into money or merchandise, long term enterprises that were daring and highly remunerative, relations with distant places, and the construction of ships, the transport of goods, the exchange of monies, transfers of credit, and many other commercial and industrial needs could not be satisfied except by the fullest liberty of contract, and this was constantly productive of an important intermingling of obligations.

Contemporaneously came the revival of Roman jurisprudence, in whose rules were soon discovered the means of satisfying the many new needs. All of these were not known to Roman law, but for every case men sought, and in a large part were able to draw, from the Roman law the principles needed to justify and regulate them. It should not surprise, therefore, that the Roman theories of obligations came again to be applied in their full extension, and that with them were revived very precise distinctions as to their origin, namely, the Roman classification of sources. These, recovering strength in succeeding systems of law, are still found in the present Italian Code.[1]

TOPIC 2.   FORM

§ 479. **Germanic Formalities; Pledge or "Wadia."** — An attentive examination of the laws and customs of the Germanic peoples has resulted in the conclusion, now a certainty, that obligations amongst them were not formed, as was for a long time thought by many, by simple evidence of intent, free from the necessity of definite external formalities, but, on the contrary, when arising out of contract, by the performance of formalities, required to give perfection to the acts to which they related.   That is to say, they grew out of contracts perfected by the use of established formalities.

There were certainly *real* contracts,[2] that is, formed by the delivery of the thing which was its object by one party, and of something equivalent by the other party.   In fact, as already observed,[3] none other than " real " contracts came at first into use.   To substitute a given formality for the actual delivery of the thing or for its immediate payment marked a progress both in legal ideas and in the importance assignable to the credit of the individual.   At first the latter was wholly lacking or at least was not taken into consideration in contracts; later, as the necessity demanded, it began to be admitted, though guaranteed by the evidence of the public, who were gathered at the market place, where contracts were wont to be made.   From this was derived the solemn form of the "thingatio", that is, of evidence by the popular assembly, which was retained also in later periods for certain contracts, including in general those translative of ownership.[4]   A still further progress freed the contracting parties also from this necessity and rendered possible a wider application of personal responsibility as the basis of an obligation, so that the relation between the contracting parties was not extinguished im-

---

[1] Art. 1097.

[2] [The designation "real" to contracts is of course that of the Roman law: *Justinian,* Digest, II, 14, "De pactis"; *Gaius,* III, 90, 91.   Contracts enforceable by the "jus civilis" were called formal because their validity depended upon formalities required by the "jus civilis"; those enforceable by the "jus gentium" were called formless, because symbolism did not enter into them.   The latter were again divided into "real" and "consensual."   The "real" contract arose by the physical delivery of some object or "res" (hence the name), whereby an obligation arose in the other contracting party to restore it or its equivalent as the case might be.   The sanction or seriousness of such a contract obviously resided in the parting with possession of the "res."]

[3] *Ante* § 476.   [4] *Ante* § 442.

mediately after its creation, but could continue alive for a certain period by the use of a form intended to preserve and guarantee it. Thus the first purpose of form in contracts was to make possible the postponement of the execution of the obligation, which, under the earlier theory, admitting of no break in time or place, had to be performed at the same moment that it was concluded. Such a form could therefore at first consist only in the delivery of a pledge ("pegno"), equivalent in value to the promise, the execution of which thus came to be rendered secure. Correspondence in value between the pledge and the object of the obligation, being contrary to the idea of personal credit and to economic needs, naturally, with the progress of these factors, was less and less frequently demanded, so that the next step was to admit the sufficiency of the pledge, whatever its value, and later to make it symbolic.

At this point, in place of "real", the obligation became truly "formal"; in place of the delivery of the thing which was the object of the contract, or in place of payment, a symbol was given, representing them. In the delivery of the symbol lay the perfection of the contract, since it took the place of actual performance which had hitherto perfected the "real" contract.

This sign or symbol was the "wadia" or "festuca",[1] used also in tradition accompanying the transfer of ownership. Its origin was probably the giving of a spear or rod to indicate the yielding of authority over the object of the obligation, and the surrender of any claim to defend it, which otherwise might have been asserted. The ceremony consisted in the throwing of the "wadia" or "festuca" by the obligor or promisor into the hands of his promisee, who received and preserved it as proof and guarantee of his acquired right.

§ 480. Influence of Roman Law; "Charta." — Through the influence of Roman law upon Germanic obligations,[2] another form soon arose, having as symbol the "charta."[3] Written documents were in use among the Romans in all contracts; for them formularies had been compiled, that were tenaciously held to in practice, even after they had become antiquated. These formularies, with the identical Roman name of "cauta" or "cautiones", spread among the Germanic population, principally through the clergy, to whom recourse was generally had, whenever it was desired to

---

[1] *Val de Lièvre*, "Launegild und Wadia" (1877).
[2] *Ante* § 474.
[3] *Brunner*, "Charta und Notitia" (1877).

put a contract into writing.   Indeed, the same formularies were continually employed in the drawing of documents of the Germanic period, and this explains why there was so great a similarity of ideas and expressions.

It happened, however, that among the Germanic population the written document, in a certain sense, was placed in the position of the " wadia ", in that it was given the same efficacy as the latter.   The delivery of the document figured as the life-giving formality of the contract.   It was no longer merely evidential. The "charta", or written title, and consequently its delivery, came to be the formative element of the contract itself.   The reasons were various.   In the later period of the Roman Empire, the " charta ", at least in practice, had acquired, or was tending to acquire, the character of a form essential to the existence of the legal transaction, and the Germanic invaders merely continued this practice, stabilizing and perfecting it.   In so doing, they were impelled by the need, always felt by a young civilization, to clothe rights in visible forms; or by the marked resemblance between the delivery of the " charta " and of the " wadia "; or further by the fact that, due to a certain confusion by the Germanic law between " real " and " personal " rights, whereby in both a preponderant consideration was given to the objective element, it was easy to understand an obligation as binding, when accompanied by the same formality of delivery of the document as employed in tradition (" traditio ") and investiture for the transfer of " real " rights.[1]   In fact, just as it had been said that there could be no stability in acquisitions without tradition, so now it was said that obligations gained permanent security by the written title.   The " charta " in which the right was centred, was in truth surrounded by a quasi-inviolability.   A penalty of double the value of the object of the contract was imposed upon the party who sought to evade his obligation, while payment of the penalty left the obligation unextinguished.   The obligor might refuse performance if the obligee did not present the " charta ", and, on the other hand, he might perform for the benefit of any other person who had possession of it; when performed, he had a right to the return of the " charta " and it was customary to cancel it by tearing or otherwise, since the right contained in it had terminated.

§ 481. **Reciprocal Influence of " Wadia " and " Charta."** — The coming into use of the contractual form " per chartam " did

---

[1] *Ante* § 442.

not at once cause the abandonment of that " per wadiam." Both forms could be executed at once. Delivery of the written instrument might accompany the " wadia ", of the giving of which there was secure proof and a perpetual record; or it might be provided that the performance of the contract " per wadiam " should be conditioned upon presentation of his title by the obligee. This could the more easily happen, in that the two contractual forms had between them much that was analogous, except the diversity of their origin and significance; for with respect to these the " wadia " was a substitute for the ancient effective delivery of the object of the contract and the reciprocal guarantee between the parties, while the " charta " indicated a perfected manifestation of consent.

Nevertheless, what could not result suddenly, came with time, as the two forms of obligations sought in turn to prevail.

At first it seemed as though it was the Germanic form which would give character to the Roman; as may be argued from the laws by which the " charta " or " cautio " lost their efficacy unless renewed every five years.[1] This idea did not exist in Roman law and may have been imparted from the nature of the " wadia ", which was not of permanent character, since it did not remain with the promisee until the obligation was satisfied, but had to be redeemed by the promisor by giving sureties, in accordance with his obligation, within a certain time.[2] Much more important and enduring, however, was the opposite influence, that of the Roman upon the Germanic form, for the contract " per chartam " so prevailed that the old form was wholly superseded by the new. All contracts, just as in the case of acquisition by tradition and investiture, came finally to be entered into in writing, with the symbolic delivery of the document.

§ 482. Influence of Canon Law. — To these elements the canon law should be added as a third factor in the historical evolution of the form of obligations. Its presence was rich in consequences. It brought to obligations the moral element, which led to the doctrine that an obligation might be valid quite independently of form, because of the duty of all to keep faith; for to do otherwise was to violate truth and to offend God, who was identified with truth. This theory was the more generally acceptable in that it was consonant with the early sentiments of the Germanic peoples. Among them, according to early custom, the word given must be unalterably kept. If defeated in games in which they had pledged their freedom, they suffered themselves

[1] *Liutprand*, 16.   [2] *Post* § 490.

to be disarmed, bound, and treated in all respects as slaves by their victorious companions.[1] In this was not absent that religious sentiment which, among all youthful peoples, and so among the Germanic nations, must have been the first basis for the efficacy of obligations. For their earliest form of contract required that it be entered into before the gods, who were made its witnesses and the avengers of its violation, so that a breach became an offense against the gods themselves. Their new religion was not hostile to these sentiments, but indeed confirmed them. This correspondence of sentiment further appears in the fact that the canon law, like ancient Germanic customs, used the oath as a mode of validating obligations. All formalities were, therefore, considered superfluous by the canon law. It did not recognize in form a sufficient force to invalidate (where the form was lacking or imperfect), or to validate (when properly employed), the intent of the contracting parties, clearly manifested, by whatsoever mode. Hence the consequence that even those obligations must be performed which, for lack or imperfection of form, gave rise to no civil action, as in the case of the " nudum pactum " of the Romans; so finally also those which were not civilly valid or which could be annulled, such as the obligations of minors or others against which the law provided defenses. The sole condition required for the validity of obligations under oath was that their " cause " (" causa ") should be lawful.

Yet another consequence of greater importance arose. The oath came to be regarded as the act which perfected the obligation, as the reason of its validity, as the element constituting its very essence. When an oath had been taken, nothing further was sought in support of the validity of the obligation and no contrary reason was admissible to overthrow it. So the oath was added to the " wadia " and the " charta " as a third form for the making of obligations.

It is interesting to observe their reciprocal relation. These three forms corresponded to the three classes of Roman obligations, i.e., " real ", " literal " and " verbal." The " wadia " corresponded to the " real " obligation, in the sense that it took the place, and remained the symbol, of the giving of the object, by which this form of contract was at first perfected; the contract concluded " per chartam " had its counterpart in the Roman " literal " form, since the basis of its existence was found in the written document which was delivered; finally, the obligation

---

[1] *Tacitus*, "Germania", 24.

under oath was analogous to the Roman "verbal" contract, because it was created by the words of the oath itself, invoking the testimony of the divinity, just as the Roman "stipulatio" was formed by words promising the solemn faith of the parties.

§ 483. **The Consensual Element.** — These principles, which the canon law was especially influential in introducing into the theory and form of obligations, did not go far before opposition arose, chiefly from the jurists who set the Roman before the canon law. But the effect was not such as to root out the non-Roman elements, for in their turn they suited the new social conditions and above all benefited commerce, which, during the period of the mediaeval communes, gained an impetus not hitherto known in Italy.[1] Jurisprudence dared not return unqualifiedly to the Roman law, but tried to reconcile it with the new law, to explain upon Roman theories situations derived elsewhere. The jurists thus necessarily brought uncertainty and confusion into legal science, but, on the other hand, science permanently acquired through them the new principles, which were thus enabled to remain alive, and to demonstrate and produce all the effects of which they were capable. In the course of this renewal, supported in the name of the Roman law, the external formalities of obligations, above all those of Germanic origin, had to be abandoned. But by this very fact, the element of consent, till then hidden under the necessary and appropriate form of the contract, was brought into greater relief. From this movement the law has never since receded. Indeed, the subsequent theories of the school of natural law, which based everything, including the very existence of society, upon the consensual element, gave added validity to the theory that this element should be given major consideration. So it came about, and so it is in the Italian law of today, that consensual contracts alone are recognized, with the exception of certain solemn forms, in which consent has to be manifested in the ways prescribed by law.[2]

[1] *Ante* § 474.
[2] [Civil Code, arts. 1098, 1104, 1108 *et seq.*]

CHAPTER XXIV

GUARANTEES OF PERFORMANCE

§ 484. **Earliest Modes.** — The earliest modes of securing or guaranteeing the performance of obligations were, like those of the formation of contracts, linked with religious sentiment. Invocation of the intervention of the gods, in whose presence and name the obligation was considered to have been concluded, made the fear of punishment hold the obligor to his promise. The rites used for this purpose varied with time and place, but the most common, at least among the earlier, were those of sacrifice and of feasting (derived from the sacrifice), in both of which it was thought that the gods took part. By such rites, indeed, do we find the more important acts of public and private life undertaken among all ancient peoples, and they did not disappear even after the ideas which had stirred their adoption had vanished. Sacrifices and banqueting, as essential elements, perfected, or, as incidental elements, accompanied marriages, international treaties, funerals, the reception of guests, the beginning of all important undertakings, everything in short of which there was an interest in assuring the successful outcome or accomplishment. Of such rites every age has long preserved traces, down to the popular usages, with altered significance, still surviving in market place and countryside, where the contracting parties conclude by drinking together, in order better to seal their bargain.

§ 485. **Oath.** — The oath became the most frequent mode of insuring an obligation and long remained unaltered, because this method, unlike the others, tainted by paganism and so unfavored, was approved and supported by the new religion. The Germanic invaders, therefore, made large use of the oath and their laws record that they customarily swore upon the Gospel, upon arms which had been blessed, upon the altar, the Cross, and on the relics of saints. As to effect, the oath, considered as a means of insuring

763

performance, supplied the coercive element, either by substituting for the civil validity of the obligation, if lacking or liable to attack, a religious sanction, based upon the oath itself and enjoying in the ecclesiastical court an ever ready authority for enforcement; or by subjecting the perjurer to serious penalties. In this respect the temporal laws were faithful followers of the canonical laws. The Lombards, employing the very words of the canons, condemned perjury, sought to repress it, and punished it no less severely than the Church;[1] the Frankish laws[2] and others throughout the Germanic epoch[3] followed the same course. In addition, the penalties for the non-performance of a sworn obligation were increased by the parties themselves, who in their agreement subjected themselves to others extra-legal, pecuniary or spiritual, which the party making oath invoked upon himself and his descendants.

The efficacy of the oath, added to the obligation, received an important confirmation and application in the "authentica",[4] "Sacramenta puberum . . .", a constitution of the Swabian Emperor Frederick I. An ancient Roman constitution had provided that a minor might not be excused from performance of a contract which he had confirmed by oath. This referred to those obligations which the minor by favor of the law might rescind, as is evident from the example given of a contract of sale. The Emperor Frederick I, on the other hand, apparently following the advice of the jurist Martinus and rejecting the contrary counsel of Bulgarus, extended the efficacy of the oath so as to validate also those contracts which would not otherwise have been enforceable by the civil law.[5]

It was not long before a reaction set in, and the principal reason, besides the fact that Roman doctrines began to prevail over canonical, lay in the new movement, which aimed to keep the field of law entirely distinct from that of morals. The Glossators were generally opposed to the Emperor Frederick's law. They did not spare their disapproval of Martinus, its supposed author, and

---

[1] *Liutprand*, 72, 133, 144; *Rachi*, "Preamble", 2.
[2] *Charlemagne*, 10, 21, 38; *Pepin*, 43; *Louis the Pious*, 15; *Lothar*, 53.
[3] *Otto I*, 1.
[4] ["Sacramenta puberum sponte facta super contractibus rerum suarum non retractandis inviolabilites custodiantur." This was inserted as an "authentica" or note to the text of *Justinian*, Code, II, 28, 1. *See Salvioli, cit.* (6th ed., 1908), p. 632. For a description of "authentica" *see* "Continental Legal History Series", Vol. I, "General Survey", pp. 169, 170.]
[5] *Justinian*, Code, II, 28, 1; *Savigny*, "Storia del diritto romano nel medio evo", *cit.*, Vol. II, § 57. Italian translation by *Bollati* of original German ed.

rejoiced that one of his family, through the use of the oath, had wasted his estate.   They persuaded Henry VII to repeal Frederick's constitution, and that this was not done, was due to the premature death which cut short all that prince's undertakings. They did succeed, however, in having the law disregarded and in introducing into several statutes of the mediaeval cities provisions directly contrary to it.   Indeed, besides the fact that in some of these Frederick's constitution was declared abolished, the statutes generally began to deny to acts, valid under the civil law, any greater efficacy derived from the oath: in other words, unless valid under the civil law, no other action could be brought based on the breach of the oath, perjury being left to punishments analogous to those for the crime, that is, to spiritual penalties.   As a consequence, also, when a civil right of action was lacking, it could not be supplied by another, by reason of the oath accompanying the contract; that is, an obligation could no longer acquire validity through the oath, which it did not have by law without it. And finally, to avoid confusion, it was prohibited to add the oath to contracts; in 1770, the Piedmontese laws forbade public officials to insert them in the acts within their jurisdiction.   By such a course, the oath came to be without effect upon the validity of contracts and this is the Italian law today.

§ 486. **Seizure of the Person.** — Some modes of insuring performance of obligations were related to that early condition when the individual was authorized to obtain justice for himself, for want or inadequacy of public powers instituted to that end.

The promisee might have a guarantee of his right in the person of his promisor, for the personal preceded the pecuniary guarantee amongst all ancient peoples.[1]   In antiquity this was a consequence of the right itself of the creditor, who, in case of breach of performance, without more, took possession of the person of his debtor. But when for individual action was substituted that of public authority, as the custodian of the rights of all and the avenger of their violation, it became necessary, if the creditor was to gain power over his debtor's person, that there should be an antecedent pact between them, by which the debtor, or another for him, promised to surrender himself as a hostage to his creditor, in case he did not satisfy the obligation, and to remain in such status until its complete performance.

§ 487. **Distraint** ("**Pignoramento**"). — Besides the person, the property of the debtor was also guarantee of the rights of the

---

[1] *Cf.* "Actio legis per manus injectionem" of the Roman law.

creditor, who could in antiquity, of his own authority, lay hands
upon it, when his claim was not satisfied.   This too was at first a
consequence of each person's recognized right to exact his own
justice.[1]   But, as in the case of the guarantee of the person, a
stipulation came to be necessary, and this was implied in contracts
concluded with the " wadia ", of which the earliest aim and significance was said to be the renunciation by the debtor of his
personal defense against the possible acts of his creditor, that is,
as happened in the contract with " nexum " of the Roman law, to
render the obligation capable of self-redress, without the necessity
of seeking the authority of the magistrate.   In measure, however,
as political authority grew and laws came into being regulating
even the relationships between individuals, this mode of enforcing
obligations was at first, as in the Lombard law, limited and systematized, and then generally prohibited, in order to substitute
in all cases justice by the State for justice by the individual.   Thus,
for private was substituted judicial attachment, a point really
reached by the laws of the Franks.   In the Lombard period it was
already known and admitted, but it existed alongside private
distraint, for which it appeared rather as a subsidiary.   The Lombard laws, indeed, provided that not everything might be the object
of private seizure.   For example, they excepted the animals
necessary for grazing and agriculture, which could not be seized
without the permission of the king or without prior express authority from the debtor.[2]   If this authorization was not secured, the
attachment of such animals might not be private, but had to be
by judicial act.   The latter is thus seen developing through the
rules circumscribing and limiting private distraint.   The requirement of authorization makes evident another fact.   Between the
ancient distraint, derived from the powers of the creditor, and the
new, authorized by the magistrate, was created, in the period of
transition, a third form, namely, that permitted by leave of the
debtor.   It might have a penal character, as where it was agreed
that the creditor should become owner of the pledged object in the
case of non-performance of the obligation, without extinguishing
the obligation ; or it might operate as a substitution of values,
where the appropriation of the pledge was understood to be in
place of payment.   If objects were given in pledge, over which
another besides the debtor had rights, such other person's consent

---

[1] *Del Giudice*, "La vendetta nel diritto longobardo", in "Studi di storia
del diritto" (1889), p. 246.
[2] *Rothar*, 249, 251, 252 ; *Liutprand*, 109 ; *Lothar*, 76.

was required to distrain them. This was also true later of feudal property and offices, which might not be distrained without the consent of the seignior.[1] After the Lombard period, as already shown, judicial distraint was subjected to a more fixed and definite procedure. A creditor who wished to assure himself of the payment of his debt, presented himself before the magistrate, that is the sheriff or count,[2] depending upon whether he sought to attach movable or immovable property, and obtained from him, according to these two circumstances, either the right of sequestration or of admission to possession, notifying the debtor at the same time that he might no longer use the sequestered objects, or place foot upon the seized land, under pain of punishment. The other steps in the seizure referred to the satisfaction of the obligation and not its security.

§ 488. **Penal Contracts.** — A third class of means of insuring the performance of obligations embraced neither those based primarily on religious sentiment nor those which were the product of a system of justice executed by the creditor himself, but depended upon the act of the debtor, who guaranteed payment of what he owed.

Among the number of such modes were penal contracts, *i.e.* with penalties, for the most part pecuniary, to which the debtor subjected himself in his promise, in case he did not perform his obligation. In these may be seen a link with the ancient private revenge for an injury, in that they may be considered as a stipulated composition,[3] intended to compensate and so to reconcile the creditor, injured by the violation of his right. One proof of this may be seen in the fact that the payment of the penalty did not exonerate from the obligation, which shows that its purpose was not to satisfy the obligation itself but to repair the wrong and the damage arising from non-performance. It is certain that Roman law contributed much to spread the practice of adding penal stipulations in contracts, as is evident from the measure of double the amount of the debt, borrowed from the Roman eviction, and recurring more frequently than any other in the ancient documents, in fixing the amount of the penalty. This was not, however, the sole measure employed in contractual penalties. There were examples of triple the debt; or of a fixed sum without relation to the value of the obligation, the latter payable in one sum,

---

[1] "Libri feudorum", II, 55.
[2] [*Ante* § 34, 35, abridged from *Calisse*, "Storia del diritto italiano", Vol. II, "Diritto publico", § 110, 113.]
[3] *Ante* § 46.

or repeatedly at stated intervals; sometimes by each debtor in full, if more than one,[1] sometimes by apportionment among all, when the rule was moderated by later laws, which, however, always substantially followed Roman principles.

§ 489. **Suretyship ("Fideiussione"): Obligatory Form.** — Besides contractual penalties, a promisor might guarantee his promisee by means of a surety, a method understood from an early period. Among the Germanic peoples it might be either obligatory or voluntary. The obligatory was certainly the earlier of the types, because it owed its origin to the solidarity of the family, who, having to answer for the acts of its members,[2] shared also in their obligations, whatever their origin, but especially in those arising from crimes, the most frequent source in antiquity.[3] If the person committing the crime, who thus became the debtor, did not pay, the family was held to satisfy the obligation. At first, because of the indivisible and inalienable character of the family patrimony,[4] there could not have existed the remedy later provided by the laws, of relieving the relatives of all responsibility by assigning over the debtor's own share in the family estate.[5] As this idea developed, the creditor was prohibited from turning against the members of the debtor's family, unless they were his legal heirs, since these had rights over the estate.[6] And as from the union of several families a wider social unit arose, first the " sippe ", then the village,[7] having characteristics proper to the family, so to this latter group was adapted the same rule of mutual guarantee of its component members. The co-responsibility of a neighboring group was long maintained, and for a long time also the principle that co-owners must answer for the obligations of their group, especially those originating from delicts. In the feudal period the rule obtained that the vassal must answer for the obligations of his immediate seignior; and in the Middle Ages it not infrequently happened that the communes, as an entity or in the persons of all their citizens,[8] and for the obligations of individuals, were held responsible by the government of the city itself, which, for the wrongdoing of a few individuals, would inflict the penalty upon the whole commune; and also by other communes which, when one of their citizens did not receive satisfaction of his rights or was otherwise injured by a member of another commune, granted the former the right of reprisal against the city and its inhabitants.[9]

[1] *Liutprand*, 107.   [4] *Ante* § 408.   [7] *Ante* §§ 22, 312.
[2] *Ante* § 312.   [5] *Liutprand*, 57.   [8] *Ante* § 310.
[3] *Ante* § 476.   [6] *Rothar*, 247.   [9] *Ante* § 49.

§ 490. **Voluntary Suretyship.** — Voluntary was the natural substitute for obligatory suretyship. Just as the creditor had a guarantee in those persons who, by ties of family or other common interest, were jointly liable with the debtor, so it was also possible to have as sureties those who, by their own intention, placed themselves in a like situation. Indeed, the creditor might not refuse, when the debtor offered such sureties and no disqualifying cause was found in them. For they had to meet certain qualifications. First was the possession of property at least equal in value to the amount of the obligation; otherwise the creditor might refuse to accept the surety and to restore the " wadia ",[1] without incurring the fine to which he would have been subject had the refusal been unjustified.[2] The debtor then had to present other sureties, not being freed by his first effort from his promise to provide them.[3] It was also required, in consequence of their early character, that sureties should preferably be chosen among persons in a position to have a certain knowledge of the debtor's condition. The best sureties would therefore be his relatives. But these not always being willing or able to act, the next choice fell among the residents of his locality, his peers, *i.e.*, those who, being of the same station, might have a certain knowledge and exercise a constant vigilance.[4] Thirdly, the sureties must not, through some personal quality, lack capacity to act as such, or be privileged to repudiate their obligation. By Germanic law women were not acceptable because of their status in the family,[5] nor were they later by reason of the re-adoption of the " Senatus-consultum Velleianum." The clergy likewise lacked competency by the canon law, which had been accepted by the Roman law [6] and repeated in the Frankish capitularies. The statutes of the mediaeval communes sometimes declared citizens without capacity to act as sureties for foreigners; the guilds were accustomed to enact similar rules for their members; in the so-called " ordinances of justice ",[7] the capacity to act as surety was withdrawn from the nobles and lowest classes; and analogous rules continued through subsequent periods.

The provision of a surety was promised by the debtor upon concluding the contract. He did not, however, give the surety at once, being allowed a certain period, which in Germanic law was three days. If he delayed longer, he was punished by fines which increased in severity in proportion to the time. When he offered

---

[1] *Ante* § 481.
[2] *Rothar*, 359.
[3] *Liutprand*, 128.
[4] *Id.*, 38.

[5] *Ante* § 305.
[6] *Justinian*, Novels, CXXIII, 36.
[7] *Ante* § 85.

the surety, he had a right to retake the "wadia", which, on assuming the obligation, he had delivered to the promisee, and the latter was in turn punished if, without justification, he refused to restore it.[1]   This was the reason that the "wadia" and surety were so closely related that the laws did not speak of one without the other.[2]   Indeed, in its early conception, the surety had the same purpose as the "wadia", that is, to be towards the promisee in the position of a pledge, just as the debtor might have given himself in pledge.

[1] *Rothar*, 359; *Liutprand*, 36, 128.
[2] *Rothar*, 360, 361, 366; *Liutprand*, 15, 36–40, 128.

Chapter XXV

EXTINGUISHMENT OF OBLIGATIONS

Topic 1. Performance

Topic 2. Non-Performance

Topic 1. Performance

§ 491. **Early History.** — Performance caused the natural extinguishment of the obligation. The Roman principle that performance, as the doing of that which had been promised, must take place in the manner and at the time and place agreed, was substantially repeated in Germanic law, as in all other systems. The Lombard law provided that the debtor must do all which he obligated himself to do on giving the " wadia."[1] Upon this point, namely, the execution of what had been promised on entering the obligation, a disagreement might arise. The law itself, therefore, established that a debtor who denied what the creditor affirmed was due him, must prove his denial by oath, unless there were witnesses to the contract, in which case the matter was to be left to their decision. If a party suspected such witnesses, he might claim that they be substituted by others, and if such a claim were put forward by both sides, the matter had to be settled by judicial duel.[2]

As to the time of performance, Germanic law required that for the obligation to be considered unperformed, the promisee should demand fulfilment of the promisor, not once, but twice or thrice, and without any distinction between contracts having no definite term and those having a fixed date of performance.[3] The contrary Roman principle, " dies interpellat pro homine ", was introduced

---

[1] *Rothar*, 360; *Rachi*, 5.
[2] *Rothar*, 366; *Liutprand*, 8, 15; *Rachi*, 5; *Louis the Pious*, 15.
[3] *Rothar*, 245, 246.

later into Lombard law, through the work of the commentators, although even they were not in agreement, some holding to the old and some to the new tendencies. Some indeed, as Ariprand, declared that, in obligations of fixed term, the expiration of that period sufficed; others, on the other hand, as Albert, held that in this case also a repeated demand by the creditor was necessary. Nevertheless, although the Germanic rule continued for yet some time, as in the statutes of the mediaeval communes, the Roman principle eventually prevailed everywhere and completely.

As to the thing, the object of the obligation, it must be given as agreed. If the thing had been determined as to kind and was lost, the law from the Lombard period, at least in certain cases,[1] permitted an equivalent object to be substituted in performance. This question arose with regard to money when, during the feudal period and the mediaeval communes, its varieties constantly multiplied, and when princes, treating coinage as regalia, might change and debase it according to their interests.[2] To escape possible damage, the contracting parties reciprocally guaranteed one another by various stipulations, among which one in general use provided that, so long as money was changed only as to form, as by substitution even of paper money for metallic currency, a practice which began in Italy in the 1200s, the debtor might pay in a different money; but if the change affected the intrinsic value, a different currency might be used only by addition or deduction in such wise as to equal the sum promised.

§ 492. **Commercial Methods of Payment.** — When commerce reached a considerable development, the natural mode of payment by an actual disbursement of money might be substituted by other forms, among which were quite usual those of cancellation ("scontrazione") and of the bank-order ("scrittura del banco"). The "scontrazione" consisted in this: when there were several persons of whom the first was creditor of the second, the second creditor of the third and so on, the last being creditor of the first, the first ordered his debtor to pay the debt to the last and all the other creditors did similarly; finally the last was reached, who, by this process of delegation, became debtor of the first, toward whom he originally stood as creditor, and in this way the two obligations cancelled one another and were extinguished. This mode was much used at the fairs where debits and credits intercrossed, and

---

[1] *Liutprand*, 43.
[2] *Ante* § 63 [abridged from *Calisse*, "Storia" etc., Vol. II, "Diritto publico", § 160, p. 287.]

was very convenient in dispensing with the transportation of money.

The " scrittura " or " promessa in banco ", that is, bank-order, was also effected without disbursing or transporting money. It consisted of writing an order on a banker for the sum due the creditor, who, in commercial debts, might not refuse this mode of payment, although in matters other than commercial he was not so obliged. At Venice, for example, he might refuse it for sums not in excess of 100 ducats. When there was an open account (" conto corriente ") between debtor and creditor, the credit order might be entered directly in the books of account of the debtor. By these methods of payment commerce was greatly benefited and this was the cause of their extended and long use.

§ 493. **Substitutes for Performance.** — Equivalent methods of discharging the obligation might also take the place of performance. One such method, set-off between two opposite obligations, was not known to Germanic law, according to which, in order to modify one legal relation by the effect of another, it was necessary to extinguish the first and enter into the second through legal formalities.[1] It is certain that in the 800 s there were laws forbidding " causam pro causa anteponere ", that is, a refusal to pay and the setting up of some other instrument giving a claim against the creditor. Whoever attempted this, saying to the plaintiff creditor " si non reddis hoc, non tibi faciam justitiam ", would be forced by the State to pay and also punished by a fine.[2] Through the reception of the Roman law, set-off entered into the statutes of the mediaeval communes and, like cancellation (" scontrazione "), being useful in commerce, it found favor and developed, while giving rise to questions and divergent opinions upon its legal nature and effect.

Prescription also could, without payment, extinguish an obligation. Lombard law declared void all unexecuted written instruments (" titoli di credito "), unless renewed within five or ten years, and the promisee was shorn of his right if, within that period, he had not begun suit against his promisor, at least unless prevented by serious cause, as, for example, becoming a slave.[3] These periods of the Lombard law were also found in the statutes of the mediaeval communes, confused, however, with the Roman period of thirty years and others of various duration, besides also those, the shortest of all, established for obligations of a special nature, such as con-

[1] *Blandini*, "Il tempo", etc., p. 196.
[2] *Pactum Sicardi*, 18, in M. G. H., ed. *Bluhme*, "Leges" and *Padelletti*, "Fontes."
[3] *Liutprand*, 16.

tracts for the payment of money at interest, for the hire of services to be performed, for compensation for damage, or for the creation of an annuity. Besides regulations as to time, these statutes established, by a long series of rules, all the other conditions for this sort of prescription, thus preparing the way for the analogous legislation of subsequent periods.

Finally should be mentioned the extinguishment of obligations by release ("dispensa") of the promisor from performance, as a result of a declaration of the termination of the right by the promisee. So, too, it was not rare in the Middle Ages for excommunication,[1] among other effects, to deprive the creditor of his right to force his debtors to fulfilment; and the same loss befell the Jews, when pursued or persecuted by the State of which their debtors were citizens. Indeed, the debts owed them were for the most part the cause of their expulsion.[2] Even in the communes there were examples of the liberation of debtors from the claims of creditors of a hostile commune. But with the progress of civilization such repudiation of others' rights ceased.

§ 494. **Surrender of Document: Receipt.** — Upon performance the obligation was extinguished. The promisor thereupon had a right to have restored to him the instrument upon which his obligation was founded; in fact, if it was not presented to him by his promisee, he might refuse payment, or, to avoid the effects of default, he might deposit the sum due with the judge. As the obligation was extinct, so the instrument or title, which was a necessary element of it, had to be destroyed, and this was effected by tearing or more commonly by cutting in half ("instrumentum incisum").

It might, however, happen that the title to the right had been lost, in which case the creditor gave the debtor a letter called "epistola evacuatoria", because by it he pronounced the lost paper "vacua", that is, deprived of all effect. This was necessary, because the instrument was not only means of proof, but was of itself a valuable right. Thus there were two ideas or purposes in the letter: one a declaration that payment had been made, that is, a quittance or receipt, and the other an annulment of the obligation of which the document was the basis or title. The latter idea was closely related to the conception of the formal obligation, "per wadiam" or "per chartam", and was, therefore, the earliest illustrated in the "epistola evacuatoria", and was already found

---

[1] *Ante* § 302.
[2] *Ante* § 301.

in the formularies of the Franks.[1] As obligations shook themselves free from formalities, the idea of the simple quittance took precedence.

Topic 2. Non-Performance

§ 495. **Early History.** — An obligation might remain partially or wholly unfulfilled by the promisor when performance was not effectively made, or one of the equivalents mentioned was not substituted for performance. Failure of performance might furthermore result from several causes and in several ways. The object of the obligation might be accidentally destroyed, in which case, as in Roman law, the promisor was not generally held responsible. But the Germanic law was more severe in that it recognized responsibility even in the case of accidental loss, if the promisor had had all the benefit of the possession of the object, as was true of one who had received it on a gratuitous loan for use (" comodato "), or had distrained it as a guarantee of a debt due, or accepted it on a bailment for hire (" deposito "). The only way to avoid responsibility in these cases also was to swear to have neglected nothing possible which would have avoided the accidental damage. The greater severity of the Germanic law is explained by its peculiar rules governing the recovery of movable property. For, the right of action in certain cases did not belong to the first owner, where possession had been voluntarily relinquished, but to the possessor from whom, for example, the object had been stolen.[2] In such case, if the possessor, even without fault, had not been made responsible towards the owner, the latter would have lost, along with the object, the right to reclaim it or its value.[3] These principles, however, gradually yielded the field to the milder ones of the Roman law, supported by the commentators of the Lombard law itself,[4] and thence passed, without further obstacle, into the statutes of the mediaeval communes.

The greater severity of the Germanic law was also seen when the promisor was at fault, because, without distinguishing between fraudulent intent (" dolo ") and different degrees of fault (" colpa "), it always called upon him to answer unless by oath he proved that there had been no negligence. Here too Roman law finally prevailed. But a trace of the Germanic law remained

---

[1] "Formulae Marculfi", *cit.*, II, 27, 35; "Formulae Andegavenses", *cit.*, 17, 18; "Formulae Sirmondicae", *cit.*, 24, in M. G. H. ed. *Zeumer.*
[2] *Ante* § 447.
[3] *Liutprand*, 131.
[4] "Expositio" to *Liutprand*, 131, §§ 3, 4.

among the later jurists in respect to that degree of negligence described as "very slight" ("levissima"), which, classed along with that termed "grave" ("lata") and "slight" ("levis") of the Roman law, was thought to have been recognized by the latter, whereas it was only a consequence and transformation of the liability, admitted by Germanic law in those cases where it was denied by the Roman law.

On the other hand, the Germanic rules as to *hidden defects*, which vitiated the performance of the obligation as executed, were various.   If the hidden defects were discovered in the object given by the promisor, he escaped all responsibility by swearing that he did not know of them at the moment of delivery;[1] if, however, the vice inhered to the right transferred, as where the transferor sold or gave something that was not his, so that the transferee was liable to have it reclaimed by a third person, the alienor was always responsible, and judgment was entered against him,[2] unless he swore that he had not acted with fraudulent intent.   His liability ended with a simple reparation for the damage, as by repaying the price, or by substituting an equivalent object for the property of the other which he had sold.[3]   Even these principles changed when, in the period of the mediaeval cities, the influence of the Roman law reintroduced its rules upon eviction and the actions granted by the aedilian edict.

§ 496. **Slavery, Personal Attachment, Imprisonment.** — If the promise was not performed by the obligor, the consequences might be of several sorts.   It might be a question of a promise whose fulfillment, if not voluntary, could not be demanded.   In such a case the promisor in default suffered the penalty agreed upon or another determined by law, whereupon he was freed from all further liability.   This was true, for example, in the obligation to marry, resulting from the promise of the betrothal;[4] and similarly when, after breach, performance was no longer possible, as where the promisor had done what he had agreed not to do, or had not performed within the time fixed.   But so long as performance was possible, the promisor might be constrained in one way or another and the promisee might always exact satisfaction of his rights.

The first means to this end was recourse to those agencies by which performance of the obligation had been guaranteed.

First of all, the creditor might seize the person of his debtor,[5]

---

[1] *Rothar,* 230.   [3] *Rothar,* 231; *Liutprand,* 43.
[2] *Ante* § 449.   [4] *Ante* § 325.
                    [5] *Ante* § 484.

who, if unable to find some one who would redeem him, ended by becoming his creditor's slave.   In fact one of the causes giving rise to slavery was the non-payment of debt.[1]   Ancient Germanic law, by an historical progress analogous to that of the Roman law, was in time mitigated in several ways, especially by limiting the creditor's power to hold the debtor as a slave solely until such time as, by the latter's labor, he had obtained what was due.   In other words, slavery for debt was changed from a permanent to a temporary condition.   This was first admitted by the Lombard laws;[2] it was later the regular rule among the Franks;[3] finally it was opposed in itself and came to disappear, for the same reasons that brought an end to the excessive powers of the individual and abolished slavery.

Of the right of the creditor over the person of his debtor a considerable trace, however, remained.   In the first place laws were still found in the 1200 s and 1300 s which allowed the creditor to compel his debtor to satisfy his obligation by forcing him to labor for him.   Besides, a stipulation in the contract was substituted for the law; the debtor might offer himself as a hostage, and in consequence he or another in his place was bound, upon failure to perform the obligation, to go and live in a designated place at his own expense until the debt was satisfied.   If he fled, a sentence of "infamy" was passed upon him, his name was posted upon the gallows, his disloyalty was published by notices posted upon the doors of the churches and in other frequented places; finally he might incur ecclesiastical censure, and might always be forcibly led back by public authority to his creditor.   This method, too, came to an end because of the many difficulties to which it gave rise, and almost its last trace disappeared during the 1400 s.

One of these, however, survived to modern times, namely, imprisonment for debt.   It originated in the stipulation to deliver one's self up, not to the creditor, since his powers of execution were constantly limited, but to the public authority, which in the interest of the creditor had consequently to take over the custody of the debtor in the public prison.   The laws favored this stipulation, as one contributing to the supremacy of public over individual authority.   Thus, from the time of the statutes of the mediaeval communes, imprisonment for debt became very common, and was not abandoned by the law until the present generation, when all

---

[1] *Ante* § 292.
[2] *Liutprand*, 152.
[3] *Charlemagne*, 31, 34, 72, 107; *Louis the Pious*, 8.

traces of the ancient personal power of the creditor over his debtor disappeared.

§ 497. **Distraint.** — After the debtor's person his property stood as a guarantee of performance. And so, next in order after his person, and subsequently in place of the person, the creditor had a right to turn to his property for satisfaction. Having already made the seizure, he proceeded to execution, either upon his own authority or through the action of the judge, according to the period of the law and depending upon whether the distraint was private or judicial.[1] Under Lombard law, in which private distraint was admissible, the creditor himself was given the right of execution. He was required, however, to make three summonses upon his debtor to pay, otherwise all his actions were illegal and punishable; and he might take possession only of such objects as were legally distrainable.[2] For other objects, the authorization of the magistrate was required and he might not grant it except in total absence of all other guarantees.[3] Moreover, the laws looked upon such a distraint as made, not so much to satisfy the creditor directly, as that the debtor, to redeem his property, should be constrained to pay his debt. This explains why, on the one hand, the creditor did not become, at least for a certain time, the owner of the object distrained, but remained responsible for any damage which it suffered; [4] and why, on the other hand, he might distrain property of greater value, indeed, up to double the amount of the debt; [5] and finally, why, notwithstanding the distraint, he might still demand performance of the obligation.

In the period of the Franks there was a change, because as already explained,[6] the judicial distraint was regularly introduced. After the time had run during which it was necessary to make demand upon the debtor, which, from the time of obtaining the right of sequestration or of entry into possession, was twenty-four days for personalty and a year and a day for land,[7] the creditor might pay himself out of the property attached, provided that no defences could be interposed either with regard to the debt, as that it was unlawful or uncertain, or with regard to the debtor's person, as that he enjoyed an immunity, *e.g.* that of soldiers while absent and for a certain period preceding departure and following their return. The peculiar factor was that, under Frankish as under Lombard

---

[1] *Ante* § 487.
[2] *Rothar*, 245, 246; *Liutprand*, 15.
[3] *Rothar*, 251.

[4] *Id.*, 252.
[5] *Liutprand*, 108.
[6] *Ante* § 487.

[7] *Ante* § 440.

law, in the cases in which judicial intervention was prescribed, the judge acted in the place of the creditor and executed the transfer of the debtor's goods, a procedure that was certainly advantageous. For not only was the creditor deprived of the power, which he might abuse, of remaining owner of the distrained property or of selling it at his pleasure, but the debtor enjoyed the assurance that all subject to the distraint in excess of the debt would be restored to him. This was in fact the function of the " boni homines ", to whom the judge entrusted the execution upon the debtor's goods.

Subsequent systems of legislation continued to protect the debtor's interests without injuring those of the creditor. From the period of the statutes of the mediaeval communes, the system of public auction was prescribed for the sale of attached property and the classes of objects which were immune from distraint were increased. The sale had to take place in the locality where the property was; and in general all those powers were withdrawn which had at first been left to the creditor.

Nevertheless, a remnant of the old power of the creditor still remained in the case of the seizure of animals or persons, caught in the act of damaging property. In this case, private seizure might still be employed, since it served better than any other means of proof of the injury, when it came to obtaining reparation. In antiquity it was permissible to kill an animal found damaging property, and traces of this right were still found in Lombard law.[1] Later this was forbidden and seizure alone was allowed. Repeated public notice had to be given by the party making the seizure, who only in this way liberated himself from responsibility for the harm which might come to the animal.[2] The owner might redeem it, but on condition of repairing the damage; or of paying a composition, also determined by the laws;[3] or of giving a guarantee to pay the damages, assessed by neighbors. If the owner did none of these, the party who had seized the animal might, without further responsibility, make use of the animal to satisfy his claim.[4] So persons, found committing damage in the fields, might be captured or a pledge taken from them, in order to secure the subsequent payment of the composition fixed by law.[5]

After the Germanic period these rules were preserved in the statutes of the mediaeval communes, where the Germanic

[1] *Rothar*, 349; *Liutprand*, 151.
[2] *Rothar*, 343; *Liutprand*, 82, 86.
[3] *Rothar*, 349.
[4] *Id.*, 346.
[5] *Liutprand*, 146.

principles are found unaltered. They were then preserved, with slight modifications, in subsequent laws and have not been entirely abandoned even today, especially in certain regional customs.

§ 498. **Sureties.** — If, either through his person or his property, a debtor had not been able to satisfy his creditor, the latter might turn against those who had become sureties. The idea, however, that a creditor must proceed against the sureties only as a secondary recourse was unknown to Germanic law. According to it, sureties having been given as a gage, in place of the " wadia ",[1] the creditor might as a consequence go against them with equal right and at the same time as against the debtor,[2] without any obligation to seek payment of him first. In other words, there was no such right in the sureties as the Romans called " beneficium excussionis." The surety, however, when invited by the creditor to pay, had a right to turn against the principal debtor, seize his property and hand it over to the creditor to satisfy the latter and liberate himself.[3] Thus the Germanic surety was fundamentally distinguishable from the Roman in this other respect also : that he was an intermediary used by the creditor to obtain satisfaction from the property or person of the debtor.

In the time of the statutes of the mediaeval communes and of the Glossators, the Germanic characteristics of the surety disappeared before those acquired in agreement with Roman principles. The privileges conceded to the surety, the determination of his relation with the debtor on one hand and the creditor on the other, the causes of incapacity to act as surety and their effect, together with all the other rules which the Roman law provided on this subject, came to be known and applied, and formed the basis of the provisions of the present Code.[4]

§ 499. **Persecution, Bankruptcy.** — Finally, if the obligation still remained unsatisfied, in that the creditor not only remained unpaid, but also lacked further means of obtaining payment, the debtor was declared insolvent. This status involved grave consequences, varying with the period of the law's history.

In antiquity the unpaid debt gave rise to slavery. When this type of slavery had been abolished, not only did the debtor continue to be held in a status of dishonor in respect to the exercise of his civil and political rights, but the creditor was permitted to persecute him. Examples were not rare of cases in which creditors broke open the houses of their debtors, sealed their doors, or even

[1] *Ante* § 490.
[2] *Liutprand*, 108.
[3] *Id.*, 40.
[4] [Ital. Civil Code, arts. 1898–1931.]

prevented their burial with ordinary rites.   This, too, came to an end; but the debtor did not go unpunished, for, as already noted, imprisonment for debt was universally applied down to modern times, without mentioning the degradation, moral and legal, involved in the status of insolvency, when in the field of commerce, bankruptcy was added.

TITLE II

PARTICULAR CONTRACTS [1]

§ 500.	Effect of Family Law on Gifts and Sales.	§ 502.	Influence of the Church.
§ 501.	Effect of Property Rights.	§ 503.	Assignment of Contracts.

§ 500. **Effect of Family Law on Gifts and Sales.** — The nature of particular kinds of contracts was in agreement with that common to obligations in general, as well as to the law governing family and property rights.   Having analyzed the more important of the principles when treating of those branches of private law which have been under review, their application to various contracts will now be considered ; through them these contracts will be better understood and their historical development more easily followed.

Beginning with the family, then, we have seen that its early organization revealed itself chiefly in the unseverable unity of its estate and in the resulting want of authority in its members to dispose of this in a way to diminish it.

The first consequence of this principle is observable in gifts. They were at first forbidden ; and when no longer wholly forbidden by law, they still remained the most serious offense against relatives and a cause of hostility, which the law itself, in some of its effects, considered as justified.[2]   But as changed conditions in family and social organization brought about a constant slackening of the early ties binding the individual and his property, the time arrived to grant him freedom to dispose of his own property, while surrounding such an act with formalities that served as expedients to harmonize the new needs with ancient traditions, and to minimize their contrast, so that the period of transition should pass almost unobserved.   Gifts were supported by the "launegild."   The word merely meant money ("geld"), given in compensation ("lohn").   It meant price, but price understood in a

[1] *Pertile, cit.,* § 156 *et seq.*; *Salvioli, cit.,* part IV, chap. 40; *Schupfer,* "La donazione fra vivi nella storia del diritto italiano" in "Annalli della giurisprudenza italiana", V (1871); *id.,* "Launegildo e Gairethinx", in "Archivio giuridico"; *Lattes,* "Il diritto communale nella legislazione statuaria delle città italiane" (1884); *Salvioli,* "I titoli al portatore nella storia del diritto italiano" (1883).
[2] *Rothar,* 360.

special sense. Consisting in some piece of money or some object, such as arms, clothes, or the like, it lacked the economic element of equivalence of value, and was of importance only from a legal point of view, in serving to make the gift appear as a transfer for value received and so removing it from those attacks which might be directed at it as an act of pure generosity.[1] Its application to gifts was not its primitive use. It had already probably been employed in all those transactions, especially purchase and sale, in which a price was necessary, where it became the symbol of the price itself, so long as unpaid, and produced the same effect, above all that of perfecting the transaction, binding the vendor and guaranteeing the vendee. Its necessity in gifts was by custom always admitted in Lombard law, but it did not become express in the Lombard Edict until a law of Liutprand, who desired to remove all doubt upon the point.[2] Once the subject of legislation, it continued to be required by law for a long period, very frequent examples of it still existing in the 1100 s. It was then slowly abandoned in favor of a return to Roman forms. It always remained true, however, that gifts, because of their importance and the dangers to which they might give rise, must be surrounded by solemn formalities: publicity or writing, the presence of witnesses or of a judge, or inscription in a public registry.

Family rights involved still other consequences in particular contracts. It has been shown that, for a long time, not every kind of property might be the object of purchase and sale, because of the right of the family to the preservation of the estate,[3] and that, in the instances where alienation was permitted, the relatives had a right to intervene in the giving of their consent;[4] and that relatives and neighbors had a right of preëmption or the corresponding right of redemption.[5]

§ 501. **Effect of Property Rights.** — Other peculiarities derived from the special character of the law of ownership. In this respect, although the individual element finally prevailed, the social element long remained powerful, as is shown by the numerous limitations which the latter imposed.[6] The tradition of the early communal state of ownership prevented the public from being deprived of all control, and this gave rise to the principle of publicity in all acts involving the alienation of land. At first the people themselves took part in the transfer, which had to be executed with the

---

[1] *Rothar*, 175, 184; *Liutprand*, 43, 54; *Astolf*, 12; *cf.* "donatio nummo uno" of the Roman law.
[2] *Liutprand*, 73.
[3] *Ante* § 422.   [4] *Ante* § 408.   [5] *Ante* § 423.   [6] *Ante* § 417.

formality of the " gairethinx ", in the public assembly.   An example is seen in gift by adoption,[1] and in the formality of tradition in the transfer of ownership by whatsoever title.[2]   For the active participation of the people, there was substituted, by a procedure analogous to that of the Roman law, the presence of representatives.   Hence arose the contractual forms which in several instances had to be entered into in the presence of a magistrate or witnesses.[3]   To the early reasons for requiring publicity others were added, principal among which was the protection of rights that others might have in the property.   Thus was extended the necessity of witnesses; and later in the period of the statutes of the mediaeval communes, there came into use the public ban, crying, notice to the city council, and various other systems of publicity, which changed in form but remained in substance in all subsequent legislation.

It has been shown how social interest limited the exercise of the right of ownership.[4]   Of this contracts were also to feel the effect. It was evidenced in *sales* by the prohibition against selling outside the district to which one belonged; or except at an established time in the case of agricultural products; or save at a fixed scale of prices; or to persons or in ways to cause public injury.   Examples of these restrictions were seen in *leases*, in which the rental and other obligations between the owner and the cultivator of the land were regulated by law; the terms and times when they were to begin and end; and sometimes even the charges that might be asked for farm implements were established.

And thirdly, to the law of property may also be traced the close connection between the influences of private interests and those dictated by political or economic policy.   We have already seen that contracts received the mark of this relation, especially those whose purpose was the possession and improvement of land, principal among which was the contract of emphyteusis.   But there was a large array of others having many characteristics akin to, though no longer confused with, emphyteusis or with each other.[5] And so from the character of ownership were derived those special qualities of the contracts of rent charge,[6] apanage [7] and others, already described.

§ 502. **Influence of the Church.** — We must not omit mention of the influence of the Church upon the formation of contracts. It has been seen how the Church wrought constant changes, more

---

[1] *Ante* § 336.   [3] *Liutprand*, 79.   [5] *Ante* § 455.   [7] *Ante* § 386.
[2] *Ante* § 443.   [4] *Ante* § 421.   [6] *Ante* § 463.

or less extensive, in every branch of the law, and it necessarily followed that contracts reacted to her principles. As an example, the loan for consumption ("mutuo") may be recalled, with which ecclesiastical legislation was much concerned, because of the prohibition against interest, as already illustrated in the case of rent charges.[1] Exaggerating certain biblical precepts, the canon law prohibited loans at interest and treated all interest whatsoever as usury. These prohibitions, often repeated, received definite confirmation at the Lateran Council of 1139 and that of Vienna of 1311. The temporal followed the ecclesiastical law, commencing with the Frankish capitularies and extending down to the 1700 s, until loans at interest were again permitted.

But if the prohibition against interest for the use of money was unjust, when the rate was moderate, it was also unfavorable to the development of credit and absolutely contrary to the needs of commerce. There, money was placed out at interest, and in large sums, but it was necessary to use expedients to avoid the ecclesiastical and civil punishments. Such expedients were found in great numbers. There was a continuous struggle on the one hand between the merchants, who, with their stipulations for the profits arising from the debtor's land ("anticresis"), fictitious sales at excessive price, purchases of products at a price below their real value, bills of exchange for sums larger than the amounts received for them, and other devices, sought to escape censure and the civil penalties; and, on the other hand, the laws, ever intent upon discovering such subterfuges, preventing them and punishing them. In practice the result was harmful to commerce and to persons in need of capital, since the interest rate kept rising, either in compensation for the lender's risk, or for lack of any legal limit or supervision, or because lending money under such circumstances was the business of those who really were usurers: of the Jews chiefly, who were a concern neither of the Church, to whom they were irreparably lost, nor of the civil authority, which could at any moment deprive them of all rights. And this power, indeed, it exercised with art, when the Jews became creditors to the damage of the Christians and perhaps indeed of the State itself, which at a moment of need had had recourse to them.[2]

Such a condition demanded a remedy, and it was not long before it was secured through the efforts of the Romanists, who sought to make Roman rules prevail over the canon law. The Reformation and the economists later only aimed to permit and justify

[1] Ante § 463.   [2] Ante § 301.

interest when stipulated within proper limits. Thus even the
Catholic Church had to modify its ideas. Having first sought to
temper the severity of its principles by appropriate measures,
aimed to avoid excessive interest, and especially by the formation
of pawn offices, where money was loaned upon pledge without or
at very low interest, it came eventually to modify its own principles. Thus Pope Benedict XIV in his Encyclical of November 1,
1745, directed to the bishops of Italy, admitted the legality of
moderate interest, provided it did not result of right from the loan
itself, in which case it would be usurious, but from a stipulation
annexed to the contract of loan.

§ 503. **Assignment of Contracts.** — Lastly, the peculiar qualities
of the law of obligations, arising out of the various elements
entering into Italian law, found reflection in turn, both in cause
and effect, in the qualities of particular contracts. In the gratuitous loan for use (" commodato ") and in the bailment for hire
(" deposito "), for example, was applied the principle of strictest
responsibility, with which the Germanic law surrounded the
property of another, held for the benefit of the possessor.[1] The
bailee in both these contracts, when supported by a consideration,
was, therefore, a guarantor of the owner against the damage which
the article might suffer by accident, and the same principle was
also applied to the creditor who was secured by a pledge, and to
other similar situations. These rules were subsequently moderated, by dividing the loss equally between the contracting parties,
or limiting still further the cases of responsibility for the loss or
deterioration of an object belonging to one person but in the possession of another, or by substituting the Roman rules. How
deep-rooted were these principles has already been illustrated in
the recognition of " very slight " negligence (" culpa levissima "),
added to the existing Roman degrees, though unknown to the
Roman law itself.[2]

But the consequences of the new qualities of obligations are best
illustrated in contracts of a commercial nature. Here the ascendancy of the economic element [3] resulted in the possibility of sepa-
rating such contracts from the persons by whom they had been
undertaken. Though still requiring two parties, a promisor
and a promisee, they became capable, as though by themselves,
of transmission from one person to another by a transfer of
the title or instrument, represented at first by the " wadia " and
later by the " charta ",[4] with which it became identified. Of the

[1] *Ante* § 495.   [2] *Ante* § 495.   [3] *Ante* § 476.   [4] *Ante* § 480.

transmissibility of obligations — a very powerful factor in the extension of commerce — there developed in various forms highly useful applications, which the Roman law, arguing from contrary doctrines, had not known, or had known but imperfectly. These forms modern law has accepted with the full implications of which they are capable.

Besides admitting the principle of representation in legal undertakings and recognizing the legality of the contract founded upon a presumed tacit agency, in the name and for the benefit of a third party, which would have been impossible had obligations not been considered essentially transferable, the law reached the point of making the assignability of rights in action the common rule and of viewing these rights as incorporated in the title or document. From this was derived the whole of that important theory of instruments payable to bearer, the chief basis of modern credit, and of the bill of exchange, the most potent of the means by which commerce attained the universal extension and social importance which it enjoys today.

PART VI

PRIVATE LAW SINCE THE UNIFICATION OF ITALY

PART VI

PRIVATE LAW SINCE THE UNIFICATION OF ITALY

CHAPTER XXVI

NATIONAL CODIFICATION

§ 504. Codification of 1865; Re-   § 506. National Legal Conscience.
      codification.   § 507. Return to National Tradi-
§ 505. Conditions of Recodifica-   tion.
      tion.

§ 504. **Codification of 1865; Recodification.**[1] — In 1848 Charles Albert granted a constitutional charter to the Kingdom of Sardinia. By it parliamentary power, representing the will of the nation, was substituted for the absolute will of the monarch in the confection of law. Under Victor Emanuel II, parliamentary government continued legislative reform, completing what had preceded and introducing the modifications called for by the new political conditions.

In 1854 was published a Code of Civil Procedure, already prepared by Charles Albert, and with it ended the work of codification of the common law, as designed by him in imitation of the French Codes. The undertaking comprehended five codes, Civil, Criminal, Commercial, Criminal Procedure and Civil Procedure.

A revision was very soon necessitated by the fact that the Kingdom of Sardinia, through the territorial addition of Lombardy, resulting from the victory of 1859 over Austria, and by the subsequent annexation of other regions by plebiscite, no longer had the same separate existence but was making way for a national, united Kingdom of Italy.

The Law of March 17, 1861, adopted by the national Parliament at Turin, proclaimed the Kingdom of Italy, though as yet neither Venice nor Rome, with their territories, belonged to it politically. The former was united after the Prusso-Italian war of 1866 against

[1] [This section was specially prepared by Professor *Calisse* for this translation. It is more properly a continuation of his "Sources" ("Fonti"), translated in "Continental Legal History Series", Vol. I, "General Survey", part II, chap. III, end of § 91, p. 194.]

Austria, and Rome was entered as a result of the military occupation of the city, which occurred in September, 1870.

All the ancient States of Italy, which by their act of union now formed a single national State, had, though more or less confusedly, already achieved systematization of their own laws. But legislative, like political difference, was destined to cease among the Italian people; and this was the task to which Italy immediately set herself when political unity had been won.

At first no single, uniform direction was followed; nor would such have been possible, in view of the diversity of conditions between regions only just united. In a few of these, the provisional governments at once set up the Piedmontese Codes. This was true of the Emilia, Umbria, and the Marches. In other regions some of the preëxisting codes were left in force, with necessary modifications, until a new and uniform national body of law should be provided. Thus in the southern provinces the early codes covering civil (private) law, civil procedure, and in large part commercial law were preserved, and elsewhere the earlier law was not always substituted by new. Unity of legislation was thus not obtained at once for the whole Kingdom. But upon this problem, without interruption or delay, parliamentary labor centered from 1860 to 1865 and in the last of these years the goal was in large part attained. By the Law of April 2, 1865 the Government was authorized to publish for the whole Kingdom the codes which those years of labor had prepared, namely, those covering civil (private) law, commercial law, civil procedure and criminal procedure, and these all came into effect January 1, 1866. They were extended to the territory of Rome, November 27, 1870 and to Venice March 26, 1871. In the field of commercial law, the recognized exceptions to the Code of 1865 became numerous, especially in Venetia. To reduce the whole subject to uniform rules, a study was undertaken which led to the adoption of a new Commercial Code throughout the realm, January 1, 1883.[1]

[1] Upon the legislative work of this period and the sources of Italian law in general, should be cited, in addition to the general histories already mentioned, the new ed. of *Salvioli*, "Storia del diritto italiano" (Turin, 1925); *Solmi*, "Storia del diritto italiano" (Milan, 1918); *id.*, "Guida bibliografica" (Rome, Fondazione Leonardo, 1922); *Del Giudice*, "Storia del diritto italiano (Milan, 1923), Vol. III; *Schupfer*, "Storiadel diritto italiano" (Rome, 1908).

Upon special topics see: *E. Besta*, "La persistenza del diritto volgare italico nel medio evo" (Palermo, 1905); *F. Brandileone*, "Il diritto romano nella storia del diritto italiano" (Modena, 1921); *B. Brugi*, "Saggi per la storia della giurisprudenza e delle università italiane" (Turin, 1915–1921); *P. Cogliolo*, "La legislazione di guerra nel diritto civile e commerciale" (Turin, 1917); *Manacorda*, "Storia della scuola in

The Civil Code still remains that of 1865. Over it has passed the second half century of our modern period, during which so many and extraordinary events agitated and altered economic, social, intellectual and political problems. The whole course of development has been made more swift and far-reaching by the late war and its world-wide consequences. The lawmaker has had to guide the State within this current and has sought to do so by adopting a large number of special measures, which now more and more strew his legislative course, introducing disorder and inconsistency, and raising a clearer and more urgent demand for a new systemization.

The Italian Government has decided to effect this change. On February 10, 1923, it presented to Parliament a bill to secure the power needed to reform existing legislation; more precisely, to modify the Civil Code by bringing its provisions into accord with actual conditions, to draft and publish new codes of civil procedure, commercial law and maritime law, and to co-ordinate with these changes other laws, including those actually in force in the new provinces of the Trentino and Istria. When approval of the proposal has been granted by both houses, the actual legislative reform will be undertaken by the Government, with the collaboration of a commission composed of Senators and Deputies and the decrees by which the reform itself will be put into force will then be submitted to Parliament.

§ 505. **Conditions of Recodification.**[1] — Codification for more than a century has been a legislative method common to most civilized peoples. For the historical school of law, which arose as an opponent of codification, it was doubtless a frank defeat. But the fundamental idea of this school, that law is a social phenomenon, subject to the general law of evolution, and the logical consequences derived from this idea, have received and still receive the clear proof and confirmation of facts. Even when confined within the covers of codes, law continues to develop by following the course of social change, until that point is reached, foretold by the historical school, when, as codified, it no longer corresponds

Italia" (Palermo, 1914); *P. Sella*, "Costituzioni Eginiane del anno 1357" (Rome, 1921); *A. Solmi*, "Guida bibliografica per la storia del diritto italiano" (Rome, 1922); *Trifone*, "La legislazione Angioina (Naples, 1921); *A. Tannitti*, "Manuale legislativo del periodo di guerra" (Rome, 1919).

[1] [This section and the following §§ 506, 507 were specially prepared by Professor *Calisse* for this translation. They are substantially a restatement of §§ 93–95, part II, topic 3 of "General Survey", Vol. I of "Continental Legal History Series", in the light of World War and post World War conditions.]

to the interests of the society which it should serve.   At that point arises the necessity of revision and reform, in order to re-establish between the law and its purpose the relationship which has been lost and which is a necessary condition of a useful and even possible application.

Such a situation repeatedly arose in Italy during the 1800 s; it has now again been reached; once more all those conditions concur that necessitate a reform of the Codes.

The first of these requisites is that a real and recognized need should have arisen for new provisions to care for new interests which, under existing law, do not receive sufficient protection. When it is remembered that the existing Civil Code dates from a time (1865) when Italy was but entering the period of national restoration, and that since that time the nation has undergone profound political and economic changes, it can not be denied that between the new conditions and the old laws the necessary harmonious relationship is lacking and that new and evident interests arise on every hand, for which the legislator must promptly provide.

A second requisite is that the manner of providing for these needs must be already known, though the particular rule may not yet have been given technical form.   This stage is reached largely through the work of legal science, which is not circumscribed by the fixed solutions of the Codes, but derives force also from other sources, the more relevant in that they attach more directly to the realities of individual and social life.   A powerful impulse was, therefore, imparted to the progress of legal science by the historical method, which, from the middle of the 1800 s, has deeply penetrated the study of Italian law.   Similarly it has used to advantage the results of investigations undertaken in the economic and social sciences, which in turn have themselves been aided by historical research and the comparative method.   There has thus accumulated a mass of scientific material upon the legal institutions today needing reform, and to it the legislator may have recourse with the assurance of discovering there solutions that will satisfy public sentiment and demand.

This becomes, then, the third condition of effective legal reform: that such a task should be the externalizing of what has already matured in the internal legal consciousness of the nation.   For not only has public opinion become so important an element that no government may ignore it, but also a general concensus, originating in the satisfaction of the people's legal instincts, is necessary if the law is to have complete effectiveness of application and to attain the full ends to which it is directed. Law can not govern solely through the force of the authority emanating from it. Force is necessary to repress the rebellious; but for law to be effectively and usefully observed, the great mass of the people must fully consent to it, and they can only consent. to it when the changes conform to their interests and sentiments, that is to what may be called public conscience.

And even public conscience has its history, for it can not be recognized and determined save by reference to the facts of social life, as these vary from period to period and from region to region.

§ 506. **National Legal Conscience.**[1] — At first was discernible the predominance of a sentiment of a religious character in the conception of law. During the Germanic period legal rules had the authority of tradition; they reflected the distant voices of ancestors, for whom a cult formed a bond of union for family and tribe. The Middle Ages conceived law solely as an emanation of divine command. By observing the law of human authority, man obeyed God. This conception remained substantially unchanged under the absolute monarchies. It was still the hand of God that conferred upon the prince his sovereignty over the people; thus, by a religious duty as well, were they bound to accept his commands. The juridical was founded upon the religious conscience.

Then a change took place. The philosophical conception of the basis of law arose, of which the 1700 s furnish the example. Its foundation was a presumed contract, according to which legislative power arose by delegation of authority to the legislator by the people, who were bound to obey him because of it, and because society could not otherwise survive and men attain the ends for which they had associated themselves. For the very reason that this was a philosophical conception it could not sink into the understanding of the general mass of the people, strangers to public life and observers of law either as a principle of authority or as a lack of means to oppose authority.

When, by the constitutional revolutions of the 1800 s, the people were called to take part themselves in government, their juridical consciousness was awakened. The content of the law was examined, but not the source from which it emanated; and approval was given in so far as it was seen to be adapted to the satisfaction of public and private interests. Such a recognition inclined men's minds to acceptance of the law, for the benefits it conferred strengthened the popular conscience.

[1] [*See* note 1, § 505.]

Thence sprang the doctrine that the reason for municipal law and its mutations must be sought in the universal economic laws governing all social phenomena. Of these phenomena one is law, which must thus also be regarded as a product of the social structure, which is founded upon economic interests. Economic interests, being the cause, reveal the real reason of the conditions of a people and, therefore, also of the laws which are formed upon them. Accord with these interests becomes the law's justification and renders it harmonious; its efficacy is assured by the popular conscience, which is thus established as merely the recognition of what is proved to be useful to human needs, individual and social.

If history constantly teaches that rules of law are born of economic facts, it is, however, also rich in examples demanding other explanations. Not unseldom the common conscience has recognized as unjust under some particular aspect what, under another, was justified by economic needs. This was so of slavery and usury. If economic interest is recognized as the sole generative force of law, we fall into the error of a too utilitarian conception. This conception is generally relative. Social utility, for example, is merely that which is beneficial to the predominant social class of the particular period. Hence for the other classes of the population, law, under such conditions, resolves itself into an expression of force, which is the denial of the free consent of their conscience.

From this it may be concluded that the content of the idea of a popular jural conscience is made up of several component elements and that, therefore, a partial consideration, that is, a consideration of one or another alone, is insufficient to illuminate fully this phenomenon, admitting of course also that one or another of the elements may become preponderating according to the conditions of the society producing it. Elements of social origin and character are not substantially different from those that fix upon each people their specific nature, their own peculiar national qualities. To these, as history shows, law does in fact correspond. Consequently, as a nation has in its constituent elements something that remains substantially constant, that impresses upon it its characteristic physiognomy, so the law which belongs to it attaches its successive adaptations to a core of continuity and tradition from which it may not be violently broken. If such should in fact happen, the organic union will re-establish itself the moment the violence which caused the rupture ceases.

§ 507. **Return to National Traditions.**[1] — A clear illustration of the historical principle in the formation of law is furnished by the developments that are now taking place in Italian law.

Throughout the 1800 s, especially in the field of private law, the new principles of French legislation prevailed in Italy. The French Codes, as we have seen, were suddenly imposed by the conquerors, without appropriate preparation and without any period of transition or adaptation. There necessarily intervened an interruption in the natural development of law, which had already received a strong impulse from the legislative reforms of the various Italian States during the second half of the 1700 s; all practical value was removed from Roman, canon and customary law, which for centuries had been the chief springs of Italian legal doctrine and practice. It is true that Italy later proceeded freely and of her own accord to codify her legislation. But she was forced to do so hastily, when her political constitution was not yet complete and grave problems and perils threatened her life. For these reasons the Italian codes of the 1800 s were in great part but imitations of the French, already known and tried; for this reason the codified law of Italy was not infrequently unadapted to the sentiments and needs of the people, and created the need of reforms. These legal science has now prepared and to them the legislator is today putting his hand.

The reform will in large part be but a renewal of early institutions, or, at least, of early principles adapted to present conditions. The historians of law have been busy in their research of these principles and have brought into the light those that have been most neglected. Today they provide material for a restoration of national law, especially of private law.

The adaptation of the right of property to collective or social uses, the mode of utilizing it to the greatest good of all, its guarantees and limitations, will find helpful examples in the early concepts, in the study of early doctrine, and in the practice and unbroken trial of centuries. Especially in the field of family law the historical regard for Italian institutions will be beneficial; for the changes already announced in subjects which intimately affect the order of the family, such as the status of illegitimate children, research into paternity, paternal authority and guardianship, the matrimonial bond, the status of woman — all are but reforms in as many fundamental conceptions, elaborated by Italian law, but which because of the strength of French imitation, were

[1] [See note 1, § 505.]

797

excluded from the Italian codes of the 1800 s.   While as yet vague, the idea has nevertheless been broached of unifying contract law, giving it international force, so that it may be common to all peoples of a similar stage of civilization, and united in frequent social and economic relations.   If such a proposal is to materialize in any degree, history must show that a common law of Europe already exists, formed and preserved by the dual civilization diffused from Rome and Italy, the classic and the Christian; two civilizations of universal character, which, even during the darkest periods of history, were a center of unity and progress for all peoples.   They have not certainly lost their vitality for the future. And because to their study peoples are turning with strong and earnest hope, from it we may draw fresh reason to look for results of universal benefit.

CHAPTER XXVII

PRESENT DEVELOPMENTS IN PRIVATE LAW[1]

§ 508. Twentieth Century Ready   § 511. Property.
          for Change.   § 512. Legislative Extensions of
§ 509. Marriage.   Existing Law.
§ 510. Family.

§ 508. **The Twentieth Century Ready for Change.** — More than one historian of the various institutions of private law has observed

[1] [This chapter has been specially prepared by Professor *Calisse* for this translation, in order to indicate the tendencies in private law since the beginning of the 1900 s and more particularly during and since the World War. Sections 508–512 are therefore properly a continuation of his Vol. III, "History of Private Law" ("Storia del diritto privato"), p. 337, concluded in this translation at the end of § 503, *ante.*]

Among the most recent Italian works of an historical character, on the subjects treated in this chapter are: *Gaspard Ambrosini*, "Transformazione delle persone giuridiche" (Turin, 1910–1914); *Guido Bonolis*, "Svolgimento storico del diritto di assicurazione in Italia" (Florence, 1901); *id.*, "Il diritto marittimo dell Adriatico" (Pisa, 1921); *Carlo Calisse*, "Gli usi civici nella provincia di Roma" (Prato, 1906); *id.*, "L'Elemento sociale nella proprietà" (Rome, 1910); *Chiovenda*, "Riforma del procedimento civile" (Rome, 1920); "Cinquanta anni di storia italiana" (1860–1910), in "Academia dei Lincei" (Milan, Hoepli, 1911); *Gabriele Fagella*, "La legislazione bellica in relazione al diritto publico ed alle riforme" (Milan, 1918); *Francesco Ferrara*, "Persone giuridiche" (Naples, 1907); *Giannino Ferrari*, "Ricerche sul diritto ereditario in Occidente" (Padua, 1914); *Andrea Finocchiaro*, "La comunione dei beni fra coniugi" (Palermo, 1902); *Leicht*, "Studi sulla proprietà fondiaria nel medio evo" (Padua, 1903–07); *id.*, "Ricerche sul diritto privato" (Siena, 1914); *Gino Luzzatto*, "Storia del commercio" (Florence, 1914–1915); *Mauro*, "Il contratto di enfiteusi nel diritto comune e consuetudinario" (Naples, 1912); *Cesare Nani*, "Storia del diritto privato italiano" (Turin, 1902); *Benvenuto Pizoeno*, "La legitimazione nella storia delle istituzioni familiari" (Sassari, Satta, 1904); *Silvio Pivano*, "I contratti agrari in Italia nell' alto medio evo" (Turin, 1904); "Relazione della Commissione Reale per il dopo-guerra" (Rome, 1920); *Melchiorre Roberti*, "Le origini dell' esecutore testamentario nella storia del diritto italiano" (Modena, 1913); *id.*, "Le origini romano-cristiane della comunione dei beni fra coniugi" (Turin, 1919); *Alfredo Rocco*, "La scienza del diritto privato in Italia negli ultimi 50 anni" (Milan, 1911); *Luigi Rossi*, "Sulle riforme del codice civile" (Turin, 1923); *Francesco Ruffini*, "Guerra e riforma costituzionale" (Turin, 1920); *Giuseppe Salvioli*, "Storia del diritto italiano" (Turin, 1925); *Francesco Schupfer*, "Manuale di storia del diritto italiano" (Rome, 1908); *id.*, "Il diritto privato dei popoli germanici con speciale riguardo all' Italia" (Città di Castello, 1910–1914); *id.*, "Il diritto delle obligazioni in Italia nella età del risorgimento"(Turin, 1921); *V. Simoncelli*, "Della enfiteusi, con noti di *B. Brugi*" (Turin, 1922); *Arrigo Solmi*, "Storia del diritto italiano" (Milan, 1922); *Nino Tamassia*, "Il testamento del marito" (Bologna, 1905); *id.*, "La famiglia italiana nei secoli XV e XVI" (Palermo 1911); *Romualdo Trifone*, "Feudi e domani. Abolizione della feudalità" (Milan, 1909); *id.*, "Il fedecommesso. Storia del istituto in Italia" (Rome, 1914).

that Italy, at the opening of the 1900 s, stood upon the threshold of a new development, of which the moving causes were already discernible.   Then intervened the World War, longer and more terrible than had been foreseen.   The multitude of needs which it created or sharpened hastened the beginning or the preparation of this development, forcing the legislator to new and rapid provisions, and stirring popular activity and conscience.

The law deeply reflects the consequences; and of these the most evident have been and remain those that affect private law.   The codification of 1865 has held back the development of this branch, and, indeed, it is still inadequate in this new age; private law had been drawn away from national traditions by the over-powering influence of the French Civil Code; and, more than any other department, private law touches the immediate interests of the individual and mankind.

§ 509. **Marriage.** — More important than all others was the question of the family.   From a certain point of view the war may have stengthened family sentiment; but it has also shown which of its ancient regulations have need of better adaptation to the interests of community and society, interests which, under present conditions, may be neither neglected nor subordinated.

A beginning of reform was made during the war.   Thus, in the case of combatants all trace of whom had been lost, the presumption of death was admissible, contrary to the provisions of the Civil Code; those killed in the war, who left an irregular family, were presumed to have desired legitimization, even in the absence of the specific proof required by the Code; the law governing marriage through a representative was extended; natural children were granted rights, especially as regards pensions, but also in other beneficial ways not possible under prior existing law; much was accomplished for orphans by the creation of a true State guardianship, under special officers and regulations.

As Italy now approaches a revision of her Codes, the need of which has already been recognized by one of the two legislative Chambers, these and other provisions of family law will pass into and become modifications of the general and permanent body of the law.   Revision, as a method, will be possible, indeed in several matters may be employed with assurance of success, because of the preparatory labors of legal science, the studies made by the Government before presenting to the Chamber of Deputies the proposal for revision, and because of the work of parliamentary Commissions.

In general it may be said that the social factor has been given greater weight than before; that the aim has been to strengthen the family unit, while at the same time tempering with equity and justice the exercise of rights over subordinate members of the family, rights which derive from the family relationship.

In a brief history it is impossible to enumerate all the instances of modification or repeal of existing law. It must suffice, by way of example, to note that in marriage, the principles of indissolubility and the impossibility of divorce remain firmly established. There is, however, a broad tendency to extend, beyond the extremely limited cases recognized by the Code, the causes of annulment, that is, of the declaration of the legal non-existence of the marriage relation, for reasons existing prior to the contract. Thus, if the wife of one declared dead, by a presumption arising from long absence, takes a second husband and the first returns, the second marriage, though legally contracted, is dissolved; not, however, by divorce, but because there existed from the beginning, though unknown, the impediment of the prior tie, whereby the new could not be effectively formed.

§ 510. **Family.** — When we consider the various members of the family, we find their interests more effectively protected than under the Code. Through numerous administrative orders, the husband's authorization, required by the Code for the legality of his wife's acts, has been abolished. This limitation will not be re-established, and, by opportune measures of reform, the law will seek to avoid injury to the matrimonial union and the good order of the family. In the case of children, special concern is shown those who, in case of conflict with the father, need the law's aid to insure their natural rights. The paternal authority (" patria potestà ") is conceived as a natural duty and a social function. The fact of paternity, solely and of itself, is considered the source and reason of duties, so that it shall not be permissible to avoid responsibilities for one's acts, to the irreparable injury of guiltless offspring. The present Civil Code does not go so far, for, on imitating the French Code, it departed from Italian national traditions. Towards these the law now returns. Thus the reforms that have been announced will regulate, in a more liberal spirit, the voluntary recognition of natural children, and their legitimization and adoption. These reforms will not only prevent abuses due to excessive or inadequate exercise of the paternal authority, guardianship (" tutela "), and in general of family authority, but, and in spite of the protests that have been voiced, they will concede to natural children the right of research into their paternity. Public opinion has at length accepted this reform, indeed demands it; jurists have safely cleared the way; their careful studies have pointed the perils to which such research may give rise and because of which it has been prohibited in the past; they have suggested necessary restrictions, which the legislature will undoubtedly accept and introduce.

These principles have also been applied to the laws of inheritance, which have undergone modification. On the one hand the right of the State has been increased, by narrowing from ten to six the degrees of relationship beyond which an estate escheats. On the other hand, greater consideration is given the true family group; the aim has been to foster its compactness and prosperity by wholly abolishing the tax on inheritance between parents and children and between other determined close ties of relationship.

§ 511. **Property.** — In the law of property, the influence of the social factor was powerfully felt during the war in legislation affecting immovable property. The owner's rights were limited with respect to the use of the land's products; conditions of labor were imposed upon him, for, by a summary procedure, new instances of expropriation were validated and, in the case of land, cases of immediate occupation by the laborer were recognized. Many, though not all, of these measures were abolished at the end of the war. But there has remained, in the legislative intention and in the popular mind, a stronger sense, that henceforth property, especially land, should be so viewed as to harmonize private interest with the common concern, until now too much neglected. Hence the markedly individualistic conceptions of the Civil Code are weakening and yielding to others of social equity. The vast legislative project in preparation with reference to agrarian contracts tends towards this precise goal, and has in view not only the improvement of agrarian methods and hence of production, but also the economic and moral improvement of the laborer on the land, so that he should become an element of order and social well being. It has not been the legislative desire to deprive him of his individual interests, either in respect to his property or his labor, but rather to seek to stimulate the reasons and incentives of his industry, not, however, so as to exclude the higher guardianship of the common interests or to prevent the latter from prevailing wherever necessary.

Such conceptions, imposed upon the legislator by the conditions of modern society are not new in the history of Italian law. The canon law, one of the chief elements in the formation of the common law, laid down the principle that property is in substance but the right to possess and administer in the interests of all. This principle did not produce in legislation all its logical consequences; indeed, from the time of its spontaneously national formation, Italian legislation consecrated the principle of a dominant individualism, as it had done under foreign influence. The fact has already been noted during the course of this history, where it has been observed that the present Civil Code has as a consequence abandoned more than one national legal tradition. This was true, for example, of the contract of emphyteusis, which, when the emphyteutic tenant was given the absolute right to free himself from the payment of rent and so to transform himself into a free owner, lost its original character of an instrument serving, through the reciprocal tie of owner and laborer, to improve the land. But the provisions of the Code are cautiously being modified in the direction of earlier principles. A stipulation not to affranchise the land is now lawful; that is, the emphyteuta may waive his right to liberate the land. Special enactments had already legalized this for some regions of Italy, *e.g.* Calabria and Sicily; very recent legislation has generalized these provisions. In the case of emphyteutic contracts affecting rural lands of certain extent, granted to persons personally directing the cultivation, a waiver of the right of affranchisement is now valid for a term not exceeding 50 years. This is a first step towards reforms which will certainly be progressively adopted.

§ 512. **Legislative Extensions of Existing Law.** — In the instance just cited the individual will still remain the dominant element, since the derogation from the Code respecting the lifting of burdens placed upon lands is made to rest upon mutual agreement. In other cases the legislator has come to inject into the law his own interpretation of such individual intent by extensions beyond what would have been possible under a strict application of the Code. Thus, for example, the Code declares that the promissor is not held to the fulfillment of his own personal obligation, when the object of his promise has become impossible of performance. Now, under the new law, enacted for the war period, but which will remain as the normal rule, it is established that the promise loses its binding force when its performance becomes not alone impossible but even exceptionally burdensome. This is in obedience to a principle of justice and equity, whereby the promissor is not bound to do or pay what is no longer proportionate to the com-

803

pensation assured him by the contract, to which, supposedly, he
would not have consented had he foreseen that, between the two
promises, there would not have continued the same balance that
determined his entry into it.   Here, as suggested, the law becomes
rather a legislative interpretation of the Code than a true modification.   Such instances may be multiplied.   In fact, the Government has expressly declared that the reforms actually being
effected in the Codes are to be extended to articles which still give
rise to question, or which are admittedly defective in formulation.
Such amendments will thus constitute so many additional rules
entering into the general body of existing legislation.

INDEX

Abduction: marriage form, 547, 549, 559;
  crime, 242, 249, 252, 292, 294, 299, 309, 311, 327, 332, 422, 439, 547.
Absence, 497, 800, 801.
Accession, title by, 692, 696.
Accident, 174, 224, 275, 357, 440.
Accomplice. See COMPLICITY.
Achasius, 558.
Actio: spolii, 745;
  injuriarum, 397.
Actionarius, 65.
Actions: *criminales*, 317;
  humiliores, 20;
  leviores, majores, minores, 317;
  potentiores, 80, 84;
  regales, 84, 290;
  extinguished by death, 259, 266, 398;
  id. by prescription. See PRESCRIPTION;
  "use" and "direct", 718;
  possessory, 178, 711, 742, 744, 747, 775;
  between clergy, 33, 34, 0, 121;
  involving "infamy", 424, 504;
  See also *ACTIO;* APPEALS; JURISDICTION.
Actor, 65.
Adelchi. Cited under Germanic public and criminal law and separate topics of private law.
Adjectio, 682.
Admiral, Grand (Sicily), 86.
Adoha, 113.
Adoption: Germanic, 66, 534, 563, 635, 642, 663, 682, 784;
  marriage impediment, 545;
  legitimization by, 562, 801;
  feudal, 628.
Adultery: crime of, 317, 330, 396, 427, 437;
  jurisdiction over, 79, 96, 263, 273, 402;
  by betrothed, 551;
  in slave marriage, 555;
  by husband, 231;

instigation to, 234, 251, 325, 331, 583;
  wrongful accusation of, 286, 331, 571, 585;
  impediment to marriage, 547;
  penalty for, 272, 293, 306, 308, 403, 412, 422, 570, 585.
Advocates, ecclesiastical, 59, 123.
Affinity, 545.
Agency, 787.
Aggravation: recognized, 90, 94, 174;
  causes of, 231, 324, 327, 339, 361, 447.
Agilulf. Cited under Germanic criminal law and separate topics of private law.
Agriculture: condition of, 28, 186;
  stimulation of, 214, 670, 678, 680, 721, 802.
Albergo, 160.
Albertus of Gandino, 352, 413.
Albinaggium, 507, 626.
Aldii: status of, 70, 500, 504, 506, 523, 667;
  crimes involving, 233, 236, 240, 292, 326, 334;
  marriage of, 546, 556, 561.
Allodium, 310, 665, 671.
Amputation: penalty, 95, 372, 375, 413;
  instances of, 91, 108, 235, 237, 250, 251, 252, 258, 278, 280, 306, 322, 323, 328, 347, 430, 436, 444, 446.
Amundius, 504, 566.
Angelus of Arezzo, 353.
Anger, 239, 362.
Animals: damage by, 223, 227, 228, 261, 275, 289, 346, 740, 779;
  title to wild, 693.
Annuity, 733, 774.
Anselmus of Orto, 352.
Antefatto, 582. See also *CONTRADOS*.
Anthropological School, 486, 487.
Anticresis, 738, 785.
Antrustion, 48, 55, 94.
Apanage, 107, 202, 631, 633, 670, 733, 784.

judicial powers of, 22, 34, 81, 82, 83, 86, 172, 513;
criminal jurisdiction of, 234, 278, 308, 311, 328, 333, 431;
feudal lord of cities, 101, 113, 128, 141, 159, 169, 184;
nomination of, 192.
Blasphemy, 403, 406, 412, 426, 429.
Blinding, penalty, 95, 175, 258, 306, 307, 346, 446.
Bonavoglia, 365, 502.
Bonfanti, 480.
Bonifacius of Vitalini, 353.
Boundary, wrongful alteration of, 251, 255, 347, 413.
Branding, penalty, 235, 306, 346, 415, 429, 446, 473, 475:
abolished, 472, 479.
Breviarium, 643.
Bridges, 59, 71, 107, 676.
Buccellati, 485.
Bulgarus, 352.
Burglary, 90, 238, 336, 388.
See also *CURTIS RUPTURA*.
Burning, penalty, 431, 433, 436.
Bursale, 113
Buticularius, 55.
Byzantine period: government during, 3–35;
criminal law of, 18.

Cage, penalty, 175, 424.
Camerarius, 56.
Canon law. See CRIMINAL LAW; PUBLIC LAW; and separate topics of private law.
Capacity, civil, 495, 587: limitations to, 517;
personal status affecting, 74, 159, 495, 524, 595;
loss of, 264, 268, 310, 323, 420, 423, 430, 433, 475, 481, 524.
See also *ALDII*; MINORS; SLAVES; WIFE; WOMEN.
Capacity, political, 71, 74, 159, 495:
loss of, 265, 268, 310, 323, 324, 371, 372, 401, 420, 423, 425, 430, 431, 433, 475, 511, 524;
of women, 53.
Capital punishment: kinds, 411, 511;
relation to outlawry, 303;
pecuniary in place of, 282;
civil effect of, 311, 423.
See also DEATH PENALTY.
Capitula missorum; id. legationis, 59.

Captain: of the People, 141, 144, 169, 188;
of county, 145.
Caput, 411, 423.
Carmignani, 480, 485.
Carpzov, 458
Carra, Francesco, 485.
Casa domnicata and *sundrialis*, 667.
Cassation, Court of, 210.
See also APPEALS; COURTS; SUPREME COURT.
Castellan, 145, 170, 181.
Castra, 13.
Causae. See ACTIONS.
Causidici, 100.
Censors (Italian Republic), 201.
Centenarius, 31, 63, 64, 79.
Chamber: of Deputies, 209;
of Orators (Italian Republic), 200;
of Supreme Council (Naples), 207;
of Accounts, 181, 182;
Grand Ducal, 182;
of Loans, 182.
Chamberlain: Frankish, 56;
Grand (Sicily), 86, 156, 170, 181.
Chancellor: Frankish, 56, 58;
of Naples, 206;
of Sicily, 86, 206;
Papal, 119, 152;
of absolute monarchies, 150, 152.
Charges on land, 717, 719, 731: rent, 723, 733, 784, 785;
tithes, 734.
Charlemagne. Cited under Germanic public and criminal law and separate topics of private law.
Charles III (Naples), 151, 168, 172, 176, 471.
Charles Albert, reforms of: political, 207, 209, 211, 213;
criminal, 481, 486;
civil, 522, 791.
Charles Emanuel III, 157, 172.
Charta, 504, 642, 706, 758, 774, 786.
Chartula adfiliationis, 564.
Chief, Germanic, 42, 43, 47, 53, 58, 62.
Children: unborn, 496;
recognition, exposure, sale of, 588;
of slave-free marriage, 500;
relatives' authority over, 590, 598;
property of, 591, 599, 604, 606.
See also FATHER; GUARDIANSHIP; ILLEGITIMATES; MINORS; *MUNDIUM*.
Church: and Empire, 115, 119, 129, 135, 139, 543;

Coemptiones, 28.
Cognitores, 21.
Coletta, 183.
Collectae, 108.
College of: Sixteen Wise Men (Venice), 148;
Cardinals, 151;
Italian Republic (Napoleonic), 200.
Colloquium, 99, 146.
Colonia parziaria, 724.
Coloni, 16, 27, 73, 506, 640, 667, 670, 671, 680, 700, 725.
Comes: *sacrarum largitionum*, 10, 26;
patrimonii, 10;
palatii, 56, 85;
provinciae, 12;
stabuli, 55;
Germanic, 48, 55, 63.
See also COUNT.
Comitatus, 55, 64.
Command, in: mitigation, 243, 279, 364;
complicity, 250, 386.
Commendation, 48, 55.
Commercial: conditions, 28, 72, 203, 754;
modes of payment, 772;
contracts, 786;
code, 791, 792;
courts, 207.
See also COMMUNES.
Commune, political subdivision, 157, 158, 199, 202, 204, 205, 206.
Communes, free: rise of, 65, 101, 127, 141, 161, 188;
government of, 130, 141, 153, 166, 169, 170, 184, 529;
statutes of, 131, 351;
relation to Empire, 130, 139;
decline of, 132, 156;
social structure of, 133, 141, 160, 506, 527;
commerce and industries of, 129, 145, 160, 186, 188, 680;
of south, 157.
See also FINANCIAL and JUDICIAL SYSTEMS; MILITARY ORGANIZATION.
Community régime (marital), 580, 582.
Commutation of penalty, 281, 302, 304, 321, 371, 375, 391, 394, 397, 407, 414.
Companies of Fortune, 189.
Complicity, 248: command, 250, 386; instigation, 90, 174, 346, 385, 403;

coöperation, 249, 387;
counsel, 251, 384;
comfort, 253, 300, 312, 388, 412;
punishment of, 319, 322, 327, 332, 340, 357.
Compositions: penalty, 88, 90, 102, 109, 238, 267, 276, 281, 403, 534, 767;
amount of, 69, 231;
payment of, 79, 235, 307, 337, 502.
See also CORPORAL PUNISHMENT; PENALTY.
Compurgators, 102.
Concilia, 66.
Concione, 146.
Concubinage, 432, 541, 555, 559, 570, 597.
Condottiero, 88.
Confession, 391.
Confiscation, penalty: character of, 93, 264, 296, 309, 314, 398, 408, 420, 473, 475, 686;
for homicide, 226, 234, 245, 251, 252, 257, 309, 340, 404, 409;
other instances of, 249, 254, 260, 269, 319–327, 333, 339, 431–444;
relation to outlawry, 268, 301, 303, 309, 409;
abolished, 459, 472, 479.
Congiure, 129.
Congregations, of: States of the Church, 151, 167, 206;
Lombardy, 155;
Lombardy-Venetia, 204.
Conjectus, 108.
Conjuratores, 102.
Conrad II, Emperor, 82, 86, 100.
Consiglio: *degli Anziani*, 147, 206;
Collaterale, 150, 151, 168, 169;
dei Credenza, 146, 169;
dei Diedici, 148, 167, 174, 461;
dei Dodici, 147;
Maggiore, 148, 160;
degli Otto, 147;
dei Pregadi, 148;
dei Quaranta, 147, 148, 167, 174;
Sacro regio, 151;
dei Savi, 147.
Consiliarii electi, 56.
Consistorium principis, 10, 56.
Consistory, Court of, 169.
Consortes, 659.
Consorzi, *consortiones*, 160, 664, 668.
Constable, 31, 55: Grand (Sicily), 86.
Constance: Peace of, 130, 139, 142, 143, 166, 185, 679;

examples of value, 68, 69, 73, 74, 94, 112, 232, 233, 240, 282, 284, 285, 504, 508, 520, 550;
penalty for other than homicide, 84, 286, 288, 321–341, 548, 551, 571, 585;
relation to feud, 272, 281;
enforcement of, 79, 272, 285;
right of women and State to, 286;
inheritance of, 286, 621.
Guilds, 72, 129, 142, 144, 173, 279, 769: statutes of, 161;
juristic persons, 528;
special courts of, 170;
abolished, 187.

Hair, cutting of, as penalty, 235, 307.
Haistan, 224, 242.
Hanging. See GALLOWS.
Hasta, 54.
Health, public, 152, 157, 171, 412, 678.
Heir, 611–634: nomination of, 563, 641;
adoptive, 563, 635;
liability of, criminal, 259, 266, 398;
id., civil, 612, 663;
loss of rights of, 310, 331, 332;
protection of against gifts, 578, 631, 639–641, 647, 663;
id. against alienations, 681, 684;
right to compositions, 272, 285.
See also INHERITANCE; WILLS.
Henry (Emperor), I, II, IV, and V. Cited under Germanic public and criminal law and separate topics of private law.
Heresy: crime, 24, 89, 172, 288, 324, 325, 326, 364, 392, 395, 397, 398, 409, 412, 413, 426, 430;
effects of, 515, 595, 628.
Historical School, 465, 472, 477, 793.
Hoba, 667.
Hoberos, 242, 336, 667.
Holy Office, Court of, 172, 181.
Holy Roman Empire, 41, 44, 56, 115, 133, 134, 139. See also CHURCH; COMMUNES.
Homage, 48, 51.
Homicide, 338, 439: intention to commit, 223, 275, 338, 356, 358, 440;
justifiable, 244, 258, 300, 338, 365, 421, 440, 446;
in church, 245, 247, 258, 276, 311, 339;
after concluding peace, 277, 280, 339;

complicity in, 249, 340;
by slave, 251, 255, 256, 258;
of relative, 234, 264, 309, 311, 339, 370, 441, 501;
of unborn, 240, 275, 314;
of public official, 369;
of ecclesiastic, 232.
Honor: injuries to, 87, 285, 311, 333, 334, 369;
loss of, 310, 341, 398, 423, 431, 433, 524;
woman's capacity affected by, 233, 236, 238, 285, 342.
See also DEFAMATION; "INFAMY"; UNWORTHINESS.
Honorati, 16.
Hospitality, 248, 261, 507.
Hostenditia, 113.
Hostility, legalized, 271. See FEUD.
Hundreds, 61.
Hunting, 676, 692, 693, 737.
Husband: offences against wife, 228, 234, 292, 296, 308, 386, 571, 583, 585;
authority over wife, 273, 330, 520, 537, 548, 549, 569, 581, 583, 602, 801.
See also HUSBAND AND WIFE; WIFE.
Husband and wife: personal relations, 570;
property relations, 571, 602, 623, 640;
termination of relation, 583.
See also HUSBAND; WIFE.
Hypothec, 732, 738.

Idertzon, 242.
Ignorance of law, 364.
Illegitimates: who are, 511, 556, 561;
under stigma, 525, 562, 597, 628;
legal status of, 596, 640, 797, 800.
See also INHERITANCE; LEGITIMIZATION.
Immunities, feudal, 46, 49, 64, 69, 81, 82, 86, 96, 109, 122, 298, 672, 687, 719.
Imperium, 20.
Imprisonment, 95, 308, 416, 459, 490, 511: instances of penalty, 328, 331, 346, 372, 375, 377, 420, 440, 444, 478, 502, 560, 777, 781.
Incendiarism, 258, 299, 317, 381, 403, 422, 447, 448: arson, 96, 225, 252, 289, 348, 448.
Incest, 310, 333, 396, 433, 501.
Incremento, 690.

Indicatio, 27.

"Infamy": causes of, 303, 341, 423, 427, 502, 525, 777;
consequences of, 372, 423, 462, 470, 472, 597;
instances of penalty, 399, 401, 430, 433, 434, 437, 443, 473;
abolished, 526.

Infant (*impubes*), 237, 246, 373.

Ingrossazione, 690.

Inheritance: Germanic and Roman contrasted, 611, 614;
systems of direct and collateral, 614;
disqualification for, 525, 648;
agnate preference, 535, 611, 617, 620, 622;
feudal, 627, 670;
between husband and wife, 583, 623;
from women, 622, 648;
from presumed dead, 497;
from illegitimates, 626;
from liberated slave, 504;
from foreigner, 508, 626;
from civilly dead, 511;
from Jews, 513, 626;
by direct and collateral heirs, 617;
by clergy, 628;
by women, 286, 613, 617, 620, 627, 628, 647, 664;
of emphyteusis, 723, 728.
See also ADOPTION; CONTRACTS; ESCHEAT; REPRESENTATION; WILLS.

Injuries, personal: criminal, 329, 393; civil, 754.
See also separate injuries.

Injuries, to property. See PROPERTY RIGHTS.

Inquisition, 172.

Inquisitor haereticae pravitatis, 431.

Insanity. See MENTAL CONDITION.

Insinuatio, 644, 710.

Insolvency, 525, 780.

Insult. See DEFAMATION, HONOR.

Intendant: royal (*missus*), 58, 66, 85, 91, 94, 99, 106, 116, 118, 122, 172, 278, 298, 317, 324, 328, 558, 645;
of Lombardy, 156, 182;
of Naples, 202, 206.

Intent, criminal, 90, 174, 289, 357, 366, 388, 428: not at first required, 222–224, 245, 275, 338, 341, 356;
presumed, 227, 237, 340, 373, 375;
absence of, in mitigation, 227, 335, 357, 362, 368, 373, 382, 402, 440.

Interdict, 526, 604: Roman, 745, 747.

Interdictio aquae et ignis, 320.

Interest, 328, 365, 433, 733, 739, 774, 785.

Internment, 420, 443, 475.

Interpleader (*interziazione*), 713.

Investiture: feudal, 51, 117, 629, 722;
in transfer of title, 705, 707, 716;
ecclesiastical, 129.

Italy: Kingdom of, Napoleonic, 201, 204, 475;
united, 199, 208, 482, 488, 791;
rise of States of, 132, 134.
See also STATE.

Jacobus: of Arena, 353;
of Belviso, 353.

Jews: status of, 171, 365, 433, 512, 774, 785;
marriage with Christian, 547;
right to inherit, 513, 626, 628.

John of: Andrea, 352;
Bassiano, 352.

Joseph: II (Lombardy), 172, 176, 433;
Bonaparte, 475.

Judges: higher, 21, 23, 84;
lower or ordinary, 21, 23, 34, 50, 62, 79, 83, 84, 86, 392;
minor, 20, 78;
royal, 77, 99, 177;
popular, 77, 97, 98;
provincial, 21;
lay (*scabini*), 59, 98, 141, 265;
ecclesiastical, 123, 431, 437;
deputy, 22, 392;
of usage, 177;
special, 24.
See also COURTS; *JUDICES*; JURISDICTION.

Judgment of God, 179: by battle or duel, 69, 92, 101, 104, 179, 273, 274, 280, 327, 335, 338, 339, 344, 367, 520, 703, 715, 771;
by ordeal, 98, 103, 584, 597.

Judicariae, 62.

Judices: Roman, 19;
Germanic, 57, 58, 62, 99.

Judicial system: Byzantine, 18, 33, 34;
Germanic, 24, 57, 63, 65, 76, 177, 317;
feudal, 50, 78, 81, 86, 95, 100, 105, 170, 407;
of communes, 130, 131, 142, 166, 169, 170;

of absolute monarchies, 165;
of Napoleonic States, 200;
of restoration States, 204;
of united Italy, 210;
confused with administrative, 18, 20, 24, 65, 165, 181.
See also separate countries of Italy.
Jugatio, 27.
Juniorasco, 632.
Juniores comitum, 64.
Jurisdictio, 69.
Jurisdiction: feudal, 50, 69, 78, 81, 82, 83, 95, 297, 317, 395, 407;
imperial, 19, 23, 24, 82, 85, 131, 166;
public, 80, 83, 96, 165, 173;
private, 82, 173, 442;
ecclesiastical, 22, 33, 34, 83, 121, 122, 161, 170, 172, 193, 370, 426, 431, 437, 481, 491, 513. See also BISHOP; CLERGY; COURTS;
proprietary, 82, 96, 98, 106, 165;
delegated, 22, 86, 392, 431;
criminal, 169, 170, 171, 173, 174, 201, 205, 207, 317, 378, 480;
administrative, 210;
commercial, 207;
civil, 170, 205, 207;
special, 170, 431;
of free cities, 130, 166, 169, 407.
See also APPEALS; ASSEMBLY, Germanic; *JUDICES*; JUDICIAL SYSTEM; KING; POPE.
Jury, 201.
Jus: and *judicium*, 19;
curiae, 82, 101;
naufragii, 509;
congrui, prothimiseos, 681;
possidendi, possessionis, 741;
recadentiae, revolutionis, 620, 684.
Justiciar, Grand (Sicily), 86, 156, 170, 174.
Justinian's reforms. See BYZANTINE PERIOD.
Justitia familiaris, 50.

Kierzy, capitulary of, 48, 100.
King: Germanic, 9, 11, 43, 53, 63, 80, 106, 108, 109, 116;
feudal, 47, 49, 52;
absolutist, 132, 137, 150, 165, 181, 198, 411;
also Emperor, 116, 118;
military powers of, 9, 30, 43, 54, 112, 321;

ecclesiastical powers of, 121, 133;
judicial powers of, 54, 83, 84, 97, 167, 317;
power over penalties, 175, 263, 411, 452. See also PARDON;
courtiers of. See COURT;
special protection by, 54, 62, 232, 298, 324, 508, 512, 520, 606;
mundium of, 65, 567;
offenses against, 231, 320, 378, 427.
See also ATTEMPT; CRIME, public;
of united Italy, 209.
See also FINANCIAL SYSTEM; INTENDANTS; PEACE.
Kinship: marriage impediment, 543;
computation of degrees of, 544;
fixes inheritance, 614.
See also PREËMPTION; REDEMPTION.
Knighthood, 113.

Labor, forced, 472, 480, 490.
Land: Germanic division of, 11, 15, 27, 70, 656, 658, 662, 665, 681, 689, 696, 742;
feudal, 46, 49, 654, 669, 671;
public, 71, 106, 110;
social and economic influence of, 69, 666, 671;
rights in, 654;
rights of common in, 71, 110, 184, 659, 668, 675;
charges on, 717, 719, 723, 731;
modes of alienation of, 662, 664, 681, 783;
confiscated, 107;
abandoned, 107, 109, 670, 696;
unclaimed, 109, 696;
the *mansus*, 666;
regulations as to use of, 680;
relation of, to army, 111, 654, 658, 668, 672, 732;
actions to recover, 714;
record of titles to, 183, 186, 670, 709, 740;
injuries to, 346, 754;
allotment of to World War veterans, 214.
See also CHARGES; *FIDEICOMMISSUM*; LEASES; PROPERTY RIGHTS.
Lateran, 119.
Latifundia, 28, 46, 186, 668, 721.
Laudemium, 109, 629, 722, 730.
Launegild, 550, 582, 636, 782.

Munera, 49.
Municipalities, 12, 13, 23, 24, 26, 39, 71, 128, 157. See also COM-MUNES.
Muratori, 456.
Mutilation, penalty, 95, 175, 274, 471, 472. See also AMPUTATION.

Naples, Kingdom of: government of, 151, 168, 170, 171, 181, 190, 202, 206, 209, 471;
criminal law of, 471, 475;
communes of, 157.
See also FEUDALISM; SICILY; TWO SICILIES.
Napoleon I, 149, 204, 210: Italian States of, 200;
influence on criminal law, 475.
See also CODE, FRENCH, CIVIL; EMPIRE; FRANCE.
Natural Law, School of, 134, 137, 176, 453, 455, 463, 465, 471.
Negligence: degrees of, 776, 786;
liability for, 90, 174, 223, 224, 356, 440, 754;
of bailee, 775, 786.
Negotiable instruments, 786.
Negotium criminale, 317.
Neighbors: right of preëmption and redemption, 682;
co-responsibility of, 768.
Nobility: Byzantine period, 16, 28;
Germanic period, 42, 53, 57, 67, 86, 104;
feudal, 47, 82, 101, 112, 158, 627;
of communes, 143, 144, 147, 158, 161, 188, 521;
of absolute monarchies, 158, 162, 183, 186;
protective societies of, 160, 664, 668;
hereditary titles of, reëstablished, 202;
loss of status, 525.
Nomenclator, 119.
Notary, 10, 56, 119.
Notatorio, 710.
Notitia, 706.
Numeri, 30.

Oath: mode of proof, 98, 101, 123, 178, 459, 703, 715, 745;
exculpatory, 227, 256, 274, 712, 771, 775, 776;
contracts under, 761, 763.
Obedientia, 73.

Obligations, 751: sources of, 753;
charges on land as, 731;
guarantees of performance, 763, 776;
performance of, 771, 803;
non-performance of, 775;
assignability of, 786.
Occupation, acquisition by, 500, 693.
Odoacer, 3, 9, 12, 13, 15, 18, 26, 30, 33, 208.
Onere reali. See CHARGES.
Opera Nazionale dei Combattenti, 214.
Optimates, 16.
Optiones, 31.
Ordeal. See JUDGMENT OF GOD.
Ordinary courts of: Byzantine period, 21, 23, 34;
Germanic period, 50, 59, 62, 79, 83, 84, 86;
free communes, 169;
absolute monarchies, 167, 170;
modern period, 201, 205, 207, 210.
Ospizio, 160.
Ostrogoths, 3–39, 208.
Otto (Emperor), I, III, IV. Cited under Germanic public and criminal law and separate topics of private law.
Outlawry: origin and character of, 88, 268, 300, 342, 365, 393, 401, 420;
consequences of, 303, 338, 421, 423, 462, 511, 595;
penalties derived from, 303;
instances of, 316, 340, 376, 404, 422, 432, 441, 443, 444, 446, 447;
aiding outlaw, 253, 254, 422.
Oviscarius, 65.
Ownership: nature of, 657, 670, 693, 696, 699, 741;
limitations upon, 674, 784, 802;
transfer of, 681, 704, 757, 783;
extinguishment of, 686;
recovery of, 711, 747;
direct and beneficial, 717, 729;
defective title to, 776.

Pacieri, 173.
Pagano, Mario, 465, **487.**
Pagus, 42, 61.
Palatini, 26.
Palatium publicum, 107.
Pardon, 175, 210, 262, 263, 302, 304, 307, 376, 384, 393, 398, 401, 408, 413, 524.